# Contemporary Dickens

EDITED BY
EILEEN GILLOOLY
AND
DEIRDRE DAVID

THE OHIO STATE UNIVERSITY PRESS · COLUMBUS

Copyright © 2009 by The Ohio State University.
All rights reserved.

Library of Congress Cataloging-in-Publication Data
Contemporary Dickens / edited by Eileen Gillooly and Deirdre David.
     p. cm.
  Includes bibliographical references and index.
  ISBN 978-0-8142-0285-2 (cloth : alk. paper)
  1. Dickens, Charles, 1812–1870—Criticism and interpretation. I. Gillooly, Eileen.
II. David, Deirdre
  PR4588.C639 2009
  823'.8—dc22
                       2008034051

This book is available in the following editions:
Cloth (ISBN 978-0-8142-0285-2)
CD-ROM (ISBN 978-0-8142-9045-3)

Cover design by Amelia Saul
Typesetting and design by Jennifer Shoffey Forsythe
Type set in Adobe Sabon

∞ The paper used in this publication meets the minimum requirements of the American National Standard for Information Sciences—Permanence of Paper for Printed Library Materials. ANSI Z39.48-1992.

9 8 7 6 5 4 3 2 1

# Contemporary Dickens

For Steven Marcus

# Contents

Acknowledgments　　IX
Abbreviations　　XI

Introduction　　1
　　DEIRDRE DAVID AND EILEEN GILLOOLY

## PART ONE: ETHICS AND NARRATIVE

1　Dickens, Secularism, and Agency
　　GEORGE LEVINE　　13

2　Dickens and the Goods
　　ROBERT NEWSOM　　35

3　The Poverty of Charity: Dickensian Sympathy
　　NANCY YOUSEF　　53

4　Uncanny Gifts, Strange Contagion: Allegory in *The Haunted Man*
　　JOHN BOWEN　　75

5　Storied Realities: Language, Narrative, and Historical Understanding
　　RICHARD H. MOYE　　93

## PART TWO: MATERIAL CULTURE

6　So, This Is Christmas
　　JOSEPH W. CHILDERS　　113

7　Green Dickens
　　KAREN CHASE AND MICHAEL LEVENSON　　131

Contents

8   Commodity Criticism and Victorian Thing Culture:
    The Case of Dickens
    ELAINE FREEDGOOD                                          152

9   Funny Money
    TATIANA M. HOLWAY                                         169

10  Enumeration and Exhaustion: Taking Inventory in
    *The Old Curiosity Shop*
    JAMES BUZARD                                              189

PART THREE: CONTEXTUAL READING

11  Paterfamilias
    EILEEN GILLOOLY                                           209

12  Reading with Buzfuz: Dickens, Sexuality, Interrogation
    JAMES ELI ADAMS                                           231

13  *Little Dorrit*'s Theater of Rage
    DEIRDRE DAVID                                             245

14  The Making of Dickens Criticism
    DEBORAH EPSTEIN NORD                                      264

Bibliography                                                  289
Notes on Contributors                                         305
Index                                                         309

# Acknowledgments

This collection traces its beginnings to a gathering of scholars at the annual CUNY Victorian Conference in 2003, a conference famous in nineteenth-century British studies circles as much for its collegiality as for its intellectual quality. Several of us who were gathered together at lunch that day—some of whom had never met before—discovered in conversation that we had all written our dissertations, over a span of two or more decades, under the supervision of Steven Marcus. One or two colleagues at the table—Oxonians, we recall—commented that "it showed": that is, that the work of those of us who had been students of Marcus (many of whose work is represented in this volume) shared not only an enduring fascination with Dickens but—regardless of great differences in interests, style, and theoretical or critical allegiances—an identifiable interpretive ethos. As Marcus remarks on the occasion of the reissue of his *Representations: Essays on Literature and Society* in 1990, "the critical study" of literature and language "in an actual historical world, and in a culture in which we are all intractably situated, seems to me still a worthwhile thing to do" (x). And so, too, does it seem to those whose essays are included here and who have learned so much from his example.

We wish to thank a number of colleagues who in various ways assisted *Contemporary Dickens* into being. Among these are Gerhard Joseph and Barry Qualls, as well as all who participated in "The Long Nineteenth Century" conference at Columbia University in October 2005, including Jonathan Arac, Rita Charon, Arnold Cooper, Andrew Delbanco, George Levine,

*Acknowledgments*

Eric Lott, Deborah Epstein Nord, James Olney, Jonah Siegel, and Patricia Meyer Spacks. The contributing authors to this volume were remarkable not only for the quality of their essays but also for their eager participation, unfailing good humor, steady (though not untested) patience, and noteworthy timeliness in meeting deadlines. Deb Nord deserves special thanks—being, in the initial stages of this project, a coeditor in all but name—as do Jesse Rosenthal, for willing and able indexing, and Sandy Crooms, our editor at The Ohio State University Press, for her enthusiastic and energetic support.

A part of Elaine Freedgood's essay, "Commodity Criticism and Victorian Thing Culture: The Case of Dickens," first appeared in a different form in the Coda of *The Ideas in Things: Fugitive Meaning in the Victorian Novel* (Chicago: University of Chicago Press, 2006). We wish to thank the University of Chicago Press for permission to reprint. We also wish to thank the University Seminars at Columbia University for their help in publication. Many of the ideas herein benefited from discussions in the University Seminar: Modern British History.

A note on the text: Following John O. Jordan's example in *The Cambridge Companion to Charles Dickens,* we give parenthetical references to chapter numbers of Dickens's novels (or to book and chapter number where applicable) rather than to specific editions, since too many of these are in circulation to make such citation useful to our readers. Unless the text under discussion is clear in context, it is identified by its initials (e.g., *PP, OT, NN,* etc.). *The Letters of Charles Dickens* (Pilgrim Edition) and John Forster's *Life of Dickens* are also noted parenthetically (see Abbreviations).

# Abbreviations

References to the novels are by book (where applicable) and chapter, unless otherwise noted.

| | |
|---|---|
| BH | *Bleak House* |
| BR | *Barnaby Rudge* |
| CC | *A Christmas Carol.* References are to stave. |
| DC | *David Copperfield* |
| DS | *Dombey and Son* |
| ED | *The Mystery of Edwin Drood* |
| GE | *Great Expectations* |
| HM | *The Haunted Man* |
| HT | *Hard Times* |
| LD | *Little Dorrit* |
| MC | *Martin Chuzzlewit* |
| NN | *Nicholas Nickleby* |
| OCS | *The Old Curiosity Shop* |
| OMF | *Our Mutual Friend* |
| OT | *Oliver Twist* |
| PP | *The Pickwick Papers* |
| SB | *Sketches by Boz.* References are to title of sketch. |
| TTC | *Tale of Two Cities* |
| UT | *The Uncommercial Traveller* |
| Forster | *The Life of Charles Dickens.* References are to volume and page. |
| LCD | *The Letters of Charles Dickens.* The Pilgrim Edition. Madeline House, Graham Storey, Kathleen Tillotson et al., eds. (Oxford: Clarendon Press, 1965–2002). References are to volume and page. |

# Introduction

DEIRDRE DAVID AND EILEEN GILLOOLY

No other author in the English-speaking world occupies quite the place in both the popular consciousness and the literary tradition as Charles Dickens. On the one hand, he is, as John Jordan has noted, "widely recognized as the preeminent novelist of the Victorian age and a major figure in world literature"—at once both quintessentially English and internationally influential, animating the novels of Dostoevsky as vividly as those of Mark Twain or, more recently, Peter Carey.[1] On the other hand, he is known to millions who have never read a word he penned. Only the Bard enjoys greater name recognition, yet the adjective "Dickensian" conjures a more vivid set of associations than does "Shakespearean," and Scrooge cuts a more familiar figure in our market-driven global economy than Lear or Hamlet or Macbeth. Although the Victorians as a whole constitute a source of nostalgic fascination for contemporary audiences (witness the relentless production in recent decades of television miniseries based on nineteenth-century novels), Dickens's appeal is of a special kind—owing not only to his formidable powers of imagination and description, his staggering output, and his persistent presence in our collective unconscious, but also to his having himself personally ruminated upon so many of the social problems, values, and ways of knowing that currently engross us. Almost every contemporary concern that can be traced back to the nineteenth century—from financial credit and social welfare to secularism and commodity culture—seems to have elicited some sort of response from the Inimitable.

It is not surprising, then, that Dickens—sneered at, condescended to, or simply dismissed by a great many early-twentieth-century modernists—should have become, as Deborah Epstein Nord notes (in the final essay of this volume), a favorite object of critical inquiry during our own historical period. Since the mid-twentieth century, scores of monographs and essay collections attest to his remarkable and eclectic topicality. As the *Longman Critical Reader* (1996), edited by Steven Connor, points out, "the very contradictions within Dickens's writing which posed such a problem for earlier critics, now offer enormous interpretive opportunities for contemporary issues such as language, gender, selfhood, space and power."[2] As a whole, Dickens criticism currently values the ease with which his literary corpus yields to the pressure of late-twentieth-century theoretical preoccupations. *Dickens Refigured: Bodies, Desires and Other Histories* (1996), for example—a collection of essays edited by John Schad—sets out to identify "the foreign bodies" and their "desires, histories" that populate "Dickens's fiction and prose."[3] *Dickens and the Children of Empire* (2000) and *Dickens, Europe and the New Worlds* (1999) are similarly focused on "foreign bodies," but of a more material sort: while the former seeks both to unpack the imperial analogy—pervasive in Dickens's writing—between children and colonized peoples and to reconsider Dickens from a postcolonial perspective that has "re-envisaged" the center and the periphery, the latter considers Dickens from both "global" and "regional" points of view, often placing him within new conceptual worlds as well: "new media (film, television, the internet) and new theoretical frames (feminist, postcolonial)."[4] Perhaps the most satisfying, because the most comprehensive, of the recent essay collections is the *Cambridge Companion to Charles Dickens* (1999), which covers "the full span" of Dickens's fiction from a number of thematic, formal, and theoretical approaches. In offering considerations of Dickens on "childhood, the city, and domestic ideology" as well as of his serial publication, his "distinctive use of language," and his "relation to work in . . . illustration, theatre, and film," it suggests both the variety of Dickens's own investments and the diversity of critical engagements his work prompts.[5]

Although *Contemporary Dickens* is similarly committed to presenting some of the most intriguing work being undertaken in Dickens studies today, it differs conceptually from recent collections in two important respects. First, it seeks to disclose the nineteenth-century origins of many of those issues that currently absorb us: not only was Dickens fully contemporary with his age—his concerns, enthusiasms, and ways of knowing and representing being shared by, often shaping, those of his contemporaries—but he is also our contemporary. As Anny Sadrin points out, Dickens was both "a great Victorian" and "a great precursor of Modernity."[6] From constructions of gender and sexuality to environmentalism and Englishness: such areas of inquiry currently in high fashion—areas often assumed to have been epistemologically unavailable to critics before the late twentieth century—are shown in these essays to have been identified, pondered, and sometimes even problematized by Dickens himself. In their Introduction to *Disciplinarity at the Fin de Siècle*, Amanda Anderson and Joseph Valente argue that "interdisciplinarity"—"dominated by the figure of Michel Foucault" in its most popular and recognizable guise as cultural studies—"can only lay claim to the kinds of theoretical and practical 'breaks' that it assigns itself by distorting or suppressing its relation to the past."[7] Like the essays in *Disciplinarity* and other recent work by Anderson and others, the essays collected in *Contemporary Dickens* explore the genealogy of contemporary ideas and question the originality of our current ways of knowing: upon examination, postmodern epistemology appears to be less a "break" from our Victorian past than a feature of its development.[8]

The second primary contribution of this volume lies in its illuminating the particular importance of Dickens, particularly late Dickens—as a novelist, reformer, activist, ethicist, psychologist, anthropologist, and biographical subject—in the critical reassessments being undertaken across the disciplines. As we are clearly not the first to notice, the popularity of "high theory" in departments of literature has subsided, and though "new historicism" remains strong, there are new currents in twenty-first-century literary criticism, new approaches—often eclectic or hybrid—to topics that once seemed, to critics writing in the final decades of the late twentieth century, to be exhausted of interest. Moral philosophy, the psychology of the emotions, liberal theory, life writing, nationalism and national character: all are being rediscovered as compelling objects of study, competing successfully for attention with race, gender, class, sexuality, ethnicity, and other such modes of analysis that have dominated professional inquiry in recent years. Far from representing a nostalgic return, however, *Contemporary Dickens* looks at these once-familiar topics from fresh perspectives that take into account the vital contributions made by Marxist, feminist, deconstructive, psychoanalytic, new historical, and other late-twentieth-century strategies of reading.

■ ■ ■

We have grouped the essays under three headings that we believe raise questions and concerns that not only are of current critical interest but also, in many cases, caused Dickens himself to ponder. The essays collected in Part One, "Ethics and Narrative," explore the multiple and sometimes conflicting ways in which Dickens gave narrative form to the moral and religious anxieties of his age. In chapter 1, "Dickens, Secularism, and Agency," George Levine begins with the claim that the Victorian novel resists at almost every turn a providential explanation for social difficulty. Dickens's novels, perhaps more pervasively than those of any other Victorian writer, strikingly and paradoxically reveal this secularity in their own insistence on the providential. With *Little Dorrit* as his representative example, Levine analyzes Dickens's elaboration of the raw secularity of the world that presses upon the overtly Christian framework of the novel, embodied in the diminutive person of Amy Dorrit. For Levine, this most somber and densely plotted of Dickens's novels reveals a struggle to fit an ethical resolution of social misery within the narrative frame of providential explanation: his analysis discloses Dickens's engagement with issues of moral philosophy that press upon us today, particularly the debates about secularism, creationism, and intelligent design.

In chapter 2, "Dickens and the Goods," Robert Newsom charts the biographical and intellectual forces that shaped Dickens's understanding and shows that virtually all of his narratives, from *Sketches by Boz* to *Our Mutual Friend,* are driven by a powerful ethical imperative: simply put, the "goods" of religion, for Dickens, rest in a duty to do good, here and now. Unembarrassed about the transparency of his moral positions, Dickens returns again and again to the simple but challenging question of what is good and what is evil, and Newsom—in showing how the novels advance an imperative to be useful, to do good, and to bring happiness to all—explores the mix of Utilitarian and "Christian" values that characterize the ethics of Liberalism, as we have inherited it from the Victorians.

Offering such moral instruction as that delivered by Betsey Trotwood in *David Copperfield* ("Never be mean in anything, never be false, never be cruel") as a remedy for social malaise has long subjected Dickens to charges of sentimentalism. In "The Poverty of Charity: Dickensian Sympathy" (chapter 3), Nancy Yousef defends Dickens against what some critics have seen as an embarrassing aspect of his art. Arguing that such charges betray a general suspicion of affective display, Yousef considers Dickens's engagement with the problems of philanthropy as part of an intellectual tradition reaching back to the eighteenth century and forward to contemporary debates within ethical theory. If Levine and Newsom find unresolved conflicts and unambiguous moral imperatives in Dickens's narratives, then Yousef places Dickens's engagement with those conflicts and imperatives in a history of moral philosophy.

Whether ambiguous or transparent, Dickens's ethical narratives depend upon storytelling, yet, as Richard H. Moye notes, the Victorians regarded the making up of stories with moral suspicion. Taking *Hard Times* as his example, Moye argues in "Storied Realities" (chapter 5) that while Dickens accepted the inevitability of making fictions (how else, after all, can we know our own past or understand our nation's history?), he also insisted that we choose our narratives wisely if we are to constitute a viable moral community: we must have healthy stories, enabling fictions, that allow us to know and to love one another. In *Hard Times,* Dickens teaches us to recognize the "good" fiction from the "bad," to marvel at Sissy Jupe's inventive imagination and to despise Bounderby's self-serving fictional biography.

The ethical significance of narrative is equally crucial in John Bowen's analysis of *The Haunted Man,* a strange, melancholy, and neglected text. Exploring the relationship between adult life and childhood misery (Dickens wrote *The Haunted Man* just before beginning *David Copperfield*), Bowen shows in chapter 4 that Dickens's exploration of memory has a close affinity with certain nineteenth-century psychological theories of split and doubled minds and with debates about the nature of material and psychic conservation. Identifying a narrative of family thick with strange figures, weird repetitions, and ghostly effects, Bowen also elaborates its ancillary meaning as a social and political allegory that emphasizes the nature of ethical responsibility to the poor. *The Haunted Man* thus both investigates the persistent strangeness of the self and defines the nature of our ethical and social obligations to others.

By virtue of the Inimitable's seemingly inexhaustible interest in everything around him, the essays gathered in Part Two under the rubric "Material Culture" explore such phenomena as Dickens's participation in the Victorian construction of Christmas, his preoccupation with the environment, his obsession with a world of things, his appearance on a ten-pound note, and his postulation of a tension between a world of stilled moral perfection and a world of movable, mutable objects. In "So, This Is Christmas" (chapter 6), Joseph W. Childers sets out to answer many questions that arise from the conjunction of Christmas and English national identity: among them, what different roles, depending on social class, did individual English people play in constructing a national experience of Christmas? Childers argues that the best-known version of Christmas, coded in Dickens's *A Christmas Carol,* is specifically and indelibly English: its concerns include the contemporary problem of the poor, a particularly English school of political economy, and the traditions of English Christmases past. At the heart of this version of Christmas is a basic contradiction: on the one hand, an insistence on a muted Christian socialism that restores human sympathy and, on the other, a celebration of the individual's ability to effect social change.

*Introduction*

"Was Dickens green?" is the question posed by Karen Chase and Michael Levenson in chapter 7. From *Sketches by Boz* to *Our Mutual Friend,* they trace Dickens's engagement with contemporary environmental issues—issues that, by the middle years of his career, had reached emergency status in London, always the site of what they term his "green reflections." Not only was Dickens a passionate campaigner for the retention of some "green spaces" in the metropolis: the memory of pastoral is a constitutive principle of his fiction. Linking modernization and social trauma, Dickens—from the coming of the railway in *Dombey and Son* to the crisis of rags and paper explored in *Our Mutual Friend*—emerges in this essay as a committed social activist, likely supporting organic farming and protesting global warming, were he alive today, as well as continuing to advocate for land conservation.

Elaine Freedgood's primary interest (in chapter 8) is in making us grasp the difference between what she terms a Victorian "thing culture" and what we now broadly term "materialism." We have lost our ability to appreciate Dickens's world of "things"—a world that he did not always present to the reader as damning evidence of a heartless commodity culture. In an innovative turn, Freedgood claims that it is the criticism of Dickens's fiction that has led us to underestimate the value of "things," and she critiques that criticism to unveil its misreading of the crowded Dickensian instantiation of the particular. Freedgood asks us to look through and beyond the materialist prism that preoccupies so many in Dickens studies today: in Dickens and in Victorian culture at large, not all objects are bad objects. If Nancy Yousef seeks to recuperate Dickens's oft-disdained sentimentalism, then Freedgood aims to rescue Dickens from readings undertaken from the perspective of a reductive materialist analysis.

Dickens on a ten-pound note—his many modes of utterance represented by the titles of his novels appearing in small, faint print on the front of the note and swirling behind the assertion "I Promise to Pay"—is the paper object that constitutes the subject of Tatiana Holway's essay (chapter 9). Where Chase and Levenson concern themselves with the production of paper that may be said to produce the ten-pound note, Holway is interested in what the note itself signals: Dickens as literary capitalist, the embodiment of the convergence of money, written language, and identity. Examining in great detail the origins of modern attitudes toward paper money, Holway explores the dramatic growth of a credit system that in mid-nineteenth-century England led to the burgeoning of middle-class wealth through the accrual of interest and to Dickens himself becoming a literary capitalist in more ways than one: making investments with profits from the sale of his novels, expanding and diversifying his business ventures, capitalizing on the republication of novels in cheap editions, inventing himself through his writing, and using his name as the ground for all of these representations.

While Holway draws our attention to both the symbolic and the literal circulation of paper and representation, James Buzard (chapter 10) focuses on Dickens's delight in inventorying a world of literal and symbolic circulating currency. For Buzard, *The Old Curiosity Shop* is the most anti-Dickensian of Dickens's novels: the figure of Nell, always moving yet always emblematic of a perfect stillness, threatens to negate the fecund power with which Dickens multiplies characters and incidents and puts himself into circulation, as it were, in the literary marketplace. If *The Pickwick Papers* is a novel whose miraculous comic inventiveness may be described by the trope of inventory— a list of separate items (characters and incidents) placed one after another, preserved in their plurality—then in *The Old Curiosity Shop,* Buzard argues, Dickens hurls against his own narrative-propagating powers the story-negating inertia of Nell. Her stillness—symbolic of a refusal to become an inventoried item—tends to make all the going to and fro that exists around her seem empty and meaningless.

As we hope is apparent, close reading is a common trait of all of the essays in *Contemporary Dickens,* but an especially important one to those in Part Three, "Contextual Reading," which examines select scenes and characters within the context of Dickens's personal history or his greater historical circumstances—circumstances that often resonate powerfully with our own. Eileen Gillooly draws our attention in chapter 11 to Dickens's parental affections, anxieties, and ambivalences. Beset by the challenges of his ever-increasing family and the disappointments presented by his children (particularly his sons, for whom he was especially ambitious), Dickens comes to find wish-fulfilling relief in inventing alternatives to the nuclear family. The aggrieved child, of course, is always at the center of Dickens's narratives, but Gillooly shows that Dickens occasionally pauses to consider the parent-child relationship from other affective positions as well (Nicholas Nickleby's mothering of Smike, for example). Father to scores of children, fictional and otherwise, Dickens consistently found his imaginative offspring easier to identify with and to project upon than he did the biological sort. Indeed, in *Bleak House,* he rewrites his personal domestic script with an altered cast of characters, directing them in their roles as the ideal children missing from his own household.

By closely questioning the ways in which literary and cultural criticism describes itself as a mode of "interrogation," James Eli Adams in chapter 12 shows how the novel has become the principal territory for a hermeneutics of suspicion. For contemporary critics, the Victorian novel, in particular, always has something to hide: it postulates the existence of a fundamentally private subjectivity that results in making everything the subject of interrogation, in bringing everything under suspicion, including the agency of the author. For Adams, the *Bardell v. Pickwick* courtroom scene of *Pickwick Papers* is the *locus classicus* within Dickens of such a way of reading. There Pickwick functions as the innocent screen onto which are projected the interrogating sexual suspicions of his audiences. Adams urges us to abandon our naïve assumption that Victorian novelists did not know what they were up to in representing sexuality, demonstrating that Dickens's own engagement with sexuality is a good deal cannier and more knowing than we have previously acknowledged.

Deirdre David also asks us to reconsider what we think we know about Dickens, to take into account not only the sentimentalized virtue of Dickens's women characters but also their destructive fury. "*Little Dorrit*'s Theater of Rage" (chapter 13) examines Dickens's ambiguous political response to "the condition of women" question at the very moment he was composing a novel giving powerful expression to some of his female characters' feelings of injury, injustice, and revenge. Miss Wade and Tattycoram, for two, reject social codes of feminine conduct and instead stage numerous theatrical scenes of vengeance—a mode of protest that utilizes nineteenth-century theatrical "attitudes," specifically rage and martyrdom. At the end of the novel, we see Dickens beating a fainthearted retreat from a politically feasible, if fictional, remedy for the social malaise that is the origin of women's anger both in *Little Dorrit* and in the public sphere at the time of its composition.

Whether we read Dickens from the perspective of narrative ethics, moral philosophy, or materialist analysis, we do so within the context of prior Dickens scholarship. In the final essay of this collection, Deborah Epstein Nord considers how Dickens came to be such a rich and enduring subject of contemporary interpretation. "The Making of Dickens Criticism" (chapter 14) examines the terms in which the best-known of Dickens's detractors—George Henry Lewes, Henry James, Virginia Woolf, and F. R. Leavis—evoked and depreciated his fiction: the infantilism of his imagination, the inappropriateness of his novels for the adult reader, his instinctive but uneducated talent. Such disparagement was, nationally speaking, English. It was not until the mid-twentieth-century, with the postwar emergence of Freudian and Marxist readings of literature, that Dickens became, particularly in America, a complex subject of sophisticated critical analysis. The "childishness" of his novels was discovered—notably by Edmund Wilson and Lionel Trilling—to be a fecund source of Freudian explications of the persistence of childhood within adulthood, and his brilliant metaphor of society as prison (expressed most fully in *Little Dorrit*) spoke powerfully to a population raw with memories of World War II and yet tinged with political idealism.

Nord reminds us, too, of the importance of Steven Marcus to Dickens studies. If Wilson and Trilling—along with Philip Collins, Humphry House, and J. Hillis Miller—brought *Bleak House, Little Dorrit,* and *Our Mutual Friend* to our critical attention, we owe the serious study of the early Dickens to Marcus and his still-influential book *Dickens from Pickwick to Dombey* (1965). Marcus is also among the first to have shown that a close reading of texts widely judged to be nonliterary could be richly productive of local literary meaning and broad cultural concepts. Indeed, as the author of *The Other Victorians: A Study of Sexuality and Pornography in Mid-Nineteenth-Century England,* which Michel Foucault famously acknowledged to have prompted him to write *The History of Sexuality,* he can be said to have inspired a new mode of inquiry, one that we would now call cultural studies.[9] Equally attuned throughout his writing to the political and the psychological, to the material specificity of historical life as well as to the transhistorical aspects of lived experience, Marcus has helped not only to make Dickens our contemporary but to shape our contemporary habits of critical exploration and analysis as well.

## NOTES

1. Jordan, Introduction, *Cambridge Companion to Dickens,* xix.
2. Connor, *Charles Dickens,* back cover.
3. John Schad, ed., *Dickens Refigured,* 1.
4. Wendy Jacobson, ed., *Dickens and the Children of Empire,* 11; Anny Sadrin, *Dickens, Europe and the New Worlds,* xiii, x.
5. Jordan, *Cambridge Companion,* back cover, xx.
6. Sadrin, *Dickens, Europe and the New Worlds,* xiii.
7. Anderson and Valente, *Disciplinarity at the Fin de Siècle,* 8, 15.
8. Suzy Anger also traces the genealogy of our ways of knowing to the Victorians. See *Knowing the Past: Victorian Literature and Culture,* edited by Anger, and her critical study *Victorian Interpretation.*
9. Foucault, *History of Sexuality,* 4.

# Part One

ETHICS AND NARRATIVE

# 1

# Dickens, Secularism, and Agency

GEORGE LEVINE

It would be silly and demonstrably untrue to argue that the novel is an inevitably secular form. Religion, in a myriad of ways, gets affirmed in a myriad of novels. And yet the novel as a form tends to resist the pressures put upon it by many writers to transcend the limits of the "secular" world. Fully flushed narratives demand the kinds of details that embody and flesh out ideas and faiths and inexplicable spiritual mysteries. The Victorian novel, written in the midst of culture-wide conflicts about just such matters, tends toward the secular even as it so often insists on the providential order of things. In constant tension between the conventions and intentions of its worldliness and its entirely understandable aspirations beyond the worldly, Victorian fiction is a secular form if ever there was one.[1]

To make a clinching case for this proposition, it would be necessary to treat in some detail a wide variety of Victorian fiction well beyond the established canon: Dinah Mulock Craik might then have to figure as importantly as Charlotte Brontë, Mrs. Oliphant as Thackeray, and Maria Corelli as Trollope. One would have to confront Newman's two novels, *Callista* and *Loss and Gain*. But any study of this problem would require close attention to Dickens, and particularly to his most overtly religious novel, *Little Dorrit*. So it will be with *Little Dorrit,* that most religious of Dickens's novels, that I will attempt here to build my broader argument.

*1: Dickens, Secularism, and Agency*

## WORLDLINESS VS. RELIGION

Most mid-twentieth-century critics, reacting to denigration of the Victorians by early modernists, came to them accepting the cliché that all of Victorian England was undergoing a crisis of faith. We were attracted to them—despite the shift in aesthetic expectations that called all things Victorian into question—just because we could see how their culture had opened the way toward an expanding and richer secular society. Of course, the kind of criticism that has dominated in recent years has forced us to qualify much of this initial enthusiasm for the Victorians. But many of us, who have perhaps become somewhat cynical of late, have been dismayed to discover that more than a century later, the thinking of skeptical Victorians (be it Mill or Darwin or George Eliot or Leslie Stephen) is still controversial and even inflammatory. The jury of popular opinion, in twenty-first-century America at least, is in, and the Victorian skeptics are out. It is in response, in part, to my shock at that discovery that I, a child of Victorian skepticism—though a child no longer—began to worry the question of secularism itself. Might it have been a mirage after all? Does a position that had seemed, perhaps to historically naïve eyes, so inevitable and at the same time so epistemologically necessary, so aesthetically engaging and even ethically imperative, turn out to have been either unreal or culturally ineffectual or both?

Our view that Victorian culture was on the fast track to secularism gave us a distorted sense of that culture and was based largely on the reading of a select group of intellectuals. There at the gateway was Carlyle thrashing about in his "everlasting No," and John Stuart Mill deep in depression, while George Eliot would soon refuse to go to church with her father and brother. And there at the far end of the century was Herbert Spencer doggedly systematizing the world according to a theory of equilibrium, and brilliant scientific naturalists like T. H. Huxley, John Tyndall, and W. K. Clifford being cockily iconoclastic, and, of course, there was Leslie Stephen, making his agnostic's apology. All of these famous instances point to a culture from which religion seemed to be being driven almost daily, and despite some very impressive rearguard actions like those of W. H. Mallock or William Balfour, driven successfully to secularity.

But if the perspective of philosophical radicals and overwrought intellectuals has been somewhat deceptive, the novel—a medium that reached deep into the stalwart middle classes—is another matter entirely. I argue here that the Victorian novel becomes a kind of battleground in which the developing conventions of the form itself often resist the pressures of the moral and sometimes explicitly religious energies that drive the narrative. It aspires overtly to represent the ordinary (even as we realize that the very concept of the ordinary is constrained by the contingencies of time, place, and perspective) and to give voice to the common experience of common people leading ordinary lives. Its strategies—from Dickens's satirical assaults on forms of cultural and governmental pomposity, to Thackeray's mock-epic similes, to George Eliot's transformation of St. Teresa into Dorothea Brooke—are deflationary and, as we all know, domesticating. Its concern in all arenas is not the strictly rational but the richly experienced: it was the Victorians who gave our culture the first big pre-Freudian dose of the Unconscious and who transferred the powers of Romantic poetry into realist narrative. That being the case, the Victorian novel is full of piety and is frequently constrained or structured by explicitly (or inexplicitly) Christian values, pointing to Christian morals with occasionally repellent ease. Although there are plenty of instances in which skepticism or even deconversion is dramatically central, for the most part it would have been difficult to infer from the Victorian novel that secularism was on the march.

But despite the piety, the novel as a form was intrinsically secular. Barry Qualls has definitively traced the parallels between Victorian narrative and the Puritan tradition, suggesting not only that the novelists were "determined that their words could still lead 'Christian' of the latter day to the Celestial City," but also that they found the belief in "a transcendent reality behind the world of appearances" finally "quite impossible."[2] Inspired in part, as was capitalism itself, by a Calvinistic ethic, the novel made its way in the secular world with ease. As Qualls has shown, it even secularized, as it utilized, the tradition of emblem and symbol through which the transcendent might be glimpsed in a secular world.

That the novel was intrinsically secular is not exactly news. But in what ways, given its frequently religious directions, might that have been so? How did it exercise a secularizing and compromising pressure on religious ideals, and how might that pressure have been extended to resist even the religious inclinations of its practitioners, exposing dramatically the contradictions built into the development that allowed the Protestant ethic to become a condition for the spirit of capitalism? The novel's determinedly detailed look at the new industrial and capitalist society put pressure on the providential narratives bequeathed to it by Christianity, disclosing tensions and instabilities as it moved from comic to tragic structures, implying alternate modes of value. Worldliness and otherworldliness do not make comfortable bedfellows. Secularity was not simply an epistemological argument of the radical intellectuals; it was also a way of living and imagining the moral life within the day-to-day world. Insofar as it did take hold, it did so not on strictly rational, epistemological grounds (of the sort that William James denigrated in the iconoclastic writings of W. K. Clifford), but on the grounds of deep feeling, deep emotional need, and a kind of Pascalian, pragmatic bet.

I focus, then, on the recognition implied in the novel, both in its earlier comic forms and in its later, more ambivalent and tragic ones, that a fully naturalized world is one in which the virtues affirmed by Christianity and Western culture, however desirable and admirable, are only fragilely sustainable, being easily corrupted and compromised: the fully religious narrative and resolution can be fully realized only in death. The realist novel needed something like the "Nemesis" George Eliot invoked so often in order to imagine the possibility that virtue would be rewarded, and vice punished, in the natural world. If providence is to make itself known in that world, it can do so only at the point of leaving it: to imagine a narrative of development in which merit is appropriately—if only roughly—rewarded, in which the conditions of virtue are compatible with the conditions of Vanity Fair, or in which uncorrupted virtue is even possible—as in Mulock Craik's *John Halifax, Gentleman*—entails a fundamental violation of the rules of the novel, of the canons of plausibility. The Victorian realist novel resisted and explored the consequences of that fact. Even so extravagant a one as *Wuthering Heights* moves toward compromise and recognition of the impossibility of the ideal. The failure of Victorian secularism can be understood in part through the movement of realistic fiction from comic to tragic form—the movement from a sense of the compatibility of the natural world with moral order to a deep recognition of their incompatibility. From *Pickwick Papers* and *Oliver Twist* to *Little Dorrit* and *Our Mutual Friend,* Dickens enacts something like that movement[3] and struggles imaginatively and I think almost heroically with it as he attempts to imagine a place for decency and love in a world that promises no rewards for them. The strains evident in his resistance to raw secularity are an impressive indicator of a culture-wide sense of the social and moral contradictions built into the partnership.

Indeed, it is the clear presence of a Christian moral framework in Dickens's work that makes the question of secularity in the novels particularly interesting. Whatever their extravagances, Dickens's novels, like those of most of his contemporaries, bind themselves to the conventions of probability and, implicitly, to the priority of the "real." His defensiveness against charges that he was not realistic is notorious. "There are such men as Sikes," he asserts in his Preface to *Oliver Twist;* and as to spontaneous combustion, we all remember his insistence in his preface to *Bleak House,* "I shall not abandon the facts until there shall have been a considerable Spontaneous Combustion of the testimony on which human occurrences are usually received."[4]

The novel as a form has from the start made drama of the relation between worldliness and religion and for the larger part of the eighteenth and nineteenth century has produced comic endings consonant with, but distinctly not the same as, the providential plot inherited from the Puritan tradition that it attempted partly to defy, partly to emulate. As Leopold Damrosch has argued, "'the faith of the reader' that Fielding invokes is a belief in plausible events, not miracles."[5] The conventions of comic fiction took precedence over the conventions of divine intervention. But whatever the convention, even in the work of a less literary and more pious writer like Richardson, virtue and worldly success were certainly not fictionally incompatible. It is the tension between a wished-for Christian ideal and a pervasively secular imagination that gives Dickens's novels their peculiar quality. And his is only the most extreme example of the way in which the novel can combine a self-evident relish for life with a not quite fully articulated aspiration toward moral ideals clearly based in Christianity and gesturing toward a transcendent reality that might somehow redeem the abundant disorders of modern England. The doubleness is intrinsic to the novel as a form, which, largely through its fascination with material particularities, in effect blocks access to the transcendence it can nevertheless attempt to intimate.

## SCIENCE AND "THE BATTLE OF THE EVIDENCES"

How, then, does the intrinsic secularity of the novel form sustain itself even as it dramatizes or overtly expresses sincere religious commitment; how does the genre itself trump the content? I come at this point indirectly by developing an analogy with the science that was contemporary with the growth of the Victorian novel, both because its commitment to register the natural world empirically parallels the novel's dominant commitment to realism and because it was largely in the hands of practitioners and theorists who were themselves religious and did not think of their work as incompatible with their religion. The question, in a way, was whether the form of scientific experiment and thought, determined by a basically empiricist epistemology, would be compatible with the scientists' own religious commitments.

The fundamental principle of Lyell's *Principles of Geology* is an axiom for all modern science: to understand any natural phenomenon, one must confine consideration to laws recognized as *verae causae,* that is, true causes, recognized now to be in operation.[6] In a letter to a friend written while he was working on *Principles,* Lyell explains that his book "will endeavour to establish the *principle[s] of reasoning* in the science; and all my geology will come in as illustration of my views of those principles, and as evidence strengthening the system necessarily arising out of the admission of such principles, which, as you know, are neither more nor less than that *no causes whatever* have from the earliest time to which we can look back, to the present, ever acted, but those *now acting,* and that they never acted with different degrees of energy from that which they now exert."[7] If there has never been at any time in any place any cause not now in operation, there are no miracles; God could not have created the world as the Bible describes him to have done; no supernatural intervention in this world is conceivable. Scientists might well be religious, but their science required of them that they make "reference exclusively to natural agents."

Perhaps the most prominent scientist of the time, John Herschel, in his still-fascinating *Preliminary Discourse on the Study of Natural Philosophy,* lays out the methods by which a genuine science might be practiced; he begins by rejecting the complaint that religion and science are incompatible. No, he claims, that cannot be right: "Truth can never be opposed to truth."[8] We can and must continue scientifically looking for scientific answers, but we may be certain that those answers will never conflict with true Christian doctrine. In effect, the claim is that if there is a god (and undoubtedly, for Herschel, there is), his works must be manifest *in* the world, and scientific scrutiny of that world will reveal him.

There came a time, of course, most obviously with Darwin and the extension of naturalistic description to the human, when the doctrines of Christianity and the laws of science would come so obviously into conflict that one truth would have to yield to the other. And it is striking, in reading Darwin, to notice how insistent he is that any *single* "fact" inconsistent with his explanations would be, as he says eight or so times in the *Origin,* "fatal to his theory." Only naturalistic explanations were acceptable, and they had to obey Lyell's actualist principles. If religion were to survive this development in science, which increasingly claimed to be able to describe all of the natural world, it would have to do so in a non-natural space.

Although few of the great scientists of the era were Calvinists, most of them were religious, just as most of the novelists were religious—in their way. And it is just the commitment to religion that makes so clear the generic secularity of their science. This is perhaps even better inferred from William Whewell's contribution to the Bridgewater Treatises. These apparently last gasps of natural theology—until our recent flirtations with "intelligent design," alas—insistently claim that the natural world gives evidence of its creator. But Whewell, perhaps the most original thinker about science in the first half of the nineteenth century, is very cautious about what constitutes a legitimate scientific argument, insisting that "final causes are to be excluded from *physical inquiry*."[9] We are not "to assume that we know the objects of the Creator's design, and put this assumed purpose in the place of a physical cause." The "physical philosopher has it for his business" to explain the physical world according to the laws of nature, and it is only "through this philosophical care that our views of final causes acquire their force and value as aids to religion." Religion can follow from science, Whewell thinks, but cannot be inside the science, which is generically constrained to adhere strictly to the laws of the physical world.

Max Weber, a century later, approaches the subject in a manner very different from Whewell's, but with results just about the same. "That science today is irreligious," he claims, "no one will doubt in his innermost being, even if he will not admit it to himself."[10] But with exactly the same kind of commitment to the responsibility of science to keep within the confines of natural explanation, he adds: "science 'free from presuppositions' expects . . . no less—and no more—than acknowledgment that *if* the process can be explained without . . . supernatural interventions, which an empirical explanation has to eliminate as causal facts, the process is to be explained the way science attempts to do. And the believer can do this without being disloyal to his faith."

Interestingly, it is the commitment to piety among scientists that helped open the way to some of the critical tensions between science and religion. Natural theology takes the evidence of the natural world as the proof of God's existence. It was, of course, common, even usual, that those who argued for natural evidences of the creator believed also in revelation and even miracle. Bishop Butler's subtle and careful arguments about using the analogy of nature as evidence are part of a large argument that in effect begins with belief in revelation. But once the field of natural theology is established, it is obliged, in itself, to demand of natural phenomena that they be clear evidences of divine creation. And it was just this move that John Henry Newman, so subtle and careful a thinker on this matter, rejected, recognizing as he did its tendency to level Nature and God.[11] The true evidences of religion are not naturalist at all: God is not just "the natural world with a divine glow upon it" (268). But once the natural world is given priority in the argument, there is trouble for religion, even if the intent is to show that the natural world is evidence of divinity.

Hugh Miller was of another mind, and I turn to him briefly here because he conveniently formulates the condition I am getting at. That brilliant and pious stonecutter geologist believed that science would, in fact, yield conclusions not only consonant with religious belief but fully confirmatory of it. He chastised Victorian clergy for being "a full age behind the requirements of the time" as they continued to build their arguments for divinity on metaphysics. He warned them as early as 1850 that there was coming what he called "a battle of the Evidences" and that the battle "will have as certainly to be fought on the field of physical science."[12] The novel too is a battleground of evidences, and a similar difficulty arises: probability and mimesis ought to reveal a divinely ordered world inside a providential plot; but probability and mimesis always threaten to fail to do this. Although Miller is ready to stake his faith on the evidences of God's presence that he will find *in* nature, it always remains possible that the evidence will not point to the divine despite Miller's confidence that science cannot be disruptive of fundamental Christian beliefs—or despite Dickens's apparent confidence, evident in the very friendly treatment of the *Origin* in both *Household Words* and *All the Year Round,* that science will not be incompatible with his ideal values.

While scientific discovery constantly puts pressure on religious explanation, the secular epistemology of the novel puts pressure on religious interpretations of life and morals. It tests pious forms and conventions in large part by forcing readers to recognize the full, personal engagement of the pious and the moral in the details of ordinary life. The novel is, then, the perfect venue for George Eliot's or Trollope's worldly and sympathetic representations of clergy and of people of faith, for it does not require either the author's or the reader's acquiescence in the faith so sympathetically registered. It is obviously no accident that George Eliot's first fictional works are about clergy, about true believers who are seen as humans subject to human desires and mistakes. Dickens often does the reverse, exposing the clergy as sweaty, greedy, hungry, selfish beings who exploit religiosity for their own interests. Ironically, however, such satiric attacks on the clergy are more likely to indicate some sort of serious belief in the realities of religious views than is George Eliot's compassionate treatment. The anger of the exposure suggests that Dickens wants to believe in the religious purity of the ideals that these clergy merely exploit. But the exposure secularizes as fully as the sympathy does. There is no necessary connection in fiction—or perhaps in life—between goodness and belief. The tensions between the secularity of the form and the religious, even transcendental, objectives of the narratives parallel the problem of religious science depending for evidence on naturalistic phenomena.

The novel as a form indeed did much to sanction the displacement of doctrinal and institutionally supported religion by its insistence on personal consciousness and personal belief, narrative being a mode that requires our engagement with particulars. When Dickens has Sissy Jupe oppose compassion for individuals to a general, averaging, rationalizing sense of overall benefits, he does so not by appealing to the transcendent but by insisting on the value of individual feeling. Think only of Louisa Gradgrind sinking to the ground at her father's feet. But fictional commitment to the validity of personal feeling might also be traced back to philosophical and at least quasiscientific roots. The connection of the realistic enterprise with the development of empiricism was long ago classically established by Ian Watt, who, as Michael McKeon has succinctly explained, connects the development of "formal realism" with "a set of socioeconomic developments at whose center are the rise of the middle class, the growth of commercial capitalism," and the "validation of individual experience."[13]

As I have previously suggested, the argument that the spirit of capitalism depended upon a Protestant ethic implies a providential narrative. When Fielding rewrote Richardson's *Pamela* as a sham, he was identifying one of the central problems of the novel form that was to grow inside the new capitalism: is it possible to be piously virtuous and to achieve worldly success? What is it that constitutes success in the novel world? Is it possible to be successful and not have money? If money is a moral disaster, the embodiment of material values, the equivalent of Boffin's dust heaps, can one acquire it without morally dirtying one's soul? If so, narrative becomes comic, which is the characteristic form of early realist fiction. But later realist fiction is less comically inflected. Reward tends finally to be fully dissociated from virtue, which, along with the religion that sanctioned it, becomes a mere cover for self-interest and greed.

## CAPITALISM AND THE PROTESTANT ETHIC

As the novel committed itself to the most authentic possible registration of the details of the sorts of lives their readers were ostensibly living, it became particularly difficult to imagine behavior leading to material success that was not tainted by acquiescence in a society built on the profit motive. How might a heroically decisive figure convincingly be shown to fight his way with full consciousness toward success and *not* be exposed as complicit in an economy operating ruthlessly in pursuit of profit? Weber provided a narrative that explains how success in business might be understood as a symptom of religious virtue and compatible with the most ferociously aggressive capitalist behavior: "earning money within the modern economic order is, so long as it is done legally, the result and the expression of virtue and proficiency in a calling" (53–54). The providential plot thus enters realist narrative, though with the wry ironies of Jane Austen, the romantic enthusiasm of Scott, or the romantic and Puritanical seriousness of Dickens.

While the economic history that Weber theorizes reveals a culture in which a rejection of worldliness, systematic self-repression, and hard work might yield worldly rewards, the novel, often playing out this very story, could rarely manage it untroubled. The strain in George Eliot's imagination of a "Nemesis" that somehow is built into a fully secular world is apparent in the very self-consciousness with which she manages appropriate punishment for Bulstrode, for example, or appropriate rewards for Caleb. The secular vision makes it very difficult to accommodate providence or to imagine the neat fit between moral virtue and temporal success, and this is particularly true when the protagonist is active and decisive. The opposition between material success and virtue is a consistent theme of Victorian fiction, even where virtue is, indeed, rewarded materially.

The uneasiness of nineteenth-century novels with their own heroes is a characteristic of the genre itself and seems largely a consequence of this opposition and the tension it produces, sometimes inside the narrative, sometimes in the narrator's relation to the story. Novelists need the success of their protagonists to bring off their comic endings, but they are hard-pressed to imagine ways, within the textured representation of middle-class life and economy, to represent it without radically compromising the protagonist's moral integrity. Ideal moral behavior is for the most part dramatized as incompatible with success within the new economic system, or, more frequently, the incompatibility is disguised by investing women with ideality and focusing on flawed male protagonists who must mature. Wherever the Protestant ethic drives successful capitalists, the narrated story of life inside the economy, inside "vanity fair," keeps the divine hand out and registers some rather seamy doings.

Although women characters, too, in the conditions of nineteenth-century realism, must suffer compromises—as does, most obviously, the overly idealistic Dorothea Brooke, or the very practical Jane Eyre, or the carefully self-abnegating Lucy Snowe—they are rarely threatened by the kind of corruption intrinsic to ambition in the economic system. Women characters can be unequivocally good, importing into their behavior the ideals of the truly religious life owing to their tightly constricted place within the economic system; yet they must live in novels with men, and they must be subject to the critique implicit in the famous "but" with which Arthur Pendennis arrived at the romantic-comic conclusion of his story. The "but" intimates the realities that Franco Moretti says the English novel largely avoids.[14] It embodies—with a sort of Thackeraryan fatigue—the secularity that imposes itself on the most religious aspirations of the English novel. The "but," Pen explains, "will come in spite of us." "But" is the secular caveat and the mark, also, of the characteristically weak protagonist of nineteenth-century fiction. It registers the fact that nobody is "exempt from the fall," as Pen puts it, particularly not the weak and wavering hero.[15] It becomes the word for the inevitable compromise that secularity entails.

## THE CASE OF *LITTLE DORRIT*: *RADIX MALORUM EST CUPIDITAS*

I turn now to *Little Dorrit,* in which the tension between the religious and the secular is thematically and formally central, and the motif that most fully embodies the tension is money itself: almost all of the major moments of the book show money marking the lives of the characters. The preoccupations and problems characteristic of the novel as a genre are prominent: the pervasiveness of money as energizing force, guilt-accruing object, and point of concern; the centrality of a weak and indecisive hero; and an elaborate plot forcing itself toward some comic harmony but strained intensely toward the possibility of matching merit, virtue, and reward. Arthur Clennam is almost the quintessential weak hero whom Scott described, about whom Thackeray complained, and around whom a striking proportion of nineteenth-century novels spin.

In *Little Dorrit* Dickens seems both more overtly religious and more self-conscious about secularity than he had ever been before. In one of his working notes he wrote, "Set the darkness and vengeance against the New Testament."[16] As others have noted, at this point in his life and career Dickens strenuously cultivated a New Testament sensibility that emerges in the language of his books and of his correspondence and public lectures. The apparent thrust of *Little Dorrit* is, as Dennis Walder has put it, "to show that one can free oneself from the imprisoning forces associated with a narrow Old Testament faith of stern self-denial and wrathful vengeance by means of the broadly redemptive, loving spirit of the New."[17] But the religious intensity runs parallel to the increasing disgust Dickens himself expresses for the social and material conditions of contemporary England. The religion, then, is paralleled by a marked world weariness, even world abhorrence, that has about it at the same time something of the Calvinist severity and anger that Dickens attacks through his analysis of the demoralized character of Arthur Clennam and of Mrs. Clennam's relentless vengefulness. The famous prison imagery entails a quasireligious vision of the world as secular prison: "Far aslant across the city, over its jumbled roofs, and through the open tracery of its church towers, struck the long bright rays, bars of the prison of this lower world" (*LD*, II, ch.30).

Self-evidently, it is in this prison of the lower world that everything in the novel must unfold, and the novel is consistently troubled by a determined registering of this prison as repulsive and destructive, while it is particularly outraged by the austere and world-hating religion exemplified by Clennam's mother. Religion and secularity constantly play off against each other, for the raw secularity of the bleak, imprisoned world is recognizable here only in the language that religion itself provides. Moreover, throughout the novel, biblical allusions comment on the degraded and degrading secularity of the realist world. The aspiration to a transcendent vision struggles with an entirely secular understanding of how the world—or at least the social world that Dickens chooses to describe—works. One might say that *Little Dorrit* dramatizes the necessary compromise between Dickensian New Testament ideal (which, as Moretti suggests, is the characteristic ideal of the English novel) and the secularity that his commitment to realist probability entailed.

The problem was to find a way to squeeze into the secular surfaces of the book some intimation of spiritual possibility. The dreary and ugly world into which Clennam moves on a representatively dreary Sunday is evidence of real fatigue and disgust, as is the surrealistically charged description of the area around Clennam's old home, to which at the start he makes his sad pilgrimage. Moving through some of the "crooked and descending" streets, he passes the "mouldy hall of some obsolete Worshipful Company," the "illuminated windows of a Congregationless Church," and then "warehouses and wharves, and here and there a narrow alley leading to the river, where a wretched little bill, FOUND DROWNED, was weeping on the wet wall" (*LD*, I, ch.3). The corruption of the propped-up house, in the midst of these squalid evidences of decay and death, gives a rough sense of the underside of the world, which the novel describes with so much satiric contempt, in fancier areas of the city. Where, in the midst of these realistically and symbolically described manifestations of a world rotting away in its sheer materiality, might there be glimpses of true spirit and transcendence?

It is in the figure of Little Dorrit that Dickens struggles not only to imagine what transcendence might look like in a world in which religion itself has become secular, but to do so in a way that will satisfy the secular and realist constraints of the novel form. A victim of the economic system from the start, Amy is born into just such physical and moral conditions as Clennam finds around and in his old home, but in a literal prison, the Marshalsea. While Clennam is trapped inside the sordidness and decay emblematized in his sad secular pilgrimage, Amy Dorrit is somehow immune to the material and psychological conditions in which she grows and lives: "Worldly wise in hard and poor necessities, she was innocent in all things else. Innocent, in the mist through which she saw her father, and the prison, and the turbid living river that flowed through it and flowed on" (*LD*, I, ch.7). She is imagined as deeply *of* the material world, as any character in a novel with realist claims must be; but Dickens figures her also as untainted by the turbid flow of secular time, by its materiality, its hard and poor necessities.

As the anti–Becky Sharp, impervious to the demeaning pressures of secularity, Little Dorrit strains the limits of the genre and is even, on occasion, allowed the voice of transcendence, as when she preaches the divine mercy that the book's last chapters attempt to embody:

> "O Mrs Clennam, Mrs Clennam . . . angry feelings and unforgiving deeds are no comfort and no guide to you and me. My life has been passed in this poor prison, and my teaching has been very defective; but let me implore you to remember later and better days. Be guided only by the healer of the sick, the raiser of the dead, the friend of all who were afflicted and forlorn, the patient Master who shed tears of compassion for our infirmities. We cannot but be right if we put all the rest away, and do everything in remembrance of Him. There is no vengeance and no infliction of suffering in His life, I am sure. There can be no confusion in following Him, and seeking for no other footsteps, I am certain." (*LD*, II, ch.31)

Such preaching is uncharacteristic of the always self-effacing Little Dorrit. The book knows all too well—not least in the determined creation of its almost saintly heroine—that nobody in the secular world, the only world the novel knows, is able to follow this injunction unfailingly, not even Amy herself, who for one brief moment earlier on had railed against the injustice done to her father and throughout the narrative has nurtured a not entirely repressed secular love of Arthur Clennam (who notes at last, in his own weakness, when Amy comes to help him in the Marshalsea, that she "looked something more womanly" [*LD*, II, ch.20]).

Juxtaposition of the two women almost makes a morality play: Amy the New Testament counterpart to Mrs. Clennam's Calvinist and hate-filled religiosity. When Amy asks Mrs. Clennam to "remember" those latter and better days, the days that lie outside secularity, she can only remind the reader that the book cannot trespass on such places except in the imagination of its titular heroine. As the novel winds down, the religious imagery and influence grow more intense, diffusing even to the point of softening the inexorable

## 1: Dickens, Secularism, and Agency

Mrs. Clennam, who rises, "as if a dead woman had risen" (*LD,* II, ch.30), and shows for the first time understanding and compassion for both Amy and Arthur, although she continues to keep the secret of Arthur's birth, and thus of her own shame. It is not beside the point that Amy's last dramatic act within the novel is morally ambiguous, although it is also clearly designed to heighten further our sense of her deference to secular promises: she burns the evidence that Arthur is not Mrs. Clennam's son, and thus keeps him forever in the dark.

Within the tradition of comic realism to which *Little Dorrit* marginally belongs, the providential plot succeeds, but here it is radically compromised. Although worldly success is not allowed, the success that is allowed is distinctly, explicitly, in this world. As what seems like a self-conscious anti-*Pamela, Little Dorrit* does not reconcile merit and worldly reward. The religious imagery continues, virtually concluding at the marriage "with the sun shining on them through the painted figure of Our Saviour on the window" (*LD,* II, ch.34), but the intimation of life and transcendence lives only in the image, not in the narrative itself.

The story labors to provide reasonable explanations for effects that seem designed to appeal to forces outside the realm of mere plausibility. It is here, in the very straining of the plot, that the tensions between the religious and the secular are most evident. For everything about the story, from Clennam's return to the collapse of his mother's house, describes what would seem a natural movement toward decay. Only some movement from beyond the natural could change this direction. The constant movement of degradation—the mud around Mrs. Clennam's house; the decay that the dominion of the Barnacles guarantees to an ailing nation; the disasters produced by the Merdle bubble enticing everyone, from William Dorrit to Pancks to Arthur Clennam, to pursue unmerited money—is counteracted by Dickens's pursuit of something else at work that will be redemptive at last.

The major redemptive event in the book is the marriage of Arthur and Amy. And that depends entirely on the withdrawal of money from their connection. Only through such straining could the comic tradition of English realism be sustained inside conventions of probability and verisimilitude. It required a plot more complex and confused than any other in Dickens's work to achieve the form of providential order. To write the final installments of the novel, Dickens had to summarize the previous action in his notes, almost as every reader must do in the reading.

Mary Poovey's comments about *Our Mutual Friend* apply as well to *Little Dorrit:* "on the one hand, the novel struggled against the modern disaggregating of domains by insisting that economic behavior not be freed from a moral analytic; on the other hand, *Our Mutual Friend* betrays the anxieties generated *by* this disaggregation."¹⁸ The moralizing of money matters is consistent with the idea that the "Protestant spirit" was at the heart of a developing capitalism. But in *Little Dorrit* there is a difference. We have Merdle's famous financial bubble, a financial success built on speculation and falsity rather than self-abnegation and honorable hard work, with the inevitable consequences. And we have Casby, who radiates a false charity around his brutal grasping for money, as well as Gowan and the entire Barnacle family, for whom work is anathema and demeaning: "how not to do it" is the perfect anticapitalist formula, as it is also the perfect anti-Calvinist formula. Dickens's deep hostility to these kinds of self-interested and lazy indulgences in wealth runs parallel again to the very Old Testament attitudes that he condemns so mercilessly in Mrs. Clennam. These figures confirm the corruption that comes with an unmoralized or a falsely moralized relation to money and worldly success.

But there is, finally, no moralizing money. In the later Dickens, there is simply no touching money without being dirtied. On the one hand, survival in secular society depends on the possession of at least some money, and only moralized money can begin to be consonant with the virtue required of Dickens's protagonists. On the other hand, it is virtually impossible in Dickens to find a way to acquire money that is not fatally tainted. Pip's moral redemption in *Great Expectations* depends on his losing the fortune that Magwitch would bestow on him. Money has real value only in its absence. "I have no use for money," Amy passionately exclaims to Clennam. "I have no wish for it" (*LD*, II, ch.29). But the book is obsessed with money nevertheless, and its workings are registered with an almost Thackerayan attentiveness. It is obviously not irrelevant that Amy's first effort after Clennam's visit to the Marshalsea is to prevent him from making any more of those euphemistically disguised "tributes" to her father.

Although there is plenty in Dickens and in most of the other great novelists of the period to support Weber's thesis, *Little Dorrit* will have nothing of it. Here, it is not enough that people must be honorable with their money: they must renounce it entirely to be morally saved. Money is the key emblem of that corrupt and depressing secularity that Dickens describes so powerfully and with a quite awful grasp of living detail. It is the circulating material that makes for moral decay, that draws even the finest away from the ideal aspirations that Little Dorrit preaches in her speech to Mrs. Clennam. Only Daniel Doyce embodies unequivocally the Protestant ethic in his relation to work, and there it is marked by his fundamental lack of interest in money. He delegates all financial matters to Clennam, while he applies all his energy and ingenuity to his work. He is not even upset when Clennam's speculation bankrupts him.

By the end, what stands between Arthur and Amy is only the Dorrit money. The virtuous protagonist cannot accept the virtuous heroine's merely fortuitous wealth. And thus the final love scene, if that's what it might be called, is in effect a mutual and joyful renunciation of money. The irony is that, even if upside-down, the relationship depends entirely on money: on Clennam's early guilt that something is owed to the Dorrits, on the attempt to discover the source of William Dorrit's debts, on the attempt to recover his inheritance, and on Amy's inheritance and loss of wealth. Money is everywhere. Love and personal commitment become possible only through a kind of negotiation in which money is entirely banished.

The proposal comes not with an expression of overt affection but with a discussion of money. The joy of the scene is worldly loss. The excitement is in Amy's eagerness to tell Clennam, another bankrupt protagonist, that she is penniless: "Do you feel quite strong enough to know what a great fortune I have got?" she asks. "I have been anxiously waiting to tell you. I have been longing and longing to tell you" (*LD,* II, ch.34).

There is a touch of playfulness here, which comes about because Amy is confident in her poverty and certain that not having money will win her loved one. "You are sure," she asks Clennam, "that you will not take it [that is, her wealth]." "Never," the honorable Clennam necessarily replies. Laying her face down on Clennam's hand in a gesture she could not indulge if she were wealthy, Amy joyfully exclaims: "I have nothing in the world. I am as poor as when I lived here." Dickens gives no words to Clennam, ever the passive figure, even here. He sheds "manly tears" (what else?), but it is Amy who takes the initiative in a way distinctly uncharacteristic of Dickens's other heroines or of Victorian heroines in general. She begins again, clasping his hand, "Never to part, my dearest Arthur; never any more, until the last" (*LD,* II, ch.34). Although Amy relies on Clennam's former expression of a wish that he had recognized that she was a woman earlier (*LD,* II, ch.29), and although she swears absolute submission, Amy is positively aggressive. And she can be aggressive precisely because she is penniless. The most convincing and touching aspect of Little Dorrit's character throughout the novel, as she is made to embody Dickens's sense of a reality beyond the secular, is her unmistakably secular love for Clennam. Real joy, it turns out, is itself secular.

For Dickens's project in *Little Dorrit* to succeed, it was necessary that virtue and social and economic success be separated. The cruel conditions of the life that Dickens so intensely describes make it impossible for him to imagine that the world is really accommodated to virtue. If in earlier novels (even *Bleak House*) the happy ending brings virtue together with some kind of worldly success, in *Little Dorrit* what is worldly is inevitably implicated in corruption. As Poovey argues, "Taking money literally, as a good and an end in itself, leads to the literal commodification of human beings" (166). The very initiating energy of the plot implies just this idea. When Arthur returns to see his mother for the first time, he is driven by a guilt that is justified only by his understanding of money itself. "In grasping at money and in driving hard bargains," he says to his mother, "someone may have been grievously deceived, injured, ruined" (*LD,* I, ch.5). Little Dorrit thus enters his life as a victim of money. The implication of this initiating energy of the plot is that only life outside the economy is to be trusted. And in the novel there is virtually nothing outside the economy, except, perhaps, Little Dorrit herself. Virtue may be rewarded, after all, but only when money is transformed into other forms of nonmaterial wealth: "I never was rich before," Little Dorrit exclaims to Arthur.

Unlike Becky Sharp, the book implies, Amy's character would be no different if she were rich. On the European tour, wealth makes her unhappy because she misses the opportunity to assist her father, which poverty had afforded her. With Oliver Twist, one feels a touch of authorial naïveté about the boy's innocence in the midst of an actively corrupting environment. But when Dickens makes Little Dorrit a literal "child of the Marshalsea," he self-consciously affirms the possibility of a spiritual condition in which social context—the bread and butter of realism—is irrelevant to character. The final love scene, enacted in the Marshalsea—the purest symbol of the constraints and corruptions of the dominant economic system—strains probability just because, in its resistance to traditional novel form and to the idea of a secularity that is consistent with Christian morality, it insists so doggedly on a religious ideal.

Secularity triumphs nonetheless, even if it is a secularity chastised and modified by the experience the book narrates. Money is indeed at the root of all evil; and because it is so, despite everyone's—even a saint's—need for it, the realist protagonist loses virtually all powers of agency. Criticism has long regarded Clennam, in his unusual interiority, to be an autobiographical surrogate for Dickens himself. But there is no Dickensian energy in Clennam, and were it to appear, it would necessarily manifest itself as a moral violation, like any action in a world so manifestly corrupt. Clennam must be the post-Scott insipid hero trying to *do* something. He insists, to the horror of the Barnacles, on wanting to "know," as a condition for being able to act justly. And his vainly pursuing the Barnacles for knowledge of the source of William Dorrit's debts is about all that he can do as an agent without compromising himself. At least there is virtue in struggling hopelessly against secular inertia and selfishness. But, in his weakness, the great system entangles and corrupts him. Not only does Dickens emphasize the weakness of the "hero"—something that other novelists often tried to disguise by means of the hero's good nature, good intentions, and good looks—but he also dramatizes that weakness through the soliloquies in which Clennam sees himself as "nobody": "I have no will," says Clennam, right at the start (*LD*, I, ch.2), and asks himself repeatedly "what he was to do henceforth in life" (*LD*, I, 16). Although Little Dorrit gives him a vocation, as Mirah Lapidoth, for example, gives Daniel Deronda (another, though quite different, indecisive young hero), Clennam acts independently really only once: when he invests via Pancks in the Merdle bubble and is consequently ruined, subjected to the Marshalsea and a near-fatal illness. Whereas Deronda finds a nation to establish, Clennam sinks back into passivity and is saved by his poverty.

Through the contortions of the plot and the weakness of the hero, the novel finds a way to point toward a New Testament mercy that might ease the pain of this prison of a lower world. But it is a resolution for two. There are casualties everywhere else, most particularly in Amy's family. Father and uncle die together; Fanny is stuck in a stupid marriage she arranged for all the wrong reasons; Tip dies. The natural narrative of decay and decline is played out everywhere in the novel except in the lives of the protagonists. They escape because they have renounced the conditions of survival in the society that the novel has so persuasively and repulsively described.

*Little Dorrit* develops extravagantly tensions basic to almost all Victorian fiction, particularly in its attempt to reaffirm the possibility of transcendence in a world that is so radically fallen. The last pages are dominated by Dickens's transformation of the rays of the sun from the prison bars of this lower world earlier in the book to rays that carry with them the image of "Our Saviour" from the stained glass windows of the church. And the wonderful, deeply moving last paragraph of the book is preceded by the moment when the lovers stand at the portico of the church looking at the street "in the autumn sun's bright rays." It is as though the sun is not a prison but an invitation to new life. But the possibility of a truly new life outside this lower world is intimated by Dickens only in images. The power of the last paragraph lies in its resolute, utterly necessary return to that world: the key phrase is "went down."

Each sentence of the last paragraph reiterates that phrase. There are no "latter and better days" here, but only the lower world. And the novel resolves itself powerfully precisely because it can only generate a hope for such days, acceding as it does to the condition of all life—to the condition of being "down" here. Formally, the ending of *Little Dorrit* retains the quality of the "happy ending" that is the mark of the early modern realist novel. But, of course, it is a happy ending manqué: not only is there no longer any possibility of material reward for the good protagonists, but happiness depends entirely on the absence of such reward. Ironically, the last paragraph is one of the few critical places in the novel where money does not figure prominently. Yet there is a kind of evasion at work in that paragraph—an evasion that somewhat perversely allows Dickens and the novel to slip into the attitudes toward work and money that mark the "Protestant ethic."

We know from the preceding chapter that Clennam will go back to work for Doyce, will be given a second chance. And we know, as Meagles describes it, that Doyce is flourishing overseas, "directing works and executing labours over yonder, that it would make your hair stand on end to look at. He's no public offender, bless you, now! He's medaled and ribboned, and starred and crossed, and I don't-know-what all'd, like a born nobleman. But we mustn't talk about that over here" (*LD,* II, ch.34). Dickens's unwillingness to show Doyce active and prosperous in England is not simply an aspect of his ironic attack against English bureaucracy and Barnacalism, though it is certainly partly that. He simply has no way to dramatize the acquisition of wealth that is not radically compromised, and so Doyce's success happens offstage, abroad. But Doyce can be invoked as a means by which Clennam can gain access to money without being tainted by it himself. Given the novel's commitment to social and contextual precision, no character, not even Clennam or Little Dorrit, can get on without money. The novel cannot finally reconcile the polar opposites—as they are established in the work and largely inherited from the novel form itself—of secularity and religion, of ethics and money.

But, like its protagonists, the book does what it can do, given the fact that it must necessarily "go down." The power of the book's last words may keep us from wondering how Amy and Arthur will sustain their integrity in a world populated, as the last grim and wonderful sentence tells us, by the "noisy and the eager, and the arrogant and froward and the vain," fretting and chafing and making "their usual uproar." But the prose does not let Dickens off the hook, even if it does allow him to intimate the possibility that transcendence lies behind the secular. Most importantly, Dickens dramatizes the limits of secularity: no redemptive acts, no heroism, only "a modest life of usefulness and happiness," lived in a world where some few people benefit briefly from that modesty and usefulness, but where the "arrogant and the froward and the vain" remain in command, and where it must be sufficient even for the best of us to live.

## NOTES

1. In this chapter there will not be time for anything resembling a full discussion of the idea of secularity. Part of what I mean by it is belief that all of experience must be recognized as nontranscendental, as operating entirely in terms of the natural world, without miracles or supernatural interventions. This is the "epistemological" aspect of it, and the one that will get most of my attention here. But beyond this, I mean something like what Charles Taylor describes in his essay "Modes of Secularism" (Rajeev Bhargava, ed., *Secularism and Its Critics*), in which he—a believing Roman Catholic—sees secularism as a kind of moral imperative in the modern world, one that allows for the extraordinary range of beliefs among people and that makes possible democracy, a social organization that is not governed by any one of those myriad beliefs but is willing to acquiesce, in order to make civilized life possible, in an "overlapping consensus" on culture-wide decisions about the particulars of ordinary and social life, on the law, and rules of social behavior. The secularism of the Victorian novel that I am discussing, derived so directly from its commitment to realist representation of society and individuals, which always registers "mixed conditions" and tends to expel excess even when it most values it, tends clearly in the direction of Taylor's ideas.

2. Barry Qualls, *The Secular Pilgrims of Victorian Fiction,* ix, 109–10.

3. In *Charles Dickens: The World of His Novels,* J. Hillis Miller lays out something of this argument in his very first chapter, on *Pickwick Papers:* "The crucial event of the novel is Pickwick's discovery that transcendent power and goodness are no longer immanent in the world" (35). And he goes on to say that the critical question with which Dickens would then be wrestling for the rest of this career was "How is a person who cannot withdraw going to avoid being destroyed by the evil forces in the world?"

4. See George Ford, *Dickens and His Readers,* 129–55, for an excellent discussion of Dickens's views on probability in fiction. While Dickens was criticized harshly in his own time for his failures of probability and for the extravagance of his prose and the flatness of his characters, he saw himself as simply investing reality with the extravagances of art. While Ford wants to show that Dickens's strenuous public defenses of the reality of his novelistic treatments put him in an awkward position and belied his own artistic commitments, he also shows that Dickens did indeed see himself as committed to representing reality precisely, with an excitement that no other writer might achieve. He was committed, that is, to the romantic side of familiar things.

5. Leopold Damrosch, Jr., *God's Plot and Man's Stories: Studies in the Fictional Imagination from Milton to Fielding,* 283. Damrosch argues that there was a major Puritan influence on the development of the novel, which, as a form, he sees as having tested out alternative religious positions. Here is his major point: "The relevance of Puritanism to the novel does not really lie in particular doctrinal points . . . [but] rather in the peculiar power, as a basis for fiction, of a faith that sees human life as a narrative invented by God but interpreted by human beings" (4). Damrosch wants to insist on the presence of Christianity in fictional narratives. My argument, rather, is that the pressures

of secularity increasingly tested and strained the providential narrative. The compromise by which the novel acts out Weber's thesis about religion and the rise of capitalism forces it increasingly to recognize the incoherence of a religious view with a commitment as well to worldly success.

6. According to Lyell, James Hutton finally set geology in the right direction because he was the first to attempt "to dispense entirely with all hypothetical causes, and to explain the former changes of the earth's crust, by reference exclusively to natural agents" (Charles Lyell, *Principles of Geology*, Vol. 1, ed. Martin J. S. Rudwick, 61). Hutton showed that "all past changes on the globe had been brought about by the slow agency of existing causes" (630).

7. Cited by Rudwick, ed., *Principles of Geology*, Vol. 1, xii–xiii.

8. John Herschel, *Preliminary Discourse on the Study of Natural Philosophy*, 9.

9. William Whewell, *Astronomy and General Physics Considered with Reference to Natural Theology*, 303–5.

10. Max Weber, *The Protestant Ethic and the Spirit of Capitalism*, 27. Subsequent references are made parenthetically in the text.

11. As A. Dwight Culler puts it, Newman "cared less for Paley . . . than he did for Darwin." Culler quotes Newman as saying that Natural Theology he had "ever viewed with the greatest suspicion." It has a tendency, Newman thought, with great prescience and insight, "if contemplated exclusively, to dispose the mind against Christianity, because it speaks only of laws and cannot tell of their suspension, that is, of miracles" (A. Dwight Culler, *The Imperial Intellect*, 267–68).

12. In a fascinating discussion of the nature of evidence for the existence of the creator in nature, Hugh Miller takes a strong scientific stance and attacks clergy for lingering in metaphysics when the true evidence must be derived from nature itself. Miller argues that "ere the Churches can be prepared competently to deal with it [that is, with the current arguments for development, which Miller sees inevitably to lead to atheism, even if not atheistic in intention], or with the other objections of a similar class which the infidelity of an age so largely engaged as the present in physical pursuits will be from time to time originating, they must greatly extend their educational walks into the field of physical science. The mighty change which has taken place during the present century, in the direction in which the minds of the first order are operating . . . seems to have too much escaped the notice of our theologians. . . . [I]t is in the departments of physics, not of metaphysics, that the greater minds of the age are engaged. . . . The battle of the Evidences will have as certainly to be fought on the field of physical science, as it was contested in the last age on that of the metaphysics" (Hugh Miller, *Foot-Prints of the Creator, or, The Asterolepis of Stromness*, 43–45).

13. Michael McKeon, *Theory of the Novel: A Historical Approach*, 382.

14. Franco Moretti, *The Way of the World: The Bildungsroman in European Culture*. See Moretti's entire discussion of the way the English novel differs from the Continental in its treatment of youth, development, and possibility. He emphasizes the English novel's failure in fact to deal with the mixed conditions that radically compromise moral choice and that make any notion of a decisive and unambiguous ending virtually impossible. From one point of view, he writes, the Bildungsroman tradition in England gives us "but one long fairy-tale with a happy ending, far more elementary and limited than its continental counterparts" (213). The implication of his argument is that my own general

*1: Dickens, Secularism, and Agency*

argument here would work better with the continental novel, and I believe that is true. But the English novel is also, willy-nilly, a fully secular form no matter how traditional many of its devices may be, and part of what is most striking about the English novel is just the tension the best of them produce between the obligatory romantic-comic resolution and the possible alternatives it has, in various ways, so carefully averted.

15. Thackeray, *Pendennis*, Vol. II, 343.
16. Quoted in Peter Ackroyd, *Dickens*, 778.
17. Walder, *Dickens and Religion*, 179.
18. Mary Poovey, *Making a Social Body: British Cultural Formation, 1830–1864*, 156. Subsequent references are made parenthetically in the text.

# 2

# Dickens and the Goods

ROBERT NEWSOM

All readers of Dickens notice that he is an insistently judgmental writer with strong opinions and especially strong ethical opinions. Even in the earliest writing the force of the writer's judgments is palpable:

> We have always entertained a particular attachment towards Monmouth-street, as the only true and real emporium for second-hand wearing apparel. Monmouth-street is venerable from its antiquity, and respectable from its usefulness. Holywell-street we despise; the red-headed and red-whiskered Jews who forcibly haul you into their squalid houses, and thrust you into a suit of clothes, whether you will or not, we detest.

So begins "Meditations in Monmouth Street," one of the early *Sketches by Boz*.[1]

This is not to say that there was anything very unusual in a writer's striking such a tone in such a piece in the early 1800s. It is easy to find similar passages in Charles Lamb, William Hazlitt, and Leigh Hunt—older writers, all of whom influenced the young Dickens. Nor was it unexpected that such a writer might grow up to be an earnest Victorian and write, in very much longer works, more focused and coherent polemics exposing institutions and practices he felt to be evil: workhouses and prisons, Yorkshire Schools, slavery, the Court of Chancery, bureaucracy and patronage in the civil service, as well as such personal vices as selfishness, hypocrisy, greed, and pride. We expect Victorians to be earnest, to denounce evil, and to exhort us to be good. We can see in the major novelists who came into prominence a decade or more after Dickens (the Brontës, Thackeray, Trollope, and George Eliot) a reaction against Dickens's didacticism accompanying what they believed to be their own greater realism—especially greater psychological realism. And all of these latter writers took exception to particular aspects of what they in their own ways understood to be Dickens's conventional values and the sentimentality in which he couched them (though they all themselves protested whenever they were charged with amorality, much less immorality, in their writings, and they were certainly very far from having reached the strong reactions against earnestness embodied in the aestheticism of Walter Pater or Oscar Wilde). But Dickens's ethical force was undiminished throughout his work and unapologetically conspicuous to the end.

Consider, for example, the final scene of his last completed novel, *Our Mutual Friend*, in which the elderly and shabby-genteel Mr. Twemlow—whose mildness and confusion have from the novel's very first chapter provided both the elevated circle in which he moves (in spite of his own financial dependence) and the reader much amusement—bravely defends, before a circle of both the old-rich and the newly rich, the marriage of a gentleman, Eugene Wrayburn, to a waterman's daughter, Lizzie Hexam, who has worked in a factory and, most damagingly, has no money. After all the company round the dinner table of the aptly named Veneerings (who themselves are not merely *nouveau riche* but frauds who, we are told, will "make a resounding smash next week") report their uniformly disapproving opinions of the marriage in what the narrator characterizes as "The Voice of Society," Twemlow finally expresses the view, "rather less mildly than usual," that it is really none of society's business, being "a question of the feelings of a gentleman." And when pressed, he adds, "If such feelings [of gratitude, of respect, of admiration, and affection] on the part of this gentleman, induced this gentleman to marry this lady, I think he is the greater gentleman for the action, and makes her the greater lady. I beg to say, that when I use the word, gentleman, I use it in the sense in which the degree may be attained by any man" (*OMF*, IV, ch.17). It is the climax not only of the chapter but of the whole book, and in spite of some lingering ironic touches with which the narrator concludes the narrative, it plainly offers us the narrator's and the author's ethical, moral, and social judgment. We know that the marriage is a good thing, and we know that Twemlow is brave and authentic and right in what he says (although many readers who prefer Thackeray or Trollope would point to just such forceful judgments as among the things they least like in Dickens).

Strong though the judgments in these two quotations are, nevertheless it is not an easy thing to say exactly *what* they are or where, precisely, they locate the good, which is, after all, what ethics is all about. The "true and real," the "venerable," the "respectable," and possibly "antiquity" and "usefulness": we can infer from "Mediations in Monmouth Street" that these are all goods, while being a Jew who forcibly hauls potential customers into squalid houses is clearly a bad. Being a gentleman, at least "in the sense in which the degree may be attained by any man," *Our Mutual Friend* clearly implies is a good. But the goods of "Monmouth Street" do not cohere, and the good of *Our Mutual Friend* is awfully hard to define. What, exactly, *is* the sense of "gentleman" in which "the degree may be attained by any man"?[2]

So it is not surprising that while every reader feels Dickens's insistent ethical force, there is, in fact, much disagreement or just vagueness about what his ethical force actually upholds and what conduct he urges us to engage in. Critics have variously figured him as of the Right and of the Left; as conventional Anglican and rebellious Unitarian, and even Utilitarian; as Family Values man and Bohemian and Dandy; as Patriarchal and Proto-Feminist; as Pillar of the Community and Vagabond Flâneur. Everyone knows he loves Christmas, but what exactly does Christmas mean to him? Is it about Divinity or Mistletoe and Turkey?

There are several possible explanations for confusion on this score, the least charitable of which would be to say that Dickens was himself highly confused and inconsistent. More sympathetically, we might suspect that his ethical difficulties reflect the Victorians' and our own. It is no great critical challenge to find positive evidence from the works and the life supporting any of the positions listed above or evidence of powerful conflicts in Dickens's sympathies. But being conflicted does not necessarily mean that one is confused. Dickens certainly was not a systematic thinker. He may have read some moral philosophy and political economy and theory. (At this point it is customary to point out that he applied for a reader's ticket admitting him to read in the British Museum—now the British Library—on his eighteenth birthday, the earliest possible date, and that he was evidently anxious to read as much as possible to make up for the deficiencies of his formal education, which had ended when he was barely fifteen and had previously been interrupted for more than a year as his father fell into debt and eventual imprisonment, while Charles, just turned twelve, went to work at Warren's Blacking factory.)[3] But his reading was extremely heavily tilted toward the literary, and he avoids alluding to philosophy except in distant and indirect ways and to individual philosophers almost completely. He confronts religious controversies somewhat more directly but is far more outspoken about religious positions (or poses) he cannot abide than doctrines to which he subscribes. Especially in the novels, he relies far more on his sheer rhetorical power and ear for logical absurdity to guide our moral sympathies than on explicit appeals to philosophical and other moral authorities.

And yet I do think that, for all his indirection and avoidance of explicit theory, it is possible to chart Dickens's ethical and religious beliefs, a chart that turns out to be readable and potentially useful today in understanding our own ethical and religious divides. We can do this from the fiction alone, but Dickens in his letters is more forthcoming, and the version of the New Testament he wrote for his children helps fill out some important gaps.

The task will be much more manageable if we first lay down a grid that delineates the ethical and religious territory in which Dickens lived.

The Victorian ethical landscape was defined for philosophers by Utilitarianism and its various interpreters and opponents. Utilitarianism is defined classically by Jeremy Bentham and the "Greatest Happiness" principle. Bentham's position is that all actions are good or bad to the degree that they increase the pleasure or diminish the pain of the greatest number of the people (or, more broadly, sentient beings) whose interests are in question. Bentham sweeps away all versions of the good or goods that do not reduce to pleasure and all evils that do not reduce to pain. And pleasure, somewhat circularly, though for Bentham appropriately, is defined as that which individuals themselves experience as good or that which presents itself to them as self-evidently good. "Utility" for Bentham *means* pleasure and is synonymous with such terms as benefit, advantage, good, or happiness. Likewise, pain is synonymous with mischief, evil, or unhappiness. Bentham is strongly opposed to ethical systems that assume that people have trustworthy *intuitions* about the good, because he believes that we do not have reliable intuitions about ethics and that tremendous harm has in fact been done by both institutions and individuals who, based upon nothing more than their own sympathies and dislikes, exalt their preferences into absolutes: "One man says, he has a thing made on purpose to tell him what is right and what is wrong; and that is called a *moral sense:* and then he goes to work at his ease, and says, such a thing is right, and such a thing is wrong—why? 'because my moral sense tells me it is.'" [4]

Certain features and difficulties in Bentham's definitions quickly become apparent. It is both a relativistic and a subjective theory—relativistic because it can be applied to individuals, families, tribes, nations, all sentient beings, to whatever "the party whose interest is in question"—and subjective because only the subject is authoritative as to what, in fact, is pleasurable or not (2). It is psychologically egoistic, but ethically altruistic, since only individual selves can experience pleasure or pain, and yet, without any attempt at logical justification, it counts everyone's pleasures as important as everyone else's. Such givens might seem to be enough to prevent it from ever getting off the ground. But Bentham assumes that we can safely establish various fictions (such as "community" and "rights") and that we can assume various collective regularities from individuals' psychologies such that analytical and systematic thinking about ways to implement the theory are workable. For example, Bentham assumes that feeling personally insecure is a significant evil, and therefore legislation and institutions designed to protect individuals or groups within the larger community so as to promote feelings of security are of fundamental importance (a line of thinking that John Stuart Mill, Utilitarianism's greatest Victorian proponent, follows in *On Liberty*).

The Utilitarians in general and Bentham in particular have had perhaps the worst press outside of academic philosophy of any major philosophical movement. This is not the place to explore the reasons for this in detail, but their bad press plays an important part in the story of how Dickens understood the ethical landscape, because, though hardly alone in this, he bought into many of the most invidious charges and even elaborated them (famously in *Hard Times*), in spite of agreements with Bentham of the most fundamental kind. Indeed even Bentham's defenders, like John Stuart Mill, whether intentionally or not, effectively denigrated him—with help, it must be admitted, from Bentham himself, a writer with a horrendous prose style who relied on editors to turn many of his works into publishable form and still left scores of thousands of pages of both highly unreadable and almost illegible manuscript behind when he died.[5]

Bentham's favored practical projects were reform of legal abuses (inherent in England's legal code), penal reform, and development of constitutional codes. He was highly influential among the philosophical radicals who were the chief theorists of the first Reform Bill of 1832 (coincidentally the year of his death) and was also regarded as the guiding force behind several important pieces of legislation, notably, if posthumously, the New Poor Law of 1834. He obsessively championed the building of his famous Panopticon, a prison with a circular and radial design such that its inmates could be continually observed from a central watchtower, a plan that was never realized. The New Poor Law proved a disaster, and partly because of that and partly because of the grim rationality and austerity of so many of Bentham's followers (James Mill, David Ricardo, Edwin Chadwick), Utilitarianism's fundamental commitment to pleasure was all but effaced. Thomas Carlyle's attacks on what he took to be the Benthamite devotion to the Mechanical, beginning already in 1829 with "Signs of the Times," and the supposedly laudatory, but in fact highly qualified, essay "Bentham" by John Mill in 1838, further degraded Bentham's reputation at the beginning of the Victorian period. Things only got worse. Carlyle never slackened his attacks throughout his long life, and Dickens's ostensible attack on Utilitarianism in *Hard Times* was joined by such major figures as John Ruskin, John Henry Newman, and Matthew Arnold, who, as late as *Culture and Anarchy* (1869) was cheerfully announcing, after pouncing upon an unfortunate remark by Bentham about Socrates and Plato, "From the moment of reading that, I am delivered from the Bondage of Bentham!"[6]

In our own time, Bentham has most notoriously been identified with the carceral by Michel Foucault in *Discipline and Punish*,[7] but there are signs of a turn in the critical tide, chiefly because Bentham's writing positively about the equality of women, the ethical claims of animals, and the utility of sodomy (just as much fun as other forms of sex, without the drawbacks of increasing the surplus population) have led many to read him more thoroughly and thereby to discover the distortions of the stereotypes.[8]

If there is any one thing we can locate in Bentham's theory that has most contributed to the bad press, it is not so much its hedonism (and, we have noted, its locating the good solely in pleasure is often misunderstood or turned on its head) as its antipathy to intuitionism and the idea that people can have innate moral sentiments that are somehow tuned in to a fundamental or transcendental reality, whether the Nature of Natural Law or a supernatural Divinity. Although, as John Mill notes in *Utilitarianism,* the theory has no objection to belief in God, it cannot endorse a god who does not wish the happiness of the souls he has created above all else. It is nevertheless deeply antagonistic to any claims made by religious (or secular) authorities to have a better understanding of the good than anyone else's or to know what is good for everybody.

Dickens was almost as uninterested in detailed theological issues as in systematic philosophy. But we should nevertheless lay out some basic issues and controversies that even the most uninterested could not avoid. England, of course, has an established church, created when Parliament broke with Roman Catholicism after the excommunication of Henry VIII subsequent to his attempts to have the Pope grant an annulment of his marriage to Catherine of Aragon. Although the split technically allied Anglicanism with the Reformation, Anglicanism need not necessarily be interpreted as doctrinally anti-Catholic, though it has since 1689 been technically Protestant. Victorian Anglicans embraced a spectrum from High Church (including the Romeward-leaning Oxford Movement—conservative, antiquarian, and ritualistic), to Broad or Latitudinarian (the church of Thomas Arnold and Charles Kingsley's "Muscular Christianity," liberal and tolerant, steeped in Enlightenment thought), to Low (often evangelical and veering toward dissent). Evangelicals could be found among Anglicans (generally at the Low end) as well as among Dissenters or Non-Conformists (who found themselves unable to subscribe to the Church of England's Thirty-Nine Articles defining the Anglican faith) and emphasized close reading of Scripture, conversion or second birth, private judgment over the authority of church hierarchy, the importance of Christ's atonement and a corresponding sensitivity to human sinfulness, a fervent and public profession of faith, and the need both to spread the Gospel and to do good works through organized philanthropy. Dissenting sects included Baptists, Congregationalists, Presbyterians, and, most prominently, Methodists (or Wesleyans), as well as Unitarians, who, in denying Christ's divinity (and the Trinity—hence the name), were arguably non-Christian. Dissenters and Roman Catholics (as well as Jews and anyone else incapable of subscribing to the Thirty-Nine Articles) suffered under a gradually diminishing number of civil disabilities throughout the Victorian period (for example, limiting access to Oxford and Cambridge) and, through Church Rates, were obliged before 1868 to support the Church financially.[9]

There was between the Utilitarians and Christians more intellectual overlap and more active practical collaboration than our contemporary experience of cultural and religious wars might lead us to expect. William Paley, probably best known today for his argument for the existence of God based on an argument from design (the ancestor of "intelligent design"), was a Cambridge don who lectured on moral philosophy before taking up a career as a clergyman. *The Principles of Moral and Political Philosophy* (1785) is based on his lectures and became the standard textbook at Cambridge for much of the early nineteenth century. Paley's ethics are heavily indebted to Enlightenment thought and are Utilitarian and anti-intuitionist. They are also from a logical or an argumentative standpoint rather a mess. Paley did not believe that we have an innate moral sense, and he believed that God wants us to be happy and that we can understand that Will by looking into the consequences of actions and their tendency "to promote or diminish general happiness."[10] It is Paley more than anyone else who stood behind the stereotypical Anglican clergyman (commonsensical and kind, enjoying hunting and drinking and flirting) and provided him with such philosophy as he might have. Indeed, in order to find Victorian religious thinking that has *nothing* in common with Utilitarianism, one has to venture fairly far—for example, to such an extreme statement as this from John Henry Newman in his *Apologia pro Vita Sua:* "The Catholic Church holds it better for the sun and moon to drop from heaven, for the earth to fail, and for all the many millions on it to die of starvation in extremest agony, as far as temporal affliction goes, than that one soul ... should commit one single venial sin, should tell one willful untruth, or should steal one poor farthing without excuse."[11] That is truly an anti-Utilitarian sentiment (one that explains some of the mutual dislike between Newman and those he called Liberals). In spite of the deep antipathy felt by Evangelicals and Dissenters for Roman Catholicism, it is a thought that shows Newman's Evangelical roots perhaps more than it accurately reflects orthodox Roman Catholic doctrine. Among Catholics and High Church Anglicans alike, there were many who would have been shocked by the extremity of Newman's formulation.

If there was little intellectual common ground between Evangelicals and Utilitarians, nevertheless there was quite a lot of common ground when it came to actual social and philanthropic projects. Indeed, Utilitarians and Evangelicals were more likely to find themselves collaborating on prison and sanitary reform, abolition, temperance, or the moral and intellectual improvement of the lower classes, than they were to find themselves working alongside people of the broad religious center; and, in spite of their technical hedonism, Utilitarians in practice, by the mid-nineteenth century, came in largely ascetic flavors.

Dickens's parents were both Broad Anglicans, though neither seems to have had any real religious interests, and they were apparently irregular and inconsistent in their observations.[12] We can infer from "City of London Churches" in *The Uncommercial Traveller* that the Dickens family, when Dickens was quite little, briefly attended a Baptist chapel—something thoughtful Broad Anglicans might be expected to avoid. We know that Dickens became sufficiently disenchanted with the Church of England that he took sittings in Unitarian chapels in the 1840s and that he counted several Unitarians among his friends (including his biographer, John Forster) long after the sittings ceased. But it is as likely that his disenchantment with the Church of England was political (the Church establishment was largely Tory) as it was theological: Dickens thought the Thirty-Nine Articles self-contradictory (*LCD*, 3:498n3). He eventually returned to the Church of England, though the regularity of his church attendance is difficult to gauge, and his will includes a somewhat equivocal profession of faith: "I commit my soul to the mercy of God through our Lord and Saviour Jesus Christ, and I exhort my dear children humbly to try to guide themselves by the teaching of the New Testament in its broad spirit, and to put no faith in any man's narrow construction of its letter here or there" (Forster, 2: Appendix, 422). The reference to Jesus is orthodox, the warning about any particular "man's narrow construction" less so.[13]

The novels give a few clues to the state of Dickens's faith, and the letters and a version of the Gospels written for his children—not intended for publication—provide much more explicit evidence. In the novels there is early on some very harsh satire of Evangelical Dissenters. The vignette on the title page of *The Pickwick Papers* shows Toby Weller nearly drowning the Reverend Mr. Stiggins, an Evangelical preacher. Women who are moved to the verge of hysterics by hypocritical preachers who fatten themselves while preaching about human sinfulness are a staple: for example, Kit Nubbles's mother in *The Old Curiosity Shop,* Mrs. Snagsby and her circle in *Bleak House,* and Mrs. Jerry Cruncher in *A Tale of Two Cities.* Equally damaging are Evangelicals (Mrs. Jellyby in *Bleak House*) and High Church Anglicans (Mrs. Pardiggle in the same novel) who either ignore home responsibilities or terrorize their children while working their philanthropic projects. More damaging still are the Old Testament–obsessed Calvinists and Puritans like the Murdstones (*DC*), Miss Barbary (*BH*), and Mrs. Clenham (*LD*), all of whose intensely oppressive parenting is brutally traumatic. But most damaging is Roman Catholicism, which for Dickens epitomized the evils of the past and remained a constant danger. The interpolated tale of the Five Sisters of York in *Nicholas Nickleby* (ch.6) warns against Catholic otherworldly asceticism. *Pictures from Italy* (1845) and *A Child's History of England* (1852–54) are far more outspoken about the cruelty, superstition, indolence, and sensuality of Romanism, and only months before his death Dickens refers to the Roman Church as "that curse upon the world" (*LCD,* 6:466).[14]

On the positive side, there are remarkably few examples of admirable clergy, and those who are exemplary are far removed from the center of power, like the meek and kind Reverend Milvey in *Our Mutual Friend,* who is, tellingly, "wretchedly paid" (*OMF,* I, ch.9).

Forster summarizes Dickens's religious belief by quoting a long letter to his youngest son, "Plorn," upon his being sent off to Australia in 1868 when he was only sixteen:

> Never take a mean advantage of anyone in any transaction, and never be hard upon people who are in your power. Try to do to others as you would have them do to you, and do not be discouraged if they fail sometimes. It is much better for you that they should fail in obeying the greatest rule laid down by Our Saviour than that you should. I put a New Testament among your books for the very same reasons, and with the very same hopes, that made me write an easy account of it for you, when you were a little child. Because it is the best book that ever was, or will be, known in the world; and because it teaches you the best lessons by which any human creature, who tries to be truthful and faithful to duty, can possibly be guided. As your

brothers have gone away, one by one, I have written to each such words as I am writing to you, and have entreated them all to guide themselves by this Book, putting aside the interpretations and inventions of Man. (Forster, 2:379–80)

As Philip Collins has noted, "These lessons were succinctly conveyed in Betsey Trotwood's advice to the young David [Copperfield]: 'Never be mean in anything, never be false, never be cruel.'" (*DC*, ch.15).[15]

The "easy account" of the New Testament referred to by Dickens was written in the late 1840s, a few years before Plorn was born. It was first published as *The Life of Our Lord* in 1934 and was not meant, as I've said, to be published. Forster says that "nothing would have shocked himself so much as a suggestion of that kind" (Forster, 1:465n51).

Dickens's reluctance may have followed a recognition that the very attempt to make the life of Christ intelligible to small children would be liable to introduce significant if innocent error. Or it may have been that he was perfectly aware of some more fundamental deviations from orthodoxy. Or it may have been that he recognized that he could not consistently at one and the same time preach against public professions of faith and publish his own—even posthumously.

On the orthodox side, *The Life of Our Lord* presents a good deal of uncritical narration of miracles and the resurrection. The miracles are introduced early, and there is no waffling about them: "For God had given Jesus Christ the power to do such wonders; and He did them, that people might know He was not a common man, and might believe what He taught them, and also believe God had sent Him. And many people, hearing this, did begin to believe in Him; and great crowds followed Him in the streets and on the roads, wherever he went" (24). His accounts of the crucifixion and resurrection are similarly full and accepting of the supernatural. But if the supernatural aspects of Christianity gave Dickens no trouble, nevertheless there is a good deal here that deviates from the Thirty-Nine Articles.

There is often ambiguity about Jesus's divinity in Dickens's *Life*. There is no mention of the Virgin Birth, and there is no interest in the Atonement. And here is how the angel announces Christ's birth to the shepherds: "'There is a child born to-day in the city of Bethlehem near here, who will grow up to be so good that God will love Him as His own Son; and He will teach men to love one another, and not to quarrel and hurt one another; and His name will be Jesus Christ; and people will put that name in their prayers, because they will know God loves it, and will know that they should love it too'" (13). This is Unitarian, approaching adoptionism (the heresy that Jesus *became*

God's son), and Christ is presented here simply as a model of good behavior and the best of teachers. Indeed, he is called "Saviour" not on account of redemption or atonement, but for just these qualities: "He was always merciful and tender. And because He did such good, and taught people how to love God and how to hope to go to Heaven after death, he was called *Our Saviour*" (33).

If Dickens is happy with miracles in private, in public he downplays the supernatural altogether. Nowhere is this clearer than in his accounts of Christmas, as Joseph W. Childers demonstrates in chapter 6 of this collection. Dickens's devotion to the celebration of Christmas was lifelong and, of course, plays a tremendous role in how it is celebrated still today, but his accounts of Christmas are highly secularized. Christmas at Dingley Dell is central to *The Pickwick Papers,* but it is all about dancing and kissing and feasting and being with friends. The interpolated tale of "the Goblins who stole a Sexton," told by Mr. Wardle, concerns Gabriel Grubb, an early version of Scrooge, who was "a morose and lonely man, who consorted with nobody but himself, and an old wicker bottle which fitted into his large deep waistcoat pocket" (*PP,* ch.29). He experiences a conversion similar to Scrooge's, though whether the spirits who have visited him and shown him visions much like those revealed by the Ghost of Christmas Present are of the supernatural or entirely natural but intoxicated kind remains unclear. These visions teach Gabriel "that men who worked hard and earned their scanty bread with lives of labour, were cheerful and happy; and that to the most ignorant, the sweet face of nature was a never-failing source of cheerfulness and joy. He saw those who had been delicately nurtured, and tenderly brought up, cheerful under privations, and superior to suffering, that would have crushed many of a rougher grain, because they bore within their own bosoms the materials of happiness" (ch.29). Happiness is here not just good, but *the* good we are ethically obliged to pursue, especially under difficult circumstances, for the simple reason that if we do not actively pursue and even create it, we are not likely to get it.

An especially jarring note in the context of the season is sounded in the next chapter, where Mr. Pickwick spends Christmas morning meeting Bob Sawyer and Ben Allen, who are smoking cigars by the kitchen fire, drinking brandy and eating oysters and fowl, and joking about their medical studies. "Nothing like dissecting to give one an appetite," says Bob, and there follows a positively ghoulish discussion of legs, arms, heads, and brains all the while they are stuffing themselves (ch.30).

We might well suppose that the secularizing of Christmas is part of an intentional program that distances Dickens's private beliefs from what he knew to be inevitable discrepancies between his own and those of many of his readers, who included the whole spectrum of Christianity as well as non-Christians, agnostics, and nonbelievers. That supposition conforms nicely with Dickens's dislike of detailed discussion of doctrine, as well as his suspicion of those who profess their faith loudly and publicly. But it does not explain the ghoulishness, which persists throughout his career, even when he allows himself to write more feelingly and explicitly about the Resurrection—as, for example, in *A Tale of Two Cities,* which in its final scene sees Sidney Carton quoting John 11:25, "I am the Resurrection and the Life" (*TTC,* 3, ch.15) but which also plays ghoulishly with the details of Jerry Cruncher's career as a "Resurrectionist" (i.e., grave robber). Without delving into the well-known question of Dickens and the macabre, we can say that whether ghoulishness is meant seriously to undermine specific religious beliefs, it certainly effectively undermines moves toward the otherworldly, moves that Dickens consistently distrusts as liable to distract attention from the here and now.

This brings us to the heart of things. Whenever Dickens imagines the goods of religion, they are always figured as doing good in the here and now. In 1850, he advises a young woman troubled by thoughts of death and evidently musing about big religious questions: "The world is not a dream, but a reality, of which we are the chief part, and in which we must be up and doing something. . . . Be earnest—earnest—in life's reality and do not let your life, which has a purpose in it—every life upon the earth has—fly by while you are brooding over mysteries. The mystery is not here, but far beyond the sky. The preparation for it, is in doing duty. Our Saviour did not sit down in this world and muse, but labored and did good. In your small domestic sphere, you may do as much good as an Emperor can do in his" (*LCD,* 6:25–26). This is advice very much in the Esther Summerson line and may well have been in Dickens's mind when he has Esther write, against the intrusive philanthropy of Mrs. Pardiggle in *Bleak House,* "I thought it best to be as useful as I could, and to render what kind services I could to those immediately about me; and to try to let that circle of duty gradually and naturally expand itself" (*BH,* ch.8).[16]

Even when Dickens imagines the goods of the other world—the heaven we may "hope to go to . . . after death"—they too are figured simply as continuations of the goods of the here and now. Here is how Dingley Dell imagines heaven: "And numerous indeed are the hearts to which Christmas brings a brief season of happiness and enjoyment. How many families, whose members have been dispersed and scattered far and wide, in the restless struggles of life, are then reunited, and meet once again in that happy state of companionship and mutual good-will, which is a source of such pure and unalloyed delight, and one so incompatible with the cares and sorrows of the world, that the religious belief of the most civilized nations, and the rude traditions of the roughest savages, alike number it among the first joys of a future condition of existence, provided for the blest and happy!" (*PP*, ch.28). It is not difficult to see that doing good or being useful means easing pain and spreading happiness. Dickens clearly has in mind immediate domestic pleasures and, to use one of his favorite words, "comfort." Given his professed faith, this makes him a Christian Utilitarian very much in the William Paley mold. But there are two significant complications: first, the public Dickens consistently secularizes his Utilitarian ethics; and second, he is an Intuitionist. The first makes him look *more* like a secular Utilitarian—a Benthamite—while the second makes him look *less* like either a Benthamite *or* a Paleyan.

The first complication also raises an interesting question, though one which we do not have sufficient space to consider fully here: whether the private or public Dickens is the more "authentic." From the standpoint of criticism, it is, of course, the public self presented through the published work that matters. But I suggest that in this case the published work may well have represented a truer picture of what Dickens privately believed than what the letters and *The Life of Our Lord* (both unpublished in his lifetime) express. The argument for this would assume that the "private" views are actually aimed at family, friends, and biographers and that, ironically, they mask deeply held beliefs that are more consistent with the fiction.

The second complication is significant only to the degree that the debate between Empiricists and Intuitionists is significant. Clearly, that debate was enormously significant to everyone working in formal moral philosophy throughout the eighteenth and nineteenth centuries, and it entails far-reaching consequences for metaphysics, psychology, and theories of education. Metaphysics interested Dickens himself, however, not at all, though he was a good deal interested in at least some aspects of psychology (dreams and hypnoid states and what we might call the psychology of extreme states—fear, anger, guilt, shame, passion of any kind) and much interested in education. If one believes we have innate moral intuitions, education and the upbringing of children in general become a matter of creating the conditions under which these will be fully brought out. If not, educators and parents have the more difficult job of inculcating what John Stuart Mill calls "the feeling of unity with our fellow-creatures" so that it "shall be (what it cannot be denied that Christ intended it to be) as deeply rooted in our character, and to our own consciousness as completely a part of our nature, as the horror of crime is in an ordinarily well brought up young person."[17]

Dickens unquestionably believed that most people have some innate moral intuitions or sympathies, and he rejected psychologies that posit inborn selfishness.[18] The clearest evidence is supplied by children like Oliver Twist or Florence Dombey or Esther Summerson, whose upbringings are so harsh that the only explanation for their moral sweetness is inborn goodness. There are also many of what we might call naturally nurturing women who suggest not only innate moral sympathies but also (in line with the conventional figure of the Angel in the House) that women are more richly endowed with these than men. But there are also enough young ones who seem to have been born with an eye only for Number One and enough adults who are apparently irredeemably bad to complicate the picture further. (Dickens is, moreover, consistently scornful of the nobility of savages.) He famously writes in his Preface to *Oliver Twist*:

> It has been observed of Nancy that her devotion to the brutal housebreaker does not seem natural. And it has been objected to Sikes in the same breath—with some inconsistency, as I venture to think—that he is surely overdrawn, because in him there would appear to be none of those redeeming traits which are objected to as unnatural in his mistress. Of the latter objection I will merely remark, that I fear there are in the world some insensible and callous natures that do become utterly and incurably bad. Whether this be so or not, of one thing I am certain: that there are such men as Sikes, who, being closely followed through the same space of time and through the same current of circumstances, would not give, by the action of a moment, the faintest indication of a better nature. Whether every gentler human feeling is dead within such bosoms, or the proper chord to strike has rusted and is hard to find, I do not pretend to know; but that the fact is as I state it, I am sure.[19]

This is equivocal on the subject of human nature, to say the least. Perhaps we can sum up such thinking as Dickens has on the subject by saying he believes that most people have innate moral intuitions and that women generally have a better supply of these than do men. Further, there are beings who naturally lack such intuitions, and there are also plenty of people who have had them effectively destroyed by unhappy experiences (mostly in childhood), as well as some few whose extremely unhappy childhoods have nevertheless *not* been sufficiently horrible to destroy their innately and powerfully good natures.

Under the circumstances, it seems impossible to say anything general about Dickens's Intuitionism that is not liable to serious qualification. As a practical matter, it is safe to say that, however much Dickens may have believed in innate moral sentiments, he is never willing actually to rely upon them. His belief gives him occasion to praise the good-natured and naturally generous; it never is so strong that it obviates the need for spelling out the moral lesson for readers who may not be so naturally well-endowed as an Esther or a Nancy.

We can much more confidently characterize the content of those intuitions—and the accompanying lessons—that entail the familiar domestic goods of security and comfort. They may come to us from some other world, but they all point us, like Esther's manifesto, or Dickens's advice to Plorn, or Betsey's to young David, to this world. One of the most eloquent examples of what Dickens often simply figures as "heart" appears in *The Old Curiosity Shop* and describes Kit Nubbles's sadness contemplating the Old Curiosity Shop after it has been abandoned by Nell and her grandfather: "It must be specially observed in justice to poor Kit that he was by no means of a sentimental turn, and perhaps had never heard that adjective in all his life. He was only a soft-hearted grateful fellow, and had nothing genteel or polite about him; consequently instead of going home again in his grief to kick the children and abuse his mother (for when your finely strung people are out of sorts they must have everybody else unhappy likewise), he turned his thoughts to the vulgar expedient of making them more comfortable if he could" (ch.14). Notice that Kit's moral intuitions are explicitly distanced from the form that Victorians most usually understood them to take—*as moral sentiments* that underlie sentimentality. In this his most sentimental novel, Dickens most seriously qualifies a fashionable understanding of sentimentality. (And notice too that the angel in the house here is male.)

Another important statement that sheds light both on Dickens's location of the good in domestic pleasure and on his thinking about how to inculcate that ideal (thus having a bearing again on the question of Intuitionism) appears in a letter to the Baroness Angela Burdett Coutts in which he proposes founding a halfway house for prostitutes to be recruited chiefly from prisons with an eye to preparing them for emigration and respectable lives abroad:

> What they would be taught in the house, would be grounded in religion, most unquestionably. It must be the basis of the whole system. But it is very essential in dealing with this class of persons to have a system of training established, which, while it is steady and firm, is cheerful and hopeful. Order, punctuality, cleanliness, the whole routine of household duties—as washing, mending, cooking—the establishment itself would supply the means of teaching practically, to every one. But then I would have it understood by all—I would have it written up in every room—that they were not going through a monotonous round of occupation and self-denial which began and ended there, but which began, or was resumed, under that roof, and would end, by God's blessing, in happy homes of their own. (*LCD*, 4:554)

Miss Coutts was deeply religious, and the first two sentences are alert to that. The subsequent "but" is telling, however, and the burden of the argument is that, while "discipline must be maintained"—to quote Mr. Bagnet's domestic motto (*BH*, ch.27)—the training is to be "cheerful and hopeful" and has as its goal not self-denial, but personal and secular happiness.

If there is anything that might have surprised mid-Victorian intellectuals about ethical beliefs a century and a half later, it would likely be the simultaneous flourishing of pursuits of pleasure and the persistence or even rise of Evangelicalism and what we today call religious fundamentalisms more generally—that is, beyond Christianity. Liberals like Mill or Arnold or Dickens looked forward to a progressive refinement in the pleasures people sought and no doubt expected progress in science to erode or at least to qualify religious beliefs and behavior. (Dickens expected science also actually to enhance religion even as it altered it.) [20] They could not have imagined a world obsessed with cosmetics, gyms and spas, plastic surgery, recreational and prescription "quality-of-life" drugs, travel for pleasure, television, movies, DVDs, CDs and MP3 players, pornography, sports, or video and computer games; but neither could they have imagined the enormous successes of the Christian Right, televangelism, Creationism, Islamism, and the like. What they would have made of it all—whether the shock of twenty-first-century hedonism would have pushed them toward twenty-first-century spirituality, or vice versa—is anybody's guess.

But it is not clear what we make of it either. Extraordinarily diverse ethical systems now violently compete with one another, but also often exist peacefully side by side. The incongruity of it all might have killed an Arnold or a Mill. Dickens, I trust, would have had a lot of fun with it, at least before the bombs started going off.

## NOTES

1. First published in the *Morning Chronicle*, 24 September 1836, and reprinted in *Sketches by Boz*, New Series, No. 2. The sketch appears in most modern editions as No. VI of the "Scenes."

2. I address the question of the meaning of "gentleman" in *Charles Dickens Revisited*, 161–63, 175.

3. Edgar Johnson, *Charles Dickens: His Tragedy and Triumph*, 1:47, 58. See also William Miller, "Dickens Reads at the British Museum," 83–84. The most complete listing of books that Dickens owned is an inventory prepared in 1854 (*LCD*, 4:711–25). Among the more than 2,000 volumes, the only primary philosophical text is a two-volume edition of David Hume's *Essays and Treatises*.

4. Bentham, *The Principles of Morals and Legislation*, 17. The first two chapters of *Principles*, first published in 1789, though written and printed a decade earlier, lay out

Utilitarianism's philosophical foundation. Subsequent references are made parenthetically in the text.

5. John Stuart Mill also effectively diluted the foundations of Utilitarianism by introducing qualitative distinctions among pleasures that he believed could be hierarchized, as summed up in his famous saying, "better to be Socrates dissatisfied than a fool satisfied." See *Utilitarianism*, ch.2, 14. Bentham would have disagreed, as is evident from *his* famous saying (and made so by being quoted derisively by Mill in his essay on Bentham for the *London and Westminster Review* in 1838), "Prejudice apart, the game of push-pin is of equal value with the arts and sciences of music and poetry." See *The Works of Jeremy Bentham*, 2:253. Bentham is defending the pleasures of the masses against the dictates of arbiters of "Taste." His reasoning is very much in line with Dickens's in *Hard Times:* "People must be amuthed" (I, ch.6).

6. Arnold, *Culture and Anarchy*, ed. Stefan Collini, 77.

7. Foucault, *Discipline and Punish*, especially the chapter "Panopticism," 195–228.

8. For some relatively recent representative writings sympathetic to Bentham, see: Frances Ferguson, "Canons, Poetics, and Social Value: Jeremy Bentham and How to Do Things with People"; Richard Dellamora, *Masculine Desire;* Louis Crompton, *Byron and Greek Love;* Janet Semple, *Bentham's Prison;* Ross Harrison, *Bentham, The Arguments of the Philosophers;* and, among older works not blinded by the reputation, Mary Mack, *Jeremy Bentham: An Odyssey of Ideas*, and Charles Everett, *The Education of Jeremy Bentham.*

9. For more on Victorian religion and Dickens's various attitudes toward it, see my contributions on the subject to the *Oxford Reader's Companion to Dickens:* "Church of England"; "dissent, religious"; "evangelical religion"; "Jews"; "*The Life of Our Lord*"; "Religion"; "Roman Catholic Church"; "sabbatarianism"; and "Unitarianism."

10. Quoted by J. B. Schneewind in his *Sidgwick's Ethics and Victorian Moral Philosophy*, 125. Schneewind's is by far the best study of Victorian academic ethics. For Paley's relationship to John Stuart Mill, see Alan Ryan's excellent Introduction to *John Stuart Mill and Jeremy Bentham: Utilitarianism and Other Essays*, which also very intelligently surveys Victorian ethical theory.

11. Newman, *Apologia*, 190.

12. Johnson, *Charles Dickens*, 1:19.

13. Forster gives the following account of Dickens's changing engagement with the Church of England: "One of the last things he did at the close of the year, in the like spirit, was to offer to describe the Ragged Schools for the *Edinburgh Review*. 'I have told [Macvey] Napier [editor of the *Edinburgh*],' he wrote to me, 'I will give a description of them in a paper on education, if the Review is not afraid to take ground against the Church Catechism and other mere formularies and subtleties, in reference to the education of the young and ignorant. I fear it is extremely improbable it will consent to commit itself so far.' His fears were well-founded; but the statements then made by him give me opportunity to add that it was his impatience of differences on this point with clergymen of the Established Church that had led him, for the past year or two, to take sittings in the Little Portland Street Unitarian chapel; for whose officiating minister, Mr. Edward Tagart, he had a friendly regard which continued long after he had ceased to be a member of his congregation. That he did so cease, after two or three years, I can distinctly

2: *Dickens and the Goods*

state; and of the frequent agitation of his mind and thoughts in connection with this all-important theme, there will be other occasions to speak. But upon essential points he had never any sympathy so strong as with the leading doctrines of the Church of England; to these, as time went on, he found himself able to accommodate all minor differences; and the unswerving faith in Christianity itself, apart from sects and schisms, which had never failed him at any period of his life, found expression at its close in the language of his will" (Forster, 1:282–83).

14. Letter to Miss Burdett Coutts, 22 August 1851. For more on Dickens and Roman Catholicism, see my "*Villette* and *Bleak House:* Authorizing Women," 54–81. Both Dickens and Charlotte Brontë were very curiously more ambivalent, at least unconsciously, about Roman Catholicism than it appeared. Brontë's heroine Lucy Snowe, against all her prejudices, wanders into a Catholic church and takes confession. In 1844, Dickens was visited in a dream by his late and much beloved sister-in-law, Mary Hogarth, who had died suddenly in his arms when she was only seventeen, and, in response to his question whether Roman Catholicism might not after all be the best religion, answers, "for *you*, it is the best!" (letter to Forster, *LCD*, 4:196).

15. Collins, "morality and moral issues," in the *Oxford Reader's Companion to Dickens,* ed. Paul Schlicke.

16. The advice also echoes Carlyle's in *Sartor Resartus:* "*Do the Duty which lies nearest thee.* . . . Thy second Duty will already have become clearer" (196).

17. Mill, *Utilitarianism*, ch.3, 35.

18. Fred Kaplan's *Sacred Tears* is the standard work. But see also Malcolm Andrews, *Dickens and the Grown-up Child* for an extremely intelligent account of Dickens's thinking about children, as well as my "Fictions of Childhood," in *Cambridge Companion to Charles Dickens,* ed. John O. Jordan.

19. Relevant, too, is the famous discussion of human nature that begins chapter 47 of *Dombey and Son.*

20. Dickens is silent about Darwin but saw no contradiction between religion and science, which he regarded as part of a continuing revelation. See his letter to W. W. F. de Cerjat, 28 May 1868, *LCD*, 10:251–52.

# 3

# The Poverty of Charity

Dickensian Sympathy

**NANCY YOUSEF**

Dickens's representation of the blindness, misguidance, and self-aggrandizement that undermine charitable endeavor is typically viewed in relation to social and political phenomena of his own age. This essay proposes to consider Dickens's engagement with the problems of philanthropy as part of an intellectual tradition extending back to the eighteenth century and forward to contemporary debates within ethical theory. *Bleak House* presents several memorably quixotic schemes aimed at helping others: ill-defined missions to imperial outposts, evangelical projects of salvation, campaigns for temperance and literacy. But the novel also includes numerous renderings of small acts of charity. These episodes collectively contrast with the absurdly ineffective philanthropic activity of characters such as Mrs. Jellyby and Mrs. Pardiggle; they are also careful explorations of the complex psychology of moral responsiveness. Snagsby's half-crowns for Jo, Woodcourt's visits to Miss Flite, Gridley's attentions to Charley and her siblings, Esther's handkerchief-shroud for Jenny's dead infant: these isolated, spontaneous, impulsive acts of kindness are characteristic instances of a sentimentalism that is typical of Dickens—and typically viewed as an embarrassing or objectionable aspect of his art.[1] In aesthetic terms, sentimentality is frequently regarded as factitious excess, a criticism easily conflated with the ethical condemnation of sentimentality as mere emotional indulgence, a substitution of feeling for reasoned judgment or effective action. However legitimate in many cases,

3: *The Poverty of Charity*

such charges also betray a general suspicion of affective display, raising questions about the authenticity or propriety of emotional response that assume precisely what needs to be established: that (genuine and appropriate) emotion is constitutive of moral experience.[2] The sentimental scene in Dickens might be seen to do no more—and no less—than foreground feeling as a form of moral discernment.

With their emphasis on the motivating force of affections and their rendering of the sudden impact of particular circumstances in inspiring responsiveness to the need of others, the novels of Dickens have proved inviting for philosophers interested in how narrative might inform ethical argument. Cora Diamond, for example, writes of Dickens as providing "paradigms of a sort of attention" that itself bears "moral significance" as an alternative to the overvaluation of "systematic generality" in her own discipline. Philosophical *style* shapes, and thereby restricts, what counts as philosophically meaningful argument, according to Diamond. "We take the explicit formulation and testing of principles" as entailing an "exercise" in our capacities as thinking beings that is central to morality, "but not the bringing of imagination to bear on observation." The alternative Diamond finds in Dickens's novels is that "they take as the root of morality in human nature a capacity for attention ... what it would be fair to call loving and respectful attention."[3] Diamond is not alone in setting the density of literary representation against philosophical writing on ethics: literature (and very often the nineteenth-century novel in particular) is often presented quite generally as the *alternative* to philosophy by those aiming to expand the interpretive and analytic range of their discipline.[4] However, the specific formal and historical relationships between particular works of literature and philosophy within distinct periods certainly merit more detailed consideration. It might seem clear enough, at the most general of levels, that a Dickens novel engages the moral sensibility of its readers through imagination, detail, and emotional appeal rather than by establishing principles or prescribing reasons for action. Dickens is neither a Benthamite nor a Kantian.[5] What is perhaps more difficult to appreciate is that the "grace of sympathy" as it is named and represented in a novel such as *Bleak House* illuminates central problems in its closest philosophical antecedents.

Dickensian sympathy is worth recognizing as an inheritance of an influential strain of ethical psychology that prevailed in English culture *prior* to the dominance of Utilitarianism and that Utilitarianism did not fully displace. As a powerful alternative to the rationalistic and egoistic implications of theories that assume human behavior to be determined by self-interest, eighteenth-century sentimentalism is an important cultural source not only for nineteenth-century challenges to the prevailing ethical theory of the time, but also for contemporary critics of the same tradition. Philosophers of "moral sense" (principally Shaftesbury, Hutcheson, Butler, and Hume) had defended what Hutcheson called the "bright side of humane nature" against the pessimistic, Hobbesian view of men as "all injurious, proud, selfish, treacherous."[6] Their affirmations of the essentially social nature of human beings, of innately benevolent inclinations and altruistic tendencies, and of the relationship between emotion and virtue—all of which have long been pushed outside the main lines of philosophy—are now receiving renewed attention from moral philosophers seeking alternatives to the idealist and utilitarian positions that have dominated the discipline.[7]

Although his use of sentiment can usefully be seen as a Victorian inheritance of eighteenth-century moral psychology, Dickens is no moral sentimentalist. To understand how *Bleak House* exposes crucial problems within ethical theories centered on the working of sympathy is to see the literary work *collaborating* in moral inquiry rather than simply representing an alternative to its typical philosophical modes. In what follows, I will be arguing that the tension between individual instance and long narrative trajectory in *Bleak House* both illuminates and redefines several impasses in eighteenth-century theories of sympathy: the vexing question of whether feeling for others necessarily entails knowing others; the relationship between sympathy and perceived similitude or identification with the other; and the potential conflict between the partiality of sympathetic feeling toward family, friends and other intimates and a broad, undiscriminating sympathy for human beings as such. Before turning to the novel, it will be useful to review how these tensions arise in some important eighteenth-century writings on moral sense.

## THE EIGHTEENTH-CENTURY BACKGROUND

"No sooner are actions viewed, no sooner the human affections and passions discerned (and they are most of them as soon discerned as felt), than straight an inward eye distinguishes and sees the fair and shapely, the amiable and admirable, apart from the deformed, the foul, the odious, or the despicable": thus Shaftesbury confidently assumes a natural sense of right and wrong.[8] This positive affirmation in *The Moralists* of reliable moral responsiveness based in a "natural sense of fellowship" is, to say the least, complicated by his conclusion to the *Inquiry on Virtue and Merit,* where one finds that the integrity of moral feeling, as Shaftesbury imagines it, is somehow disconnected from perception of a real world of real others: "Let us carry skepticism ever so far, let us doubt, if we can, of everything around us, we cannot doubt what passes within ourselves. Our passions and affections are known to us. They are certain, whatever the objects may be on which they are employed. Nor is it of any concern to our argument how these exterior objects stand—whether they are realities or mere illusions, whether we wake or dream. For ill dreams will be equally disturbing, and a good dream, if life be nothing else, will be easily and happily passed."[9] The "natural affections" from which the sense of right and wrong is derived would appear to have no sure correspondence to any "objects." The social feelings collapse back into the restricted sphere of lonely subjectivity. The avowed defiance of skepticism is in fact a surrender. A realm of certainty is claimed—"what passes within ourselves"—but that inner certainty seems secure only because we can indeed doubt "everything around us." If it does not matter whether "exterior objects"—including other persons—are real or illusory, then for whom, or for what, does the individual feel? What does a term such as sympathy mean if it is only a feeling *within,* unaffected by (indifferent to?) the apprehension of another person?[10]

Shaftesbury's unqualified confidence in benevolent inclinations and natural affections toward others is compromised by an indifferent epistemology. "Any kind of rejoicing or pity presupposes, in principle, some sort of knowledge of the fact, nature, and quality of experience in other people": thus Max Scheler, the preeminent twentieth-century theorist of sympathy, initiates his discussion of "fellow-feeling."[11] Certainly Hume's sustained and complex treatment of sympathy in the *Treatise of Human Nature* (1739–40) and the *Enquiry into the Principles of Morals* (1751) suggests an awareness that prior philosophical work on sympathy fails to theorize the *knowledge* of others which it necessarily entails. In Shaftesbury (as in Adam Smith, a later, even more influential theorist of natural sympathy), affirmation of the "self-evidence" and "naturalness" of the feelings of love, fellowship, and compassion that engage us with others stands in strange and unresolved tension with admissions of the possibility that we have no good way of knowing exactly what we share with others and, more surprisingly, that we have *no need* to trouble ourselves over that uncertainty. For Hume, however, to be sure only of one's "passions and affections" without knowing "whatever the objects may be on which they are employed" is to be tormented by questions the very formulation of which is symptomatic of radical alienation: "Where am I or what?" "Whose favour shall I court, and whose anger must I dread?" "What beings surround me?"[12] The well-known conclusion of the first book of the *Treatise*—among the most dramatic expressions of skeptical despair—is a dramatic articulation of the psychological and ethical implications of radical epistemic instability. Fear, dread, and estrangement—a "temper full of suspicion"—afflict the philosopher who cannot reason himself free of doubts about the reality of things.

Famously, the "disconsolate" thinker of Book I, "Of the Understanding," unsure of what beings surround him, disappears in Books II and III, "Of the Passions" and "Of Morals." Genial and reassuring assertions of the "resemblance," "parallel" nature, and "similarity" of human minds and hearts appear instead of the anticipated "dispute, contradiction, anger, calumny." The *Treatise* proposes that human beings stand in a special epistemological relationship to one another—that of "sympathy"—which is at once a feeling, a faculty (a way of knowing), and an irresistible relation of "correspondence" between individuals. "Considering anew the nature and force of sympathy" in the concluding section of Book III, "Of Morals," Hume writes, "The minds of all men are similar in their feelings and operations; nor can any one be actuated by any affection, of which all others are not . . . susceptible. As in strings equally wound up, the motion of one communicates itself to the rest; so all the affections readily pass from one person to another, and beget correspondent movements in every human creature" (368).

However, and rather surprisingly, a cleavage between knowledge and ethical inclination appears in Hume's argument. Though "the very aspect of happiness, joy, prosperity, gives pleasure; that of pain, suffering, sorrow, communicates uneasiness" because of the "correspondent movements" of the heart, this intersubjective phenomenon is *not* necessarily a moral phenomenon for Hume.[13] In the context of eighteenth-century sentimentalism, the *amorality* of Humean sympathy is a crucial and distinctive element. He is careful to emphasize that no morally responsive act necessarily follows from sympathetic feeling: "One may venture to affirm, that there is no human creature, to whom the appearance of happiness . . . does not give pleasure, that of misery, uneasiness. This seems inseparable from our make and constitution. But they are only the most generous minds, that are thence prompted to seek zealously the good of others, and to have a real passion for their welfare" (*Enquiry*, 52).

That human beings perceive one another's pain or happiness is a quasi-anthropological fact in Hume's account ("inseparable from our make and constitution"), but to sympathize with another is to some degree only to identify (with) the other's feeling: it is not necessarily, irresistibly to wish the other well, let alone to do well by the other. In fact, Hume's account even raises questions about the ethical ramifications of indulging sympathetic feeling. In Shaftesbury, love of "father, child, or brother" naturally evolves into a universal "love of mankind, merely as such"; "each friendly affection in particular" is necessarily related to affection for "mankind in general."[14] In Hume, by contrast, sympathy is naturally partial, inspired by and restricted to our most intimate relations with family, friends, and acquaintances—and as such it is always potentially in conflict with concern for the well-being of others in general. This very issue seems to drive the important Appendix to the *Enquiry*, which is devoted to explicating the differences between justice and sympathy. Hume explains that the "social virtues of humanity and benevolence exert their influence immediately, by a direct . . . instinct" (*Enquiry*, 93). Examples of such virtually automatic response include a "parent fl[ying] to the relief of his child; transported by that natural sympathy which actuates him" and "a generous man chearfully embrac[ing] an opportunity of serving his friend." Such "passions," writes Hume, "have in view a single individual object, pursue the safety or happiness alone of the person loved and esteemed," and are to be distinguished from the "social virtues of justice and fidelity," which have in view the considerably more abstract collective object of "mankind" (*Enquiry*, 93–94).

It is a paradox of Hume's ethics that sympathy turns out to be a powerful natural affection potentially in conflict with a sense of justice that *itself* seems to require another order of sympathy. It is as if there are two kinds of profound "correspondence" between minds: that which binds us to and engages us with one another in all forms of habitual and intimate encounter and that which requires us to adopt what Hume calls a "common point of view," thereby placing us in relation to the "humanity of everyone" by bringing us to share "some sentiment common to all mankind."[15] Moreover, the conflict Hume envisions does not only emerge between concern for "a person loved and esteemed" and regard for a broader public welfare. Any "particular regard to the particular right of one individual citizen" can come into conflict with the wider execution of justice, which is to say that a perception of particular need in particular circumstances might have to be overlooked. The point is elaborated in the *Treatise*:

> When I relieve a person in distress, my natural humanity is my motive; and so far as my succour extends, so far have I promoted the happiness of my fellow-creatures. But if we examine all the questions that come before any tribunal of justice, we shall find that, considering each case apart, it wou'd as often be an instance of humanity to decide contrary to the laws of justice as conformable [to] them. Judges take from a poor man to give to a rich; they bestow on the dissolute the labour of the industrious; and put into the hands of the vicious the means of harming both themselves and others. The whole scheme, however, of law and justice is advantageous to the society . . . [and]

is *naturally* attended with a strong sentiment of morals; which can proceed from nothing but our sympathy with the interests of society. (370)

The argument is that sympathy for accidentally proximate others (close relations, suffering strangers immediately in our way) may actually *undermine* that other sympathy with "the interests of society."

As a mere perception, or apprehension, of the other, the partiality of sympathy has everything to do with proximity, with exposure to particular others at particular moments. In the immediate presence of another, sympathy makes no distinction between friends and strangers. "*All* human creatures are related to us by resemblance," and it is the irresistible *perception* of that resemblance which makes us as liable to feel the distress of a loved one as to apprehend the distress of a stranger in need" (*Treatise*, 207). However, in the case of strangers, Hume appears to argue that we ought to *ignore* what we cannot help seeing, that we ought to resist the impression of immediate suffering. Here, for example, is Hume's account of "pity" which he defines as "concern for the misery of others, without any friendship": "Pity depends, in a great measure, on the contiguity and even sight of the object; which is a proof that 'tis derived from the imagination. . . . Women and children are the most subject to pity, as being most guided by that faculty. The same infirmity which makes them faint at the sight of a naked sword, tho' in the hands of their best friend, makes them pity extremely those, whom they find in any grief or affliction" (239). The "infirmity" that afflicts women and children presumably has to do with failing to distinguish actual and apparent occasions of concern; their hearts leap to emotional conclusions. Yet, even on its own terms, this derogation of pity is inconsistent. The woman who fears the sight of the sword imagines the wound that such a weapon might inflict instead of seeing that dreadful object in the harmless "hands of her best friend." But the pity for a stranger she finds in "grief or affliction" arises straightforwardly from perception of need. And if she acts on her pity, she would be moved by none other than the "social virtues of humanity and benevolence" Hume elsewhere praises. The problem with pity, in this case, has nothing to do with femininity or imagination, and everything to do with the disturbing tension between sympathy and justice in this account of moral sentiment.

Remarkably, Hume's argument against charitable response requires one to ignore the evidence of grief and affliction, to turn away from immediately perceived needs of the poor in particular. He explains in the *Enquiry*, "Giving alms to beggars is naturally praised; because it seems to carry relief to the distressed and indigent; but when we observe the encouragement thence arising to idleness and debauchery, we regard that species of charity rather as a weakness than as a virtue" (*Enquiry*, 19). Presumably pity is a "weakness" from the point of view of "justice," which looks past the person immediately in need and imagines instead the "well-being of mankind."

■ ■ ■

The split between a sympathy stirred by the vivid and immediate presence of an other and the distanced humanitarianism of justice that one finds in Hume is clearly at issue in Dickens, but in a manner that involves the complex rendering of moral psychology and careful distinctions among types of sympathetic response. The small act of charity in response to an immediate instance of need is indeed an expression of sympathy in *Bleak House*, but with each reappearance the condition of the neediest characters is shown to be intractable, unimproved—as desperate as ever in spite of the good will of the novel's most generous characters. The long, temporal arc of this narrative, composed of coincidental recurrences and interconnections, has the effect of exposing the poverty of charity itself, even as it represents the compelling force of sympathetic feeling in individual episodes.

## FROM EPISTEMOLOGY TO ETHICS: "DON'T KNOW NOTHINK"

While the Shaftesburian sentimentalist is surprisingly untroubled by the possibility that his feelings might not correspond to any real objects—and the Humean philosopher rather mysteriously shifts from despairing uncertainty to unqualified confidence in intersubjective harmony and transparency—Dickens constructs a world in which interpersonal relations are notably opaque, but one in which the pervasive exigency of poverty is never invisible and never in doubt. The "fog everywhere" with which *Bleak House* famously begins and the impenetrabilities of Jarndyce and Jarndyce ("so complicated that no man alive knows what it means") establish the existential obscurity and mystery of the social realm (*BH*, ch.1). Suspicion is the psychological fog pervading the novel, from the secret combat between Lady Dedlock and Tulkinghorn at the center of the plot, to the estranging mistrust that afflicts Richard Carstone ("His blood is infected and objects lose their natural aspects in his sight," laments Jarndyce [ch.35]), to Mrs. Snagsby's jealous torments ("Go and see Othello acted. That's the tragedy for you," observes Bucket [ch.59]). Richard's apostatic distrust of Jarndyce appears to Esther as pathological distortion of irresistible impressions of the senses: "is it possible that you can ever have seen him and heard him . . . and can yet breathe . . . such unworthy suspicions?" (ch.37). But insofar as Richard's response allows for the possibility that appearance and reality might not coincide (i.e., Jarndyce's "outward indifference" to his interests in the Chancery suit might cover a hidden design to cause others "to become lax about their interests"), he makes a point repeatedly proven in the novel.

"I'd rather trust my own self than another!" offers Krook in explanation of his laborious, futile efforts to teach himself how to read, but the orientation toward others that he articulates is not in itself extraordinary (ch.14). At the level of everyday exchange, thoughts and desires are obscured or hidden by conversational conventions that allow for evasive denials and inhibit direct confrontation. Letters and documents (often lost, damaged, misplaced, or at risk of falling into the wrong hands) seem to be the fragile repositories for a sincerity and an authenticity stifled in ordinary intercourse.[16] Even the privileged inmates of the quasi-utopian community Jarndyce forms at Bleak House are impenetrable to one another in important matters. Jarndyce at first hides his interest in making Esther his wife and then hides his interest in making her Woodcourt's; Esther keeps her engagement hidden from Ada, and Ada keeps her marriage hidden from both Esther and Jarndyce. The very possibility of maintaining such secrecy while living in such intimacy and with such affection is itself remarkable.

Into this world in which no one really knows what lies in the hearts of others, Dickens introduces three figures of extraordinary penetration. The sinister Tulkinghorn, whose "calling is the acquisition of secrets, and the holding possession of such power as they give him" (ch.36), devotes his time, intelligence, and money to the hoarding of intimate knowledge about others. His motives remain mysterious, however, and his discrediting of Lady Dedlock deferred; exposure is evidently not his aim. The damaging secrets he holds, like his cellar of precious old wines, afford him a peculiarly private pleasure. He savors his remarkable knowledge alone. Neither isolated nor feared (as Tulkinghorn is), Jarndyce is nevertheless also not fully related to anyone else. His extraordinary generosity is characterized by an extraordinary capacity to divine the needs of others, to provide what others want before they themselves are aware of their desires. Frequently compared to a god or an angel by Esther, the "guardian" of Bleak House appears to his dependents to be a source of absolute knowledge. "I am quite sure that if there were anything I ought to know, or had any need to know, I should not have to ask you to tell it to me," Esther professes; "If my whole reliance and confidence were not placed in you, I must have a hard heart indeed" (ch.8). It is precisely this extraordinary knowledge that ultimately drives him to forsake his hope for the real intimacy of filiation, which marriage would create. "I saw with whom you would be happier . . . I penetrated his secret," he explains to Esther (ch.64), and in so seeing and so penetrating he definitively sets himself apart from the circle he had drawn around himself at Bleak House. Though it may seem perverse to link the two figures, it is not entirely coincidental that the sinister Tulkinghorn and the benevolent Jarndyce, exceptional readers of the minds and hearts of others, are also unrelated to others in the most ordinary sense, their childless bachelorhoods a sign of utter singularity.

Bucket, by contrast, who seems to be "everywhere, and cognizant of everything" (ch.47), is fully enmeshed in familial and social relations of all kinds and achieves his extraordinary knowledge by dint of labor and experience. Tireless in his investigations, he "pervades a vast number of houses, and strolls about an infinity of streets" such that he appears "in all manner of places, all at wunst." But what he can achieve by this committedly empiricist method is tragically restricted in the novel. Though Bucket "never relaxe[s] in his vigilance a single moment" (ch.57), he ultimately fails to discover Lady Dedlock before her demise. Moreover, his successful identification of Tulkinghorn's murderer owes nothing to his exhaustive way of working. His suspicion of Hortense is a wild insight, an unmotivated surmise, an uncanny intuition ("By the living Lord it flashed upon me!" [ch.54]) that exceeds the bounds of his empiricism and thereby suggests its limitations.

Taken together, Tulkinghorn, Jarndyce, and Bucket are exceptional in the novel precisely because they seem, by dint of obsessive investigation or remarkable insight or unstinting labor, to penetrate appearances, solve mysteries, and divine hidden desires. They are epistemologically gifted, but their extraordinary knowledge appears to bear no relation to their moral character. Jarndyce is benevolent, Tulkinghorn villainous, Bucket devoted and dogged: these inclinations may be strengthened by their epistemic achievements, but are not determined by them. Thus the novel suggests a distinction between the limitations of intersubjective knowledge and the possibilities of ethical orientation toward others. The problem of goodwill is not necessarily connected to desires for, or doubts about, interpersonal transparency.

Indeed, the fog that everywhere conceals thoughts, intentions, and desires in *Bleak House* does not conceal real need. Representation of destitution forms a "primary matrix of interest" in the novel, as Steven Marcus has pointed out, one particularly marked by sensory impressions of unmistakable intensity: the dizzying visual clutter of Krook's rag shop, the "foul and filthy air" of Nemo's room, the "filth begrime[d]" body of Jo, "dirty, ugly, disagreeable to all the senses."[17] The unknowability of others is an existential truth in the novel, but one that has little to do with the capacity to perceive misery and privation. This might seem an abstruse distinction, but to conceive of epistemological and moral forms of recognition as separate or separable is already to issue a certain ethical challenge. The novel in effect rejects Scheler's proposition that rejoicing with or pitying others presupposes access to their experience. But then what does inspire sympathy in *Bleak House*? What is it to recognize another's need if it is not to know the other? What in such recognition is compelling, and how does recognition fail?

## RECOGNITION AS RESEMBLANCE?: "I—I . . . SEEMED TO ARISE BEFORE MY OWN EYES"

Irresistibly intuited likeness is the foundation of Humean sympathy: "'Tis obvious, that nature has preserv'd a great resemblance among all human creatures, and that we never remark any passion or principle in others, of which . . . we may not find a parallel in ourselves." It is precisely this "remarkable resemblance" which allows us to "enter into the sentiments of others, and embrace them with facility and pleasure" (*Treatise,* 207). Such an idea is presented in *Bleak House* but is also decisively rejected as a basis for ethical response.

Esther's sudden "recognition" of an inchoate connection to Lady Dedlock is composed of a murky compound of intuition, perception, and spontaneous emotional connection—an experience sparked by their uncanny, undeniable resemblance. The surface reflection of her own face in that of the stranger stirs the early memories that intimate their relation to one another. "I knew the beautiful face quite well. . . . And, very strangely, there was something quickened within me, associated with the lonely days at my godmother's. . . . And this, although I had never seen this lady's face before in all my life—I was quite sure of it—absolutely certain. . . . Why her face should be, in a confused way, like a broken glass to me, in which I saw scraps of old remembrances . . . I could not think" (ch.18). The spontaneous recognition is apparently mutual; Esther later learns that on this occasion Honoria too "had been startled; and had thought of what would have been like me, if it had ever lived, and lived on" (ch.36). The correspondence of Esther's and Honoria's appearances ("a something in her face that I had pined for and dreamed of when I was a little child; something I had never seen in any face" [ch.36]) functions simultaneously as the sign and the inspiration for a natural, irresistible bond of affection.[18] "I told her that my heart overflowed with love for her; that it was natural love," Esther recounts, a profession requited by Lady Dedlock's maternal embrace: "she caught me to her breast, kissed me, wept over me, compassionated me" (ch.36). Deftly brought together in these scenes of filial recognition are the sentimental hypothesis that natural benevolence is both rooted in and evinced by the affective bonds of family and the Humean idea of sympathy arising from the remarkable resemblance between human beings ("the minds of men are mirrors to one another" [*Treatise*, 236]).

"Natural love" flows irresistibly, but in so emphasizing the power of resemblance in sparking it, Dickens also evokes the idea of similitude as the basis for mutual recognition. To say that Esther and Honoria feel so powerfully for one another because they are child and mother is, almost, to venture a tautology. Less obvious is Dickens's representation of the powerful feeling stirred by likeness itself, in the absence of any familiarity with the other. The *feeling* of recognition that both Esther and Honoria experience at first sight is based solely on their resemblance—a basis for recognition that the novel elsewhere radically undermines. Similitude is certainly a discernible sign of connection: Guppy, for example, guesses at the relationship between Esther and Lady Dedlock by piecing together an array of apparently unrelated details, but he is inspired to do so after being struck by their "undoubted strong likeness" (ch.29); and Jo is at first terrified of Esther, mistaking her for the lady who made him guide her to Nemo's gravesite. But insofar as the emotional bond between mother and daughter is avowed and established only *after* their resemblance has been destroyed by Esther's illness, it is not represented as the *basis* for their mutual recognition. Esther is grateful "that I was so changed as that I could never disgrace her by any trace of likeness" because her disfigurement obscures the resemblance between them from strangers ("nobody could ever now look at me, and look at her, and remotely think of any near tie between us" [ch.36]), but the accident of the illness and its seemingly gratuitous consequence also suggests the arbitrariness of the face as sign of similitude, mover of affections, and locus of identification.

## GENEROSITY ACROSS IRON BARRIERS: SYMPATHY WITHOUT IDENTIFICATION

The series of events and circumstances leading up to the disfiguring change in Esther's appearance suggests an alternative to the idea of identification and resemblance as the basis for sympathetic recognition of others. The illness is contracted through a chain of charitable acts: Esther becomes infected while nursing Charley, whose infection follows her attendance on Jo (it is she who goes "to and fro" from Bleak House to the loft-room by the stable where they house the sick boy). The contagion originating with Jo is perhaps most readily seen as a flagrant manifestation of unremedied social ills. Like the typhus fever afflicting Carlyle's poor Irish widow, Jo's fever is communicated because he is left to circulate, indeed compelled to "move on," within a social world that affords him no home, but cannot banish him altogether.[19] At the same time, contagion has long served as a figure for the communicability of thoughts and susceptibility to feeling associated with sympathy. "The passions are so contagious," writes Hume, "that they pass with the greatest facility from one person to another and produce correspondent movements in all human breasts" (*Treatise*, 386).[20] Thus the disease that ultimately alters Esther's face may be seen as a trace of sympathetic response, retrospectively marking a narrative path that connects earlier, isolated episodes of seemingly insignificant acts of kindness. Recall that Esther herself learns of Jo's existence only through the wives of the St. Albans brickmakers who temporarily shelter and seek medicine for the boy ("he had once done as much for her," Liz tells Charley; "I've kept him here all day for pity's sake," adds Jenny [ch. 31]). The brickmakers' wives themselves are familiar to Esther from her first days at Bleak House, her visit to their home with Mrs. Pardiggle offering among the most memorable juxtapositions of insensitive, ineffective philanthropy and genuine sympathetic response in the novel.

However, to see that Jo's illness is inextricably bound up with small acts of charity *as well as* being evidence of irremediable poverty entails recognizing the productive tension that the novel establishes between individual instances and an overall narrative trajectory that allows for nothing good to come of its moments of goodness. In what follows, I will be suggesting that the particular sophistication of Dickens's representation of sympathy is manifested not in a few individual, praiseworthy acts, but in the cumulative effect of generosities that ultimately count for very little. The failure of charitable efforts to ameliorate the condition of the novel's neediest recurrent characters marks both a refusal to sentimentalize the social impact and efficacy of sympathy and an insistence on the psychological and ethical complexity of sympathy.

■ ■ ■

The illness that disfigures Esther's face comes about through a chain of coincidences that binds together several conspicuous charitable occasions, and returns, in particular, to the first occasion for kindness in the novel, one that seems inspired by no more and no less than the phenomenological immediacy of suffering. Far from entailing identification, the experience appears instead to involve enduring aversion, coming face-to-face with the failure

### 3: *The Poverty of Charity*

to identify. Entering the brickmakers' cottage where "nobody gave us welcome," hearing the brickmaker's hostile catechistic response to Mrs. Pardiggle ("An't my place dirty? Yes, it is dirty. . . . How have I been conducting of myself? Why, I've been drunk for three days; and I'd a been drunk four, if I'd a had the money. . . . And how did my wife get that black eye? Why, I give it her. . . ." etc.), finding the space itself "damp and offensive," Esther and Ada feel "uncomfortable . . . intrusive, and out of place" (ch.8). If sympathy entails the irresistible recognition of similitude, then the visitors appear to be experiencing just the opposite: "We both felt painfully sensible that between us and these people there was an iron barrier," admits Esther.

The barrier remains even through the death of Jenny's infant, an event Esther records principally through *Ada's* pained response: "Such compassion, such gentleness, as that with which she bent down weeping . . . might have softened any mother's heart that beat. . . . The woman at first gazed at her in astonishment, and then burst into tears" (ch.8). Whose heart is softened here? That of the suddenly grief-stricken mother, or Esther's own, feeling for Ada? Is it by means of observing Ada that Esther comes to see the bereaved mother? Does Esther see the woman's tears as a response to Ada's emotion rather than as a spontaneous expression of distress? Dickens's mediated representation of Esther's sympathetic response to the shock of this moment raises such questions without detracting from the simple kindness of the gestures inspired in such a complex and disturbing way: "I took the light burden from her lap; did what I could to make the baby's rest the prettier and gentler; laid it on a shelf and covered it with my own handkerchief. We tried to comfort the mother, and we whispered to her what Our Saviour said of children. She answered nothing, but sat weeping—weeping very much" (ch.8). Have awkwardness and discomfort disappeared? Is the weeping woman touched by the words and attention offered, or does her "answer[ing] nothing" bespeak indifference to the presence of these strangers at this most isolating moment of grief? Nothing in the episode suggests that the genteel visitors have passed through the "iron barrier" separating them from these uncomfortably proximate, evidently anguished others. Indeed, as if to counter that comforting notion, a sharp contrast between Esther's kindness and the sympathy of a true friend brings the scene to a close.

> An ugly woman, very poorly clothed, hurried in. . . . She also had upon her face and arms the marks of ill-usage. She had no kind of grace about her, but the grace of sympathy; but when she condoled with the woman, and her own tears fell, she wanted no beauty. I say condoled, but her only words were 'Jenny! Jenny!' All the rest was in the tone in which she said them. I thought

it very touching to see these two women, coarse and shabby and beaten, so united; to see what they could be to one another; to see how they felt for one another; how the heart of each to each was softened by the hard trials of their lives. (ch.8)

Liz can condole with Jenny not so much because she is *like* Jenny but rather because she actively participates in her friend's grief, living *with* her rather than (simply) feeling for her. The "grace of sympathy" in this context, a compound of friendship, familiarity, and intimacy, is powerfully distinguished from the strangers' charitable efforts to comfort. Such closeness is neither possible, nor necessary, for Esther and Ada, who, appropriately enough, find "it better to withdraw" at this moment.

Nevertheless, the simple acts of kindness proffered by the uncomfortable visitors properly constitute the *ethical* substance of the scene. Upon returning to the brickmakers' cottage in the evening with "some little comforts" and finding Liz still watching over her sleeping friend and the small shrouded form of the dead infant, Esther and Ada praise her: "'May heaven reward you!' we said to her. 'You are a good woman'" (ch.8). Liz's response—"'Me, young ladies?' she returned with surprise"—compels reflection on what is meant by the term "good." Her rhetorical question suggests more than humility. Her presence and her attendance on her friend are touching acts of love and are meaningfully distinguished from moral response. Love is neither good nor evil, yet neither is the mere charity doled out by Esther and Ada depreciated because uninspired by deep affection. The unspecified "little comforts" the two strangers carry to the cottage are not to be confused with the succor of the true friend (whose "familiar voice" alone has the power to "calm" the grieving mother), but it is precisely in not being friends, in not feeling sympathetic identification and yet responding to need, that Esther and Ada can be seen as "good." Between Mrs. Pardiggle's judgmental condescension and Liz's intimate familiarity are simple acts of kindness by strangers who overcome discomfort and aversion: it is a terribly narrow sphere for the "good," but it is all Dickens allows us to imagine as sufficient and necessary to charitable response.[21]

Esther, it is worth recalling, initially resists the invitation to accompany Mrs. Pardiggle on her rounds, seeing her as one of those "charitable people" who "did a little and made a great deal of noise" (ch.8). However, her stated reasons suggest an ambitious view of what charitable work entails emotionally and epistemically: "I then said . . . that I was not sure of my qualifications. That I was inexperienced in the art of adapting my mind to minds very differently situated, and addressing them from suitable points of view. That I had not that delicate knowledge of the heart which must be essential to such a work ... and that I could not confide in my good intentions alone. For these reasons, I thought it best to be as useful as I could, and to render what kind services I could, to those immediately about me; and to try to let that circle of duty gradually and naturally expand itself" (ch.8).

Articulated here are several presuppositions about the sympathy necessary to assist a stranger: entering into the mind of the other, knowing what the other feels, fully apprehending the other. We have seen how *Bleak House* as a whole presents this ideal of interpersonal transparency as an impossible kind of knowledge and one, moreover, that does not necessarily correspond to good will toward others. The figure of the "gradually and naturally" expanding "circle" also assumes a continuum between kindness to "those immediately about me" and kindness to those at a distance. However, the visit to the brickmakers proves a paradigmatic episode for the novel insofar as it separates emotional intimacy and identification from the possibility of ethical response to others. Esther is proven wrong on her visit: although she feels that an "iron barrier" separates her from the hearts and minds of "these people" whom she would help, her good intentions alone do suffice. Indeed, the challenge appears to be to relinquish the fantasy of sympathetic identification, to offer "little comforts" without aspiring toward the affective involvement of true familiarity or being deterred by aversion. To do less is to confine one's kindness to a narrow "circle," to settle for the partialities of proximity, intimacy, and acquaintance.[22]

## THE POVERTY OF CHARITY

To say that *Bleak House* offers an unsentimental view of charity is to say that it refuses to confound the aspiration to do well *for* an other with the establishment of a relation *to* an other. Whether seen as coextensive with the "natural affections" of family (as in Shaftesbury) or as entailing intersubjective harmony and transparency (as in Hume), theorization of sympathy as a moral response frequently bears with it some expectation or assumption of achieved intimacy—of being moved to act precisely because one has drawn close to the other and entered his or her experience. I have suggested that the novel attempts to distinguish sympathetic response to strangers in need from ideals of intimacy, familiarity, and identification with others.

This is not to say, however, that sympathy is devalued: it entails a genuine perception of and readiness to respond to the other's neediness or pain. While the sight of a stranger in need does not necessarily evoke a sense of kinship, it does constitute something more than mere seeing. Consider, for example, the idiomatic pattern woven around the figure of Jo, the novel's exemplary, recurrent object lesson in poverty and social marginality. Outside any circle of relationship ("No father, no mother, no friends"), invisible to those philanthropists such as Mrs. Jellyby who can "see nothing nearer than Africa," he is also largely unseen in his own neighborhood. Entering the narrative as a rejected witness at the Coroner's inquest into Nemo's death (the "nobody" who, like him, has no friends), Jo recalls their first meeting thus: "One cold winter night, when he . . . was shivering in a doorway near his crossing, the man turned to look at him, and came back, and, having . . . found that he had not a friend in the world, said, 'Neither have I! Not one!' and gave him the price of a supper and a night's lodging" (ch.11). Nemo's seeming identification with Jo is less significant than the act that precedes it, which is his turning to look and then turning to address. Similarly, Woodcourt's sympathetic eye falls on the boy because he "pauses to look after him" (ch.46). "It must be a strange state to be like Jo!," observes the narrator, "to be perplexed by the consideration that I *am* here somehow, too, and everybody overlooked me until I became the creature that I am!" (ch.16). "Overlooked," or seen as "dirty, ugly, disagreeable to all the senses" and so to be "moved on" out of sight, Jo is elaborately imagined as the victim of a pervasive moral blindness that the novel works hard to expose.[23] Given the absolute neglect of a social world that finds "nothing interesting" about him, the occasional kindnesses he does receive (Nemo's coins, Snagsby's half-crowns, the brickmakers' shelter, Woodcourt's final ministrations) are instances of a kind of attention or perception of the other that the novel presents as a genuine ethical achievement.

But Jo is also exemplary of the poverty of charity. His meager existence, really only a staving off of death ("Jo lives—that is to say, Jo has not yet died" [ch.16]), is the pathetic record not only of an indifferent social and political system but also of the generosity of good people. Unfolded and developed through each brief appearance, Jo's degradation, homelessness, illness, and death suggest how the novel refuses to sentimentalize the effects of charitable response, even as it presents numerous instances of inspired moments of giving. With the exception of the fairy-tale-like adoption of the orphaned Charley into the Jarndyce household (itself suggesting that true philanthropy calls for no less than permanent involvement), the narrative arc of characters such as Jo, Liz, Jenny, and the brickmakers is one that leaves them fleetingly touched but fundamentally unchanged by the sympathies they evoke and the charitable acts they inspire. Thus, although Esther receives a "morose nod of recognition" from Jenny's husband when she appears at St. Albans in pursuit of Lady Dedlock, the brickmaker is as hostile and defiant as always ("I'm not partial to gentlefolks coming into my place.... I let their place be, and its curous thy can't let my place be" [ch.57]). Liz, intimidated into silence by her abusive husband, is likewise unchanged: "there's something kept back," Bucket observes, but he also recognizes that "a poor creetur like her, beaten and kicked and scarred and bruised . . . will stand by the husband that ill uses her, through thick and thin" (ch.57).

Liz's constraint at the end of the novel is especially poignant because she is the character who comes nearest to articulating the relative insignificance of fleeting sympathies, however genuine. Bucket appears in their squalid room ("offensive to every sense") at Tom-all-Alone's in search of Jo; he softens at the sight of Liz's newborn infant and Jenny's affection for the boy, and then is shocked to hear Liz say, "'Much better to think of dead than alive, Jenny! Much better!'" (ch.22). Her response to Bucket's rebuke ("'Why, you an't such an unnatural a woman, I hope,' returns Bucket sternly, 'as to wish your own child dead?'") both acknowledges a "natural" maternal altruism ("'I'd stand between it and death with my own life'") and sadly complicates the sentiments stirred by the newborn. Urging Bucket to *look* more attentively at their condition, she conjures a future condition the shadows of which darken even present joy at the new life.

> "If it was never to wake no more, you'd think me mad, I should take on so. I know that very well. I was with Jenny when she lost hers.... But look around you, at this place. Look at them;" glancing at the sleepers on the ground. "Look at the boy you're waiting for.... Think of the children that your business lays with often and often, and that *you* see grow up!"
>
> "Well, well . . . you train him respectable, and he'll be a comfort to you, and look after you in your old age, you know."
>
> "I mean to try hard.... But I have been a-thinking . . . of all the many things that'll come in his way. My master will be against it, and he'll be beat, and see me beat, and made to fear his home, and perhaps to stray wild . . . and if he should be turned bad, 'spite of all I could do, and the time should come when I should sit by him in his sleep, made hard and changed, an't it likely I should think of him as he lies in my lap now, and wish he had died, as Jenny's child died!" (ch.22)

Certainly maternal anxiety, poverty, and exhaustion inspire these thoughts, but they are also wise projections into a future that Liz does not look toward with any expectation of substantial aid or relief. The life of her child, like that of Jo, is one of a deferred mortality, survival on sufferance. Bucket looks gently on the sleeping newborn in the miserable room; Snagsby "coughs his cough of sympathy" and "lay[s] upon the table half a crown, his usual panacea for an immense variety of afflictions" (ch.22), but neither imagines what they both cannot fail to know and what Liz bids them see: that such moments make little difference over time.

The episodic structure and long temporal span of *Bleak House* allow Dickens to explore two distinct problems with the ideal of sympathy as the basis of moral response. On the one hand, the phenomenological detail of episodes such as the visit to the brickmakers presents a form of genuine, admirable, charitable response that does not sentimentalize its effects by imagining a magically achieved identification or recognition of the other. On the other hand, the condition of characters such as Jo and the brickmakers, seen over time, does not allow for complacent appreciation of the novel's instances of generosity. Moments of kind attention to the impoverished and the overlooked effect little change.

■ ■ ■

In closing, I return to Cora Diamond's claim that literature in general—the work of Dickens being particularly exemplary—offers some instruction in an emotionally inflected mode of attention constitutive of moral experience and that, in so doing, it presents a substantive alternative to the characteristic emphases of philosophical argument. I take it that what Diamond would emphasize as the special achievement of Dickens's art is the creation of a figure such as Jo, the rendering visible of the overlooked, the mere taking of interest in him. But Diamond's valorization of literary form risks reduplicating the "systematic generality" and oversight of the particular that she is eager to redress in her own discipline. Certainly a novel such as *Bleak House* provides what Diamond calls "paradigms of a sort of attention" associated with moral sensibility. And yet, sympathetic attention is complex and unstable in the novel as a whole, and sympathy itself was a complex and variously defined concept in the ethics and the moral psychology that formed part of Dickens's cultural context. If *Bleak House* can be read not simply, or not only, as presenting an alternative to philosophy, but also as responding to a range of philosophical ideas and assumptions specific to its age, then it becomes possible to see that as significant as the representation of attention is to the novel, so too is the valuation of its failure. For more philosophically challenging than Jo's mere inclusion in the world of the novel is Dickens's representation of his isolation even among those who do attend to him—the failure of even those who do see him to touch him.

3: *The Poverty of Charity*

# NOTES

Work on this essay was supported by a grant from the PSC-CUNY Research Foundation of the City University of New York.

This essay is dedicated to my father, Ibrahim (1940–2006).

1. See, for example, John Kucich's discussion of melodrama and sentimentality in *Excess and Restraint in the Novels of Charles Dickens*, 45–57.

2. For a helpful effort to disentangle aesthetic and ethical objections to sentimentalism, see Robert C. Solomon, "In Defense of Sentimentality." Solomon argues that the charges of "excess" and "self-indulgence" and "artificiality" need to be distinguished from a more general and problematic objection to the moral relevance of feeling as such. In his view, the appeal to the emotions in sentimentally charged scenes aims to represent "the precondition for ethical engagement" (305).

3. Cora Diamond, "Anything but Argument?," 299, 305, 306.

4. See, for example: Colin McGinn, *Ethics, Evil, and Fiction*; Martha Nussbaum, *Love's Knowledge: Essays on Philosophy and Literature*; Robert Pippin, *Henry James and Modern Moral Life*.

5. The question of Dickens's engagement with utilitarian thought should not be oversimplified. Kathleen Blake has recently made a compelling argument for the Benthamite basis of Dickens's social criticism in *Bleak House*, focusing on the incorporation of principles of political economy in the novel ("*Bleak House*, Political Economy, Victorian Studies"). While Blake is convincing on the influence of specific Benthamite proposals in Dickens, her argument does not address itself to the more fundamental question of utilitarian assumptions about motivation. John Stuart Mill, for one, clearly acknowledges Bentham's constrained imagination of human interests: "Even under the head of *sympathy*, his recognition does not extend to the more complex forms of the feeling—the love of *loving*." That this criticism comes from Mill is itself a telling indication of awareness that certain aspects and complexities of ethical psychology appear to be excluded from theoretical accounts of human interests and aims. Mill, "Bentham," *Collected Works*, 10:96.

6. Francis Hutcheson, "Reflections on the Common Systems of Morality," 100. Published in the *London Journal* in 1724, "Reflections" is an essayistic preview to the work that made Hutcheson's reputation, *An Inquiry into the Original of Our Ideas of Beauty and Virtue* (1725). For a useful review of the "sentimental revolution" in eighteenth-century English ethics, see Norman S. Fiering, "Irresistible Compassion: An Aspect of Eighteenth-Century Sympathy and Humanitarianism."

7. Among contemporary recognitions of eighteenth-century sentimentalism as an important precedent for alternatives to Utilitarianism and rationalism in moral philosophy, see especially, Annette Baier, "Hume, the Woman's Moral Theorist?"; Stephen Darwall, "Empathy, Sympathy, Care"; Joseph Duke Filonowicz, "Ethical Sentimentalism Revisited"; Alasdair MacIntyre, *After Virtue*; J. B. Schneewind, *The Invention of Autonomy* (especially 285–306 and 330–73).

8. Shaftesbury, Anthony Ashley Cooper, Third Earl of, *The Moralists; A Philosophical Rhapsody*, in *Characteristics of Men*, 326.

9. Shaftesbury, *Characteristics*, 229.

10. The tension between the assumption of radical subjectivism of experience and natural sympathy is startlingly present in the opening paragraphs of Adam Smith's *Theory of Moral Sentiments* (1759), which is probably the best-known exposition of sympathy among literary historians. Smith begins by affirming: "That we often derive sorrow from the sorrow of others, is a matter of fact too obvious to require any instances to prove it." The next paragraph begins from the proposition that since "we have no immediate experience of what other men feel, we can form no idea of the manner in which they are affected." The correspondence of feelings Smith theorizes is in fact an imagination of what one's own feelings would be in a given "situation," rather than knowledge of the feelings of the other. Thus one might sympathize with another's calamity by experiencing "a passion of which he seems altogether to be incapable" because the "passion arises in *our breast* from the imagination, though it does not in his from the reality." Paradoxically, sympathy would here mean not feeling what the other feels. Given Smith's assumption that "we have no immediate experience of what other men feel," it is not surprising to find that his descriptions of sympathy frequently emphasize the limitation of the feeling as well as the distance between subjects. Smith, *The Theory of Moral Sentiments*, 9 and 12.

11. Max Scheler, *The Nature of Sympathy*, 8.

12. David Hume, *A Treatise of Human Nature*, 175. Subsequent references are made parenthetically in the text.

13. David Hume, *An Enquiry Concerning the Principles of Morals*, 43. Subsequent references are made parenthetically in the text.

14. Shaftesbury, *Characteristics*, 256–58 and 205.

15. Dickens's skepticism about the efficacy of imagining "mankind" as a collective object is foregrounded at the outset in *Bleak House* through the presentation of Mrs. Jellyby's telescopic philanthropy from the perspective of Esther, for whom it is categorically "right to begin with the obligations of home." However, as we shall see below, Esther's partiality does not escape criticism either.

16. On the role of documents and other writings in the novel, see J. Hillis Miller's Introduction to *Bleak House*, 11–35.

17. Steven Marcus, "Homelessness and Dickens." The quotations are from *Bleak House*.

18. For a contemporary phenomenological account of response to the human face as a compounding of epistemic and ethical appraisal, see Emmanuel Levinas, *Entre-nous*, 1–38.

19. For Carlyle's influence on Dickens, and both writers' use of disease as a metaphor for "moribund social conditions," see Michael Goldberg, "From Bentham to Carlyle: Dickens's Political Development."

20. Hume, *Treatise*, 386. "Communication," "susceptibility," and "infusion" are also frequently used by Hume to describe the immediacy of sympathetic response. On sympathy as emotional contagion, see Darwall, 264–65.

21. Insofar as the episode sets Liz's intimate care in contrast to the small, material "comforts" brought by Esther and Ada, it foregrounds the distinction between acts of affection and acts of "good will" that Kant draws in the *Groundwork of the Metaphysics of Morals*. Indeed, the scene may be read as a highly sympathetic explication of Kant's argument that a "good-natured temperament" and generous "inclinations" have nothing

to do with the "genuine moral worth" of an action or character. Dickens grants Esther and Ada good natures, but he neither reduces the generosity of their actions to that sentimental inclination nor detracts from it by drawing attention to the limitations of their sympathy.

22. Taking particular note of his use of "pathetic scenes of physical and emotional suffering," Mary Lenard has placed Dickens's fiction within the context of a culturally gendered moral sentimentalism with roots in the eighteenth century ("'Mr. Popular Sentiment': Dickens and the Gender Politics of Sentimentalism and Social Reform Literature"). On her reading, Esther's "spontaneous, private" acts of charity, "always the result of personal sympathy for those afflicted," deliberately limit the scope of social action to the "domestic sphere" (59). In my view, the constraints and failings of that limitation are subtly brought to attention through the reappearance, in ever more miserable conditions, of characters like Jo and the brickmakers. Individual episodes do indeed critique and satirize the "businesslike" philanthropy of a Mrs. Pardiggle by setting it in stark contrast to Esther's perceptive sensibility, but if the former is obviously condemned, the latter is not necessarily advocated. Single "pathetic scenes" might foreground Esther's sympathy, but the power of that sentiment is dissipated by the accumulated number of scenes showing unameliorated suffering.

23. In a related argument on the interrelationship between love and justice in *Bleak House*, Joyce McClure posits that "the malicious refusal to see" epitomizes Dickens's "indictment of social injustice" in the novel and, correspondingly, that "visual impairment" is symptomatic of the failings of justice and charity represented in the novel ("Seeing through the Fog," 23–44).

# 4

# Uncanny Gifts, Strange Contagion

Allegory in *The Haunted Man*

JOHN BOWEN

On 27 July 1848, Charles Dickens wrote to one of his most intimate female friends, the Hon. Mrs Richard Watson, about his memories of their meeting a few years before in Switzerland:

> Were you all in Switzerland? I don't believe *I* ever was. It is such a dream now. I wonder sometimes whether I disputed with Haldimand—or found it impossible to dispute with Cerjat, because everybody's opinion was his exactly. Whether I ever drank mulled wine on the top of the great St. Bernard, or was jovial at the bottom, with company that have stolen into my affection. Whether I ever was merry and happy in that Valley on the Lake of Geneva ... I am quite clear that there is no foundation for these visions. But I should like to go somewhere too, and try it all over again. I don't know how it is, but the ideal world in which my lot is cast, has an odd effect on the real one, and makes it chiefly precious for such remembrances. I get quite melancholy over them some times—especially when, as now, those great piled up semicircles of bright faces at which I have lately been looking—all laughing, earnest, intent, —have faded away like dead people. They seem a ghostly moral of everything in life to me. (*LCD*, 5:378)[1]

It is a remarkable letter, written under the shadow of the fatal illness of Dickens's sister Fanny, which brings into conjunction three things: the vocation of the writer and the world of imaginary representations that he or she inhabits; dreams and visions; and the processes of human memory. All are similarly "ideal" and dreamlike, all in some sense "ghostly."[2] Dickens's work as a writer in an "ideal world"—an imaginary one consisting of ideas, not real presences or material things—has an "odd" or strange effect on the real, which seems to fade like the dead, the imagined or the dreamed. In memory too, the dead and the living, the imaginary and the "real" are akin, not safely distinguishable. This kinship of memory, dreams, and haunting is marked by their shared *ideality,* and the response to it is "melancholy." Everything in memory is both derealized, like a dream, and marked by death, like a ghost. Such an insight seems to Dickens an allegory (or "ghostly moral") of "everything in life to me."

This resonant letter was written at a significant time. Dickens was shortly to begin the composition of *David Copperfield* in which he incorporated many of his own childhood memories, in particular the loathed time as a child worker in Warren's Blacking factory. But before *David Copperfield* and shortly after the letter to Mrs Watson, he wrote the extraordinary 1848 Christmas Book, *The Haunted Man and the Ghost's Bargain,* which, like the novel, is concerned with memory—in particular, the relationship between adult life and childhood misery.[3] *The Haunted Man* is the most compact and mysterious of Dickens's explorations of memory, one of the more remarkable explorations of the theme of the psychic double in nineteenth-century fiction and an allegorical and melancholy text full of uncanny effects. It has a close relationship to certain contemporary psychological theories of split and doubled minds, as well as to mid-nineteenth-century debates about the nature of material and psychic conservation.[4] But its ambition does not stop there, for it also wants to link its exploration of the uncanny and haunting nature of memory to questions of political, ethical and social responsibility, and the ways in which social or psychic forces become *contagious*. Like Marx and Engels's *The Communist Manifesto,* also published in 1848, it begins with a ghost or spectre and concerns itself with class difference and poverty.[5]

Dickens was an experimental writer throughout his life, and *The Haunted Man,* his fifth Christmas Book, is one of his most experimental texts: its central character, the chemist Redlaw, is himself an experimenter. It was, perhaps unsurprisingly, greeted with hostility and puzzlement on its first publication. The satirical paper *The Man in the Moon,* for example, put Dickens on trial for writing a work that was "entirely unintelligible," and *Macphail's Edinburgh Ecclesiastical Journal* thought that it abounded "with the Author's worst mannerisms."[6] Subsequent criticism has done little to redeem its reputation, and, like all the later Christmas books, it seems destined to live perpetually in the shadow of *A Christmas Carol*.⁷ One of the more common objections to *The Haunted Man* over the years has been that it is too explicitly theoretical, philosophical, or ideological: *Bell's Weekly Messenger* in 1848 said that the ideas of the story "might well pass for a chapter of pure metaphysics."⁸ This is at least in part a consequence of the hostility that Romantic and post-Romantic critics have often felt toward allegory, a mode that lends itself to both highly rationalistic and deeply uncanny effects and one that is often seen as intrinsically inferior to both fictional realism and the poetic symbol.⁹ The charges of confusion often leveled at *The Haunted Man* are nevertheless somewhat puzzling, for, at one level, its purpose is straightforward enough: Redlaw is offered by his double the opportunity to forget entirely the memory of his unhappy and neglected childhood and the resentment and anger that accompany it; but, in losing his memory of past unhappiness, he also loses his capacity to sympathize or feel with others.¹⁰ As Dickens puts it, "my point is that bad and good are inextricably linked in remembrance, and that you could not choose the enjoyment of recollecting only the good" (*LCD*, 5:443). It is, we could say, a theory of memory or, perhaps more accurately, *A Theory of Moral Sentiments* that, like Adam Smith's, begins with sentiment as the basis of human compassion and ethical obligation. When Dickens first told his friend John Forster of his idea for the story, however, he called it "a very ghostly and wild idea" (*LCD*, 4:614).¹¹ In this chapter, I will analyze the strange narrative figures and repetitions of this story in relation to both Freudian and earlier nineteenth-century psychological theories of the relation of memory to selfhood and ethical being in order to explore the relation between the story's ghostliness, its wildness, and its "idea."

At the heart of *The Haunted Man* is the question of the relation between memory, as embodied in resentful and bitter memories of childhood neglect and suffering, and adult subjectivity. Dickens returns to this question throughout his writing career, but at the time of *The Haunted Man*, it is a particularly significant and insistent theme. Sometime between 1845 and 1849, he wrote a document or group of documents that have come to be known as "the autobiographical fragment" and that contain an account of his childhood poverty and his father's imprisonment for debt; early in 1850, he was to begin *David Copperfield*, which incorporated significant portions of the text from which the fragment is taken.¹² *The Haunted Man,* written between the unpublished autobiographical fragment and its partial incorporation in *David Copperfield,* also seems to draw on this material, at once linking and dislocating the two different autobiographical projects. The spectral Redlaw, for example, says to his other self, in a passage with clear echoes of the sentiments and content of the autobiographical fragment: "'Look upon me! . . . I am he, neglected in my youth, and miserably poor, who strove and suffered, and still strove and suffered.... My parents, at the best, were of that sort whose care soon ends, and whose duty is soon done; who cast their offspring loose, early as birds do theirs; and if they do well, claim the merit; and, if ill, the pity'" (ch.1).[13] *The Haunted Man*'s relationship to Dickens's autobiographical writings at this time is not, however, a simple one; it seems both to intensify the resentment of the autobiographical fragment and to attempt to move beyond it. But it also tries, in a way that is perhaps unique in Dickens's work, explicitly to "theorize" some of the central issues and problems it is troubled by, in particular, the nature of memory and the relation of the self to the past. Its allegory makes it a more self-consciously *conceptual* reflection on those processes than either *David Copperfield* or the autobiographical fragment, as well as being a strangely disturbing and mysterious narrative. The dialogue between present self and the memory of past resentment that it describes, for example, is the product of an agonizing and potentially fatal self-division. Whereas in *David Copperfield,* David is torn between the safely externalized Steerforth and Agnes, here he is own bad angel. Redlaw's double, who is also, of course, his self, all but destroys him.[14]

Dickens is one of the great poets of memory; more strangely and disturbingly, he is, with Proust, the great poet of not forgetting. The most famous (and most criticized, particularly by Victorian readers) passage he ever wrote about memory concerns his mother's wish that he return to work at Warren's Blacking factory after his father was released from jail: "I never afterwards forgot; I never shall forget, I never can forget, that my mother was warm for my being sent back" (Forster, 1:32). A reiterative, compulsive remembering dominates past, present, and future. *The Haunted Man* wishes to show that the desire to forget is no better, indeed much worse. Its vision of a world of selfishness and matter—later, the world of Gradgrind—is one without the memory of suffering. Dickens's work is concerned on the one hand with the persisting, constitutive strangeness of the self, with the "others" that inhabit any self, and on the other with the nature of our ethical obligations to others, to strangers such as the wild child that Redlaw encounters. *The Haunted Man* is about the relationship of those two strangenesses, about how, in Julia Kristeva's words, "foreignness, an uncanny one, ... irrigates our very speaking-being.... [W]e know that we are foreigners to ourselves, and it is with the help of that sole support that we can attempt to live with others."[15]

*The Haunted Man* tells the story of the eminent chemist Redlaw, who encounters his own double ("the Spectre," "the Ghost," "the Phantom"), who offers a gift that will enable him to forget his past unhappiness. It is an infectious gift, which he must give to others so that their memories too are transformed. It is presented as a kind of blessing; it is, in fact, a curse. Redlaw, in losing his memory of unhappiness, also loses his compassion for others. He becomes, like the feral child that he encounters, wholly outside human congress and warmth, and he infects others with a similar indifference to the needs of others. To place a scientist at such a central position in the narrative is an unusual choice for Dickens—Redlaw is the only significant scientist in all his fiction—but it enables him both to foreground and to attempt to go beyond a number of topics within contemporary scientific and psychological debate. There is a repeated return in the story to the idiom of contemporary science—of matter, the immaterial, conservation, and the elemental—and to figures and tropes of mental self-division. In a key speech, the Spectre, drawing a parallel between the wild child and Redlaw himself, says: "he is the growth of man's indifference; you are the growth of man's presumption.... from the two poles of the immaterial world you come together" (ch.3). The scientific matter of the story—ideas of conservation, combination, and contagion, for example—is used to figure psychological or social processes and to draw both parallels and contrasts with artistic and other kinds of human endeavor. Redlaw's gift, for example, is an inversion, almost a parody, of Dickens's fictional purpose: whereas the novelist attempts to invoke memory and foster compassion, Redlaw spreads selfishness and forgetfulness. The ghost's gift destroys memory, and the task of the writer of fiction is to restore it, to "keep ... memory green" (ch.3).

*The Haunted Man* explores how the mind retains memory, how its experiences relate to one another, and how, if at all, it is unified. In these concerns, Dickens is very close to some central questions in nineteenth-century psychology.[16] The idea of mental conservation in the story, for example, is explicitly paralleled with ideas of conservation in the material world. Redlaw, at the climactic moment of anagnorisis at the end of the second chapter ("The Gift Diffused"), says: "in the material world, as I have long taught, nothing can be spared; no step or atom in the wondrous structure could be lost without a blank being made in the great universe. I know, now, that it is the same with good and evil, happiness and sorrow, in the memories of men." In very similar terms, Forbes Benignus Winslow argued, in his 1860 *On Obscure Diseases of the Brain and Disorders of the Mind,* "Annihilation exists but in the fancy. It is an illusion of the imagination, dream of the poet, the wild and frigid phantasy of the sceptic. Nothing obvious to sense admits of destruction. This is a well-established axiom in physics. It is not in the power of man to destroy the slightest particle of matter ... God has not delegated to poor puny man the power of destroying any portion of the physical universe by which he is surrounded ... What is true with regard to material holds good, à fortiori, respecting psychical phenomena. Hence the tonic, permanent, and indestructible character of the impression made upon the cerebrum."[17] Redlaw's work as a chemist in the story is seen as predominantly a matter of resolving complex materials into their elements, of uncombining them. By contrast, Milly Swidger, the voice of redemptive compassion in the tale, finds the elements hostile: "'Mrs William may be taken off her balance by Earth . . . by Air . . . by Fire . . . by Water'" (ch.1). In the course of the story, Redlaw seeks to uncombine his memories, to separate the good from the bad, but such psychological chemistry is impossible, both for him and those whom he influences. Milly's intuitively integrated knowledge is seen as superior to Redlaw's analytical elementalism.

The question of memory is also explored through the issue of double consciousness. Contemporary psychology was deeply interested in the phenomenon of "double consciousness"—in the possibility, as in the celebrated case of Mary Reynolds, of differing personalities (without shared memories) within the same person, or of the brain as "double organ" with each half "capable of a distinct and separate volition."[18] Dickens's treatment of this material both resembles and differs markedly from that of his scientific contemporaries. Whereas nineteenth-century psychology stresses the cohabitation of apparently independent consciousnesses—whether for organic reasons or through failure of mental association—Dickens creates a self and a double who are physically separate (although identical in physical appearance), share the same memories, and are in conscious communication with each other. This leads to some deeply enigmatic effects. In the penultimate paragraph, for example, we are told that "some people have said since, that he [Redlaw] only thought what has been herein set down; others, that he read it in the fire[;] . . . others, that the ghost was but the representation of his gloomy thoughts" (ch.3). The Spectre is constitutively mysterious: it does not simply represent the past; it is not a cohabiting consciousness with distinct memories or personality; and it does not resemble a Freudian superego or id. Nor is *The Haunted Man* a simple ghost story, for it is his *own* self that haunts Redlaw, not one of the dead. The Spectre may be, it is implied, a form of self-projection by Redlaw, the figure of an internal dialogue externalized, but the story never allows us to be certain. The Phantom in consequence is a deeply troubling figure, to both Redlaw and the reader, in which identical and different, self and other, internal and external, human and ghostly, memory and forgetting come together not in unity or melancholic loss but in dispossession, struggle, and contagious brutality.[19]

In the creation of this figure and the telling of this story, despite their different conceptions of the mind and psychic topography, Dickens in some ways is closer to the work of Sigmund Freud than to the psychological thought of his contemporaries. Freud was particularly concerned with the relationship between memory and past unhappiness and trauma, the human ability or inability to overcome or be reconciled to painful or traumatic past events.[20] In trying to understand these topics, Freud was, like Dickens in *The Haunted Man*, drawn to *uncanny* narratives concerned with compulsive repetition, doubles, and haunting, most notably in his discussion of E. T. A. Hoffmann's "Der Sandmann" ("The Sandman"). Both Redlaw's and the reader's experiences are very akin to the Freudian uncanny, "that class of the frightening which leads back to what is known of old and long familiar," which is characteristically manifested in doubles, animism, repetition, hauntings, and telepathic influence, all of which appear in *The Haunted Man*.[21] It is not only, however, a thematic link that exists between these two texts, but also a *cognitive* one. In his discussion of the semantic fields of "unheimlich" and shortly before his famous assertion that "unheimlich is in some way or other a species of Heimlich," Freud offers two examples of the idea of an uncanny knowledge: "*Heimlich,* as used of knowledge—mystical, allegorical . . . *Heimlich* in a different sense, as withdrawn from knowledge."[22] Redlaw is at home (which is also his place of work) when his unhomely, uncanny double appears, and the knowledge that he is pursuing is similarly both "heimlich" and "unheimlich": both modern, rational, and scientific and also mystical and akin to alchemy. In his laboratory, for example, he is described as "motionless among a crowd of spectral shapes" (ch.1). His double will shortly offer him the chance to withdraw from certain kinds of knowledge, through the ability selectively to edit his memory. *The Haunted Man* thus both explores, and in some sense attempts to be, a knowledge simultaneously canny and uncanny. Dickens was an author deeply identified by his contemporaries with domesticity and the homely, but this story is concerned with the competing claims and often violent conflict of "what is familiar and agreeable, and . . . what is concealed and kept out of sight," of the linked and conflicting powers of the heimlich and unheimlich in both cognition and narration.[23]

*The Haunted Man* begins:

Everybody said so.

Far be it from me to assert that what everybody says must be true. Everybody is, often, as likely to be wrong as right. In the general experience, everybody has been wrong so often, and it has taken in most instances such a weary while to find out how wrong, that the authority is proved to be fal-

## 4: Uncanny Gifts, Strange Contagion

lible. Everybody may sometimes be right; "but *that's* no rule," as the ghost of Giles Scroggins says in the ballad.

The dread word, GHOST, recalls me. (ch.1)

It is at first a matter of knowledge, of the relation of truth to what is familiarly known and said. This question is then interrupted by the six simple words that begin the story: "The dread word, GHOST, recalls me" (ch.1). What follows is a response to a call from memory and language that is both a calling away from what everybody thinks and a calling back to the self, and to narrative. But to recall is also to remember, to produce a memory that is both a repetition and a summoning: all this is announced and recalled in the sentence—as, too, is the "GHOST," who will come again, and again, to both bring and take away recall.

So far my analysis of *The Haunted Man* has been concerned with the nature or form of memory in the story. But that memory has a content. Briefly put, the back-story is this: Redlaw has a friend (whose name we later discover is Longford) and a sister whom he loves and with whom he lives.[24] Longford is engaged to Redlaw's sister, and Redlaw is engaged to another woman whose name we do not learn. Longford and Redlaw's fiancée then betray their lovers and run off to be married. Redlaw's sister subsequently dies. It is classically a tale of what René Girard calls triangular or mimetic desire.[25] Longford's desire is copied from Redlaw, and the friendship, in classically triangular fashion, becomes rivalry. This is fatal to the friend, who begins to degenerate at once; to the sister, whom he rejected for Redlaw's fiancée; and to the chemist himself, who is caught within a compulsively repetitious resentment that is a kind of living death: Redlaw looks haunted, is almost buried underground, and his deserted lecture theater is "a ghostly place" and "an emblem of Death" (ch.1). His home—"so quiet, yet so thundering with echoes . . . rumbling and grumbling till they were stifled in the heavy air of the forgotten Crypt" (ch.1)—is clearly a psychic as well as a physical space. But when his doubled self offers him the ability to forget once and for all, no longer to hear the echoes or to have them stifled in the crypt, its effect is to intensify the deathliness and repetition within which he is caught, a therapy that is worse than the cure. The figure of the double, Freud argues, which was "originally an insurance against the destruction of the ego, an 'energetic denial of the power of death,'" reverses its aspect and "becomes the uncanny harbinger of death . . . an agency . . . able to treat the rest of the ego as an object."[26] Split off from Redlaw, his double acts first as a kind of defensive repository or crypt of anger and resentment but rapidly becomes a threat, whose apparently benevolent promise would leave him a simulacrum, merely "the animated image of himself dead" (ch.1).

The narrative dissolution of the deathlike repetition that both compulsive remembering and absolute forgetting represent occurs through the self-sacrificing, quasimaternal love of Milly Swidger, who rescues Redlaw and restores memory to him and those whom he has infected. Redlaw, like Dickens in the autobiographical fragment, places maternal neglect and selfishness at the core of his resentment: "No mother's self-denying love . . . aided me" (ch.1). Milly, who has no children—we learn at the climax of the story that her only child was stillborn—is, in compensation, compulsively maternal to those she meets: "There's a motherly feeling in Mrs. Williams's breast that must and will have went . . . being a sort of mother to all the young gentlemen that come up from a wariety of parts" (ch.1). She is also the spokeswoman for the overt Christian moral of the story, which is united with the maternal in her climactic statement of faith: "even when my little child was born and dead but a few days, and I was weak and sorrowful . . . the thought arose, that if I tried to live a good life, I should meet in heaven a bright creature, who would call me, Mother!" (ch.3). Happiness and the hope of breaking the cycle of mimetic violence seem, then, to be figured in the story through the reconciliation of the dead, the remembered, and the ideal within a maternal presence and bosom (the story's privileged metonymy of Milly) that also represent Christian charity and love.

But the story's overt ideological commitment to a Christian thematics and the restoration of the mother-child bond takes place within a strangely twisted and unfaithful religious allegory. After he has received the terrible gift, for example, Redlaw feels that he makes the busy streets a desert and "the multitude around him . . . a mighty waste of sand" (ch.2), akin to an inverted Christ who has "mortal contagion in any fluttering touch of his garments" (ch.2). When he gives thanks for the restoration of his memory through Milly's exemplary love, he prays: "Oh Thou . . . who, through the teaching of pure love, has graciously restored me to the memory which was the memory of Christ upon the cross . . . receive my thanks" (ch.3). It is strangely put. The phrase—"the memory which was the memory of Christ upon the cross"—makes it uncertain whether Redlaw is giving thanks for being now able to remember Christ, for being now remembered in Christ's memory, or, most strangely, for now having the memory restored of a suffering akin to Christ's on the cross. The climax of the tale in Redlaw's peripeteia and anagnorisis at the end of chapter two is neither a return to the maternal presence nor a moment of transformation or conversion that can safely be described as either Christian or not. Outside the door of Redlaw's study, Milly begs to be let in, saying, "Pray, sir, let me in," repeating the word "pray" six times:

"there is no one else to help me, pray, pray, let me in!" (ch.2). At the same time, on the other side of the door, another prayer takes place, as Redlaw prays to himself as other:

> "Shadow of myself! Spirit of my darker hours! Come back and haunt me, day and night, but take this gift away! Phantoms, punishers of impious thoughts ... look upon me. From the darkness of my mind, let the glimmering of contrition that I know is there, shine up and show my misery! ... Shadow of myself! Spirit of my darker hours! ... Come back and haunt me, day and night, but take this gift away!" (ch.2)

It is an extraordinary moment of prayer and counter-prayer: of prayer being met by silence and of prayer addressed not to a divinity but to its own sinister other.

As the book's subtitle—"The Ghost's Bargain"—suggests, its exploration of memory is deeply intertwined with the question of economic exchange. In particular, it seeks forces that can resist or counter the deadliness and repetition that in the story are inherent to economic life. For *The Haunted Man* is full of poverty, most notably in one of the newspaper clippings that Tetterby fastens to his screen: "Melancolly case of destitution. Yesterday, a small man, with a baby in his arms, and surrounded by half a dozen little ones, of various ages between ten and two, the whole of whom were evidently in a famishing condition, appeared before the worthy magistrate, and made the following recital" (ch.3). One answer to such misery and inequity is to valorise the power of the *gift*. In one way, Dickens's Christmas books want to restore the simplicity and virtue of gift giving in opposition to the instrumental and utilitarian nature of the commodity-form and capitalistic exchange. *A Christmas Carol,* for example, moved toward the gift of the prize turkey to the Cratchets, and of Scrooge himself to life. Indeed, much of the history of the modern Christmas is of the acceleration of capitalistic commodification and exchange, and the simultaneous implication and resistance of gift giving to those processes (see Joseph W. Childers's essay [chapter 6] in this volume). *The Haunted Man,* however, has a more complex idea of what the gift represents, closer, in its contagious, sacrificial, and destructive power, to Marcel Mauss's sense of "the dangerous gift economy."[27] Whereas the act of giving is unequivocally a good thing in *A Christmas Carol,* here it is anything but. The gift that Redlaw receives (which he also then is compelled to give) is, paradoxically, the gift of loss, a gift that takes away. One could call it a poisoned gift, which, as it takes away, also closes off.[28] Those who receive the gift lose memory, and perhaps themselves, but this appears in the form of returning to themselves, of being concerned only with themselves.

The gift, then, is not simply a happy and beneficent supplement or counter to capitalistic forms of exchange, but a darker and more ambivalent force that runs below and alongside other social relations. Its most powerful forms in the story—for bad or good—are *contagion* and *sacrifice*. In February 1848, some six months before beginning the story, Dickens had written a review of Catherine Crowe's *The Night Side of Nature; or, Ghosts and Ghost Seers*, his first piece of journalism since August 1845, apart from some letters to the *Daily News* on capital punishment the previous year.[29] It contains a deeply skeptical account of doubles and doppelgangers which he sees (in this review at least) as essentially and only psychic projections. But such phenomena are also a social matter for Dickens. The belief in uncanny powers and doubles is transmitted, he writes, through a kind of mental infection, what he calls, in a resonant phrase, the "contagion of imagination."[30] Contagion was an important topic at this period. Henry Austin, General Secretary to the Board of Health and the novelist's brother-in-law, had issued an official warning of the dangers of cholera at exactly the time Dickens was writing the book, and the following year saw multiple child deaths from the disease at the notorious Drouet's baby farm.[31] The power not of contagious disease but "contagion of imagination" is central to the content and the narrative structure—as well as everything that escapes such an opposition—in, and beyond, *The Haunted Man*: in the contagion that Redlaw bears; in the contagious maternal love of Milly; and in the narrative project of the book, which seeks to infect its readers—and thus the society within which it is read—with a similarly redemptive remembering. Like sacrifice—which appears comically in the naming of the Tetterbys' baby "Moloch" (the Canaanite idol to whom children were sacrificed), tragically in Redlaw's sacrifice of his memory, and redemptively in Milly's self-sacrificing love—contagion is the gift in involuntary and hyperbolic form.

It is in this context of gift, sacrifice, and exchange that *The Haunted Man* explores the nature of social and ethical obligation to others. In its desire to relate its exploration of psychic being and the uncanniness and duplicity of memory to an understanding of the nature of our ethical obligation to others, it differs markedly from Dickens's later reworking of the autobiographical fragment in *David Copperfield*. This is particularly clear in the figure of the feral child whom Redlaw encounters, the most significant character in the story apart from Redlaw and Milly. The most important passage in this regard is the most anthologized of the book, in which the Spirit or Phantom, addressing Redlaw, says:

## 4: Uncanny Gifts, Strange Contagion

> "This," said the Phantom, pointing to the boy, "is the last, completest illustration of a human creature, utterly bereft of such remembrances as you have yielded up.... Woe to such a man! Woe, tenfold, to the nation that shall count its monsters such as this, lying here, by hundreds and by thousands!... There is not... one of these—not one—but sows a harvest that mankind MUST reap.... Open and unpunished murder in a city's streets would be less guilty in its daily toleration, than one such spectacle as these." (ch.3)

Dickens is asking here a fundamental question about the nature of ethical and social responsibility: why should we care about others? The answer on the one hand is simply that we ourselves have suffered, and the memory of that suffering enables us to feel compassion for others. This is a staple of much Victorian fiction: Estella in *Great Expectations,* for example, tells Pip that "suffering has been stronger than all other teaching, and has taught me to understand what your heart used to be" (*GE,* ch.59). But *The Haunted Man* (like many nonrealist Victorian texts) also has powerful resonances with certain kinds of modernist literary and social discourse, in particular, the work of Walter Benjamin, who was similarly concerned with the relationship between memory, allegory, and social exploitation in texts that sought to interrupt or punctuate the continuities of linear temporality. For Benjamin in "Theses on the Philosophy of History," "our image of happiness is indissolubly bound up with the image of redemption," our task "to seize hold of a memory as it flashes up at a moment of danger" in order to reinvigorate "homogenous empty time."[32] Dickens has a similarly strong sense of the redemptive power of memory, which contains the most potent possibility of change when it is most dangerous and life-threatening. In both *A Christmas Carol* and *The Haunted Man,* he uses allegorical form to arrest linear time and to figure the possibility of radical social change. Of course, Dickens's political allegiances in 1848 were very different from Benjamin's in 1940, and for him it was the power of maternal charity rather than proletarian insurrection that embodied the necessary "spirit of sacrifice" that would redeem time.[33] Yet in its sensing the potential of allegory as a privileged form within modernity to think the relation of subjectivity, temporality, and social change, *The Haunted Man* may be ahead of us in its strange doublings and contagions, in its desire to arrest time and make it just.

*The Haunted Man* is a story about strangeness and repetition, written in a strange and repetitive way, concerned with psychological processes, particularly memory, equally strange and repetitive. As I hope to have shown, repetition and the uncanny are not just topics of the book, but also deeply embedded in its rhetoric and figuration. The processes of reading and writing of and in this text are thus not free of the strange powers of splitting, doubling, haunting, contagion, temporal punctuation, and suspension that are the story's privileged tropes of both social and psychic life. Near the beginning of the story, for example, there is a remarkable passage. In what is probably unparalleled in even such a sublimely repetitious novelist as Dickens, thirty-one successive sentences, spread over eight paragraphs, all begin with the same word and temporal marker: "When." It is an attempt simultaneously ritualistic and magical, machinelike and compulsively repetitious, to invoke "the dead of winter" (ch.1), a time of death that is also strangely haunted and alive. Dickens draws on some of his own favorite passages of childhood reading to invoke the uncanny quality of a time:

> When little readers of story-books, by the firelight, trembled to think of Cassim Baba cut into quarters, hanging in the Robbers' Cave, or had some small misgivings that the fierce little old woman with the crutch, who used to start out of the box in the merchant Abudah's bedroom, might, one of these nights, be found upon the stairs, in the long, cold, dusky journey up to bed. . . . When twilight everywhere released the shadows prisoned up all day, that now closed in and gathered like mustering swarms of ghosts . . . When they had full possession of unoccupied apartments. When they danced upon the floors, and walls, . . . When they fantastically mocked the shapes of household objects, making the nurse an ogress, the rocking-horse a monster, the wondering child, half-scared and half-amused, a stranger to itself,—. (ch.1)[34]

It is a haunting passage in which the reader of the tale—like Redlaw or the child encountering, half-scared and half-amused, monsters and ogresses—may find its self a stranger to itself.

The story that follows, like the earlier Christmas books, uses both supernatural means to initiate and resolve the narrative, and allegorical form to explore the relation of time, memory, and the hope of radical social change. Like Freud in "The Uncanny" and *Beyond the Pleasure Principle*, it seeks to give full weight to the compulsion to repeat, while seeing under what terms it may be possible to overcome it.[35] It can be understood from one perspective to be a story in which Dickens through Redlaw attempts, as it were, to therapize himself but is caught (as Freud was later to be) in tangles of uncanny and compulsively repetitious power that deviate and swerve his allegorical purpose and clarity.[36] For the destination of the story—and the end of all Dickens's Christmas books—is a picture, by Dickens's close friend Clarkson Stanfield, that shows the characters of the story assembled around a Christmas table, with children playing at their feet. The printed text ends with a description of an old portrait on the walls of the room: "Deepened in its gravity by the firelight, and gazing from the darkness of the panelled wall like life, the sedate face in the portrait, with the beard and ruff, looked down at them from under its verdant wreath of holly, as they looked up at it; and, clear and plain below, as if a voice had uttered them, were the words" (ch.3). This final sentence is completed by a plea or an injunction, incorporated in gothic script within a scroll at the foot of Stanfield's illustration, the frame both of the picture and of the text, whose words are: "Lord, keep my memory green."

Stanfield's engraving shows a characteristically Dickensian Christmas celebration, sealed by a pious injunction to integrate the past and present in memory, a phrase taken from the first act of Shakespeare's *Hamlet* to speak of both the faculty of memory and of particular memories.[37] Yet what it says, how it says it, and the position in which it places the reader or viewer are all very strange: at once—neither and both—writing and speech, presence and absence, text and illustration.[38] For it is not at all clear who is speaking these final words or to whom or whether their repetition here echoes or revises the sentiments that they expressed earlier in the story. One could analyze at length the implications and modulations of the five words: as address to the self, to others, to the other, in their three occurrences in the book (twice within the text and here on its very margin).[39] But the positioning of the reader or viewer is stranger still. Twelve figures are seated or standing in a medieval hall around a table, grouped like those of the Last Supper. The viewer is in the place of the fourth wall, where the portrait whose motto he or she is reading would be hung. The motto, however, is turned toward us: the reader inhabits both the blank gaze of the portrait and the place of a festive, ghostly other, reading the words below it. Gazing both down and up, s/he is doubled and split: just as Redlaw was when he met his own ghost. It is in a way a triumph of presence, and of speech over writing, for the words are "clear . . . as if a voice had uttered them" (ch.3), and also nothing of the sort. Our voice and the dead man's voice: a wild and strangely doubled voicing.

## NOTES

1. Dickens had recently returned home following a number of public performances ("those great piled up semicircles of bright faces at which I have lately been looking") of his amateur theatrical troupe, the Amateurs. On Lavinia Jane Watson and William Haldimand, see *LCD*, 4:574n.

2. Dickens wrote to Thomas Beard, 6 September 1848, shortly after the death of

Fanny: "Poor Fanny is to be buried on Friday. I begin to think, like the Monk who spoke to Wilkie, that we are the Shadows, and Pictures the more robust realities" (*LCD*, 5:402). He makes almost the same point in a letter of 27 January 1847 (*LCD*, 5:13) and in his last ever speech.

3. One can trace the process of its composition in detail through his letters. He described himself as "dimly conceiving it" at Lausanne in July 1846 (*LCD*, 4:614), and on 12 September 1847, in a letter now lost, he told John Forster that he was "sending the first few slips of *The Haunted Man* proposed for his next Christmas book" (*LCD*, 5:165). He then decided to delay for a year. He was "thinking about" it, he wrote to Miss Burdett Coutts, 20 August 1848 (*LCD*, 5:395); "a mentally matooring" in late September 1848 according to Forster (*LCD*, 5:414); and "entered on the first stage of composition" (to Mrs Richard Watson) 5 October 1848 (*LCD*, 5:419). There is a most interesting letter of "defence" of the text, to Earl of Carlisle, 2 January 1849 (*LCD*, 5:466–67).

4. See Jenny Bourne Taylor and Sally Shuttleworth, eds., *Embodied Selves*, 123–31, 141–48, and Sally Shuttleworth, "'The malady of thought': Embodied Memory in Victorian Psychology and the Novel," 46–59. On Dickens's relation to contemporary psychological thought, see Fred Kaplan, *Dickens and Mesmerism*, and on Dickens and associationism, see Rick Rylance, *Victorian Psychology and British Culture, 1850–1880*, 55–56. For a consciously revisionist account of the "reductive, binding nature of associative memory" (141) in *David Copperfield*, see Nicholas Dames, "Associated Fictions: Dickens, Thackeray, and Mid-Century Fictional Autobiography," in *Amnesiac Selves*, 125–66. See also Vincent Newey, *The Scriptures of Charles Dickens*, 109–12. On the topic of the double in sciences of the mind later in the century, see Roger Luckhurst, *The Invention of Telepathy 1870–1901*, 99–100.

5. "A spectre is haunting Europe—The spectre of Communism": so begins *The Communist Manifesto*. See also Jacques Derrida, *Specters of Marx*, and John Bowen, "Nell's Crypt: *The Old Curiosity Shop* and *Master Humphrey's Clock*," in *Other Dickens*, 132–56.

6. Michael Slater, Introduction, *The Haunted Man*, 237. For further contemporary reviews, see Joanne Shattock, ed., *Cambridge Bibliography of English Literature, Volume 4: 1800–1900*, 1237, and Philip Collins, ed., *Charles Dickens: The Critical Heritage*, 145–46, 179–81.

7. Edgar Johnson calls it "a weak performance . . . feeble . . . sentimental, mawkish, and overmoralistic" (*Charles Dickens*, 656). For Michael Slater, it is a "strange, confused little book in which Dickens's personal preoccupations do not mesh easily with that combination of social purpose, celebration of domestic joys, and supernatural interventions which is the essence of his Christmas fiction" (*Dickens and Women*, 18). For Alexander Welsh, it is "a poor story with inconsistencies and a few unintelligible sentences" (*City of Dickens*, 101). The most sustained modern reading, that of Harry Stone, praises its "technical advances, powerful scenes and memorable characters," but concludes that it "fails and fades," becoming "huddled and implausible" (*Dickens and the Invisible World*, 141).

8. Slater, Introduction, 237.

9. See Paul de Man, "The Rhetoric of Temporality," in *Blindness and Insight*, 187–228. J. Hillis Miller has written of the many generic affiliations of *A Christmas Carol*, as "allegory or a parable . . . or a conversion narrative, or a dream vision, or a melodrama,

4: *Uncanny Gifts, Strange Contagion*

or a ghost story, or a Gothic tale, or the text for a dramatic reading or monologue, all at once" ("The Genres of *A Christmas Carol*," 199). *The Haunted Man* has a similar range of generic allegiance.

10. "The moral of Dickens's tale is quite clear," Shuttleworth notes in "'The malady of thought,'" 47.

11. It is a repeated emphasis. Dickens later said that he believed that Redlaw's ignorance of the means of his contagiousness "makes the thing wilder and stranger" (Slater, Introduction, 236).

12. "He clearly was at this time (the late 1840s) much preoccupied with his past, brooding over it and reshaping it in various fictional patterns as well as embarking on an actual autobiography" (Slater, *Dickens and Women*, 99). See also Nina Burgis, Introduction to *David Copperfield*, xv–xxi. Forster gives a variety of dates for the writing of the autobiographical fragment, which seem to vary from 1845 to 1849, but these "are not necessarily inconsistent" (*LCD*, 4:653n). Robert Langton, *The Childhood and Youth of Charles Dickens*, looking for allusions to Dickens's childhood in his published works, points out that "*The Cricket on the Hearth*, 1845, and *The Battle of Life*, 1846, have no special interest for the purposes of this book" (179). The strong use of autobiographical material in *The Haunted Man* (composed in the autumn of 1848) may point to a date within the latter end of the range given by Forster. The period between *Dombey and Son* and *David Copperfield* has been seen by many critics as marking a significant change in the quality and seriousness of Dickens's work and may be linked to the failed autobiographical project. See also *LCD*, 5:290n.

13. Redlaw has other similarities to Dickens. He is, for example, a charismatic performer: his study, where much of the first chapter takes place, is a kind of antechamber or green room of a lecture theater—a "high amphitheatre of faces, which his entrance charmed to interest in a moment" (ch.1), akin to the theaters Dickens had recently been touring. Dickens wrote during the composition of the book, "I . . . must hermetically seal myself up, in my own rooms here in the mornings," just as Redlaw seals himself away (*LCD*, 5:418).

14. See Dickens's letter concerning Mark Lemon's stage adaptation of the book: "I don't think it would do to shew the Phantom. I think it would involve an absurdity in reference to the prevailing idea of the book" (*LCD*, 5:456).

15. Kristeva, *Strangers to Ourselves*, 170.

16. "Is the self unified or divided, or multiple? How is a sense of personal identity formed through different patterns of memory, and what is the relationship between the individual's childhood and the collective, historical, and organic past?" (*Embodied Selves*, 67).

17. Quoted in *Embodied Selves*, 147. For a slightly later version of this argument, see Eneas Sweetland Dallas, "The Hidden Soul," 149: "Strictly speaking the mind never forgets. . . . Absolute as a photograph, the mind refuses nought." There was a presentation copy of Dallas's book in Dickens's library, but the pages were uncut at his death (Stonehouse, *Reprints of the Catalogues of the Library of Charles Dickens*, 26).

18. *Embodied Selves*, 123–24.

19. On contemporary parallels to Dickens's text in the work of Fyodor Dostoevsky, Hans Christian Andersen, and James Hogg, see Karl Miller, *Doubles: Studies in Literary History*, 123–31.

20. There is no reference to Dickens in *The Standard Edition* of Freud's works, but Freud's admiration for Dickens, particularly for *David Copperfield*, is recorded by Ernest Jones in *Sigmund Freud: Life and Work*, 116, 177, 190. More generally on Dickens and Freud, see "Criticism and Scholarship: Freudian" in *The Oxford Reader's Companion to Dickens*, 138–39.

21. Sigmund Freud, "The Uncanny," 340, 347, 365.

22. Ibid., 346. On Dickens and the uncanny, see Nicholas Royle, *Uncanny*, 313–15.

23. Freud, "The Uncanny," 345.

24. Edmund Denham's secret is that his real name is "Edmund Longford," a name close both to Edward Leeford (alias Monks) and Edwin Leeford (Oliver and Monks's father) in *Oliver Twist*. There is a good deal of concern with naming in the story. Milly Swidger is also known as "Swidge," and her husband says of it "better to be called ever so far out of your name, if it's done in real liking, than have it made ever so much of, and not cared about! What's a name for? To know a person by . . . Let 'em call her Swidge, Widge, Bridge,—Lord! London Bridge . . ." (ch.1). Redlaw has, according to Longford, "a generous name" (ch.2), and the feral child is "the child who had no name or lineage" (ch.3).

25. See René Girard, "Triangular Desire."

26. "The Uncanny," 356–57.

27. See Marcel Mauss, *The Gift*. Among the many gifts in the story: the Tetterbys' baby is "a gift" (ch.2) to his brother; Mrs Tetterby, when she starts to be dissatisfied with her lot, tells her husband that "when I was single, I might have given myself away in several directions" (ch.2); Redlaw offers the feral child money "more shillings than you ever saw" (ch.2), as well as trying to give Longford a gift of money while simultaneously giving him the more deadly gift of the loss of memory.

28. "If one cannot receive this gift as such, no more can one refuse it—the gift is thus always poisoned (*gift, Gift*, as Derrida reminds us, playing on English and German)." Geoffrey Bennington, *Jacques Derrida*, 191.

29. Michael Slater, ed., "Review: *The Night Side of Nature; or, Ghosts and Ghost Seers*," in *Dickens's Journalism: The Amusements of the People*, 80–91. Dickens promised to write a less skeptical second article, the following week, also about ghosts—a twin or double of the first article—but never did. He both doubles and refuses to double himself, exorcizing the ghost first and then promising but refusing to return like a ghost or to speak with ghosts.

30. "Review: *The Night Side of Nature*," 85.

31. See Dickens, "The Paradise at Tooting," in Slater, ed., *Dickens's Journalism*,147–56.

32. Benjamin, "Theses on the Philosophy of History," 256, 257, 263.

33. Ibid., 262.

34. Cassim Baba appears in *The Arabian Nights*. Abudah's bedroom figures in "The Talisman of Oromanes," in James Ridley, *The Tales of the Genii, translated from the Persian by Sir Charles Morell* (1824). Both were important texts in Dickens's childhood reading.

35. See *Beyond the Pleasure Principle*, 269–338.

36. See Jacques Derrida, *The Post Card*, 259–409.

37. Shakespeare, *Hamlet*, I, ii, lines 1–2: "Though yet of Hamlet our dear brother's

death / The memory be green . . . ." The Christmas books therefore begin and end with *Hamlet*, as the first page of *A Christmas Carol* includes this passage: "If we were not perfectly convinced that Hamlet's father died before the play began, there would be nothing remarkable in his taking a stroll at night, in an easterly wind, upon his own ramparts, than there would be in any other middle-aged gentleman rashly turning out after dark in a breezy spot—say Saint Paul's Churchyard for instance—literally to astonish his weak son's mind." The manuscript continues with a short passage (deleted at proof stage) about the weakness of "Hamlet's intellects" (see *A Christmas Carol*, ed. Michael Slater, 275). Valerie Gager, in *Shakespeare and Dickens*, points out that "Redlaw as 'a haunted man' whose 'memory is [his] curse' strengthens the connection with *Hamlet*" (277). See also Derrida, *Specters of Marx*, 17–23.

38. My discussion here is indebted to the discussion of the *passe-partout* and the *parergon* in Jacques Derrida, *The Truth in Painting*, 1–148.

39. "Dickens would not place the inscription so strategically if it did not have two meanings: both 'let me remember' . . . and 'let me be remembered after death.'" Welsh, *City of Dickens*, 198–99.

# 5

# Storied Realities

Language, Narrative, and Historical Understanding

RICHARD H. MOYE

It is a curious aspect of Dickens criticism that his novels elicit such intensely opposed valuations. With George Eliot, for contrast, there is fairly general agreement that *Romola* is not her best work and that the plot of *Daniel Deronda* is flawed. But one does not hear the refrain, repeated over a considerable span of time, that a particular novel is either a masterpiece or a failure, as one so often does with Dickens. *Hard Times* provides an interesting case in point. The critical reception of *Hard Times* is a story too well known to require extensive retelling, but it might be said that there are two primary positions on the novel. When F. R. Leavis declared *Hard Times* a masterpiece—effectively sneaking Dickens, through the side door, back into the Great Tradition from which he had initially banished him for a lack of profound "seriousness" and a "loose inclusiveness"[1]—he was following a line of response established almost immediately after the publication of the novel (first serially in Dickens's own *Household Words* and then as a single volume) in 1854. As John Ruskin, for example, put it in *Cornhill Magazine* in 1860: "The usefulness of that work [*Hard Times*] (to my mind, in several respects, the greatest he has written) is with many persons seriously diminished because Mr. Bounderby is a dramatic monster, instead of a characteristic example of a worldly master; and Stephen Blackpool a dramatic perfection, instead of a characteristic example of an honest workman."[2] Not only is Ruskin's parenthetical assessment of the value of *Hard Times* parallel to Leavis's marginalizing "appendix," but also Ruskin's valuation similarly highlights the formal aspects of the novel. Ruskin's assessment is also, like Leavis's, a response to a critique of Dickens's novel, one that clearly faults Dickens for failing to present an accurate portrayal of a "characteristic worldly master" or an "honest workman." Here then, in brief compass, are the two primary positions on *Hard Times:* on the one hand, a celebration of the largely formal qualities of the novel and, on the other, a declaration of the weakness of the novel in Dickens's "failure" to reflect accurately the "real world" phenomena central to his theme in what is clearly a "social novel."

What Leavis saw as the strength of the novel—the moral fable—is precisely the ground of complaint for those critics who see the weakness in a failure of accurate and adequate representation. For any number of possible reasons, this argument goes, Dickens's middle-class perspective prevented him from truly understanding, or truly representing, the working class and organized labor. As Terry Eagleton recently put it, following a line of valuable criticism that stretches back to Raymond Williams and beyond to George Orwell, George Gissing, and George Eliot: "The less creditable aspect of Dickens's Romantic humanism is unwittingly exposed by *Hard Times* itself, a novel which recognizes that what is at stake is a whole industrial-capitalist system, yet which can find little to oppose to it but the anarchic spontaneity of a circus."[3] The Victorian industrial novels, as David Lodge has said, "open themselves to evaluation according to the 'truthfulness' with which they reflect the 'facts' of social history," and *Hard Times* demonstrates considerable weakness in such "truthfulness."[4] While Dickens could more "truthfully" represent organized labor in his journalistic account of the strike and lockout in Preston, which he visited briefly as preparation for writing *Hard Times,* in his novelistic account he misrepresented the workers' movement and diverted what could have been a realistic story of that movement into a story of the bank robbery, into fairy tale and moral fable.[5]

The terms of this opposition—the "facts" of social history and fairy tale or moral fable—should, however, give us pause. After all, the central theme of the novel itself is the conflict between Fact and Fancy. Perhaps, since "no amount of comparison between a novel and its social-historical sources (whether specific or general) can ever settle the question of how successful it is as a work of art,"[6] we might be better served by considering Dickens's misrepresentation of the "facts" of social history not as a weakness but as a deliberate aesthetic choice manifesting Dickens's recognition of and struggle with the contradictions and tensions inherent to any representation of a social reality, past or present.

The issue here is obviously enormous. Even considering only the difficult relation between history and fiction, we are dealing with a debate that goes back at least to Thucydides, who felt called upon to distinguish his own work from the more "romantic" tales of his predecessors. "History" and "fiction" are remarkably slippery terms, which is one reason for our contemporary debate over whether or not we can distinguish between them. When we use "history" to refer both to the past itself and to our written record of it, we reveal our assumption that there is a transparent relation between the vanished past and our written record, but we also reveal the degree to which the "story" we tell of the past is the only past we know. And while "fiction" clearly carries the sense of "made up" or "imaginary" (as opposed to "real"), it also means, as the derivation from the Latin *fingo, fingere* indicates, "to shape or form, to arrange." It is this sense of fiction as a *construct* that has come to the center of the debate over the last several decades as the focus has shifted from a relatively naïve objectivism based upon truth-of-fact to a more complicated and ambiguous justification of history on the basis of truth-of-explanation.

Understanding "fiction" as "construction"—an ordering or arranging of elements into an intelligible and meaningful whole—highlights not the nonreferential, nonverifiable, imaginary aspects of fiction but the narrative element that it shares with historical explanation. But it also points more deeply to the role that narrative plays in perception, cognition, and understanding. Our sense of history, of reality, depends upon our sense of narrative, upon how "things" relate to one another to become meaningful. As Hayden White has argued, "we make sense of the real world by imposing upon it the formal coherency that we customarily associate with the products of writers of fiction. . . . [W]e experience the 'fictionalization' of history as an 'explanation' for the same reason that we experience great fiction as an illumination of a world that we inhabit along with the author. In both we recognize the forms by which consciousness both constitutes and colonizes the world it seeks to inhabit comfortably."[7] Narrative, then, to use Louis O. Mink's terms, is a "cognitive instrument," and as such, "narrative form in history, as in fiction, is an artifice, the product of individual imagination."[8]

This is not to say that fiction and history are, in fact, the same, and there have been a number of valuable efforts to redraw the boundaries between them, both by professional historians and by literary analysts. To take just the literary side, Dorrit Cohn, for example, has laid out in *The Distinction of Fiction* a thorough-going analysis of a variety of specifically narratological features that are available to fiction *as* fiction but that are seen as inadmissible in history *as* history. "Narratology," Cohn argues, "has been largely disregarded by modern theorists in the on-going discussion of fictionality. Far more often than not, borderlines between the fictional and the nonfictional realms of narration have been drawn, withdrawn, retraced, and re-effaced on various grounds—logical, ontological, phenomenological, pragmatic, speech-actional, deconstructive, semantic—without looking to the discipline that has dug most deeply into the ground of narrative itself."[9]

The problem in distinguishing on purely narratological grounds, however, is that we are ultimately relying purely on conventions and shared assumptions. As Cohn acknowledges, a "fictional history . . . might be effectively told by a narrator posing as a historian. But if an author imposed this role on the narrator of a historically realistic novel, the result would be a generic anomaly; for unless it announced its fictional status para- or peritextually, nothing would prevent such a work from passing for a historical text."[10] To put the problem another way: the crucial term missing from Cohn's list of means for investigating the borders of fiction and nonfiction is "epistemological," and the epistemological problem is at the heart both of our own contemporary discussion and of Dickens's recognition of the problematic relationship between fiction and the representation of any social or historical reality.

As Suzy Anger has argued, "Questions of historical knowledge were central to Victorian intellectual debate, as was the Victorians' sense of themselves as historical beings (which Mill famously called 'the dominant idea' of the age)."[11] Certainly there were historical thinkers who promoted a fairly naïve objectivist history, but there were others whose investigation of the problems of history and representation was equally powerful. Dickens's sense of the past and of written history was far from naïve, if highly problematic, and he was keenly aware of historical narrative as interpretation (as opposed to a recitation of the facts as they actually happened). He began *A Child's History of England,* for example, which completed its run in *Household Words* just prior to the start of *Hard Times,* specifically to counteract idealized representations of the past and to prevent his son from acquiring any "Conservative or High Church notions" of history.[12] Dickens is not simply presenting a "correct" (as opposed to a biased) interpretation. Indeed, his awareness of his own interpretive bias is evident in the frequently satiric and highly personal cast of the narrative and constitutes a crucial aspect of the *purpose* of the narrative. Similarly, Dickens is very much at play with interpretations of the past in the novel that immediately followed *Hard Times: Little Dorrit.* While *Little Dorrit* is generally not considered an overtly historical novel (as are *Barnaby Rudge* and *A Tale of Two Cities*), history and the past, as Angus Easson has shown, are among its significant themes.[13]

In fact, Dickens is playing very deliberately both with the historical novel and with the fictive nature of historical interpretation. In a distinct echo of the novel considered to have inaugurated the genre, Scott's *Waverly*, the first sentence of *Little Dorrit* reads: "Thirty years ago, Marseilles lay burning in the sun, one day." Given the subtitle of *Waverly*—"Or 'Tis Sixty Years Since"—it is likely that Dickens is not simply echoing Scott, but also suggesting that *Little Dorrit* is a "half-historical" novel. More significantly, Dickens's play with the imaginative, fictive nature of historical interpretation, as well as the ways that we use such interpretations, is clearly evident in his lighthearted "history" of the origin of the name of Bleeding Heart Yard:

> The opinion of the Yard was divided respecting the derivation of its name. The more practical of its inmates abided by the tradition of a murder; the gentler and more imaginative inhabitants, including the whole of the tender sex, were loyal to the legend of a young lady of former times closely imprisoned in her chamber by a cruel father for remaining true to her own true love, and refusing to marry the suitor he chose for her. The legend related how that the young lady used to be seen up at her window behind the bars, murmuring a love-lorn song of which the burden was, "Bleeding Heart, Bleeding Heart, bleeding away," until she died. It was objected by the murderous party that this Refrain was notoriously the invention of a tambour-worker, a spinster and romantic, still lodging in the Yard. But, forasmuch as all favourite legends must be associated with the affections, and as many more people fall in love than commit murder—which it may be hoped, howsoever bad we are, will continue until the end of the world to be the dispensation under which we shall live—the Bleeding Heart, Bleeding Heart, bleeding away story, carried the day by a great majority. Neither party would listen to the antiquaries who delivered learned lectures in the neighbourhood, showing the Bleeding Heart to have been the heraldic cognisance of the old family to whom the property had once belonged. And, considering that the hour-glass they turned from year to year was filled with the earthiest and coarsest sand, the Bleeding Heart Yarders had reason enough for objecting to be despoiled of the one little golden grain of poetry that sparkled in it. (*LD*, I, ch.12)

While the passage most immediately shows the competing interpretations of the "practical" and the "imaginative" camps, along with the presumably more authoritative version of the "antiquaries," the implications are more extended than this. The choice of tradition, or legend, is entirely dependent on temperament (or bias), if not gender, and ultimately "must be associated with the affections." Moreover, the least plausible interpretation—given that the refrain that "gives" the Yard its name is the invention of an embroidering "romantic" spinster still resident in the Yard—is the one chosen for belief by the "great majority." No one will even listen to the story the antiquaries tell, not because it is implausible, but because they are outsiders and the residents care less for "accuracy" than for their "one little golden grain of poetry." Presumably there is a "truth" in the antiquaries' version, though the word "true" (emphasized by repetition) appears ironically only in the context of the legend of the young lady. But the antiquaries' "truth" is totally overridden by the primarily emotional *use* (and perhaps moral use, considering the interpolation set off by dashes) to which the Yarders put their preferred stories.

Certainly, Dickens is not denying a reality to the past. The problem, as for Carlyle, lies in our access to that reality and the use we make of it.[14] In some ways, Dickens is not terribly far from Fredric Jameson's revision of Althusser (however distant he may be politically and otherwise): "that history is *not* a text, not a narrative, master or otherwise, but that, as an absent cause, it is inaccessible to us except in textual form, and that our approach to it and to the Real itself necessarily passes through its prior textualization, its narrativization in the political unconscious."[15] While the foregoing passage from *Little Dorrit* suggests Dickens's lighthearted play with the past and our stories about it, elsewhere he makes it clear that the reality of the past is highly significant and that how we deal with it has deadly serious consequences.

Dickens's sense of the nightmare of history, particularly in *Barnaby Rudge* and *A Tale of Two Cities,* has been too frequently noted to require much demonstration here; we might simply take Patrick Brantlinger's conclusion to his discussion of Dickens's "philosophy of history" as "grotesque populism" for one example: "Instead of the narrative of historical progress that Dickens might have offered if he had been a Whig-liberal like, say, Macaulay, both in *Barnaby* and in *A Tale of Two Cities,* he renders history as a nightmare from which we are always vainly trying to awake. . . . But whereas for Marx, the final revolution of the proletariat would dispel the nightmare, for Dickens, such a revolution, like the Gordon Riots or like the great French Revolution of 1789, would only be nightmare compounded."[16] The past, specifically as burden, as Steven Marcus has argued in his classic *Dickens from Pickwick to Dombey,* was the crucial source of the sense of "crisis and division" that Dickens had reached in *Dombey and Son,* and, more importantly, "From this point on in Dickens's career, the problem of the past and the problem of the will become the dominant themes of his novels, and the new ways in which he deals with them are part of the achievement they represent."[17]

According to Marcus, in *Barnaby Rudge*—which moves from the personal and nonhistorical to the social-historical level—Dickens sees the dysfunction of father/son relations writ large in the dysfunction of social relations that he describes by focusing on the Gordon Riots. But Dickens's power to convey a strong sense of reality comes precisely from the fictive elements: "Dickens's use of poetic and mythical images, his inclination toward parable and the elaborate, symbolic plot, are inseparable from the intensity and immediacy of registration, the energy of perception, *the vivid grasp upon actuality* which blaze out almost every moment in his prose" (200; emphasis added). Significantly, though, the fictive serves not only to convey a vivid actuality but also to act as a means of dealing with the burden of the past, as Marcus notes of Dickens's use of Staggs's Gardens in *Dombey and Son:* "The displacement of Staggs's Gardens by the railroad may represent Dickens's symbolic attempt to efface the past and creatively reconstruct it" (356).[18]

What I would focus on here is the way that Dickens turns deliberately to fictions to remediate the past, to turn it not only into something meaningful but also into something that we can live with. For example, Dickens reverses in *A Tale of Two Cities* the trajectory that Marcus notes in *Barnaby Rudge:* instead of moving from the personal to the social-historical level, Dickens subsumes the historical revolution in the story of individuals and families, both French (Defarge) and English (Manette-Darnay/Carton). It is not simply that Dickens presents the historical revolution through the mechanism of a nonhistorical but concrete individual or family. Rather, revolutionary vengeance, for example, is displaced and subsumed by the vengeance of Mme. Defarge. The representation sustains a vivid actuality, despite or perhaps because of symbol and allegory, but it also transforms history into something else.

But the way Dickens works upon and with the past is most intricately revealed in the one historical *artifact* that plays a crucial role in *A Tale of Two Cities:* the "paper," or rather narrative, that Dr. Manette secreted in his cell when he was "buried alive" and that Defarge unburied at the taking of the Bastille. It is significant that the artifact is a narrative, an interpretation, recounting events both past and present. At the same time, however, it is the voice of the past speaking in its own present, a true witness as it were. But that voice is necessarily reinterpreted from the novel's present when the narrative is read during Darnay's second Revolutionary trial before Dr. Manette himself, who has no memory of the existence of the original. For his own part, Dr. Manette's reinterpretation is inarticulate, as his only verbal response to the letter is a shriek. Presumably, the shriek signifies that he would reject or rewrite the denunciation of the descendents of the Evrémonde family that closes the narrative, but he is powerless to do that. Instead, the "literal" reading of the Revolutionary tribunal takes precedence, though clearly for its own agenda, not for "justice." There is, finally, only one way that the artifact, the dead, buried, and resurrected past, can be remediated and laid to rest: the *lie,* the fiction, that Carton is Darnay.

As the close of the novel shows, the revolution, in all its nightmarish violence, is ultimately displaced by prophetic vision. It is not an easy displacement: the revolution, to use Carlyle's terms, must eat its own children before it burns itself out; but vision, rather than represented actuality, is where the novel ends. Significantly, the character through whose eyes we see this vision has never been presented as symbolic of the historical aspect (as his mirror Darnay has); rather, Carton, as a redeemed redeemer, is associated with Christ, whose story is the most powerful "working fiction" of Dickens's culture. Dickens seems to be suggesting that the nightmare that is actual history can be remediated only by being reinscribed as fiction, and specifically as a fiction we can live by. The problem, however, is that it is all cast in terms of "if": "*If* he had given an utterance to his [thoughts], and they were prophetic, they *would have been* these: . . ." (*TTC,* II, ch.15; emphasis added).

My point here is that, having confronted the epistemological dilemma of how or whether we can know the past—or, indeed, any reality for that matter—Dickens also struggles with the ethical question of what we *do* in the face of that dilemma. That is why the choice of the circus—both as symbolic of Fancy and as the locus of the solution that allows the representative of institutional authority, Gradgrind, to avoid the legal consequences of his son's theft—is so significant in *Hard Times.* Questions of interpretation and meaning, of truth and knowledge, are inevitably linked to ethical questions, so it is no surprise that such questions should be central to *Hard Times,* one of Dickens's major novels of social reform. In fact, the issues are even more acute in *Hard Times* than in Dickens's historical novels, if only because we are dealing with a contemporary rather than a past reality.

Explanations and interpretations of contemporary reality were, of course, not confined to novels, even novels of social reform. But the kinds of epistemological questions that were raised for history in terms of access to and representation of the past were equally problematic, as Mary Poovey has shown, for the developing social sciences, particularly political economy, which is very much the competing discipline for Dickens in *Hard Times.*[19] The darkly ironic presentation of the "gospel of Fact" and its conflict with Fancy throughout the novel bear out for *Hard Times* what J. Hillis Miller has described in the context of *Bleak House* (significantly, the novel just prior to

*Hard Times*) as Dickens's dark suspicion "that all systems of interpretation may be fictions."[20] I would suggest that in *Hard Times* it is no longer suspicion but acknowledgment, and part of that acknowledgment is Dickens's recognition of the greater power of fiction *as* fiction to reach and affect an audience.

The problem for the political economist or social scientist, Poovey argues, is that "to produce systematic knowledge about society, human nature, or the market, social scientists first had to generate an abstraction—'society,' 'human nature,' or 'the market'—that somehow stood in for, but did not refer directly to, whatever material phenomena it was said to represent."[21] But the very nature of the formulation as abstraction or *construct*, as well as the fact that those abstractions did not always ring true for the reality of readers' experiences, called into question the validity of the discipline that formulated them.[22] The tools of the novelist, on the other hand, particularly those tools that Dickens wielded so well—"poetic and mythical images, his inclination toward parable and the elaborate, symbolic plot," as Marcus puts it—along with a convenient willing suspension of disbelief, allowed the constructs of fiction to stand in, vividly, for a social reality that did not explicitly ask to be verified. The fiction could be taken for, and take the place of, fact.

Dickens was clearly aware of that power, not only for his novels, but for his journalism as well. As Joseph Butwin demonstrates in setting *Hard Times* in the context of Dickens's journalistic reporting in "On Strike" and of *Household Words* as a whole, Dickens's "Preliminary Word" in the inaugural issue of *Household Words* (March 1850) could be taken as a foreword for *Hard Times* itself, presenting the journal as providing a fanciful presentation of fact for the purpose of effecting social change.[23] Butwin argues that readers were expected to move easily between the nonfictional journalistic reports and the fiction, transferring "knowledge directly from one sphere to another, from fact to fiction and back again. . . . [Dickens] teases the reader with fictions that retain the latent authority of fact."[24] The implicit conflation of the novel with journalism could backfire, calling down on the novelist the claim of inaccuracy or misrepresentation, as the history of the reception of *Hard Times* reveals. But the power of fiction to create a "vivid grasp upon actuality," as Marcus puts it, far outweighs the risk, and there is no question that the fiction, particularly the keynote of Coketown, has been taken for fact, as when Lewis Mumford, for example, in *The City in History: Its Origins, Its Transformations, and Its Prospects* (1961), borrows the name of "Coketown" to characterize the nineteenth-century industrial city in general.[25]

To see the power of Dickens's fictionalized fact, one need only compare Dickens's description of Coketown to the absolutely brilliant description of the Old Town of Manchester by Friedrich Engels in *The Condition of the Working Class in England in 1844*. After roughly six pages of extraordinarily detailed, concrete, and extended description of the unfathomable, horrifying, inhuman conditions in which the inhabitants of the Old Town live, Engels assures his reader that he is by no means exaggerating: "Such is the Old Town of Manchester, and on re-reading my description, I am forced to admit that instead of being exaggerated, it is far from black enough to convey a true impression of the filth, ruin, and uninhabitableness, the defiance of all considerations of cleanliness, ventilation, and health which characterise the construction of this single district, containing at least twenty to thirty thousand inhabitants."[26] In fact, Engels is far more specific and concrete in his description than Dickens: there is nothing, not a single foul detail, that his practiced eye misses. He is also intensely personal, as he describes from the first-person point of view, as he interjects exclamations, and as he reaches his own breaking point with "Enough!" in the midst of his description. He even reaches toward the same kind of irony as does Dickens in characterizing these literally dehumanizing conditions by conflating animal and human. Curiously enough, however, in reaching toward verifiable actuality, Engels notes that his description, far from being exaggerated for effect, does not, perhaps cannot, go far enough to convey the truth, particularly as it affects "twenty to thirty thousand inhabitants." It is there, I think—in the concrete specifics of number—that Engels loses the vivid actuality that Dickens maintains throughout, as he pushes his reader beyond the capacity to visualize or imagine. Again, Marcus encapsulates the point: "The twenty-four-year-old Engels has achieved a tour de force. I know of no representation of an industrial city before this that achieves such an intimate, creative hold upon its living subject. For anything that stands with it or surpasses it, one has to go to the later Dickens, to *Bleak House, Hard Times, Little Dorrit,* and *Our Mutual Friend.*"[27]

But Dickens surpasses Engels in the way his description is taken as representative of the industrial city. Dickens's famous description of Coketown achieves a vivid actuality different in kind and degree:

> It was a town of red brick, or of brick that would have been red if the smoke and ashes had allowed it; but, as matters stood it was a town of unnatural red and black like the painted face of a savage. It was a town of machinery and tall chimneys, out of which interminable serpents of smoke trailed themselves for ever and ever, and never got uncoiled. It had a black canal in it, and a river that ran purple with ill-smelling dye, and vast piles of building full of windows where there was a rattling and a trembling all day long, and

where the piston of the steam-engine worked monotonously up and down, like the head of an elephant in a state of melancholy madness. It contained several large streets all very like one another, and many small streets still more like one another, inhabited by people equally like one another, who all went in and out at the same hours, with the same sound upon the same pavements, to do the same work, and to whom every day was the same as yesterday and tomorrow, and every year the counterpart of the last and the next. (*HT,* I, ch.5)

Dickens's description is certainly vivid, but not exactly specific; rather, the extraordinary effect of oppression, deformation, and monotony is carried by the figurative transformations of images conflating animal and inanimate city, by evocation through color and shape, by the rhetoric, rhythm, and repetition. It is intensely visual, but precisely the opposite of the visual detail of actuality in Engels.[28] No one would expect to see precisely this city anywhere on earth, yet the fiction is taken for fact.

The crucial point here, however, is not that Dickens was successful in passing off an obviously imaginative construct as a fact of industrial life, but rather that the entire novel is wrapped up in the idea that, inevitably, we live by our fictions, and the struggle is between competing versions of reality. Nor is it simply that Dickens, as a "sentimental radical" (as I believe Walter Bagehot first called him), proposes fantasy, entertainment, and "childish lore" (*HT,* II, ch.9) as a necessary escape from the fact-bound reality of the "Utilitarian" social order of the industrial world. That social order is presented equally as socially constructed knowledge and as a particularly dangerous fiction disguised as fact.[29] While the opposition between Fact and Fancy is clearly presented in the opening chapters in the catechizing of the school children concerning representations of flowers and horses on carpets and wallpaper, the government officer's equation of fact and reality (*HT,* I, ch.2), along with socially institutionalized authority, has earlier in that chapter already been undercut by the narrator in a more problematic exchange between Gradgrind and Sissy Jupe. When "Girl number twenty" redefines herself by name as Sissy Jupe, Gradgrind invalidates her name and instructs her to call herself Cecilia. When Sissy defends her name by citing her father, Gradgrind asks not who he is or what he does, but for a definition: "What is your father?" When Sissy responds that her father "belongs to the horse-riding," Gradgrind disallows any knowledge, and therefore the existence, of such a calling: "We don't want to know anything about that, here. You mustn't tell us about that, here." Gradgrind then proceeds to redefine Sissy's father completely: "He is a veterinary surgeon, a farrier and horsebreaker." Not only has Gradgrind

## 5: Storied Realities

sought to redefine Sissy's experience, but the perfect irony is that he has done so with a total fabrication, and he has substituted that thoroughly linguistic fiction, presenting it as fact, for the reality that Sissy knows.

Dickens is even more deliberate in underlining the fictive nature of the institutional reality when he presents the "fictions of Coketown" through which the "hard-fact" men preserve the order of things for their benefit. The overt fictions, as Dickens identifies them at the beginning of "Book the Second, Reaping,"[30] include "Mr. Bounderby's gold spoon [the construct that any Hand expects to be 'set up in a coach and six, and to be fed on turtle soup and venison, with a gold spoon'] which was generally received in Coketown"; the "threat" presented by any Coketown Owner who might be held accountable for his actions that he would "pitch his property into the Atlantic"; and the reproach of "any capitalist there, who had made sixty thousand pounds out of sixpence," directed toward the "sixty thousand nearest Hands" who did not accomplish the same (*HT,* II, ch.1). While the narrator is obviously presenting these fictions ironically, the subtler problem is that they are clearly "received in Coketown" as truth by the industrialists who promulgate them, as is the far more insidious fiction, received as truth by Hands and Industrialists alike, of Bounderby's supposed autobiography.

Bounderby is, ultimately, as much a performer as any "Cackler" in Sleary's circus, though he presents himself as, and is taken for, fact. He is constantly narrating his "history"—that he is truly a "self-made" man, abandoned by his mother, abused by his grandmother, and left to pull himself up out of the ditch in which he was born to the eminence that he now occupies—as central to the meaning of himself and, by extension, Coketown. Bounderby's story is an extreme version of a common tale enjoyed by a rising middle class and immortalized by Matthew Arnold as Mrs. Gooch's golden rule: "the sentence Sir Daniel Gooch's mother repeated to him every morning when he was a boy going to work:—'*Ever remember, my dear Dan, that you should look forward to being some day manager of that concern!*'"[31] As we discover, however, from the competing narrative told by Mrs. Pegler (the suspected-bank-robber-cum-proud-mother), Bounderby is the ultimate "self-made" man in that he has literally invented himself, even to his surname.[32] While Dickens uses Mrs. Pegler's narrative to deflate the "Bully of humility, who had built his windy reputation upon lies" (*HT,* III, ch.5), the ultimate irony is that Bounderby's fiction is totally gratuitous. The alternative story that Mrs. Pegler tells—and it is presented as the *story* of a parent's sacrifice for a child's advancement—is just as inspiring a tale. Moreover, though Bounderby is the obvious butt of irony and derision, Dickens does allow for the perpetuation of Bounderby's fiction in the *artifact* of his will, which serves not only to multiply Bounderbys (in the taking of the same invented name by "five-and-twenty Humbugs"), but also to preserve a "vast amount of Bounderby balderdash and bluster" (*HT,* III, ch.9). The windy reputation built on lies becomes perpetual bluster.

The problem, when all stories are seen as competing versions of reality, is that the one *true* meaning cannot be determined. Bounderby's story is a lie, but Mrs. Pegler's is an *interpretation,* and the true meaning of the stories, even of the "good" characters, cannot be determined unequivocally. The story that Sissy Jupe tells herself about her father's leaving her is just one of several possibilities. E. W. B. Childers declares it a "remarkable fact" that Jupe could not bear to have his daughter know of his failures in the ring and suggests that he left so that she might have a chance at education (*HT,* I, ch.6). Bounderby, who "knows" something of desertion, declares that the "vagabond" has "absconded" and "deserted" Sissy, never to return. All we ever know for certain is that Jupe does not, "in fact," return and is assumed dead, as Merrylegs had somehow made his way back to Sleary's circus, thrown himself up on his forelegs despite his weakness, wagged his tail, and died, as if to announce Jupe's death. Even Sleary, who is most familiar with the ways of dogs, pronounces it a mystery "whether her father bathely detherted her; or whether he broke his own heart alone, rather than pull her down along with him" and thinks it better to say nothing to Sissy about it at all (*HT,* III, ch.8).

Ultimately, we are confronted with the failure to know and the impossibility of true communication, and hence of true community, and at the root of the problem is the one thing, for Dickens, that makes us human: language. Gradgrind's refusal in the schoolroom to "know" anything about Sissy's words and the world they represent is mirrored in her incapacity to understand his language: she "translates" statistics into "stutterings" (*HT,* I, ch.9). Mrs. Gradgrind's efforts on her deathbed to communicate "something—not an Ology at all—that [Gradgrind] has missed or forgotten" devolve into little "figures of wonderful no-meaning" that she traces on her wrappers as she dies (*HT,* II, ch.9). Gradgrind, drowning in facts, misses meaning in general and specifically the meaning of Louisa's figurative language in their discussion of Bounderby's proposal (*HT,* I, ch.15). Stephen Blackpool's "muddle," however sentimentally it is finally presented, is the perfect metaphor for the central problem, as Dickens makes clear in Stephen's final speeches. Bounderby, Stephen realizes, though he claims to "know" the Hands as he knows the bricks of Coketown (as if he built the town with his own "hands"), has never known him at all, any more than Stephen and his fellow workers have known Bounderby, given his deliberate deception. The star that brightens Stephen's muddle to some vague clarity leaves him (and us) with one final prayer: "that aw th' world may on'y coom toogether more, an get a better unnerstan'in o'one another" (*HT,* III, ch.6). The prayer, clearly, is for fuller knowledge and understanding between and among different members of the community, and that requires true communication. Certainly, it is Dickens's prayer as well, as he said essentially the same thing in "On Strike" in his own voice.[33] But even there, Dickens and "Mr. Snapper" speak at cross-purposes; communication fails, and Snapper takes himself off in silence to another carriage of the train. The star that gives Stephen light in his darkness clearly evokes the star of Bethlehem; but this star leads not to the birth of a savior, but to the death of a scapegoat. Stephen's death, however much a Christ-like innocent sacrifice, redeems nothing; instead, it "reveals" Tom as the true criminal.

The most serious problem in the recognition of the failures of language and of the fictionality of all our systems of interpretation is the danger that James Harthouse represents and that Louisa nearly succumbs to: "What does it matter?" leads to a moral vacuum. Harthouse arrives in Coketown out of boredom and has decided to "go in for" the hard-fact men because they will do better than another party if only because, he explains to Louisa, "we know it is all meaningless, and say so; while they know it equally and will never say so" (*HT,* II, ch.7). With her faith in a "wider and nobler humanity" destroyed by her father's system, she finds release in the "Harthouse philosophy": "Everything being hollow and worthless, she had missed nothing and sacrificed nothing. What did it matter, she had said to her father, when he proposed her husband. What did it matter, she said still. With a scornful self-reliance, she asked herself, What did anything matter—and went on." The "Harthouse philosophy" says that it simply does not matter what one believes or by what rules one plays, since it is all the same nonsense anyway. That, Louisa realizes almost too late, is a dangerous and finally destructive position to take.

But Dickens's irony, and the sense of the impossibility of communication and community, is not the end of the story. There is some hope, however qualified. There is the restoration of some communication, even unspoken, between Louisa and Sissy (as there is Sissy's influence on the youngest Gradgrind child, Jane, and in the household in general); there is the connection that Louisa establishes with Stephen and Rachael that is broken but partially repaired; there is the support and connection that Sissy provides Rachael as she waits for Stephen's return; Gradgrind even learns partly to speak and understand Sissy's language of feeling. Clearly, although it is not *always* Sissy, as Gradgrind says (*HT,* III, ch.7), "it" is always connected to Sissy, who proves ultimately to be the redeemer and savior. It is Sissy who directs Tom to the circus, and it is the circus and Sleary that provide Gradgrind the solution that allows him to evade the forces of law and order, of institutional authority, that he himself has stood for as Member of Parliament.

Still, this solution has its own problems. Despite being the spokesman for the circus and for the necessity of amusement, play, and fancy, Sleary never thought that he "wath tho muth of a Cackler" (*HT,* III, ch.8). And just as at the beginning there were barriers to understanding in the lingo of the circus, so there is the fundamental difficulty of understanding Sleary's speech. It is not simply that the circus is anarchic: rather, it is performance and outrageous display; it is founded upon exaggeration; its advertisements suggest obvious impossibilities; and the speech of its spokesman is literally deformed. More importantly, perhaps, the solution of Tom's escape is intimately bound up in disguise, primarily Tom's, and finally deception. Having discovered through Bitzer's dialogue with Gradgrind that Tom has robbed the bank, Sleary declares that he is ethically bound not to help Tom escape but to side with Bitzer. Of course, he is lying and, in full knowledge, takes the putatively unethical path of saving Tom from Bitzer and getting him out of the reach of law. Clearly, this solution is out of bounds and hence raises serious questions. But I think Dickens's answer is that the truly ethical choice is the one that preserves true community: the community with Sissy now at the center is preserved through Sleary's choice to stand by the "Thquire" as he stood by Sissy (*HT,* III, ch.7).

Having arrived at the epistemological recognition that all of our competing systems of interpretation and explanation are finally fictions, *constructions,* Dickens reaches—and in the final paragraph pushes the reader, too—toward the ethical stance that, in the interests of true communication and community, it very much *does matter* what fictions we choose. While we may *be* skeptics, we cannot *act* as such. In fact, there is one (perhaps only one) act of incontrovertible true communication in the novel, and that is interestingly enough between Sissy and the representative of "what does it matter," Harthouse. She commands him—without any basis as he concludes except "her plain faith in the truth and right of what she said" (*HT,* III, ch.2)—to leave Coketown, and he does so. We must acknowledge that Sissy's statement depends upon *faith,* rather than *knowledge,* and Harthouse, who simply "goes in for" any philosophy that suits regardless of an ethical ground, learns nothing. He leaves despite himself and is finally ashamed of his actions because of "a dread of what other fellows who went in for similar sorts of things, would say at his expense if they knew it." Nonetheless, despite what Harthouse may wish to believe, the victory of Sissy's truth, or at least her faith in it, is real and banishes the truly unethical. Dickens's point, I think, is that, because we live by our fictions, we must, if we are to have a viable human community, choose them wisely and well. We must have healthy stories, enabling fictions, through which we can "coom toogether" and that allow us to know one another, as opposed to disabling, deforming, distorting lies, especially those that set themselves up as the absolute truth of "fact."

## NOTES

1. Leavis, *The Great Tradition*, 19–20. Leavis's designation of *Hard Times* as a "masterpiece" comes in the final chapter, "'Hard Times': An Analytic Note," which appears essentially as an appendix to *The Great Tradition* (227–48). Of course, it should be noted that Leavis significantly revised his position, not only allowing Dickens to be among the greatest of creative writers, but, in collaboration with Q. D. Leavis, dedicating an entire work to *Dickens the Novelist* (1970).
2. Ruskin, "Note on *Hard Times*," 332.
3. Eagleton, *English Novel*, 158.
4. Lodge, "How Successful Is *Hard Times*?" 381.
5. Dickens's account of the Preston strike was published as "On Strike" in *Household Words*, 11 February 1854, shortly before the start of the serial publication of *Hard Times* in the same magazine. While Dickens does present a fuller and more sympathetic picture of the workers' movement in "On Strike," it is also true that he presents there the same fundamental position that he does in *Hard Times*. On the relation between "On Strike" and *Hard Times* and between Dickens's journalistic and his novelistic practice, see especially Joseph Butwin, "*Hard Times*: The News and the Novel," and R. D. Butterworth, "Dickens the Novelist: The Preston Strike and *Hard Times*," as well as "Dickens the Journalist: The Preston Strike and 'On Strike.'" See also Stephen J. Spector, "Monsters of Metonymy: *Hard Times* and Knowing the Working Class."
6. Lodge, 382.
7. White, "The Historical Text," 61. See also White's "The Value of Narrativity in the Representation of Reality."
8. Mink, "Narrative Form as a Cognitive Instrument," 141, 145. It should be noted that the context and background for these isolated comments is too large even to begin listing in this brief space. But it might be said that White and Mink, along with Arthur Danto in *Narration and Knowledge*, are the three most influential voices for literature, history, and philosophy respectively in the discussion of the relation between narrative and cognition and the consequent implications for the relation between fiction and history.
9. Cohn, *Distinction of Fiction*, 109.
10. Ibid., 120. It should be acknowledged that Cohn deliberately establishes clear limits at the start of her study on the use of "fiction" to avoid conflation with "construct" or the more general "narrative." Such conflation, or at least the use of the term "fiction" as synonymous with "construct" and "narrative," is central to the epistemological problem.
11. Anger, "Knowing the Victorians," 3. I cite Anger in particular on this point partly because the project she defines in *Knowing the Past* is very much what I am trying to get at here: to see a Victorian writer both in some semblance of his own intellectual

and social context and in terms of the ways in which that writer has anticipated and shaped our own contemporary discussion.

12. Quoted in Jann, "Fact, Fiction, and Interpretation in *A Child's History of England*," 199. See also John Lucas, "Past and Present: *Bleak House* and *A Child's History of England*."

13. Easson, "A Novel Scarcely Historical? Time and History in Dickens's *Little Dorrit*."

14. Carlyle is crucially relevant, as many critics have noted, for any consideration of Dickens and particularly for his sense of History as Catastrophe. See especially Michael Goldberg, *Carlyle and Dickens,* and Jonathan Arac, *Commissioned Spirits.* See also Fleishman, *The English Historical Novel,* 114–26; Daleski, "Imagining Revolution, 61–72; and Brantlinger, "Did Dickens Have a Philosophy of History?" 62–63.

15. Jameson, *Political Unconscious,* 35. While Dickens is clearly not Jameson, politically or intellectually, there is no doubt that for Dickens "narrative" is a "socially symbolic act," as the address to the reader at the close of *Hard Times* suggests.

16. Brantlinger, "Did Dickens Have a Philosophy of History?" 71.

17. Marcus, *From Pickwick to Dombey,* 356–57. Subsequent references are made parenthetically in the text.

18. Of course, such displacement and reconstruction may be no solution, as Marcus continues: "but in the world of this novel the railroad exists as a thing apart, and as the impersonal and ironic comment upon the grim, doomed, and determined lives of its principal characters" (356).

19. See Poovey, "The Structure of Anxiety."

20. Miller, "Interpretation in Dickens' *Bleak House*," 197.

21. Poovey, "Structure," 151.

22. See ibid., "Anxiety," 156–60. Obviously the same can easily be said for the historian: the absent cause that is the past must be formulated as "abstraction," as mental or imagined entity, and here too such an abstraction might not ring true for a reader.

23. Butwin, 170, 171–72.

24. Ibid., 174.

25. See Welsh, *Dickens Redressed,* 148, 219n5.

26. Engels, *The Condition of the Working Class,* 84.

27. Marcus, *Engels, Manchester, and the Working Class,* 198.

28. See also Spector, 232–33. Spector also provides a discussion of Engels in the context of Dickens (240–43).

29. On the fictionalizing of the "hard-fact" men and its relation to socially constructed knowledge, see Bodenheimer, *The Politics of Story,* 189–207. See also Larson, "Identity's Fictions," and Brantlinger, *The Spirit of Reform.*

30. The agricultural metaphor organizing the book—Sowing, Reaping, Garnering—serves both to show metaphor as an organizing principle for fiction and to set off that "vanished" agricultural metaphor as an organizing construct for life against the new industrial metaphor that has replaced it.

31. Arnold, *Culture and Anarchy,* 88.

32. See also Bodenheimer, *Politics,* 198.

33. Dickens, "On Strike," 286.

# Part Two

## MATERIAL CULTURE

# 6

# So, This Is Christmas

JOSEPH W. CHILDERS

"CHRISTMAS IS BANNED: IT OFFENDS MUSLIMS" shouted a recent headline from the front page of the *Daily Express,* a London tabloid. "Britain's proud heritage suffered a devastating blow yesterday after council chiefs banned Christmas," announced the story's lead.[1] Apparently, the tradition of British Christmas was eviscerated when the South London Lambeth council, which also has jurisdiction over Brixton and Clapham, two of the most culturally diverse residential areas in England, ordered "Christmas lights in its town centres to be called 'winter' or even 'celebrity' lights to avoid upsetting other faiths" (1). The reactions incited by the council's decision ranged from the predictable accusations that its members were "ashamed to be Christians" to the Muslim Council of Britain's unexpected reproach of the Lambeth bureaucrats for their overzealous attempts at political correctness. Some of the attacks on the council argued the need for religious freedom, diversity, and tolerance toward all, including Christians, but far more attacks focused on the connection between Christmas and Britishness or Englishness. In an op/ed piece in the same issue, the *Daily Express* pronounced Christmas "a traditional British celebration" and insisted that it "should be enjoyed as such" (12). Furthermore, asserted the editorial in a rather snide choice of words, "Britishness is being destroyed in a misplaced bid to kowtow to other ethnic sensitivities." Such deference is "just turning everything that is best about British life into something of which we are supposed to be ashamed" (12).

## 6: So, This Is Christmas

Unlike the complaints of the religious right in the United States who, in December 2005, clamored for putting "Christ" back into "Christmas," the sentiment in the United Kingdom reverberates with the tensions that accumulate in a discourse of Christmas that is reliant on classical liberal sensibilities as well as on the identification of the holiday with the national character. It is not eternal salvation and the celebration of the birth of the son of God that are at stake in the *Daily Express* as much as it is Britishness itself, an entire way of life, a national identity ostensibly struggling with guilt over its very existence. For contemporary readers, the various opinions voiced in the name of the culture of Christmas may seem merely to stake out another front in the culture wars, yet discussions of what Christmas means to the British, more specifically what it means to the English—and indeed what Englishness means to Christmas—are by no means novel.[2] In 1897, George Bernard Shaw writes, "Christmas is forced on a reluctant and disgusted nation by the shopkeepers and the press; on its own merits it would wither and shrivel in the fiery breath of universal hatred; and anyone who looked back to it would be turned to a pillar of greasy sausages."[3] Shaw takes issue not only with the materialism and sentimentalism that had come to define English Christmas by the end of the nineteenth century, but also with the Victorian culture of Christmas that began to take shape more than a half-century earlier, making it nearly impossible for Shaw or anyone else to consider Christmas "on its own merits."

The 1840s were arguably the crucible of the Victorian era, when the properties of the "national character" were so successfully formed that they established notions of Englishness for the next century and beyond. During this decade, concerns over the Condition of England rose to prominence, and the dichotomies that lie at the heart of tales such as Charles Dickens's *A Christmas Carol* first irrepressibly asserted themselves to the English, impressing upon the middle classes an urgent sense that they must assume some responsibility beyond their own immediate interests. It was also between 1843 and 1848 that Dickens published his Christmas books—*A Christmas Carol, The Chimes, A Cricket on the Hearth, The Battle of Life,* and *The Haunted Man*—and in the process created Christmas as a narrative space in which the paradoxes of the social conditions of English life could be resolved and national identity established. So "English" was Dickens's portrayal of Christmas that it became inseparable from Englishness itself. G. K. Chesterton comments that the Dickensian Christmas "is especially and distinctively English in the style of its merry-making and even in the style of its religion. For the character of Christmas . . . lies chiefly in two things; first on the terrestrial side the note of comfort rather than the note of brightness; and on the spiritual side, Chris-

Joseph W. Childers

tian charity rather than Christian ecstasy. And comfort is, like charity, a very English instinct."[4] In this symbiotic relationship, Christmas becomes English at the same time that it is also demanding a particular sort of observance as a means of reaffirming one's Englishness. As Chesterton points out, Christmas reflects, and amplifies, middle-class English proclivities toward comfort and charity. Irresistible and inescapable, in Dickens's hands Christmas is a master trope for narratives that simultaneously laud and lament the effects of classical liberalism and that, consequently, establish a model of "Englishness" for the Victorians as well as for later generations.

In this chapter, I dwell among the doubly constitutive efforts of what might well be labeled the "culture of Victorian Christmas" and consider what it meant to offer any sort of public, or for that matter private, utterance within that culture. What sorts of assumptions obtained? What place was there for expressions from competing or complementary discourses that did not immediately identify Christmas as peremptorily middle-class and English? Did Christmas and the celebration of it constitute a place where, as Dickens so often suggests, time not so much stands still but stacks up so that all narratives are synchronic, a site both familiar and *unheimlich*? Or was it, instead, yet another way of living that was not just constructed and imaginary, but experienced at such a depth, so completely imbricated in the consciousness of Victorian subjects, that it became hegemonic, having the status, as Raymond Williams might say, of common sense? Did Christmas and participation in it reassert, or reaffirm, not only what it meant to be human and part of a community that relied on its members to give back as much as they took, but also what it meant to be a child, a woman, a worker, or a clerk—or for that matter cockney or Geordie, Irish or English? That is, even as writers like Dickens were proclaiming a celebration of humanity in a season of joy, were they also specifying the particular roles each got to play in that celebration? I consider the place that certain kinds of difference had in a culture of Christmas—a culture that we often represent to ourselves as egalitarian and universal, but that also depends on hierarchy and exclusion. Indeed, the very existence of such a culture in part relies on its ability to reproduce those conditions of inequity it purports to ameliorate.

Dickens has been directly associated with Christmas since Ebenezer Scrooge, Bob Cratchit, and Tiny Tim made their first appearances 17 December 1843. By the time of his death in 1870, Dickens seemed to own the holiday. One of the most popular anecdotes recounted by Dickens biographers, and first recorded by Theodore Watts-Dunton, is of the Drury Lane barrow girl, who upon hearing of the author's death cried, "Dickens dead? Then will Father Christmas die too?"[5] The extraordinary initial popularity of *A Christ-*

mas *Carol* and its subsequent installation as a Christmas institution (it has never been out of print) have a great deal to do with the perception of Dickens as single-handedly saving Christmas from Victorian earnestness and the opprobrium of the "Hungry Forties." More precisely, however, Dickens did not so much "save" Christmas as exert considerable influence in recreating it, calling on cultural memories that were themselves yet more creations. In *The Making of the Modern Christmas,* J. M. Golby and A. W. Purdue point out that one of the most memorable of Dickensian Christmases, at Dingley Dell in *Pickwick,* is an "idealisation of an eighteenth-century Christmas" that locates the "hey day" of Christmas in that time.[6] This nostalgia, compelling though it may have been, was also apparently inaccurate.[7] Christmas in the eighteenth century did not enjoy any particular popularity and for many was not as important "a holiday as New Year or even St. Valentine's Day." For Golby and Purdue, the Victorian Christmas was an invented tradition, a refurbishment of selectively remembered Christmases, a cultural practice they label "a symbiosis of an idealised past with the preoccupations of Victorians themselves."[8]

Of course, that is not to say that everyone joyfully yielded to the Christmas spirit, especially Dickens's version of it, or that all critics appreciated Dickens's Yuletide efforts. A reviewer of *The Haunted Man* writes in *Macphail's Edinburgh Ecclesiastical Journal* in January 1849: "Let us now have a few more returns of Christmas, and Mr. Dickens will have destroyed his reputation as a tale-writer. We earnestly recommend him to quit the twenty-fifth of December, and take to the first of April."[9] Another review, this time of *The Battle of Life* in *Tait's Edinburgh Magazine,* is even more cynical and caustic:

> *The Battle of Life* is the fourth of Mr. Dickens's annual publications. *The Christmas Carol,* the first and the best, has reached only a *tenth* edition. *The Chimes* was said to be inferior to its predecessor, and is up to the twelfth edition. *The Cricket on the Hearth* had the worst character of the three, and has, therefore, attained its twenty-second edition. The facts merely show that book-buyers and reviewers do not always entertain similar opinions. The latter class pretty generally asserted that Mr. Dickens was living—so far as his Annuals were concerned—on his character—eating into his acquired literary capital, while the former has taken care that he should live upon his edition. No book of the past, or many previous issues, has been so successful as the *Cricket*.... On the ratio of increase in the previous publications, the *Battle of Life* will run into forty-four editions.[10]

Dickens's Christmas books and stories were very popular indeed, but did this mean that Dickens was creating his own market—which he was very good at doing—or was he participating in a culture of Christmas that was already strenuously at work?[11] Dickens and his writings should not be credited for inventing the modern Christmas; nevertheless, he was inarguably well attuned to the cultural imperatives of his age, recognizing the contradictions inherent to the way Christmas was thought of and functioned, as well as the seemingly endless narrative possibilities occasioned by the holiday. Dickens's early Christmas stories, whether in the novels or in a work like *A Christmas Carol,* typically concern themselves with pointedly commenting upon and describing Christmas or the Yuletide season. By the time he took up his position at *Household Words,* the stories had broken no new observational ground, existing less as comments on the holiday or the season than as the literary giant's somewhat meager gifts to an adoring public. Only a few short years after the *Carol,* Dickens himself was more a product of the English Christmas than its creator.[12]

The phenomenon of the Victorian Christmas is usefully considered in the somewhat modified light of the critic Raymond Williams's tripartite conception of culture: the residual, the dominant, and the emergent.[13] This model presents a number of theoretical problems for Williams, not the least of which is asserting culture as a totality even while seeing it as dynamic and susceptible to outside influences. Rather than presuming culture as an identifiable totality, I want instead to suggest the possibility of multiple complementary and opposing cultures that can and do exist within the same social space and that form around certain practices, such as the observation of Christmas. I wish to retain a form of Williams's triad primarily because I believe that it is in early Victorian celebrations of Christmas that we can see emergent, residual, and finally dominant characteristics of what I have labeled the culture of Christmas. Humphry House was one of the first modern Dickens scholars to recognize the force and expansiveness of such a culture in Dickens's fiction; he wrote in 1942: "The Christmas spirit is not confined to the *Christmas* Books, the *Christmas* Stories, or the set descriptions of Christmas in the novels: it is present in the very attempt to hold up benevolence as a social ideal."[14] We can further see, especially in *A Christmas Carol* but in *The Chimes* as well, how Christmas struggles against competing views of social responsibility that are likewise attempting to resolve the contradictions of the Victorian everyday in the 1840s. Both of these texts take up the issue of the poor, the other nation, and the increasing gap between the lower and the upper classes. And while Christmas, per se, receives relatively little notice in *The Chimes* (many have noted that it is more appropriate to call it a New Year story), in *A Christmas Carol* we are told explicitly that it is the job of Christmas to heal, at least temporarily, the breach between humans that has come about as a result of modern modes of producing and modern ways of doing business.

For Scrooge's nephew, Fred, Christmas should help allay the material difficulties of the working classes and assuage the consciousness of a middle class that is caught up in a frenzy of production, consumption, and profit. As Fred says to Scrooge:

> "There are many things from which I might have derived good, by which I have not profited, I dare say.... Christmas among the rest. But I am sure I have always thought of Christmas time, when it has come round—apart from the veneration due to its sacred name and origin, if anything belonging to it can be apart from that—as a good time: a kind, forgiving, charitable, pleasant time: when men and women seem by one consent to open their shut-up hearts freely, and to think of people below them as if they really were fellow-passengers to the grave, and not another race of creatures bound on other journeys. And therefore, uncle, though it has never put a scrap of gold or silver in my pocket, I believe that it *has* done me good, and *will* do me good; and I say, God bless it!" (*CC*, stave 1)

Fred's speech demonstrates how emergent, residual, and dominant imperatives combine in a hodge-podge that both characterizes and undercuts Christmas. First, he bravely takes on the concept of political economy that dominates Scrooge's character, a notion that the text ties to Malthus and Bentham but that in Scrooge's hands is transformed into a philosophy of profit and misanthropy. Scrooge is the anti-Christmas, and by implication and association his legions are those political economists who so vulgarized Benthamite economic principles as to render a simplistic code of self-interest as the means by which society might best progress. Scrooge has translated a conception of his "good" into "profit" and marks no difference between the two. Christmas, however, demands that distinction be maintained, emerging as a set of practices and utterances that directly oppose the parsimony and solipsism of Scrooge's worldview. It materializes as a means by which the hardness of *laissez-faire* economics can be made softer, gentler, kinder. At the same time, the residue of its "sacred name and origin," as Fred puts it, cannot be separated from it. Indeed, it gets re-enacted, retold, and re-interpreted repeatedly, even today.

Fred's defense also disrupts Christmas, however. Even while the holiday appears as a cultural entity at the heart of Victorian society—apparently doing battle with what Dickens no doubt would have labeled prevailing political-economic views—it is also subsumed by those views. Fred must take up the idiom of the political economists, a language of "good" and "profit," in order to define Christmas. Discursively it exists within the very culture it seeks to modify—if not to replace. The desire for a good old English Christmas is described in language that justifies a good *new* English Christmas, one that can be understood and approved by those who seem to hold sway in the English middle classes and who demand an explanation based on precisely those principles Scrooge represents. Further, Fred pointedly remarks on the temporariness of Christmas. For him, it is not something he holds in his heart all the year through, as Scrooge ultimately promises he will do. Rather, it "comes round" as a brief moment of generosity and good will in a "long calendar year." It is a time, for Fred, that may return every year, but also a time that passes and whose effects are fleeting. Finally, Christmas may indeed help the middle classes to think of those below them as fellow human beings, but the other side of that thought congratulates the middle classes first for being above and second for being able to patronize the poor.

Scrooge begins to take up his own place in this ambivalent ideological mix when he reprimands the Ghost of Christmas Present for Sabbatarianism, the movement that legislated against many sorts of commerce and leisure activities on Sunday and religious holidays so those days could be used (by the working classes) exclusively for worship. As Scrooge and the Ghost of Christmas Present walk among the Christmas revelers, the "steeples" soon called all "good people":

> to church and chapel and away they came flocking through the streets in their best clothes, and with their gayest faces. And at the same time, there emerged from scores of bye streets, lanes and nameless turnings, innumerable people, carrying their dinners to the bakers' shops.
>
> In time the bells ceased, and the bakers' were shut up.
>
> "Spirit," said Scrooge, after a moment's thought, "I wonder you, of all the beings in the many worlds about us, should desire to cramp these people's opportunities of innocent enjoyment."
>
> "I!" cried the Spirit.
>
> "You would deprive them of their means of dining every seventh day, of the only day on which they can be said to dine at all," said Scrooge. "Wouldn't you?"
>
> "I!" cried the Spirit.
>
> "You seek to close these places on the Seventh Day?" said Scrooge. "And it comes to the same thing."

"*I* seek!" exclaimed the Spirit.

"Forgive me if I am wrong. It has been done in your name, or at least in that of your family," said Scrooge.

"There are some upon this earth of yours," returned the Spirit, "who lay claim to know us and who do their deeds of passion, pride, ill-will, hatred, envy, bigotry, and selfishness in our name, who are as strange to us and all our kith and kin, as if they had never lived. Remember that, and charge their doings on themselves, not us." (*CC*, stave 3).

Like so many passages in *A Christmas Carol*, this one is both fascinating and vexing: fascinating for the number of tasks it takes on; vexing because once again the place it clears for Christmas remains shadowy and rather rough ground. The bells call the faithful to worship, to both church and chapel, indicating the universalism of Christmas, and, of course, the good people respond. At the same time, it reminds that "innumerable" crowd living in the "scores of bye streets, lanes and nameless turnings" to get their one meat meal of the week to the bakers before they close for night. The call to worship and the attendant efforts by Parliament to restrict Sabbath recreation for the working classes was not something Dickens suffered gladly, and it is not for nothing that he juxtaposes the call to worship with the poor's attempts to take care of their Christmas dinners. Readers of Dickens cannot help being reminded of another passage, in another novel more than a decade later, in which the bells are again ringing out, urging the people to "come to church, come to church, come to church." But as Arthur Clennam sits in a coffee shop in Ludgate Hill, he can hear one maddening bell begin to "realize" that "they won't come, they won't come, they won't come." Then, as if in despair, for the last five minutes before the hour, the bell "abandoned hope, and shook every house in the neighbourhood for three hundred seconds, with one dismal swing per second, as a groan of heaven." And when the hour finally strikes and the oppressive ringing ceases, Clennam reacts, ironically, by "thanking heaven" (*LD*, I, ch.3).

Admittedly, the passage in the *Carol* focuses less on the poor's heeding the call of the bells to come to church than on their getting their dinners to the bakers; yet the story's attention to Sabbatarianism and the happy throng's response to the call of the bells serve, like Fred's disclaimer, to link Christmas to religion and to its origins as the observation of the birth of Christ (and one might as well say the birth of Christianity). But the conversation between Scrooge and the Spirit, in which the miser admonishes the ghost and his kind for denying the poor their opportunities for "innocent enjoyment" also frees Christmas from the demands of too fervent and narrow a Christianity. The narrator of *Little Dorrit* tells us that the poor could have no possible secular want on their seventh day, except a stringent policeman to see to it that they observe their faith in a dour and oppressive way (*LD,* I, ch.3). At first glance, this policeman does not exist in *A Christmas Carol,* but upon closer inspection it is evident that the spirit of Christmas also needs keeping. Even the tolerance and the largesse represented by the Ghost of Christmas Present require enforcement, for the petty, bigoted, and hateful aspects of religion seem to hold quotidian sway. The Ghost fills the role of the figure who hails people into place as subjects with the Christmas "spirit." For instance, the one or two times in this scene when there are angry words between "dinner carriers who had jostled each other," the Ghost sheds "a few drops of water on them from [his torch] and their good humor [is] restored directly." Immediately they are recalled to the spirit of Christmas, believing it a "shame to quarrel upon Christmas Day. And so it was God love it, so it was!" (*CC,* stave 3).

The Ghost, then, is a benevolent policeman, perhaps, but a policeman nonetheless, as in fact are all of Scrooge's visitors. Nor is this particular spectral constable completely unschooled in a certain kind of political economy. Scrooge's brand of Malthusianism is sarcastically tossed back at him each time his heart seems to soften in this stave. When he inquires about the fate of Tiny Tim, the Ghost replies, "If he be like to die, he had better do it and decrease the surplus population" (*CC,* stave 3); when Scrooge asks if there is no refuge or resource for Ignorance and Want, the ghost mocks him with his own words, "Are there no prisons?" Especially significant is the *Carol*'s version of the language of political economy, which persists at the very moments when Scrooge experiences sympathy, indicating that neither Scrooge nor Christmas ever completely escapes the grasp of Utilitarianism. For example, Scrooge's concern over the ability of the working poor to cook their dinners on Sunday must certainly be read as an instance of the old reprobate's sympathetic connection to others; yet the residue of his place in the world as a businessman and as one who is informed by a particular version of what it means to conduct business clings tenaciously to his character. Sabbatarianism impeded commerce as well as leisure activities, and to avaricious old Scrooge this is sacrilege. Remember that Scrooge, as Marley's sole legatee, executor, and friend, "was not so dreadfully cut up by the sad event [of Marley's death], but that he was an excellent man of business on the very day of the funeral and solemnised it with an undoubted bargain" (*CC,* stave 1). Scrooge's resentment toward impediments of conducting business, for whatever reason, is even more evident in his well-known Christmas Eve exchange with Bob Cratchit:

## 6: So, This Is Christmas

"You'll want all day tomorrow, I suppose?"

"If quite convenient sir."

"It's not convenient," said Scrooge, "and it's not fair. If I was to stop half a crown for it, you'd think yourself ill used, I'll be bound?"

The clerk smiled faintly.

"And yet," said Scrooge, "you don't think *me* ill used when I pay a day's wages for no work."

The clerk observed that it was only once a year.

"A poor excuse for picking a man's pocket every twenty-fifth of December!" said Scrooge, buttoning his great-coat to the chin. "But I suppose you must have the whole day. Be here all the earlier next morning." (CC, stave 1)

This is the preconversion Scrooge, to be sure, but how complete is his turnaround? And what caused it? To some extent, the Christmas spirits open Scrooge's heart to the plight of others, but more to the point, they open his heart (and his eyes) to *his own* plight. Those events that cut Scrooge to the quick are the ones that specifically affect him. It is sad for Scrooge to think of the possible fate of Tiny Tim; it is hard for him to look upon Ignorance and Want; but it is utterly terrifying for him to witness his own mortality and his lying in an unkempt grave. Scrooge's approach to life is fundamentally no different after the visitations; he simply rethinks the source of his pleasure and his definition of value. To paraphrase awkwardly Mill paraphrasing Bentham, before the visits that source is pushpin; after, it is poetry. Scrooge's own interests are served by his keeping the Spirit of Christmas, and he completely internalizes the lessons of the "Christmas police," saying to the last ghost, "I will live in the Past, the Present, and the Future. The Spirits of all Three shall strive within me. I will not shut out the lessons that they teach." He then turns once again to his own headstone and exclaims, "Oh tell me I may sponge away the writing on this stone" (CC, stave 4), as though their lessons promised material, and not spiritual, immortality.[15]

Without completely abandoning an analysis of the *Carol,* I want to consider this culture of Christmas in its larger implications, including some of those that I mentioned at the beginning of this chapter. Not only do I want to insist that the version of Christmas articulated in the *Carol* is coded as English in its specific concerns: of the poor, of the Manchester school of political economy, of the traditions (real or imagined) of Christmases past. I also want to maintain that even in its early iterations, the Victorian culture of Christmas yokes Englishness to what it is now fashionable to label "liberal guilt." In an essay entitled "The Liberalism of Fear," Judith Shklar argues that the "divorce of religious affirmation from conscience" constitutes the earliest formative phase of liberal political theory. For Shklar, "liberalism's deepest grounding is in place from the first, in the conviction of the earliest defenders of toleration, born in horror, that cruelty is an absolute evil, an offense against God or humanity." I do not want to accept without reservation Shklar's version of the origin of liberalism, but I do want to consider how the essence of liberal theory as she puts it forth—namely, "the elimination of coercion from human life"—finds voice in so much reform writing during the early nineteenth century.[16] Daniel Born points out, however, that as the century progressed, the optimism of the first generation of liberal theorists that poverty, social inequity, and coercive government could be overcome gave way to the realization that capitalist and liberal value systems make uneasy bedfellows.[17] The confidence of the earlier generation was waning by the time we get to Dickens, even early Dickens, and prescription turned to guilt. The great liberal political and social reforms of the 1830s no longer seemed capable, in the 1840s, of eradicating the problems of inequality and suffering they had been designed to address. The facts of the two nations and the hungry masses could not be explained away; it became impossible to justify the almost unspannable chasm between the lower and middle classes in the richest country in the world. In Dickens we find no suggestion of a systematic way for society to face these problems—nor should we necessarily expect to: there is no getting rid of poverty, inequity, and ill-use; there is only individual intervention, the possibility of making things spiritually and materially better for a few. As Chesterton might put it, there is only the prospect of "comfort" and "charity," an "English" version of amelioration.

Such is Scrooge's case. In a tale that quickly transforms the humanistic shortcomings of *laissez-faire* economics into an allegory, the problem of the employer who pays the exact wages fixed by supply and demand and whose primary moral failing is his lack of sympathy for the troubles of the poor is solved by transforming the individual. The result: Cratchit gets better wages and Scrooge a better temper. The masses of poor still go about poorly fed, poorly clothed, and poorly sheltered, however; and if any other Scrooges existed in England, they no doubt slept soundly on Christmas Eve. In fact, the appearance of Mr. Chokepear—a literary forerunner of Scrooge—in the 1841 Christmas number of *Punch* signals a concern that far too many members of the middle classes were self-satisfied and complacent, that the English Christmas had become a celebration of English material success. Unlike Scrooge, Chokepear keeps Christmas well, feasting and drinking in a sumptuous manner, and never undergoes any sort of reformation ("Mr. CHOKEPEAR loves Christmas! Yes, he is an Englishman, and he will tell you that he loves to keep Christmas-day in the true old English fashion").[18] As J. A. R. Pimlott says,

"He went to church, congratulated himself on being English, a Christian, a carriage-holder, and an eater of venison," and he thought his conscience clear. Yet he ignores the shivering poor who pass his way, has his debtor imprisoned, and renounces his daughter for marrying a poor man.[19]

*Punch* goes on to remark: "If the human animal were all stomach—all one large paunch, we should agree with Chokepear that he *had* passed a merry Christmas; but was it the Christmas of a good man or a Christian? That is the Christmas of the belly; keep you the Christmas of the heart. Give—give." Such sentiments—which are echoed in the lament of Marley's Ghost, "Mankind was my business. The common welfare was my business; charity, mercy, forbearance, and benevolence were, all, my business!"—indicate a realization on the part of many of the failure of capitalism to care for those who do not prosper under it yet are enslaved by it (*CC,* stave 1). Marley's punishment for his lack of concern while alive is a hell of "no rest, no peace. Incessant torture of remorse." Marley's guilt and remorse become Scrooge's, but in life rather than in death. In a kind of trickle-down theory of salvation, Marley saves Scrooge from the eternal damnation of liberal guilt by making him temporally (and temporarily) guilty so that he can, in turn, save Tiny Tim's life and the rest of the Cratchits from material want (their souls, after all, are not in danger).

The problem that remains for the tale is that humanity and the common welfare were indeed Marley's (and now are Scrooge's) business; if the dealings of their trade are "but a drop of water in the comprehensive ocean" (*CC,* stave 1) of their business, what sorts of comprehensive *measures* are being taken so that business gets managed? In the *Carol* none, really, and in *The Chimes* only workhouses and prisons. At such points, the basic contradiction at the heart of the Victorian culture of the English Christmas is readily apparent: on the one hand, it insists on a muted Christian socialism that restores human sympathy and relieves spiritual and physical want; on the other, it simultaneously celebrates the individual's ability to effect at least small-scale, localized change. Also at stake is the individual himself, especially the condition of his soul, or even, as Scrooge's narrative corroborates, the individual's interiority—a specific emotional and intellectual relationship to the past and present as well as to the possibilities of the future. Scrooge's largesse is still an investment in his eternal destiny; that he also acquires pleasure from it is an accrued advantage, to be sure, but he is never freed from his guilt, his responsibility.[20] If anything, his position as the self-made, middle-class Englishman of business is inexorably linked to his guilt and makes him even *more* aware of it.[21] None of the spirits, or anyone else, ever suggests that Scrooge sell his business and give all the proceeds to the poor or even that he raise Cratchit's position by making him a partner; the way he can best attend to the needs of the lower classes is to remain a man of business and a successful one at that. He just needs to try a little tenderness. Thus, Christmas attempts to curb the predatory aspects of capitalism, but never does away with it altogether. This, perhaps, is the gift of the English tradition of Christmas to the rest of the world, for we can see the culture of Christmas continuing to function in this way. A well-known example is Frank Capra's *It's a Wonderful Life*. When there is a run on the building-and-loan and one of the depositors demands his money, George Bailey replies that it does not exist as cash but has been poured into another's home, and another's, and another's. The investments that the depositors have made are in each other, and when they recall those investments, they give up on the community and on beneficent capitalism, preferring instead to put their faith in a more nefarious form of individualism and Mr. Potter's more successful (because redder in tooth and claw) way of doing business.

Although Capra's is a striking twentieth-century instance of exposing what I have labeled the primary contradiction of the culture of Christmas that we have inherited from the Victorians, there are also numerous examples from the period itself. Not even the Poor Law Board could escape the effects of Christmas. In direct repudiation of the principle of least desirability that informed the New Poor Laws (and which comments yet again on Scrooge's problems with Sabbatarianism), the Board in 1842 ordered that no labor except housework should be done on Christmas Day and Good Friday. And in 1847 it gave the local Guardians discretion to provide extra food on Christmas Day at the expense of the poor rate. By 1864 the Guardians at Chepstow began to provide the paupers with a little extra, including a "modicum of tea and sugar wherein with to regale themselves during the afternoon, for the females."[22] In such moments, Christmas is calling to account the very institutions devised to help alleviate the problem of the Victorian poor, and, finding those institutions severely lacking, it steps in with a kind of communitarianism that seems to de-emphasize the rather austere notion of individualism underwriting those institutions. Yet the restorative and salvational aspect of the culture of Christmas as it functions in the Christmas books operates on a principle of least desirability of its own, insisting as it does upon the freedom of the individual to shape his or her own fate.

The result of this mélange of values is to muddle the entire concept of Christmas. The residual feudalism and patronage (whether accurately or romantically remembered) and the dominance of capitalism and the individual combine to produce a culture that depends on ethical equality, humanitarianism, and selflessness at the same time that it is starting to market itself most aggressively. Consequently, the subject caught up in the Christmas spirit is pulled in a number of directions at once. Ethical equality, for example, is read as equality of consumption. In the *Carol* the flavor of the water sprinkled from the Ghost's torch applies to the poor's dinner most of all because "it needs it most" (*CC,* stave 3). Later, after his conversion, Scrooge buys a huge turkey for the Cratchits in order to replace their comparatively meager, and much more economical, goose. In *The Chimes,* the ethical valence of consumption gets inverted in certain ways, such as when Trotty feels ashamed about his tripe because it is made "clear" to him that someone else has had to go without for him to have his treat. Repeatedly, we see the "spirit of Christmas" enforced through the application of guilt to those accused, rightly or wrongly, of failing to keep to inclusive and egalitarian consumption at Christmas.

For the middle classes this guilt is mitigated by patronage, what a number of critics of the political economy of the culture of Christmas refer to as a nostalgic return to the Middle Ages. As I suggested earlier, this particular practice in fact undermines the sought-after "egalitarianism" of Christmas by serving as a constant reminder of class difference and the political and economic power of one over the other. Scrooge is entirely aware of this when he upbraids Cratchit for being late in order to reveal his "new self" to his clerk. Such positioning allows the middle classes to define the structure of the culture of Christmas by asserting their own moral and ethical values as those best held by all: thus the inclusivity of Christmas becomes exclusive as well, and its universalism quite particular. It also commodifies the poor, for it makes them central to the culture of Christmas. Indeed, for the middle classes, Christmas becomes a time to clear the ledgers and settle the accounts. It is almost as if the English Christmas cannot exist in all its glory unless there are poor to be saved, either materially like the Cratchits or spiritually like Trotty Veck.

In terms of consumption, then, the poor become the proof of the Christmas pudding. And in a sense, they are devoured in the service of middle-class conceptions of munificence. Of course, it is not *de facto* self-serving to help out those who have less than oneself, but the representation of this practice—or even just the representation of poverty and destitution—became one of the stocks-in-trade of English Christmas pieces. Thomas Hood's "Song of the Shirt" in the 16 December 1843 number of *Punch* is a case in point, as are the Cratchits, Trotty, and legions of less memorable characters. Not only does it become important to do for those with less at Christmas time, but it also becomes important to write about the poor as well. In a rather perverse way, the poor become essential to the selling of Christmas.

All of the major periodicals of the era include some sort of report, factual or fictional, of the doings for the poor on Christmas Day. So much the better if those poor are children, since one of the effects of the culture of Christmas is the placing of the figure of the child at the center of many Christmas activities. It is better still if those children are physically afflicted in some way. A typical example is the 1850 Christmas number of *Household Words,* which offers an article by Dickens entitled "Christmas Among the London Poor and Sick." The piece begins by informing the readers that eighty to a hundred thousand of the two and a quarter million people living in London have their Christmas dinners provided to them by their respective parishes. It then goes on to report the numbers of paupers in each of the major parishes, capping its list with a paragraph that must have seemed the obvious choice for ending the section on the poor: "The largest party of children has always assembled at the Norwood Schools, where about a thousand of the progeny of London pauperism open their young hearts on the great festival of the English year."[23] The number ends with a collection called "Household Christmas Carols." The titles include "The Lame Child's Carol," "The Deaf Child's Carol," "The Deformed Child's Carol," "The Deaf and Dumb Child's Carol," and "The Blind Child's Carol," and, since it is Christmas after all, the final poem is "The Healthy Child's Carol." Each of the "carols" has the same chorus: a celebration of the coming of Christmas and its accompanying "bright thoughts and hopes," which are now awake and penetrate "each grief and make a golden radiance of our tears"[24]: a not-so-distant echo of "God Bless us, every one."

Notably, it is the "great festival of the English year" that is enhanced by the golden-voiced thousand, the "progeny of London pauperism." Time itself has a national identity in this passage, and the irony of its connection to the biological *reproduction* of poverty in the great capital is evidently completely lost on the reporter of this happy scene. Christmas allows Englishness to claim seemingly everything, making it difficult to disarticulate the associations between the two. It is equally difficult to resist the insistence of those associations. In a letter of 28 December 1843, Jane Welsh Carlyle describes the effects of this Christmas spirit on her husband after he read the copy of *A Christmas Carol* sent to him by Dickens: "A huge boxful of dead animals from the Welshman arriving late on Saturday night together with the visions of *Scrooge*—had so worked on Carlyle's nervous organization that he has been seized with a perfect convulsion of hospitality and has actually insisted on improvising two dinner parties with only a day in between."[25]

It was not merely Christmas to which Carlyle had succumbed, but apparently Englishness as well, as Thackeray's allusion makes clear in his February

## 6: So, This Is Christmas

1844 review of the *Carol* in *Fraser's Magazine:* "A Scotch philosopher who nationally does not keep Christmas-day, on reading the book sent out for a turkey, and asked two friends to dine—this is a fact! Had the book appeared a fortnight earlier, all the prize cattle would have been gobbled up in pure love and friendship, Epping denuded of sausages, and not a turkey left in Norfolk."[26] Not only does Christmas transform the dyspeptic, acerbic Carlyle into a pleasant gourmand, but it also makes him English—at least for the day. Fifty years later in *The Children of the Ghetto,* Israel Zangwill's Maida Vale middle-class Jews will keep Christmas Dinner, complete with their anglicized names, and dismiss its connection to Christianity while embracing its Englishness.

The power of Christmas has become so formidable in our own time that it is nearly impossible to imagine it without "all the trimmings" of its Victorian heritage and the unique, sometimes grandiose, articulations of liberal guilt that surround our observance of the holiday. Whatever one's religion, in the anglicized world, Christmas has transformed into an annual assertion of a set of ideological assumptions that, at least for the season, abide without serious threat or opposition. Just as for Scrooge's nephew, it is held up as a fleeting moment of universal goodwill and tolerance, of searching out and eradicating cruelty—whether in the form of feeding hungry third-world children, commuting prisoners' sentences, or simply thinking, for a brief time, of the needs and desires of others. As Fred implies, this can a very good thing indeed. Yet the idea of "virtue as its own reward," if, in fact, it ever really existed within the culture of Christmas, has been fairly successfully siphoned out of the practices that inform contemporary versions of the holiday, replaced by impulses toward self-fulfillment and consumerism: those traits of Christmas that Dickens tries to belie, but without which it is impossible for him to discuss Christmas at all. In those instances when we identify acts of generosity and thoughtfulness that are not self-directed, we tend to undercut their substance by highlighting them in the media and proclaiming them the "true spirit" of Christmas. We typically fail to see in them one of their most significant functions: as nostalgic nods toward an imaginary time within modern memory, when Christmas was divorced from the social forces that created Mr. Chokepear and Mr. Scrooge and that continue to exert considerable pressure on our own understandings of Christmas, as the *Daily Express*'s urgent proclamations demonstrate. We have indeed inherited Dickens's version of Christmas, and all its contradictory ideological baggage with it. To try to reform it may well lead us back to the dilemmas that we see bedeviling *A Christmas Carol.* To try to understand it within its context of Christian, liberal, and nationalist ideologies may produce entirely different results.

## NOTES

1. The *Daily Express*, 3 November 2005, 1. My thanks to Nick Stevenson of the University of Nottingham for telling me of this story and sending me a copy of the paper. Subsequent references are made parenthetically in the text.

2. Much recent work has been devoted to the problem of distinguishing between English and British identity, and I do not want to fail to recognize the complexity involved in disentangling the two by using Englishness and Britishness interchangeably. However, I also want to be conscious of how the *Daily Express* article is clearly invoking an English conception of Britishness. As Krishnan Kumar has argued, the co-opting of Britishness for the purpose of fleshing out a conception of English national identity has been happening for centuries. See Krishnan Kumar, *The Making of an English National Identity*.

3. George Bernard Shaw, *Collected Works*, 25:293.

4. G. K. Chesterton, *Charles Dickens: A Critical Study*, 165.

5. Theodore Watts-Dunton, "Dickens and 'Father Christmas,'" 1016.

6. J. M. Golby and A. W. Purdue, *The Making of the Modern Christmas*, 43.

7. In *The Englishman's Christmas*, J. A. R. Pimlott argues that a substantial break with an earlier culture of Christmas takes place around 1840, and he cites the differences between the Christmas at Dingley Dell and that of *A Christmas Carol*. In the *Pickwick Papers*, on Christmas Eve the revelers congregate "by the huge fire of blazing logs to a substantial supper, and a mighty bowl of wassail." Mr. Wardle explains that this is the "invariable custom"; everyone "sits down with us on Christmas eve, as you see them now—servants and all; and here we wait, until the clock strikes twelve, to usher Christmas in and beguile the time with forfeits and old stories" (*PP*, ch.28). The following day, the party goes its separate ways without further ado. In contrast, in the *Carol*, Christmas is celebrated on Christmas itself; supper is replaced by dinner; wassail by turkey, servants and noblesse oblige by children and charity, and the nostalgic rural setting with the modern city. See also Adam Kuper, "The English Christmas and the Family," in *Unwrapping Christmas*, 160.

8. Golby and Purdue, 44.

9. Quoted in Philip Collins, ed., *Dickens: The Critical Heritage*, 181.

10. "*The Battle of Life* and 'Mrs. Perkins's Ball,'" 55.

11. Mark Connelly has argued that Golby and Purdue, following J. A. R. Pimlott, somewhat overstate their case; that Christmas traditions were quite important throughout the eighteenth and early portions of the nineteenth century; and that, indeed, the Victorian period was in many ways concerned about the "disappearance" of Christmas. As regards the popularity of *A Christmas Carol* he notes: "But surely one of the reasons for the success of Dickens was that people understood and related to the tale. A society with no reference to what he was talking about could not have reacted with such enthusiasm" (*Christmas: A Social History*, 3).

12. Margaret Lane collects twenty-one Christmas stories written by Dickens (some in collaboration with Wilkie Collins) for *Household Words* and *All the Year Round* between 1850 and 1870 in *Christmas Stories*.

13. See Raymond Williams, *Marxism and Literature*.

14. Humphry House, *The Dickens World*, 53–54.

15. Cf. House's comment on Scrooge's conversion: "Scrooge does not see the Eternal

behind the Temporal, a new heaven and a new earth: he merely sees the old earth from a slightly different angle" (*The Dickens World*, 53).

16. Judith Shklar, "The Liberalism of Fear," 23.

17. See Daniel Born, *The Birth of Liberal Guilt in the English Novel*, 1–17. Born identifies the emergence of liberal guilt in the fiction of the period in *Little Dorrit* and argues that it wanes during the Edwardian period. His argument rests upon the move from novelists' emphases on individual responsibility (as in *A Christmas Carol*), which he links to a culture of Christianity, to social responsibility (apparently first observable for Born in *Little Dorrit*), which he characterizes as more secular in its motivations. In contrast, I contend that "liberal guilt" is already at work as a significant social force, owing, in part, to the overdetermined effects of political economy on the shape of increasingly compelling and numerous articulations of moral responsibility by the middle classes, at least as early as the 1840s.

18. "How Mr. Chokepear Keeps a Merry Christmas," *Punch*, Vol. 1 (25 December 1841), 277.

19. J. A. R. Pimlott, *The Englishman's Christmas: A Social History*, 87.

20. It is never entirely clear that the pleasure Scrooge receives from "keeping Christmas" throughout the year is his enjoyment of the camaraderie and humanity of the holiday or the anticipation of laying up his own "treasures in heaven."

21. Audrey Jaffe makes a similar observation regarding the readers of *A Christmas Carol*: "The story's ideological project—its attempt to link sympathy and business by incorporating a charitable impulse into its (male) readers' self-conceptions—underlies its association of charitable feeling with participation in cultural life" ("Spectacular Sympathy," 329).

22. See Pimlott, 90.

23. Dickens, "Christmas Among the London Poor and Sick," 304.

24. See *HW*, 21 December 1850.

25. Jane Welsh Carlyle, *Collected Letters*, 17: 219.

26. [William Makepeace Thackeray], "A Box of Novels," 169.

# 7

# Green Dickens

KAREN CHASE AND MICHAEL LEVENSON

Dickens lived and wrote not only through a time of massive urban transformation, but also during the first epoch of a concerted environmentalism. Was he green? At some times more than others. But his work always unfolded in relation to the material world that impinged on it. The activity of world-construction comes early into his self-understanding as a novelist: the fictional universe as an ecology that exceeds individual agents and incidents, possessing laws and dispositions of its own. With only a slight troping, we may speak of the "climate" of the Dickens world, marked as it is by large governing tones and modes that move through the work like tellurian plates or ocean currents. Then without any troping at all, we need to register the engagement with an environmental emergency that becomes inescapable in the middle years of his career.

The allure of a green refuge shows itself in Dickens's earliest novels, where the achievement of pastoral is cast with an innocent glow. Pickwick's retirement home in a "pleasant neighbourhood" in Dulwich offers an escape from the agitation of London. When Oliver Twist encounters life outside the city, the effect of rural living assumes a radiant glow and stimulates a passage of strenuous idyll.

> Men who have lived in crowded, pent-up streets, through lives of toil, and who have never wished for change; men, to whom custom has indeed been second nature, and who have come almost to love each brick and stone that formed the narrow boundaries of their daily walks; even they, with

the hand of death upon them, have been known to yearn at last for one short glimpse of Nature's face; and, carried far from the scenes of their old pains and pleasures, have seemed to pass at once into a new state of being. Crawling forth, from day to day, to some green sunny spot, they have had such memories wakened up within them by the sight of the sky, and hill and plain, and glistening water, that a foretaste of heaven itself has soothed their quick decline, and they have sunk into their tombs, as peacefully as the sun whose setting they watched from their lonely chamber window but a few hours before, faded from their dim and feeble sight! The memories which peaceful country scenes call up, are not of this world, nor of its thoughts and hopes. Their gentle influence may teach us how to weave fresh garlands for the graves of those we loved: may purify our thoughts, and bear down before it old enmity and hatred; but beneath all this, there lingers, in the least reflective mind, a vague and half-formed consciousness of having held such feelings long before, in some remote and distant time, which calls up solemn thoughts of distant times to come, and bends down pride and worldliness beneath it. (*OT*, ch.32)

London will always be the privileged arena for Dickens, a scene of modernity and the vessel of narrative. But the memory of pastoral is a constitutive principle of the fiction. Occasionally it appears in lyric effusions such as this; more often it exerts tacit pressure on the narrative and erupts in surprising places. Improbably, London itself becomes the chief site of his green reflections, and in what follows we look to disclose modernity and greenery within their productive friction.

## THE IMPROVING METROPOLIS AND ITS DISCONTENTS

The short piece "Scotland Yard," one of the early scenes in *Sketches by Boz*, evokes a metropolitan neighborhood on the point of its disappearance. For generations it had survived as a closed, nearly unknown community whose original inhabitants were "a tailor, a publican, two eating-house keepers, and a fruit-pie maker." These were joined by "a race of strong and bulky men" who heaved and carted coal, thereby bringing money into the micro-economy of Scotland Yard. The settlers and the traders achieved a simple collective equilibrium anchored at a public house, where they gathered to recall "old legends of what the Thames was in ancient times," only "to meet again in the same room, and to say and do precisely the same things on the following evening at the same hour." This is economy as ecology, a self-contained system of human exchange (narrative as well as material) that exists in organic relation to the natural world. The river brings ships; the ships deliver coal, which the traders carry into the country; and when coal has been exchanged for cash, they return to convert it into food and drink and clothes. The smooth, ancient circuit finally breaks when the modernizing world intrudes to disrupt the flow between nature and culture. The new London Bridge appears, and then a new Hungerford market and a police headquarters. Outsiders begin to pass through the secluded streets, until Scotland Yard is thrown open to novelty. In the midst of this "change, and restlessness, and innovation," the shopkeepers now compete with one another. The fruit-pie maker calls himself a pastry-cook, and the eating-house keeper solicits customers "among a new class of people"; a boot-maker arrives, and then a dress-maker: "The old heavers still assembled round the ancient fireplace, but their talk was mournful: and the loud song and the joyous shout were heard no more." Here at the beginning of his career, Dickens secures a firm link between modernization and social trauma.

The word "improvement"—as in, "Improvement began to march with rapid strides to the very threshold of Scotland Yard"—is Dickens's name for modernization, and it is, of course, not his alone. It stood generally to describe renovations of the built and the natural environment; within the context of London it came to refer to the ambitious urban transformations conducted by John Nash under the patronage of the Prince Regent. In *Metropolitan Improvements* (1828), James Elmes had prepared engravings to celebrate the changes, including the cutting of Regent's Street, the laying out of Trafalgar Square, the renovation of Buckingham Palace and the Mall, and the creation of Regent's Park and the villas that encircle it. Nash's projects often involved the destruction of closed urban spaces (like Scotland Yard) in favor of broad avenues and open squares. Dickens, who knew these precincts well, faced a difficult uncertainty in establishing a perspective on the change.

"We marked the advance of civilisation, and beheld it with a sigh" (*SB*, "Scotland Yard"): the remark captures the unstable tonality in Dickens's early thinking about the course of "improvement" and the loss of ecological equilibrium. It is clear enough that he regrets the disappearance of the past and that he casts a nostalgic eye on the waning of "old customs" and "ancient simplicity." But the mere wistfulness of the "sigh" and the staginess of the emotion suggest the unsettled attitudes. This is no doubt the case because through the 1830s and 1840s, Dickens, like others, saw modernization as inevitable. And yet he found it difficult to articulate the principle, favoring instead a skein of ironies, as in this meditation on "Hackney-coach Stands":

## 7: Green Dickens

> We have recently observed on certain stands, and we say it with deep regret, rather dapper green chariots, and coaches of polished yellow, with four wheels of the same colour as the coach, whereas it is perfectly notorious to every one who has studied the subject, that every wheel ought to be of a different colour, and a different size. These are innovations, and, like other miscalled improvements, awful signs of the restlessness of the public mind, and the little respect paid to our time-honoured institutions. Why should hackney-coaches be clean? Our ancestors found them dirty, and left them so. Why should we, with a feverish wish to "keep moving," desire to roll along at the rate of six miles an hour, while they were content to rumble over the stones at four? These are solemn considerations. (SB, "Hackney Coach Stands")

The stakes become higher in the treatment of the railway in *Dombey and Son* in the later 1840s. The iron monster brings chaos to Staggs's Garden in Camden Town. Houses are "knocked down; streets broken through and stopped; deep pits and trenches dug in the ground; enormous heaps of earth and clay thrown up" (*DS*, ch.6). The passage is a climactic account of the incoherence of modernization. Space has lost its intelligibility: "Everywhere were bridges that led nowhere; thoroughfares that were wholly impassable." Where there once stood a knowable community, however poor, now there is physical upheaval and also social convulsion: the coming of the railways has "wholly changed the law and custom of the neighbourhood." This tableau of disorder in *Dombey and Son* is a *locus classicus* of the emergency of modernity. But it is also the place where Dickens perfects the irony corresponding to his own unstable perspective. The railway derangement is rendered as overwhelming and violent, but it is also misinterpreted by those who endure its first effects. The citizens of Staggs's Gardens take up an "uncommonly incredulous" perspective; they see their wretched homes as making a "sacred grove not to be withered by railroads" (*DS*, ch.6). Transfixed by the originating violence of modernity, they miss its redemptive telos.

The pattern of irony, here and in many other places, depends on first registering the shock of modernity and then assuming (in order to surpass) the standpoint of the benighted local traditionalists. The railway in chapter six of *Dombey and Son* is brutally destructive, but it is so because it is "unfinished and unopened." By the time we reach chapter fifteen, all has changed. The deprivation of Staggs's Gardens has given way to a carnival of prosperity: "The old by-streets now swarmed with passengers and vehicles of every kind: the new streets that had stopped disheartened in the mud and wagon-ruts, formed towns within themselves, originating wholesome comforts and conveniences belonging to themselves, and never tried nor thought of until they sprung into existence. Bridges that had led to nothing, led to villas, gardens, churches, healthy public walks." The once skeptical inhabitants now boast of their connection to their new employer, the railway (*DS,* ch.15). The critique of modernization had been vivid, but in light of Dickens's radical ambivalence, the critique is identified with the ignorant traditionalists and loses force as time and progress unfold. Once irony has exposed the limits of resistance, the railway has launched "upon its mighty course of civilisation and improvement" (*DS,* ch.15), and *Dombey and Son* warns us not to stand in its way.

## "COWS ARE MY PASSION": COUNTERFEIT PASTORAL

Dickens, like those in Staggs's Garden, lived within the immediacies of space and time. His mobile tones partly reflect his uncertainty, but they also register uncertain changes in his environment. By the end of the 1840s, the return of cholera and the growing sanitation crisis changed the terms of debate. Where Nash's stucco and the spreading railways could be seen as anodyne signs of a flourishing environment, disease was an affront to the language of improvement. A narrative of inevitable progress now met a story of disorder and fatality. Moreover "improvement" could now be reinterpreted as itself a source of the danger, and this was so because it had stimulated the astonishing increase in population. The pleasure in wider streets, gleaming villas, and faster trains—"Crowds of people and mountains of goods, departing and arriving scores upon scores of times in every four-and-twenty hours, produced a fermentation in the place that was always in action" (*DS,* ch.15)—now met the inescapable reality of mass deprivation and spectacular overcrowding in the courts, warrens, and rookeries.

Dickens had paid early and vigilant attention to the degradation of the rookeries, which were mirror images to Scotland Yard with its self-enclosed community sustained by ancient practices of exchange and reciprocity. *Oliver Twist* evoked the narrow self-containment of dispossession and criminality: "Confined as the limits of Field Lane are, it has its barber, its coffee-shop, its beer-shop, and its fried-fish warehouse. It is a commercial colony of itself: the emporium of petty larceny: visited at early morning, and setting-in of dusk, by silent merchants, who traffic in dark back-parlours, and who go as strangely as they come. Here, the clothesman, the shoe-vamper, and the rag-merchant, display their goods, as sign-boards to the petty thief; here, stores of old iron and bones, and heaps of mildewy fragments of woolen-stuff and linen, rust and rot in the grimy cellars" (*OT,* ch.26). Still, as long as the blighted zones were seen as bounded and discontinuous, they did not interrupt the narrative of improvement. As Pickwick begins a journey to Ipswich, he rides with Sam through Whitechapel, described here as a "pretty densely populated quarter."

> "Not a wery nice neighbourhood, this, Sir," said Sam, with a touch of the hat, which always preceded his entering into conversation with his master.
> "It is not indeed, Sam," replied Mr. Pickwick, surveying the crowded and filthy street through which they were passing. (*PP*, ch.22)

As Pickwick and Sam pass through Whitechapel, they exercise the traveling gaze that is the early privilege of Dickens and his characters. Even as the records of distress sharpen—in portraits of the Marshalsea, Jacob's Island, Saffron Hill, Covent Garden—the novels see these as pockets of dispossession that might simply disappear in an improving age. Within this context Staggs's Gardens is a culminating epitome: the miserable tract of land that is re-created and integrated into "the railway world beyond" (*DS*, ch.15). *Dombey and Son* offers a consolidation of Dickens's initial standpoint on the environmental plight. He allows himself the warm tones of nostalgia—"Staggs's Gardens had been cut up root and branch. Oh woe the day when 'not a rood of English ground'—laid out in Staggs's Gardens—is secure!" (*DS,* ch.15)—but he inflicts brisk satire on those who cling to an unreconstructed past. No good can come of antimodern, antitechnological Luddism. The best hope seems to be for those who have been steeped in ancient custom to accommodate an inevitable modernity, which is indeed the work of the broader plot, a marriage between the eccentricity of tradition (Sol Gills's instrument shop, the mariner's life, Toots) and the new times of a railway universe.

What makes *Dombey and Son* notable, then, is its repudiation of the sacred nature celebrated just a few years before in *Oliver Twist*. In place of a "sky, and hill and plain" that give "a foretaste of heaven," we find the sham nature of Mrs. Skewton, Edith Dombey's mother. A synthetic creation herself, nothing more than a mix of cosmetics and wasting bone, Mrs. Skewton is unsparingly satirized for her affectation of green thoughts about green spaces: "'I assure you, Mr Dombey, Nature intended me for an Arcadian. I am thrown away in society. Cows are my passion. What I have ever sighed for, has been to retreat to a Swiss farm, and live entirely surrounded by cows—and china'" (*DS,* ch.21). Caught within this counterfeit discourse, the natural world loses critical force. "Nature" is left as a debased token of fashion, a privileged currency in polite conversation, but lacking any purchase as alternative to the failures of modernization. Later novels pursue the same terms of satire: Harold Skimpole in *Bleak House* is another who poses and parades in synthetic pastoral as one who "loves to see the sun shine, loves to hear the wind blow, loves to watch the changing lights and shadows, loves to hear the birds, those choristers in Nature's great cathedral" but who never breaks from the aesthetic frame that converts nature into style (*BH,* ch.26). Skimpole is "very fond of nature, very fond of art," which is exactly the problem (*BH,* ch.6). The Nature cult now appears as a sterile aestheticism, a tease and a social ploy. Mrs. Merdle in *Little Dorrit* brings the absurdity to its highest pitch. "'If we were in a more primitive state,'" she daintily says, "'if we lived under roofs of leaves, and kept cows and sheep and creatures instead of banker's accounts (which would be delicious; my dear, I am pastoral to a degree, by nature), well and good. But we don't live under leaves, and keep cows and sheep and creatures'" (*LD,* I, ch.33). Her proviso gives away the truth, without giving away the game.

By the end of the 1840s, Dickens has lost confidence in the power of the green refuge. The Wordsworthian aura that had sustained a counter-world has all but dissolved. In its place is this sustained critique of nature: discourse as nothing more than a tactic of social advantage. It is notable that in the three examples mentioned above—Mrs. Skewton, Harold Skimpole, and Mrs. Merdle—each figure veils self-interest within the language of pastoral. Although Dickens would not have put it this way, they are all cunning ideologists who look to gain competitive edge by disguising interested motives beneath a sickly-sweet nature-worship.

The difficulty, of course, is that when nature can no longer provide an outside to modernization, then the fiction must strain to imagine an alternative to debased modernity. The heightened recognition at mid-century was precisely that the outside was disappearing, that the place elsewhere—the green world, the silver river—was being absorbed by the thrusting city. In a phrase made famous by George Cruikshank, the prospect of "London Going Out of Town" crystallized the spatial emergency: the limitless metropolis that would eventually cover the island. In 1851, *Fraser's* breathlessly described the loss of boundaries that is at the same time a loss of meaning in the word "London."

> New streets, squares, crescents, terraces, and suburban villas, hardly to be distinguished, except by a gush of trees and flowers here and there, from the more compact and populous streets upon whose extremities they are grafted, grow up in thick clusters upon the frontiers with a rapidity so astounding that it is impossible at any particular moment of time to fix the actual limits of that brick-and-mortar chaos which comes under the general designations of Lon-

## 7: Green Dickens

don. Even while we are making the calculation [of the census], fields, gardens, and sleepy hamlets, are in process of obliteration by masonry and scaffolding on all sides. No man can define where the town ends, and the country begins.[1]

In an early essay for *Household Words,* "The Heart of Mid-London," Dickens and W. H. Wills brood over the scandal of Smithfield Meat Market. There in the center of the city are the noise, the stench, and above all the cruelty of animal slaughter. But when the essayists ask where the market might be moved, they uncover the confusions of space. To the proposal for moving Smithfield to the suburbs, their dejected response is, "But look at the rapidity with which London spreads. How long will you guarantee that any site you may select will remain 'out of Town?'"

In 1808, it was proposed to remove the market to the "open fields"—Clerkenwell-fields; but, twenty years afterwards, there was not a blade of grass to be seen near the place. It was covered with bricks and mortar. . . . Again, only last year, a field between Camden-town and Holloway was proposed; but since then, houses have been built up to the very hedge that incloses it.[2]

The growth of the city is seen as the invasion of a youthful metropolis into the dignified age of the countryside—the elusive shifting edge of urbanism, the sliding border. And yet, our emphasis here will fall on another spatial event: namely, the transformation of the metropolitan interior, the saturation of space within city, the disappearance of open expanses, lines of sight, and freely circulating air.

One effect of the cholera epidemics was that they undermined the reassuring spatial discontinuity of London. Dickens's fascination with (and revulsion from) the self-enclosed zones within the city will never disappear. These spaces continue to represent both the most infernal depths of the metropolis and also its refuges. But from the beginning of the 1850s, the discontinuous zones were overlain by larger networks, subterranean connections, and social webs. The movement from "Our Parish," which opens *Sketches by Boz,* to the "London" that inaugurates *Bleak House* marks a shift from localism to totality. The metropolis is not the whole world, not even within *Bleak House.* But within Dickensian geography, London is the name for encompassing modernity. Its provocation is to surpass zonal boundaries; it does so not only through the tentacular administration of Chancery law but also through the spread of contagion and the pervading effects of climate. Tom-all-Alone's may be a "black, dilapidated street," "avoided by all decent people," but it is also "in Chancery" and is the source of disease that respects no boundaries (*BH,* ch.16). The mud and damp oozing through the virtuosity of the first paragraph of that novel establish the climate of the metropolitan ecology.

## TOWARD A GREEN LONDON: COMMONS PRESERVATION AND THE OPEN SPACES MOVEMENT

Even the very technology that had first promised escape, the railways, was a central cause of the in-filling of London, the obliteration of boundaries. Notoriously, the railway companies bought huge tracts of land for their terminals, their sheds, and their lines that crisscrossed the inner metropolis and saturated the urban field. The train map spread as quickly as cholera. In 1857 the home secretary was asked whether he was "aware that the Midland Railway Company . . . are about to make an open cutting through the old churchyard of St. Pancras . . . , thereby disturbing the tombs and bodies."[3] Not to worry, responds the secretary, the Midland Railway will construct a tunnel, all of twelve feet beneath the surface. The more comfortable classes moved into new homes and flats constructed in Belgravia and Tyburnia; workers and artisans often carved up flats into one-roomed family dwellings, while the poor heaped up within already crowded courts. These events made the saturation of London space a journalistic concern, a parliamentary irritation, an imaginative crux, and an urban sensation.

As the visual imagery of the rookeries circulated in the popular imagination of the 1850s—dark, inward and tangled, branching enclosures where too many Irish bodies were squeezed into too many narrow corners—the tableau of the open field of recreation became a powerful lure. One MP spoke of the need for untamed common spaces "in all their wild and uncultivated condition," noting that "it would be a pleasant sight to see the boisterous enjoyment of the working people in places where there did not exist those restrictions which were natural and proper enough in well laid-out gardens."[4] Through many mid-century texts one finds a similar vision of caged urban creatures set free to exercise their limbs in "boisterous" expression. Metaphors of visibility (as opposed to the invisibility of the rookeries), of distance between bodies, of the harmless discharge of energies: all reflect the urgency of the concern. Part of what is striking is the abruptness of the response: the sudden resistance to urban saturation that appeared in many different discursive contexts. It is clear that the mere experience of moving through London in the 1850s created a shared metropolitan perception: that the green world was rapidly being obliterated and that fields traversed last month were covered over today. The events of the 1850s and 1860s constitute a kind of case study in the emergence of collective attitudes and public opinion.

Even as anxiety sharpened, however, the sense of helplessness increased; again within the terms of parliamentary debate: "while the necessity for open spaces was increasing, the difficulties of obtaining control over them was [sic] increasing also."[5] By what right could the great landowners, the lords of the manor, be prevented from turning their fields into another Belgravia? What legal basis could be found to prevent the paving over of gardens and the construction of new streets and squares, crescents and terraces? The Inclosure Act of 1845 had regularized the procedures for enclosing land, but it had done little to stop that "obliteration by masonry and scaffolding" described by *Fraser's*. According to the views of the Inclosure Commissioner himself, "the lord's ownership [over his land] is absolute," and the public have no defined rights in the matter.[6] A great mid-century struggle was precisely to define a public right to space and to do so on the basis of ancient usage, long-abiding custom, time immemorial. Because the public had worked and walked in Hampstead Heath for many centuries, it had a claim on its disposition. So at least it was argued during the acrimonious debates about the Heath and whether Thomas Maryon Wilson should be allowed to develop his property there, debates that would become a pointed focus in the emergent open-space campaign. The founding of the Commons Preservation Society marked a landmark date in the history of environmentalism, not least because one of its leaders, George Shaw Lefevre, became an insurgent theorist of the public ownership of land. In parliamentary debates and committees, as in his journalism, Shaw Lefevre developed a property radicalism emerging from the crisis in London. He held that the rights of ownership over the great Commons—rights enshrined in the Statute of Merton passed under Henry III—were merely feudal impositions upon the people and that more ancient rights still reside in the citizenry. We have recently learned, he wrote, that "the Commons now existing are to a very large extent a remnant or survival of [the] collective ownership of land."[7] Not the great landowners like Hampstead's Maryon Wilson but the modern metropolitan mass, relaxing in the Commons on Sunday, were the proper legal heirs to the green spaces of London.

In its most radical implication, this legal argument justified the expropriation of the expropriators and the return of private property to the people. That claim would eventually coincide with a socialist program emerging in subsequent decades, but in the early years of the Open Spaces movement, when the goal was to persuade parliament and to build public consensus, the argument took a more cautious, though still potent, form. The emphasis fell upon the time-honored right of villagers to preserve their village green. Here the law was unambiguous. As long as villagers enjoyed their green, no one had the right to appropriate it. The task of the Open Spaces movement was then to apply the law of the village green to the struggle in London. Early in the debates, Shaw Lefevre posed the challenging question: "Do you think," he asks, "that such a place as Hampstead Heath might be considered a village green to a large town like London?"[8] Here is how he put it in a letter to the *Times*: "The law . . . most fully recognises the right of the village to its green, and allows the establishment of such right by evidence as to playing games, &c., but it has failed as yet to recognise the analogy between the great town and its Common, and the village and its green, however complete in fact that analogy may be."[9] The success of the Commons Preservation Society in making this case—in persuading public and parliament that London must be seen as a large village and that its great Commons could be seen as village greens, where citizens might exercise their right to fields and free air—was a decisive event that changed the course of modern environmentalism. Moreover, the successful struggles, especially over Epping Forest and Hampstead Heath, created a new spatial recognition for London. For Dickens, not many years earlier, an afternoon in Hampstead was thought of as a day in the country, an excursion out of London; and certainly this was also true for Wimbledon Common and Epping Forest. But the subtle claim of the Open Spaces movement was that even as London extended to incorporate these large expanses—even as it became so much larger than a village—the metropolis should come to know itself as a social whole and as a spatial integrity. The notion that Epping Forest belonged to all the citizens who enjoyed it, that Hampstead Heath was a ground for all Londoners—this was the telling idea developed in public meetings, in letters to the *Times,* in parliamentary debate, and in a series of conspicuous lawsuits.

## DICKENSIAN LONDON, THE CITY OF PLEATS AND FOLDS

Dickens recognizes London as an apparatus producing modernity. But he also sees it as a complicated machine. It flattens the past; it produces homogeneity; it ravages tradition. But crucially, it fails to complete its project. London remains in his fiction as it remained in fact: the pleated city, the city of folds, the creased metropolis. Even as it endures the simplifications of modernity, it carelessly allows spaces for the obsolete, the endangered, and the elderly. We arrive at a passage from *Little Dorrit* that should be encountered in its full extravagance.

## 7: Green Dickens

> Mrs. Plornish's shop-parlor had been decorated under her own eye, and presented, on the side towards the shop, a little fiction in which Mrs. Plornish unspeakably rejoiced. This poetical heightening of the parlor consisted in the wall being painted to represent the exterior of a thatched cottage; the artist having introduced (in as effective a manner as he found compatible with their highly disproportionate dimensions) the real door and window. The modest sun-flower and holly-hock were depicted as flourishing with great luxuriance on this rustic dwelling, while a quantity of dense smoke issuing from the chimney indicated good cheer within, and also, perhaps that it had not been lately swept. A faithful dog was represented as flying at the legs of the friendly visitor, from the threshold; and a circular pigeon-house, enveloped in a cloud of pigeons, arose from behind the garden-paling. On the door (when it was shut), appeared the semblance of a brass plate, presenting the inscription, Happy Cottage, T. and M. Plornish; the partnership expressing man and wife. No Poetry and no Art ever charmed the imagination more than the union of the two in this counterfeit cottage charmed Mrs. Plornish. It was nothing to her that Plornish had a habit of leaning against it as he smoked his pipe after work, when his hat blotted out the pigeon-house and all the pigeons, when his back swallowed up the dwelling, when his hands in his pockets uprooted the blooming garden and laid waste the adjacent country. To Mrs. Plornish, it was still a most beautiful cottage, a most wonderful deception; and it made no difference that Mr. Plornish's eye was some inches above the level of the gable bedroom in the thatch. To come out into the shop after it was shut, and hear her father sing a song inside this cottage, was a perfect Pastoral to Mrs. Plornish, the Golden Age revived. And truly if that famous period had been revived, or had ever been at all, it may be doubted whether it would have produced many more heartily admiring daughters than the poor woman. (*LD,* II, ch.13)

In all its whimsy and absurdity, Mrs. Plornish's Happy Cottage celebrates the persistence of pastoral in the midst of urban hardship. The portrait of rural simplicity—thatched cottage, faithful dog, pigeon-house, all enhanced by the ancient song of her aged father—preserves a relic of what London has devoured. The city saturates space and fills in emptiness, but then, improbably, back inside a house within the metropolitan center, there flourishes an Arcadian ritual, the ceremonies of a bygone age.

Although in the last years of his life when the Open Spaces movement began to have success, Dickens can be seen as his own kind of campaigner and one who disclosed the imaginative logic underlying the social ambition. In this light we might consider a turn in the movement after its initial successes, when it became clear that still more was at stake than the important defensive acts of saving the great Commons. The turn was toward the microspaces of London. No new Heath was going to be carved out of the city's stone, but given the ongoing loss of openness—street by street and corner by corner—the struggle was to excavate green expanses even in narrow quarters. An annual report of the Commons Preservation Society acknowledged a now urgent recognition: the need "of providing in the heart of London, small lungs of unoccupied space."[10] The abolition of private rights in London squares was one brisk proposal: the breaking up of the stone in Trafalgar Square was another. More extreme was Octavia Hill's call to open up the burial grounds of London. Closed since 1852, the grounds were full of fallen headstones, overgrown vegetation, and gloomy associations, yet the fact that Hill's call was promptly heeded is a sign of the depth of need and the inventiveness of the campaigners. The prospect of harried Londoners strolling through narrow burial grounds may not have inspired everyone, but it indicates to us the determined pursuit of small lungs.

In this light, we invoke a luminous moment from *Our Mutual Friend*: the garden lovingly planted on the rooftop of Fledgeby's counting house in the midst of financial London—a garden composed of just a "humble creeper," "a few boxes" of flowers and evergreens within the "encompassing wilderness of dowager old chimneys" (*OMF*, II, ch.5). In this lineage belongs Miss Flite's threatened flock of birds in *Bleak House*, which grows in *Our Mutual Friend* into the marvelous tropical aviary inside the Harmon house off somber Cavendish Square, an aviary within the phantasmagoria of "gold and silver fish, and mosses, and water-lilies, and a fountain" (*OMF*, IV, ch.12). Wemmick's Castle in *Great Expectations*, perched defiantly against the creeping metropolis, is another strangely prodigious act of pastoral invention. Squeezed within a spread of "back lanes" and "ditches," the Castle is a working farm, with its pigs, its fowls, its rabbits, its cucumbers (*GE*, II, ch.6). What completes the recovery, of course, is the Aged P himself, preserved as if in aspic, at the very margin of life, as a kind of trophy of longevity. These are all sites of deep investment in Dickens, scenes of flourishing where the green world returns to the gray of London. The seeding of the metropolis with human relics and with the remnants of its rural past, its bygone beauty is a refusal of the false present tense—the falsity of moneyed respectability and of the cream stucco covering the truth of brick. In the face of such shams, Dickens offers a hope like that of Octavia Hill: that amid London's pleats and folds there might grow a garden—the bearer of age in a time of false youth.

Unlike the activists who were engaged in the gritty struggle for open expanse, Dickens gives a self-consciously fictive quality to the images of pastoral recovery. The novels offer the preservation, in effect, of exhibition spaces—strange inner places where the green past can be rehearsed and performed. It is, after all, a short though telling step from Mrs. Skewton's pretense to the make-believe of the Plornishes. The incongruity of Happy Cottage—its absurdity and unreality, its evocation of a Golden Age that may never "have been at all"—is shared by all the other examples: Riah on the rooftop, Wemmick at the cannon, the aviary in the townhouse. Happy Cottage is a "counterfeit cottage"; the other cases also depend on "poetical heightening" to achieve their strange force. These uncanny effects help us to see a necessarily fictive quality in the Open Spaces campaign itself. Born into belatedness, it found itself already surrounded by the developing city. It was forced to project its green onto an existing gray—to invent not only new narratives of ownership but also new images of a space to excavate and recover. And then, as the wary campaigners quickly learned, even a victory on the ground could come undone in the next railway bill, leaving behind just a memory of green.

## RAG, PAPER, AND WASTING HUMANITY

But what is London made of? What is its primal matter? What composes the grit deposited on the street, the dust blowing through the air, the mud covering the street? As he thinks ever more seriously about the contexts of human flourishing, these questions begin to loom large for Dickens. They give a startling specificity to his engagement with the environment; they also place the question of material regeneration in stark and urgent terms. Here we turn to another tableau from *Bleak House,* the early encounter of Esther Summerson with Krook's decrepit but evocative shop.

> She had stopped at a shop over which was written KROOK, RAG AND BOTTLE WAREHOUSE. Also, in long thin letters, KROOK, DEALER IN MARINE STORES. In one part of the window was a picture of a red paper mill at which a cart was unloading a quantity of sacks of old rags. In another was the inscription BONES BOUGHT. In another, KITCHEN-STUFF BOUGHT. In another, OLD IRON BOUGHT. In another, WASTE-PAPER BOUGHT. In another, LADIES' AND GENTLEMEN'S WARDROBES BOUGHT. Everything seemed to be bought and nothing to be sold there. (*BH*, ch.5)

Krook's shop is mirror and precursor of the dust heaps of *Our Mutual Friend:* a place where everything goes, the receptacle at the end of the world. In general, there is nothing surprising about the items in his window. But what are we to make of that third sentence that interrupts the catalogue of objects bought and sold: the picture of a red paper mill with a cart unloading old rags? In this patchwork of signs and notice-boards there stands this bright tableau, which is not simply an improbable image in Krook's window: it is also an opening onto an image composed nearly fifteen years later, as Dickens was bringing *Our Mutual Friend* to its close. There too he devised a picture of an idyllic mill, which will become decisive at the climax of this last finished novel. The redemption of Lizzie Hexam depends on her escape from dispossession into dignified work at the clean and serene mill alongside the river. In the novel's last conversation, Mortimer Lightwood defends the marriage between Lizzie and his well-born friend, Eugene Wrayburn. He has this exchange with the unappeasable Podsnap:

"And now, Mr Lightwood, was she ever," pursues Podsnap, with his indignation rising high into those hair-brushes of his, "a factory girl?"

"Never. But she had some employment in a paper mill, I believe." (*OMF*, IV, book 4, ch.67)

Women performed the essential work in the making of paper. For Dickens, it was elevating labor (unlike factory work) that prepared for marriage across the chasm of class. The extent of his investment in the iconic paper mill—the flourishing workplace, clean and productive, a fit place for women—offers a way into the material problem that we mean to follow here.

In the middle decades of the nineteenth century, there was a British paper emergency. Where to find enough of it, when so much more was needed every year? By the 1850s the demand for paper was increasing at ten times the rate of a fast-growing population. These years saw the emergence of a documentary society, intent to record the smallest transactions; this was also an avid newspaper-reading society, and one that needed to print fresh banknotes to circulate through industry and empire.[11] Then there were all those copies of all those novels by Dickens. And all the wills for the many dead. The paper emergency was a sudden eruption. It flared at mid-century, but by 1870 it was nearly over. Still, while it lasted, it created a visible agitation well captured in a remark by Harriet Martineau, who wrote in 1854 that "we cannot, by any means yet tried, get anything like enough paper; and the scarcity and dearness of it now constitute what may be called without exaggeration, a national calamity."[12] Meanwhile, the duty on paper kept the scarce material more expensive than it would otherwise have been. The duty had been a staple of government revenue since the reign of Queen Anne, but despite the protests of authors and paper manufacturers, it was not lifted until 1861. Still, as the paper campaigners well understood, the difficulty was not the tariff that raised the price. The urgent problem was on the side of production: how to make enough to meet the paper hunger.

The problem, in short, was rags: how to find them, gather them, and sell them to the paper mill. By 1870, as Dickens's career and his life were ending, so was the rag production of paper: the perfection of wood-based technologies, brought from America, transformed the process. But until then, paper was an industry of rags, and for mid-century London, the pursuit of rags was a ceaseless activity, and a humming part of the street economy. In the eighteenth century it had still been necessary to find white cloth for white paper, but after the discovery of the bleaching power of chlorine gas, rags of any color were greedily sought—even as foreign governments worked to block the export of their own precious rags. Under such constraint, Martineau sternly instructs her readers: "Do any of us burn rags, or allow anybody under our roof to burn them? Never let such a thing happen again" ("How to Get Paper," 242).

The picture on Krook's window—the cart delivering rags to a red paper mill—is a concise image of the essential material transaction and of the hopes bestowed on this act of manufacture: dirty rag converted into white paper at a red mill. The tableau recalls the more extensive scene painting in a short essay that Dickens composed for his then-new journal, *Household Words,* with Mark Lemon as coauthor. It is a rapturous reverie stirred by a paper mill that he had visited, a building "clean without and radiant in the sun," that excites a mix of nostalgia and technophilia: "Paper! White, pure, spick and span new paper, with that fresh smell which takes us back to school and school-books; can it ever come from rags like these? Is it from such bales of dusty rags, native and foreign, of every colour and of every kind . . . that virgin paper, to be written on, and printed on, proceeds?"[13] In this essay, as in *Our Mutual Friend,* the scene of the paper mill gives a utopian figure for what ecologically pure manufacture might be. Dickens disregards both the risk (especially the risk of fire) and the arduous demands on the employees (the heat and the air), so committed is he to finding an instance of safe and befitting labor. In *Household Words* the mill is said to be in "beautiful order" with the "workpeople so thriving," just as a decade and a half later, the waterwheel of the mill exudes a "softening influence" on its surroundings ("A Paper-Mill," 531). Partly no doubt because the factory is set alongside the untainted upstream river, it creates a rare late glimpse of a nature that can still be bountiful: "peaceful, pastoral and blooming" (*OMF,* III, ch.9).

The miracle of technology that converts dusty rag into white paper: this is the exciting image that brings Dickens toward a more subtle and difficult approach to materiality. The blank, open, virginal expanse is a sign of possibility, especially for Dickens, who is ready to pen *Bleak House* upon these sheets. But the question to be pressed is: What then? After this transformative act, what happens next? Old clothes into rag, rag into paper—a wedge of matter changes shape, alters form—it is written on and circulated—but where does it go then? Mid-century London not only saw an accumulating mass of printed matter on its streets, but that mass was also so often ephemeral: newspapers, broadsheets, flyers that exhausted their meaning as soon as they were glimpsed. What became of the hard-won products of the paper industry? With so many publishers, large and small, clamoring for so much paper, what became of the wedge of matter after the notice was scanned, the newspaper read? Sought in vast quantities, "waste paper" became a precious commodity in its own right—so common an object it was simply called "waste," and those who sold it, "waste men."

Cheesemongers, butchers, and fruit and pastry shops had an endless need for wrapping for their goods. In *London Labour and the London Poor,* Mayhew encounters these street merchants who pursue waste paper everywhere they can imagine finding it and who then store it in rented rooms until it is ready for sale. Here is a passage from one interview:

> One man, who "did largely in waste," at my request endeavoured to enumerate all the kinds of paper he had purchased. . . . He had dealt, he said . . . in "books on every subject . . . on which a book can be written." . . . I've had Bibles—the backs are taken off in the waste trade, or it wouldn't be fair weight—Testaments, Prayer-books, Companions to the Altar, and Sermons and religious works. . . . I've had Prayer-books, and . . . hymns. More shame; but you see, sir, perhaps a godly old man dies, and those that follow him care nothing for hymn-books, and so they come to such as me. . . . I've dealt in tragedies and comedies, old and new, cut and uncut—they're best uncut, for you can make them into sheets then—and farces, and books of the opera. I've had scientific and medical works of every possible kind, and histories, and travels, and lives, and memoirs. . . . Poetry, ay, many a hundred weight. . . . Pamphlets I've had by the ton, in my time; I think we should both be tired if I could go through all they were about. Very many were religious, more's the pity. I've heard of a page round a quarter of cheese, though, touching a man's heart.[14]

Mayhew goes on to describe the painful case of an "elderly and intelligent man" who "could afford, and enjoyed, no reading when I saw him last autumn, beyond the book-leaves in which he received his quarter of cheese, his small piece of bacon or fresh meat . . . ; and his wife schemed to go to the shops who 'wrapped up their things from books,' in order that he might have something to read after his day's work" (*London Labour,* 114). What fascinates Mayhew is the uncanny scene of the destruction of meaning, the sinking down of text into waste. Religion, politics, and poetry all receive a final glimpse before they decompose into stain and grease. Sentences become faint traces before they disappear at last—when meaning returns to matter. Then in the ultimate stage the waste itself disintegrates. After the cheese, after the joint of lamb or the scone, the waste paper sooner or later loses the fibrous consistency imparted by the rags. It pulverizes until we meet it as it appears at another moment in *Our Mutual Friend,* in the aspect of "that mysterious paper currency which circulates in London when the wind blows, gyrated here and there and everywhere. Whence can it come, whither can it go? It hangs on every bush, flutters in every tree, is caught flying by the electric wires, haunts every enclosure, drinks at every pump, cowers at every grating, shudders upon every plot of grass, seeks rest in vain behind the legions of iron rails" (*OMF,* I, ch.12). This is the last stage in the life cycle of London paper. After the rags have been sold, the paper milled, the *Times* printed, the waste gathered, and the cheese wrapped, then the particles finally break apart into this "paper currency" that blows in bits through the atmosphere, as part of the "abominable emanation of the streets"[15]—what Dickens elsewhere calls "the city grit" that "gets into the hair and eyes and skin" (*OMF,* II, ch.15).

This last turn in the circuit is also a turn in our account, because the material exchange that we are describing is not only conducted by persons: it is also a threat to persons. "All smell is, if it be intense, immediate acute disease": Edwin Chadwick's memorable motto captures the Victorian fear of entanglement with a foul material world that is never safely external but can always penetrate the body.[16] The years of the paper crisis were also the years of the cholera panic. And while no one thought that the disease was transmitted in the newspaper, still the rag-paper-waste circuit belongs within this phase of urban fear. The dread of incorporation, of the ingestion of particles, fluids, gases and grit that could enter the body through some open orifice and deposit their contagion: that was one aspect of metropolitan emergency. But another aspect, more immediate to our subject here, concerns the descent of human beings into the cycle of matter. Not what they might ingest, but what might incorporate them, as Charles Knight suggests in this passage from his *London.*

> Groups of women, *with dirty rags hung round them,* not put on, cower

round the doors—the old with wrinkled parchment skins, the young with flushed swollen faces and heavy eyes.... In this region there are no birds or flowers at window or on wall; the inmates can scarcely muster liveliness sufficient to exchange words, or perpetrate the practical joke of pushing each other into the kennel. Shops are almost unknown—in the interior of the district quite unknown. Half-way up Bainbridge Street is one in which a few withered vegetables are offered for sale; in George Street another, *where any kind of rags, with all their dirt, are purchased.*[17] (emphasis added)

The barely suppressed thought, extracted by our italics, is that the loose rags in the first sentence might become the commodities in the last. Torn from the back of a child or a woman, rags might change from poor clothes into dear paper. So Hollingshead in *Ragged London* writes of a court in which "the windows are everywhere stuffed with paper—rags being in too much demand at the marine store-shop, or for the clothing of the human child-rats."[18] Rags, paper, clothes, human beings: this is the wider circuit of waste at mid-century. A grim image, common through the period, is that human beings might become no more than the shroud of rags that covers them, as in *Bleak House* where Dickens evokes a poor woman who appears to be nothing more than "a drunken face tied up in a black bundle, and flaring out of a heap of rags on the floor of a dog-hutch which is her private apartment" (*BH*, ch.22).

In *Our Mutual Friend*, Mortimer Lightwood and the benevolent Boffin contest the meanings of this transaction between human beings and the rags that surround them.

> "My dear Mr Boffin, everything wears to rags," said Mortimer, with a light laugh.
>
> "I won't go so far as to say everything," returned Mr Boffin, on whom his manner seemed to grate, "because there's some things that I never found among the dust." (*OMF*, I, ch.8)

We take this exchange as capturing the mid-century poise between nihilism and humanism. Lightwood's brazen thought is that we human beings decay with the decaying objects around us, becoming waste ourselves like dirty rags and waste paper. And, after all, wasn't that a lesson that could be drawn from the cholera doctors, as it finally became clear that cholera was carried by invisible organisms swallowed with water? The body now lost the integrity of its boundaries, becoming another biofluid mixing its microbes with the grit around it.

Boffin's response to Lightwood—not everything will wear to rags, some things are not found in the dust—belongs to the other narrative of grit and particles, the story of paper. In that essay of 1851, Dickens can cheerfully imagine himself as a rag, "torn cross-wise" by the women working the paper-mill. He sees himself "pressed, and squeezed, and jammed," until he loses his "grosser nature," becoming "greatly purified," "gradually becoming quite ethereal."[19] This creation myth—ethereal paper born out of dirty rags—is a product of deep imaginative investment, not only in Dickens but in a reading public newly conscious of the expensive meanings of paper. At this moment of the 1850s, pressures toward materialism and scientism were growing briskly. The metamorphic story of paper—its virgin birth, its recovery of ethereal whiteness out of dirt—was a lustrous and consoling tale.

But, of course, what we have been meaning to show is that white paper is only a stage in a process, within which human beings play many uncanny parts: women at the mill beating cloth into pulp while chlorine gas fills the air; street traders foraging for the same rags that clothe indigent children; waste men in pursuit of documents left by the dead; and the intellectually starved poor, keen to read texts that are fast fading into grease. Although Boffin stands out for the immaterial human dignity that floats above the dust, Lightwood drops the heavy thought that will not be spirited away: People who read the papers can themselves be reduced to rags, and the elevating texts they scan will one day crumble into the gritty currency that blows through the wind and into the lungs—a reminder that the distance between the waste without and the wasting within is no thicker ... than a sheet of paper.

## NOTES

1. "London in 1851," *Fraser's Magazine*, 11.
2. Dickens and Wills, "The Heart of Mid-London," 124–25.
3. *Hansard*, 1857 June 23, col. 237.
4. Ibid., 1864 June 28, col. 435.
5. Ibid., col. 432.
6. *First and Second Reports from the Select Committee on Open Spaces*, 12.
7. Lefevre, *English and Irish Land Questions*, 188.
8. Lefevre quoted in *First and Second Reports from the Select Committee on Open Spaces*, 12.
9. Lefevre, "Our Common Land," 11.
10. *Commons Preservation Society: Report of Proceedings*, 8.
11. See Tatiana M. Holway, "Funny Money," chapter 9 in this volume, for further discussion of this issue.
12. Martineau, "How to Get Paper," 242.
13. Dickens and Lemon, "A Paper-Mill," 529.

14. Mayhew, *London Labour and the London Poor*, 113.
15. *Lancet*, 265–66.
16. Chadwick quoted in "Metropolitan Sewage Committee," 10.
17. Knight, *London*, 267.
18. Hollingshead, *Ragged London*, 72.
19. "A Paper-Mill," 530.

# 8

# Commodity Criticism and Victorian Thing Culture

The Case of Dickens

ELAINE FREEDGOOD

The commodity culture of Victorian Britain was, if our best analysts of it are right, a culture of display.[1] The activity of gazing from a distance at consumer goods replaced other kinds of literal object relations and alienated Victorians from the things of their world, as we are alienated from the things of ours. Looking became the mode of relating to things, and all things became commodities, or commodities became the only things that could be seen. In the compelling thesis of Guy Debord's *Society of the Spectacle,* first published in 1967, on which some of the most influential criticism of Victorian commodity culture relies, a historical moment arrives "at which the commodity completes its colonization of social life. It is not just that the relationship to commodities is now plain to see—commodities are now all that there is to see; the world we see is the world of the commodity."[2] Many contemporary Victorianists have collectively and implicitly agreed to project this moment backward onto a point of origin in the mid-nineteenth century and, even more specifically, onto that spectacular efflorescence, the Crystal Palace Exhibition of 1851.[3] But the idea of the commodity's "complete colonization of social space," which has been an extraordinarily productive notion for a long time, may now be due for some revision. As postcolonial theory has taught us, the idea of complete colonization underestimates the canniness of the colonized and the ruses and refusals at the disposal of even the most apparently powerless victims of imperial might. I suggest that our intense focus on the totalizing character of the commodity culture of Victorian Britain has perhaps occluded our ability to appreciate other kinds of object relations that may have preceded and survived it. The power of the commodity, I have argued and will argue here, did not entirely displace, much less destroy, other kinds of object relations.[4]

As long-term residents and resistors of commodity culture, we tend to become nervous about things—they all seem to be commodities. As Rey Chow points out, in Marx's description of the commodity fetish, the commodity becomes a "false representation," and "despite the ambiguities that may be detected in Marx's memorable portrayal, this portrayal has nonetheless given rise to a prevalent Modernist intellectual tendency to regard things as superficial and morally suspect phenomena."[5] This "tendency" operates even in Chow's analysis: we conflate or immediately equate *things* and *commodities,* so that the welter of things found in Victorian novels has made these texts seem eminently symptomatic of what we reflexively understand as the bad materialism of commodity culture. Indeed, in the generous and symptomatic estimation of Jeff Nunokawa, in the realm of discourse, "our sense of the commodity's invasiveness may owe its largest debt neither to the eloquence of social prophecy . . . nor the elaborations of social theory but rather to the Victorian novel and its narrative heirs."[6]

The Dickens novel has long been criticized for its thingfulness: it is *the* Victorian novel we might think of first when we want an example of a compelling representation of "the commodity's invasiveness." I will argue here that it is the criticism of the Dickens novel rather than anything inherent in his novels themselves that has convinced us that their thingfulness is first and foremost a representation of commodity culture. We look *past* things in the Victorian novel generally—and the crowded, Dickensian instantiation of it in particular—because we do not want to repeat the Victorian error of looking *at* them; we thereby commodify—paradoxically and, of course, unwittingly—things as we uncover commodification. We do this, in part, because we have allowed for no residual or resistant modes of object relating in commodity culture—then or now.

## VICTORIAN THING CULTURE: FUSES, OATS, PINS, AND VINEGAR

We are all commodity fetishists now, and our literary criticism is often hobbled by this problem, but our nineteenth-century forebears may well have maintained a more complex relationship to the goods that surrounded and intrigued them. Ideas, connections, and social relations swarmed in the many and various things of that world: the processes of commodification—abstraction, alienation, and spectacularization—were achieved, I contend, slowly rather than suddenly, unevenly rather than consistently or finally. I suggest that thing culture preceded commodity culture and still persists within it: thus the need for the kind of policing of the object world that we both analyze and practice. Henri Lefebvre has described the dialectic of everyday life in which "alienations, fetishisms and reifications" come up "against a hostile force": the human ability to appropriate goods for needs and desires. "In the link between pleasure and objects . . . the reification engendered by these very things tends to break up."[7]

The Great Exhibition might be imagined as the emblematic and epic face-off between thing and commodity culture, although it has usually been understood as the crystallization (if you will) of the triumph of commodity culture. It showed, Thomas Richards has influentially argued, "once and for all that the capitalist system had not only created a dominant form of exchange but was also in the process of creating a dominant form of representation to go along with it. Capitalism was now consolidating its hold over England not only economically but semiotically. The era of the spectacle had begun."[8] The enormous success of the Exhibition consisted in a "grandeur [that] does not consist in one thing," as Charlotte Brontë wrote, "but in the unique assemblage of all things."[9] The truth of Brontë's observation suggests the extent to which Victorians liked to look at things, any and seemingly *all* things, things that were not yet commodities in a spectacular sense: piles of pins, "improved fuses," ordinary cakes and biscuits, aromatic vinegar, barrels of Kildrummie oats, hemp—many displays seem to have been striking only in what to us seems like their lack of apparent interest as spectacles. The era of the spectacle may have found one of its more fortuitous points of entry at the Exhibition, as Richards argues, but the "spectacle" it presented was not the kind of consistently mesmerizing or alienating display Debord describes. It seems to me that illustrated catalogues and narrative accounts have misled us into imagining halls rife with elaborate gewgaws, baroque birdcages, and grotesquely large diamonds: a careful perusal of the written lists in these catalogues suggests that splendor and spectacle are balanced, if not humbled, by a significant showing of the mundane, the everyday, the distinctly and perhaps definitively unspectacular.

Fuses, vinegar, pins, and oats were also important to the triumph of pre-sentation Brontë describes. The success of the Exhibition was, of course, a feat of *re*presentation: like the realist novel, the Crystal Palace gave the impression of displaying everything; any selection process seems to have been annulled. This triumph was accomplished by a monumental sleight-of-hand: "the spaces of production and consumption," Andrew H. Miller points out, "were evacuated and replaced in the Exhibition by one spectacular space of exchange."[10] And yet Miller goes on to point out that exchange—literal exchange—was controversial within the Exhibition; after a long debate, price tags were banned: "all signs of commerce were banished and the objects were thus not to be considered in relation to their monetary value."[11] As a result, "relational categories of gender, nationality, labor and taste implicitly articulated objects into new practical and conceptual orders" (63–64). I would like to underscore here the originality of an insight that I think Miller makes too little of in his own argument: there is an "order of things" that is blatantly *not* commercial at work in the Exhibition; a culture that is not commodity culture is animating the "relational categories" he so vividly observes.

Thomas Richards argues that the spatial and temporal restrictions of the Exhibition altered perception, so that he too suggests that the triumph of commodity culture was not actually a done deal at the moment of what he otherwise describes as the scene of its apparent triumph: "visitors were virtually forced to acquire a limited attention span. Like it or not, they had to adjust themselves to the serial rhythm of the place. . . . [T]he Crystal Palace turned you into a dilettante, loitering your way through a phantasmagoria of commodities."[12] The Exhibition instilled in its viewers, and, more importantly, *needed* to instill in them, the frame of mind in which reification began to feel natural: things must be understood and evaluated quickly and successively. To cut to the cognitive chase is to understand that things mean something that a close inspection and consideration of their material form will not yield. Meaning is not immanent in things; meaning is created outside of them, in the organization of things into exhibitions, pictures, novels, and other "realist" representations. This split is cognitively similar to the one that divides a commodity from its use value. Indeed, the economic processes that characterize modernity—Weber's rationalization, Simmel's objectification, and Marx's abstraction—are first and foremost representational practices: we must become inured to the idea that the meaning and value of things can be separated from their materiality. And we must become comfortable with the idea that we can "know" these meanings and values only in a process apart from knowing the things from which they are so easily detached.

Yet the very impulse to visit an exhibition of "all products of industry" suggests the vestiges of a very different consciousness—one that might have belonged to the precursor of the dilettante who cannot stop to touch or scrutinize or think much about the objects on display. In that earlier consciousness, "industry" was still a largely human practice, including machine and factory as well as hand and home production.[13] In the catalogue of the Great Exhibition, things are often elaborately annotated, not only with the names of the person or company who made them and the place of their origin, but with the process or conditions of production, extraction, or cultivation: "a carved book-tray, executed by a ploughman, in the evening, by candle-light, without the aid of any model or design, and solely with a penknife," reads one entry.[14] By hand, by spade and dibble, by power loom, with a penknife, at night: the purchase and perusal of these catalogues suggests that visitors wanted to know about the provenance of these humble objects not only in terms of country, city, town, manufacturer, and person, but also by process.[15] So although, as Miller points out, process was giving way to product as the focus of display, that transition was not completed by the time of the Exhibition—nor perhaps has it ever become permanent.[16]

The visitor to the Exhibition might well have come to see the products of human endeavor and to imagine, particularly at the many very popular exhibits that featured working industrial equipment, in what that endeavor consisted. The tumble of objects on display suggests that Victorians had a relationship to things, or to things in the process of becoming commodities, that we have not fully appreciated. In their indiscriminate abundance, their literal and figurative lack of polish, their wildly varying states of manufacture, many of the items on display are products of industry only if those terms are construed so broadly as to make them almost meaningless: the autumn leaves from Vermont on display in the United States exhibit, for example. The inclusiveness of the exhibition confounds our sensibilities: we do not understand leaves as products of industry, nor do we typically find raw oats compelling. We have long taken such failures of interest as a sign of advancement—that is, our demanding and ironizing relationships to things are a sign of development rather than decline—but such failures may instead suggest the indigence of our object relations, the extent to which we are numbed by spectacular relations to commodities and the extent to which the mid-Victorian exhibition-goer may not have been.

It only makes sense that we have also lost sight of the archive of thing culture: its documents belong to no discipline; they rest in unvisited call numbers. So we remain largely unaware that the emblematic "thingful" experience of the Crystal Palace was reinforced in more quotidian practices of the mid-nineteenth century. In the huge nineteenth-century literature of industrial production—including multiple multivolume histories of goods such as cotton and pottery; periodical articles on the manufacture of buttons, umbrellas, and screws; illustrations of spinning jennies and steam engines that are impressive if indecipherable—Victorians built up reservoirs of detail from which associations could be drawn or from which they flowed spontaneously. In a parallel (and better-known) literature of empire, the writings of missionaries, explorers, travelers, and colonial civil servants and their families built up equally dense catalogues and compendia of the raw materials available in the world outside Britain.

These associations had two large perceptual consequences. In economic terms, commodities might continue to "speak" of the social relations of production to those who bought and used them. In literary terms, anarchic metonymic processes were always receiving new infusions of energy and detail. I do not mean to suggest that such "infusions" were benign or their effects utopian. The object relations of thing culture could be as exploitive as, or more exploitive than, those of commodity culture given the ruggedly referential form of their representation. Thus their virtue and their violence: we can tolerate knowing very little about the social relations of production, but our forebears (culturally speaking) had strong stomachs, including, I think, for the details of the fates of various people and places that came under the domination of the workshop of the world.

In positing the existence of Victorian thing culture, I am suggesting that commodity culture did not "win" once and for all in the mid-nineteenth century. I am assuming that there were failures in the process of commodification. They may also have been "failures," to anticipate a certain reading of my reading that might come from the general direction of Slovenia: we are never so inside an ideological formation as when we think we are outside it, looking at a glitch in its functioning. This may well be true, and I am happy to concede that commodity culture may allow for or even require the failures that I am categorizing as the practices of thing culture. Nonetheless, these failures or "failures" offer chances for reconfigurations of object relations, or for moments of remembering or of trying to remember what distinguishes the thing from the commodity—or, more precisely, what distinguishes a thing relation from a commodity relation. Such failures may be fleeting: the most hardened consumers may be visited by fits of longing for some long-lost thing or some long-hoped-for item, and the object of their inchoate desires cannot be named, much less purchased. Such failures may call for the deployment of such cultural practices as the keeping of keepsakes, the playing of the lottery, and the watching of detectives, for example. In such practices, personal, random value trumps exchange value; apparently meaningless things can suddenly become legally legible, or luminous, or life-altering. Thing culture is not utopian. It is literal; it is commemorative; it is hopeful. It allows for a kind of aspiration and belief, I will argue, for which somewhat Marxist, somewhat modernist critics of Victorian culture have developed a particularly strong and debilitating form of contempt.

It may be that it is thing culture rather than commodity culture that so often confuses and embarrasses us about the prolific, even promiscuous, object relations of these daunting cultural progenitors. Thing culture, in its profusion, intensity, and heedless variety, displays that appalling lack of irony, of distance, of coolness that we so often cringe at in the worst examples of Victorian middle-class taste. But the riot of stuff that we imagine when we imagine the claustrophobically cluttered Victorian parlor is not only—nor perhaps even mostly—composed of what can properly be called commodities. Curiously, as the work of Talia Schaffer has taught us, some of the most outré ornaments that produce that characteristic clutter are the crafts made by women, often out of rubbish. The fish-scale or cucumber-seed collage, the shell sculpture, the dried-flower arrangement: there is little, or to put it more plainly, nothing, in the way of exchange value in these home-made goods.[17] That from our point of view there is also little in the way of use value is perhaps because we cannot remember or imagine relationships to things based on such an unembarrassed sense of the elasticity and capaciousness of value; our sense of value, is after all, constrained into a rather small number of distinct categories, many of which are carefully quarantined from one another. The aesthetic, the economic, the psychological: whole disciplines are now deployed to maintain the distinctions between what we hope are incommensurable realms of worth and worthiness.

There has also been a distinct, diffused, and lasting aesthetic assault on much of Victorian thing culture by various modernist taste-makers. Paul Delany has pointed out that "the rentier culture out of which Modernism emerged was a particular class formation, hostile to 'trade,' marketing and mass consumption."[18] These "rentier" values are evident in Woolf's criticism of the Edwardian novel in the essay "Modern Fiction," which might be described as a critique of the extant Victorianism of that novel. The Edwardians in question—Mr. Galsworthy, Mr. Bennett, and Mr. Wells—are all materialists. "The proper stuff of fiction" is not stuff anymore, Woolf announces: like "Mr. Joyce," the modern writer needs to be "spiritual."[19] But there is a lingering sense that if Galsworthy, Bennett, and Wells only gave us the right stuff, their novels would pass muster (surely there is no lack of "stuff" in *Ulysses*). The problem with Bennett's characters, for example, is that we cannot imagine "what they live for" given that their highest goal seems to be to arrive at "the very best hotel in Brighton." Mr. Wells focuses on the wrong things "out of sheer goodness of heart": he takes "upon his shoulders the work that ought to have been discharged by Government officials."[20] These novelists, like Victorian consumers and craft-makers, do not discriminate enough among things.

Woolf, in distinguishing good fiction from that of the "materialists," makes a move that the keepers of high culture endlessly repeat: she works to reinforce the line between high and middlebrow culture by carefully and continually sorting out the merely well-intentioned from the truly well-executed. As Bourdieu has argued, the middlebrow seeker after high culture is a source of chronic danger to highbrow culture: "legitimate culture is not made for him (and is often made against him), [and] it ceases to be what it is as soon as he appropriates it."[21] Highbrow culture must constantly redefine itself, and redraw its own boundaries, in order to resist the encroachments of this appropriation.

We might say that one of the most profound legacies of modernism is the way in which it ceded nearly all of Victorian culture to middlebrow cultural aspirants. Such aspirants, usually members of the lower-middle class, are always behind the times in any case: why not give them the better part of a century to chew on? Modernism, meanwhile, could concentrate on small print runs and coteries of readers who would need more than a hardy case of autodidacticism to make the grade. So even now, I think there is, among those of us who study Victorian culture, an embarrassment, or the threat of an embarrassment, about its objects: Do we like them? Do we think any of them are beautiful? The uncertain relationship, for many of us, between ourselves and the objects we study—or the objects in the texts we study—makes it safe simply to lump them all together as commodities. Marxists and modernists alike—those who populate our internal and external object worlds—are likely to be satisfied by this "critical" move, this distancing relation, this paradoxical commodification of the things of the literary worlds we study.

## COMMODITY CRITICISM:
## IN WHICH ALL OBJECTS TEND TO BE BAD OBJECTS

I have suggested that the thingfulness of the Dickens novel has long been a subject of anxiety and complaint. Hippolyte Taine, in his 1883 *History of English Literature,* complains that "Dickens does not perceive great things.... Enthusiasm seizes him in connection with everything, especially in connection with vulgar objects." He takes Dickens to task for the "minute and impassionate observation of small things" and the neglect of "beautiful forms and fine colours."[22] Ruskin complained of the "diseased extravagance" of Dickens's imagination.[23] "His works," Bagehot wrote, in a brief masterpiece of ambivalence, "are full of acute remarks on petty doings, and well exemplify the telling power of minute circumstantiality."[24] There is also the disturbing sense that Dickens makes people into things. G. H. Lewes, a sort of rueful and slightly embarrassed admirer of Dickens, points out the mechanical nature of Dickens's characters: they make him think of "the frogs whose brains have been taken out for physiological purposes, and whose actions henceforth want the distinctive peculiarity of organic action.... [T]hey are as uniform and calculable as the movements of a machine."[25]

For Victorian critics of Dickens, this thingfulness is an aesthetic and compositional failure; but by the mid-twentieth century, some critics had begun to understand the failure as an aesthetic, social, political, and/or economic one belonging to the world Dickens is self-consciously criticizing. Dorothy Van Ghent in 1953 was one of the first and most perspicuous critics to understand the thingfulness of Dickens as a critique of industrial culture: "People were becoming things and things (the things that money can buy or that are the means for making money or for exalting prestige in the abstract) were becoming more important than people. People were becoming de-animated, robbed of their souls, and things... were usurping the prerogatives of animate creatures."[26] It is worth noting here that although we might reflexively accept this as a loosely Marxist critique, Marx did not criticize capitalism for turning people into *things*. Rather, the problem is that the labor of humans is commodified, so that humans become, to some extent, *commodities*. In a further slippage, Dickens is put into sympathy with this squishy version of Marxism. Dickens, in any case, complained about industrial culture differently than either Marx or Van Ghent did: his critique was essentially conservative and nostalgic.

The critique that Van Ghent makes here is, I think, a particularly mid-twentieth-century one, partly Marxist and partly modernist. Van Ghent sees Dickens as trying to rescue his readers from the fate of his characters in this description: we must decommodify ourselves in order to regain some form of humanity that industrialization is threatening to destroy. Interestingly, Van Ghent almost stops herself from conflating things and commodities: her parenthetical clause restricts the "things" in question to a subset that seems to suggest a rough definition of the commodity: "the things that money can buy or that are the means for making money or for exalting prestige in the abstract." But she cannot quite dispense with the conflation because her analysis depends on an unquestioned moral and hierarchal antinomy between people and animate creatures, on the one hand, and things, on the other: the awful thing is to be like a thing; there is no sense that we might learn something important about subjects from objects.

This tradition has, tellingly, not been interrupted by any of the many interceding waves of critical innovation. In something of a summation of one of those waves, *Practicing New Historicism,* Catherine Gallagher has noted the extent to which the object world is rendered vital in Dickens. The problem, in Gallagher's reading, is not that people are like things, but rather that things are like people in that they promise to live, and therefore people seem also to be at the disposal of animation processes outside of themselves. The materialism of the nineteenth century "dramatically expanded the zones of the organic, vastly multiplied the entities that could be described as alive or dead."[27] The novel displays a "flattened ontological space" in which the difference between subjects and objects, between animate and inanimate things, is blurred by the possibility of animation/re-animation, vivification/re-vivification. This argument, however interesting, does not change the moralized antinomy between thing and non-thing, and so the discussion of subject/object relations in Dickens has not changed a great deal: objects are still too much like subjects, which results in subjects becoming too much like objects: the dead subject, like the inert object, can live or live again.

The price paid by subjects in the Dickens novel is made clear by Taine, Lewes, Bagehot, Van Ghent, and Gallagher, but what of the price paid by objects in the process that we call, with concern and disdain, objectification? Fictional objects become exchangeable figures, used in the novel's symbolic system to make a point about the mechanicalness, one-dimensionality, and deadness of industrialized people who are dulled by the welter of detail, of stuff, of things in which they live and by which they are represented. In this way, fictional things become themselves commodified.[28] Importantly, they are commodified *by criticism.*

The social and political price of commodification is paralleled by the aesthetic toll it takes: for well over fifty years we have too often had the sense that Dickens has the same "taste" that "we" do and that he finds Victorian thingfulness excessive and ugly in the same ways that we do. I quote from Van Ghent again, in what I take to be a familiar "summary" of Victorian kitschiness that many of us assume we have in common with Dickens:

> Dickens lived in a time and an environment in which a full-scale demolition of traditional values was going on, correlatively with the uprooting and dehumanization of men, women, and children by the millions—a process brought about by industrialization, colonial imperialism, and the exploitation of the human being as a "thing" or an engine or a part of engine capable of being used for profit. This was the "century of progress" which ornamented its steam engines with iron arabesques of foliage as elaborate

as *the antimacassars and aspidistras and crystal or cut-glass chandeliers and bead-and-feather portieres* of its drawing rooms, while the human engines of its welfare groveled and bred in the foxholes describe by Marx in his *Capital*. (128; emphasis added)

The question is this: from what textual source or sources do we have this particular, *rhetorically* recognizable picture of Victorian culture? Why do its details strike us as "right"? Dickens does not give us the world that Van Ghent gives us in the above paragraph. (Nor, I think, does Marx give us foxholes.) When Dickens does give us things in detail, it is not antimacassars, aspidistras, cut-glass chandeliers, and portieres: advanced search engines turn up these things not at all. But even if they did, it is not the particular ugly object that makes a room seem unbearable and somehow overrun by industrial commodification to so many moderns; it is, rather, the profusion of things and the formal features of the novel that stretch to accommodate this profusion: the lists, the descriptions, the catalogues, the indexing of the world. In the Victorian period, such forms were probably largely regarded as comic; in the twentieth century, they are often regarded as ugly and symptomatic: signs of acquisitiveness run amok, of an industrialized private sphere, of mass-produced minds.

The list of objects Van Ghent gives us is symptomatic of something other than Victorian culture as Dickens represents it: interestingly, none of the examples for "aspidistra" in the *OED* come from Dickens, or from any other Victorian source. The aspidistra—an Asian lily that was often grown as a houseplant—is defined as a "symbol of dull middle-class respectability," and the OED's example comes, not surprisingly, from George Orwell's 1936 novel, *Keep the Aspidistra Flying*. In this novel, the aspidistra is tellingly *not* a symbol of middle-class respectability; rather, it is a chronically reappearing emblem of *lower*-middle-class respectability. Rita Felski describes the "material culture" of Orwell's "ruthlessly detailed portrayal of English lower middle class life in the 1930s" as "profoundly expressive, attesting not only to economic status but also to a complex blend of moral values and structures of feeling: respectability, frugality, social aspirations. These are epitomized in the drab, indestructible aspidistra displayed in every parlor window, the ubiquitous symbol of the pathos and triumphs of lower-middle-class life."[29] The aspidistra is "the flower of England," for Gordon Comstock, the novel's hero. He announces that "there will be no revolution in England while there are aspidistras in the windows."[30] This potted plant is for Comstock, as it seems to be for Orwell, a horrible sign of the extent to which the lower-middle class has identified with an oppressor whom it is consigned to mimic with egregious and depressing results. That many of the characters belonging to Messrs. Bennett, Galsworthy, and Wells might well be aspidistra-owners almost goes without saying.

To be clear, Van Ghent does not mean to be citing Dickens in the above description—few of us could match her for a command of apposite Dickensian detail. But she is putting "his" world before us, the Dickens world as she "sees" it in the 1950s. As I have mentioned, the keywords in Van Ghent's description of the Victorian drawing room turn up no hits for Dickens on Victorian Etexts: "aspidistra," "cut-glass chandelier," "portiere," or "antimacassar."[31] "Chandelier" turns up four times, and only once in anyone's home—that of Dombey—and it is symptomatic of a lack of proper coziness in that household, I think, rather than bourgeois excess. Van Ghent's random itemization of what was for her the disaster of Victorian interior design can be explained if we understand it as intensely inflected by the views and values of Orwell, Woolf, and other Edwardians and modernists who read that culture with such brilliant hostility.

These writers viewed Victorian culture—and its contemporary instantiation in British lower-middle-class domestic life—as dreadful precisely in what might be broadly described as its "materialism." Marx did not make this connection; neither did Dickens. If anything, both writers make profound arguments for the problematic disconnection between subjects and objects, the ways in which industrial culture makes it difficult for human beings to know things and to know each other by or through them. Materialism is a nineteenth-century problem in the opposite sense: it is in some ways a cure, explicitly so in Marxist theory and perhaps implicitly so in the rich and largely disorganized object world of the Dickens novel. "Materialism" becomes a bad thing in the aesthetic canons of modernism, and then it becomes mixed up with ideas about taste that are also, paradoxically and painfully, connected to class.

"Cut-glass," for example, is a subtly judgmental descriptor in Van Ghent's usage and often a judgmental, shaming one in modernist fiction, indicating inept social climbing through misguided material acquisition. Interestingly, it is a recurring feature of the whisky decanters that inhabit *Keep the Aspidistra Flying*: one of the boarders in Gordon Comstock's rooming house has had his head "broken" by a "cut-glass whisky decanter" flung at him by his wife. Later in the novel we learn that it is *the* weapon of choice for lower-middle-class wives in general: "what a life! Licit sexual intercourse in the shade of the aspidistra. Pram-pushing and sneaky adulteries. And the wife finding you out and breaking the cut-glass whisky decanter over your head."[32] This decanter is metonymic of lower-middle-class attempts to have "good" things so that

8: *Commodity Criticism and Victorian Thing Culture*

it might become ready to become middle class. When Van Ghent accuses a culture of partaking excessively of cut-glass chandeliers, not only does she cast a quiet but definite slur on its style of interior decoration, but she questions—more gravely—the taste and the very middle-class-ness of the Victorian middle class. The entire Victorian middle class is consigned retroactively to the lower-middle class. And this is typical of the attribution of lower-middle-class-ness: "it is a category usually applied from outside, by those of higher social status, or retrospectively, by those who once belonged to the lower middle class and have since moved beyond it. In both these cases, it becomes an object of irony, humor, or scorn rather than a notion one rallies around or identifies with."[33] Many twentieth-century critics of Victorian culture may be newly middle class, if not financially, then in terms of their cultural capital. The cultural formulae of modernism proffer a ready-made strategy to keep even with the highbrow, which, whatever else it is, is distinctly not lower middle class. This may be why so many of us remain so in tune with the mid-twentieth-century formulations of Van Ghent. The dislike of Victorian commodity culture is often a dislike of Victorian commodities, which is to say of Victorian taste, which lives on in the twentieth century in the "parlors" of people with whom, as Felski points, out, no one wants to identify and for whom no one wants to be mistaken.

The Dickens novel is more ambivalent about things than we are in our criticism of it; things have more possibilities for meaning and for making meaning about subjects than they do in the minds of commodity critics. For Dickens a chandelier meant something much different from what it meant for Van Ghent in the light-fixture-minimalist 1950s and from what it still sometimes means for us when we are not careful. In *The Old Curiosity Shop*, chandeliers are mentioned twice, both times as the central lighting fixtures in theaters, which apparently they were and are. In the first mention of this object, Dick Swiveller is bemoaning, in an apostrophe to an absent audience that would be populating the ceiling if it existed, the unfortunate fate of becoming the clerk of Miss Brass. Swiveller directs "his observations to the ceiling, which these bodiless personages are usually supposed to inhabit—except in theatrical cases, when they live in the heart of the great chandelier" (*OCS*, ch.34). There is no immediate metaphoric or metonymic connection between chandeliers and Swiveller's self-indulgence. The chandelier is a prop: it suggests the way in which one's emotional expansiveness (for good or ill) may be inhibited or allowed by the extent and variety and richness of one's object world.

We need props, literally and figuratively. The chandelier is a theatrical object, not quite a prop in the world of the novel, but a prop in the world in which we read the novel: a prop we might see used for such an apostrophe, or one that Dickens's original readers would have seen. Reading things as props might be one way to free them from the constriction of their lives as commodities. It would also free us from the conventions of literary criticism as it has been practiced on novelistic things (which is to say, not very much) and from our reflexive distaste and contempt for much of Victorian material culture, which denies us the ability to make meaning since we have been taught not to look seriously or thoughtfully at so many of the things in question.

The extent to which our sense of the commodity's invasiveness derives from the Victorian novel, to return to Nunokawa's formulation, may be due largely to the literary critical tradition that has attended that novel. We have, for too long, imagined that the realist novel "thinks" about things the way that we do or that we have learned commodity thinking from the novel and its representational traditions. We need now to develop alternative modes of reading the thingful world of those novels. Otherwise, we will proceed in the mode of M'Choakumnchild, the schoolmaster of *Hard Times*, for whom all forms of study that might provide actual objects or experiences are a waste: quantification is all. This abstraction drives the children in the novel to despair because it gives them so little *material* with which to relate to the world: it places them in a state of metonymic indigence in which no little Gradgrind can associate "a cow in a field with that famous cow with the crumpled horn who tossed the dog who worried the cat who killed the rat who ate the malt, or with that yet more famous cow who swallowed Tom Thumb" (*HT*, ch.3). Material things offer starting places for metonymic flights of fancy; it is the loss or lack of "fancy" in *Hard Times* that makes the times particularly hard (and makes the novel unexpectedly Arnoldian): the imagination can provide no relief from reality because it has no material on which to work, no things, no details from which to take flight.

The abundance of Dickens's description is the cultural cure for the material scarcity of the schoolroom and the figural scarcity of the educational texts in *Hard Times*. The Dickensian catalogue of items in a room or a shop or a street that has the potential to go on forever promises a kind of social and historical plenitude that has been banished—because of its excessiveness, its dullness, its literalness—from twentieth-century literary culture *tout court*. The descriptions we find in twentieth-century fiction, at high-, middle-, or low-brow levels, rarely approximate such exuberant cataloguing; when they come even close, they are liable to be described—in what I often think of as a form of consumer alert—as "Dickensian." I have argued elsewhere that the Dickens novel, and the mid-Victorian novel more generally, because of the rich disorganization of their object worlds, allow us, in principle, to "read" the meanings, the possibilities, the histories that abide in things. The possibility for reading things as things—of taking them literally, materially, and then returning them to the novel with lost associations and possibilities restored—has been forestalled, paradoxically, by the commodity criticism of the novel, in which most things in Victorian fiction are treated as clutter that needs to be cleared away so that we can see the meaningful stuff "behind" it.

Indeed the tradition of *not* reading things in realist fiction is much longer than can be summarized here. But in connection with the particular problem of commodity criticism, it is interesting to think that the "symptomatic reading" that has been the hegemonic mode in much Marxist, historicist, and materialist literary criticism, especially since Jameson's convincing reading and dissemination of this Althusserian idea in *The Political Unconscious* (1979), has emphasized the extent to which we must roll by what Jameson dismisses as the "inert givens" of the text.[34] Symptomatic reading might be described as a particularly pure form of commodity criticism. In this reading, only what is not there can count: the text itself is almost entirely reified, its processes entirely displaced by processes that it cannot name but that it symbolizes unwittingly.

Thing culture allowed, I argue, for the promiscuous assignment of value, of interest, and of meaning to a startling range of things: we could take a cue from it and read the things in texts instead of reading *past* them to see something behind or beyond them. We have treated fictional objects as we would now treat the barrels of oats or the piles of pins displayed at the Crystal Palace. We reproduce the restricted, constricted, and damaging object relations of commodity culture in the endless repetition of the defensive and misguidedly "sophisticated" maneuver of understanding all things as commodities: we distance ourselves from the experience of the thing.

Dickens can help us with this, but first we will need to separate the material world of his fiction from its long modernist and Marxist quarantine. And we will need to understand the class conflict at the heart of that quarantine: the consequential cultural conflict that began in the last third of the nineteenth century and continues to this day—the one between the middle and the lower-middle classes, in which irony and humiliation, knowingness and belief, taste and "the best hotel in Brighton" are painfully and consequentially at stake. Otherwise, we will continue to practice a critique of commodification that is itself a form of commodification, and more seriously, we will continue to injure people whose cultural practices we fear but from which we might learn. The awkward, inadequate expression of aspiration through the things of this world is lost to most of us who like to maintain and perform a certain level of interpretive sophistication when it comes to things. But the use of objects to maintain such hope rescues them from commodification, if only because it endows them with meanings they cannot bear, with value other than the kind we have learned to read on their "faces."

## NOTES

1. See Andrew H. Miller, *Novels behind Glass*, and Thomas Richards, *Commodity Culture in Victorian England*.
2. Guy Debord, *Society of the Spectacle*, 29.
3. Interestingly, Debord himself did not specify a chronology for the society of the spectacle until *Commentaires sur la société du spectacle,* written twenty-one years later, when he specifies the 1920s as the start of the "society of the spectacle." (For a discussion of the significance of this decade, see Jonathan Crary, "Spectacle, Attention, Counter-Memory.") Various cultural critics have freely chosen other time periods: in addition to Richards, see T. J. Clark, *The Painting of Modern Life,* who chooses the 1860s as the start date. Cited in Crary.
4. Elaine Freedgood, *The Ideas in Things*.
5. Rey Chow, "Fateful Attachments: On Collecting, Fidelity, and Lao She," 288, 289.
6. Jeff Nunokawa, *The Afterlife of Property,* 4.
7. Henri Lefebvre, *Critique of Everyday Life,* 66–67.
8. Richards, *Commodity Culture,* 3.
9. Asa Briggs, *Victorian Things,* 36.
10. Miller, *Novels behind Glass,* 53.
11. This is in distinct and paradoxical opposition to the modern museum in which you can always find a gift shop in which to buy some kind of replica of the priceless things you have just seen. Maeve Adams, personal communication.
12. Richards, *Commodity Culture,* 35.
13. "Industry" derives from the Latin *industrial*—diligence—and comes to mean productive labor of any kind in the early nineteenth century (*OED* online).
14. *Official Catalogue of the Great Exhibition,* 131.
15. In the special foldout banner of the Great Exhibition issued by the *Illustrated London News*, it is notable that many visitors are represented as in possession of a catalogue, and many are actually pictured busily referring to catalogues (perhaps an advertisement for the catalogues themselves).
16. Miller, *Novels behind Glass,* 77.
17. See Talia Schaffer, "Craft, Authorial Anxiety, and the 'Cranford Papers,'" 221–39.
18. Paul Delany, "Who Paid for Modernism?" *The New Economic Criticism: Studies at the Intersection of Literature and Economics,* 344.
19. Virginia Woolf, "Modern Fiction," 150–58.
20. Woolf, "Modern Fiction," 152.
21. Pierre Bourdieu, *Distinction,* 327.
22. Hippolyte A. Taine, *History of English Literature,* Vol. 4, 129–30.

## 8: Commodity Criticism and Victorian Thing Culture

23. Quoted in Philip Collins, *Dickens: The Critical Heritage*, 100.
24. Quoted in Collins, *Dickens*, 393.
25. Quoted in Alice R. Kaminsky, *Literary Criticism of George Henry Lewes*, 101.

I almost reflexively described this group of Victorian critics as protomodernist: that would underscore the point I am making here, but it would also be wrong. There is, in Victorian aesthetic theory, a critique of rhetorical and ornamental excess that precedes and differs from that of modernism. In addition to the criticism of Dickens mentioned here, see the discussion of debates about design and ornament in Joseph Bizup, *Manufacturing Culture: Vindications of Early Victorian Industry*. See also the bibliography on design in Asa Briggs, *Victorian Things*, 381.

26. Dorothy Van Ghent, *The English Novel*, 128.
27. Catherine Gallagher, "The Novel and Other Discourses of Suspended Disbelief," in *Practicing New Historicism*, 189.
28. See the Introduction by Margreta de Grazia, Maureen Quilligan, and Peter Stallybrass to *Subject and Object in Renaissance Culture*: "it is not only the subject that is lost in commodification: the object too is lost. . . . [C]ommodification depletes the object of its qualities" (4).
29. Rita Felski, "Nothing to Declare: Identity, Shame, and the Lower Middle Class," 35.
30. George Orwell, *Keep the Aspidistra Flying*, 44.
31. http://www.victorianetexts.com
32. Orwell, *Keep the Aspidistra Flying*, 104.
33. Felski, "Nothing to Declare," 41.
34. I owe this analysis to Sharon Marcus and her proposal for an ACLA Panel, "Beyond Symptomatic Reading," Princeton, 2006. In *Between Women: Friendship, Desire and Marriage in Victorian England*, Marcus offers a critique of and an alternative to symptomatic reading: "Just reading strives to be adequate to a text conceived as complex and ample rather than as diminished by, or reduced to, what it has had to repress. Just reading accounts for what is in the text without construing presence as absence or affirmation as negation" (75).

# 9

# Funny Money

TATIANA M. HOLWAY

In 1970, when the Bank of England began circulating paper money that portrayed famous British personages, it did so primarily with a view toward preventing counterfeiting. This has been a problem for the Bank since its founding in 1694, and the creation of the portrait series is only one of the more recent, if most superficial, means for addressing it. Among the dozen or so luminaries who have figured on this series is Charles Dickens, who appeared on the £10 note that circulated from 1992 to 2003. Serving the purpose of a security device, the depiction of Dickens was also designed to "'ensure that the currency notes themselves command the confidence of those who use them.'"[1] Hence, the £10 note was devised with a very particular Dickens in view.

Although the portrait that dominates one half of the reverse of the note is that of the mature novelist, the writer whom the Bank represents is not the "dark," polemical Dickens of the latter half of his career. Rather, he is the author of *The Pickwick Papers*—an illustration of the Dingley Dell-Muggleton cricket match occupies the other half—and of *David Copperfield,* a novel that has a small but prominent place in the top center of the note, under the figure of a star, which illuminates copies of this book as well as Dickens's forehead and brow. What appears on the Bank's issue, then, is an eminently popular image of the author who had bestowed on Mr. Pickwick the "beaming eyes" (*PP,* ch.1) and "the most sunny smiles" (*PP,* ch.39) that reflected so well on him, and whose "genius" in *Copperfield* was said at the time to be like "the sun which gives a universal glow."[2]

## 9: Funny Money

If it is understandable why the Bank should have revived this genial view of Dickens, it is equally understandable why the author of, say, *Little Dorrit*, who represented the political and economic institutions of mid-Victorian Britain as exemplifying the principle of "How Not to Do It" (*LD*, ch.8), does not appear. In fact, in its official monograph on the £10 note, the Bank dismisses the novels Dickens wrote after *Copperfield* as not "ranking with his best works." What this monograph observes instead is that Dickens was "the epitome . . . of the Victorian work ethic"[3]—a characterization that returns again to *David Copperfield,* in which Dickens asserted that "determination" and "earnestness" constituted the "golden rules" for "success" (*DC*, ch.42). Add to this model image of "How to Do It" the perception that Dickens "frequently referred to the Bank of England in a favourable way,"[4] and Dickens seems like a most noteworthy "character,"[5] as Bank officials call him, wittingly or unwittingly invoking the convergence of money, written language, and identity in a word that could itself be a synonym for "Charles Dickens."

Still, the effect of Dickens's presence on paper money is ambiguous at best. There are, to be sure, several related tendencies that make him an oddly suitable choice. One is the way in which, in producing that popular and profitable icon named "Charles Dickens," he advertised its variations as authentic, selling the reprints of portraits that depicted images of authorial character, for example, as true representations and adding his signature, scrawled under "Faithfully yours," to attest, as it did on paper money, to genuine worth in exchange. Alongside this commodification of Dickens, there arose the Dickensification—and the authentication—of commodities, wherein advertisers used not just this or that from his works to market their wares but also Dickensian realism to attest to the value of all manner of things—of prints, for example, which, being said to be "literally transcri[bed]" from Dickens's "accurate and vividly minute descriptions," promised consumers pictures of "true characters."[6] Given these complementary tendencies in Dickens's career and their persistence to this day, his recent appearance on the ur-commodity, money, is their logical extension—or consummation, or collapse, as you will.[7] Either way, a related effect is to foreground the degree to which authenticity is a value created by art, and in this way the £10 note also foregrounds the "tension . . . between [the] political nation and [the] individual imagination"[8] that was abundantly apparent in the latter half of Dickens's career.

Yet insofar as the Dickens note calls attention to the degree to which authenticity can be an effect of representation, rather than its source, it can have the further untoward consequence of highlighting the fragility of authenticity, its susceptibility to imitation, simulation, and fraud. This, of course, was a problem that preoccupied "the only true Boz" ("*Nickleby* Proclamation") as much as it did, and does, the Bank. From this point of view, the use of the pirated novelist to ensure that paper money "commands" confidence is somewhat inapt.

But then it is not Dickens's portrait alone, or any other image, that creates this confidence. Behind paper money stand the enduring political and economic institutions of Britain, if no longer the perdurable reality of gold—the "solid ground," as John Stuart Mill put it,[9] that guaranteed the validity of banknotes' claim to truthful representation and secured the confidence with which they were regarded and exchanged for much of the nineteenth century. Although that "solid ground" is long gone—the Bank abandoned the gold standard in 1931—and although Victorians would have derided what the Bank now issues as "fictitious," current notes are certainly authoritative and authentic. They are also genuine imitations, if you will, of the genuine imitations that the first fully mechanically reproduced notes brought into circulation in the 1850s. The continuing appearance of the traditional pound signs and promissory clauses provides a further trace of the Victorian past. But in the absence of "solid ground," contemporary banknotes present what amount to a patching of symbols onto symbols. For when the Bank abandoned the "perfect security" of gold (Mill, 4:79), it insured the integrity of fiduciary money through the introduction of what the Bank called "'the greatest single security'"[10]—that is, a portrait of a monarch, a symbol of authority, which is now backed by images of eminent Britons. If one effect of the portrait series is thus to suggest the degree to which "credit, or belief, involves the very grounds of aesthetic experience," the effect of the Dickens note in particular is to underscore how very slippery those grounds are in modern forms of economic and literary exchange.[11]

## A HABIT OF TRUSTING

Before considering the Dickens banknote in further detail, I will dwell briefly on mid-Victorian attitudes toward credit, beginning with the confidence with which Bank of England notes were regarded. Though a recent phenomenon,[12] this confidence was secured by the Bank Charter Act (1844), which legally established the conventional backing of paper money by gold and its convertibility at a fixed rate of exchange. Of course, "solid ground" remained invisible. Credit always entails an element of "supratheoretical belief," as George Simmel puts it, and is therefore susceptible to any of the contingencies that affect belief.[13] Nevertheless, the law that guaranteed the Bank's solvency also afforded some security—and enough so that by the 1850s, the public had acquired what Walter Bagehot termed a "habit of trusting" in the Bank's paper promises.[14] Those notes may have been "'flimsy' to a proverb," as Dickens wrote, but "no tyro need be told that these notes are representatives of weightier value" ("The Old Lady in Threadneedle Street"). The public had become habituated not just to their value but also to the value of representations.

Sustained by belief in the solvency of the Bank, this habitual trust extended to the multifarious media of exchange that collectively went under the name of "credit" and that far surpassed the circulation of paper money by the mid-nineteenth century, partly because of the security afforded by the Bank of England and partly because the confinement of its notes to the material basis of gold, along with the restriction of the fiduciary issue to a fixed amount, made those notes insufficiently flexible for an expanding economy. This expansion was effected mainly by joint-stock banks, the number of which more than doubled between the 1830s and the 1860s. Offering relatively high interest rates, these institutions attracted a wide range of middle-class investors, and, with over one-third of the national income deposited in them by the 1840s, they also appealed to a growing number of national and international enterprises that sought to extend their resources through the capital and credit these banks controlled.[15] While the checks that joint-stock banks issued were one means for effecting such transactions, the burgeoning credit system consisted of an additional, and ample, repertoire of media of exchange, which were unrestricted in their issue and unregulated in their circulation.[16] Marked by their varying and often tenuous relationship to any store of value, these interchangeable forms of credit expanded the scope for and the velocity of exchange and became the currency on which the economy came to rely. As Bagehot remarked, "It is only by this refinement ... that we are able to do the sort of trade we do, or to get through the quantity of it" (9:56).

The dramatic growth of the credit system thus involved an unprecedented augmentation of a tendency toward abstraction in capitalist exchange. Indeed, the detachment from the "solid ground" of gold appeared to be so complete to some mid-century observers that the entire British economy seemed to be supported by "one huge structure of mere paper, resting upon the basis of other paper."[17] At the same time, though, all this credit was not just an arbitrary formation. It was an organized system—that is, a system organized by and through financial institutions and, more generally, a complicated network of symbols and signs. In this system, "the tropic interaction between economic and linguistic symbolization and production" was both condensed and elaborated as the economic functions of credit were achieved through the figurative potentiality of language, with signs being substituted for substances, parts for wholes, attributes for entireties, to the point where the original propositions—gold, capital—could become effectively moot.[18] Thus "coined into currency" (Bagehot, 10:67) through metonymic processes, credit was also sustained by the written names that stood in for individuals and that procured the extension of capital, the deferral of payment, with further extenuations, further postponements, brought about by further exchanges of nominal values associated with the signatures of individuals who were far-flung, unseen and unknown, yet inextricably connected. In effect, then, the credit system transformed social as well as economic relations as the bonds of the cash nexus gave way to a more attenuated and inclusive "web-work of confidence and opinion" (Bagehot, 10:54) that was largely constituted by and through symbols and signs.

Accordingly, the character of the capitalist underwent a subtle transformation as well. By the mid-nineteenth century, the characteristics that made him worthy of receiving credit—namely, "the acquisition of a character for punctuality, or the exact performance of what one undertakes"[19]—no longer involved, in such a direct way, the ethos associated with the rise of industrial capitalism. If, in that older moral economy, worth derived principally from work, in the newer symbolic economy, it could come from qualities that were much more abstract, more detached. "Decency, regularity, . . . always . . . seen in the same place every day, and never failing in pecuniary engagements when called upon to discharge them" (Bagehot, 9:324) were the criteria for obtaining credit—that is, for contracting new obligations in the self-generating, self-perpetuating system of exchange in which the attributes that constituted creditworthiness generated more creditworthiness. Now, the capitalist could simply "deriv[e] an income from his credibility . . . and the confidence reposed in him" (9:324), Bagehot wrote, perfectly tautologically, eliding the fundamental question that credit raises: on what grounds?

To be sure, City men made much of the sound moral and mathematical principles on which the business of banking was conducted. But as Bagehot pointed out, "It is not only essential . . . that a bank should do its business well; it is at least as essential that it should be *thought* to do its business well" (9:395). Trust itself could keep the bank in business, and trust was to a considerable degree the effect of ledgers produced for scrutiny, of printed assurances concerning the minimization of risk, of published accreditations by the press and by Parliament—of representations, in a word. Where credit "confers an enormous power on *writing*"[20] and where writing itself "confers belief,"[21] the field for fraud is, of course, wide open. The fictional Montague Tigg took advantage of this: witness his Anglo-Bengalee Disinterested Loan and Life Assurance Company—"'paid up capital, according to the next prospectus' . . . 'A figure of two, and as many oughts after it as the printer can get into the same line'" (*MC*, ch.27). So did the real John Sadlier, the director of the Tipperary Bank and a model for Dickens's Mr. Merdle: instructing his brother "'to give a good appearance'" to the bank's accounts by "'treating the paid-up capital as £100,000 on the 31st of December 1855,'" Sadlier explained that such a practice, if "'kept very quiet,'" would make "'what at first was a kind of fiction . . . come gradually to be *bonâ fide*.'"[22]

While many mid-Victorian joint-stock banks became notorious for just such practices, fraud was not limited to those institutions. Any note could be struck up and made to appear bona fide, as the Bank of England was, and is, well aware. The legal term for the crime of circulating forgeries and pronouncing them to be true was, and remains, "uttering." Conversely, "uttering" is Carlyle's term for the "function" that the "Hero as a Man of Letters" performs, "which is . . . ever the highest. . . . He is uttering-forth, in such a way as he has, the inspired soul of him."[23] In between these polarities of darkness and light, "uttering" also means putting up goods for sale, bringing into currency—and, by extension, publishing, professing, puffing. In between, then, is a murky, inky zone in which all manner of transactions effected through writing take place and where there is hardly recourse to "solid ground" for determining their worth.

Although such a radical state of affairs could—and periodically did— arouse some alarm, the advantages of credit tended to eclipse the uncertainties. As Marx said, it seemed "as if this period found Fortunatus's purse."[24] Credit, according to many, was the catalyst for prosperity. It augmented Britain's already "illimitable powers of production," *The Economist* wrote (5 December 1857), using the hyperbolic terms that were becoming characteristic of discussions of credit. This "exaggerated language so often used respecting its national importance" made Mill, for one, uneasy (3:527). Nonetheless, he, too, agreed that credit "is indispensable for rendering the whole capital of a country productive" (3:529). Bagehot went further: "The refined means by which the movement [of capital] is effected is one of the nicest marvels of our commercial civilisation" (11:2); "The country leaps forward as if by magic" (9:124).

Part of this sense of magic was no doubt owing to the apparent effortlessness through which profits could accrue in a realm of exchange seemingly divorced from production. Labor and capital were, of course, involved in the exchange of credit, but middle-class investors were gaining incomes passively, as it were, from interest on previously earned surpluses, which joint-stock banks collected and extended to large-scale enterprises run by capitalists, who were themselves detached from the sources of capital they controlled.

If credit thus bore as tenuous a connection to labor as it did to gold, its very abstractness had tangible consequences. Generating profits that could materialize as visible wealth, credit could produce an economic foundation for a form of social respectability that itself became a means for obtaining more credit. Where debt, which is always coterminous with credit, was no longer felt as a negative condition of lack or constraint but as a positive one productive of wealth, and where the speculative nature of credit had come to be regarded not as a pervasive problem but as a widespread beneficial force, a profound transformation had occurred in Victorian society. Imbued with the modern magic of credit, this society was captivated by its sheer potentiality.

If the perceived—and the projected—results of the credit system tended to assuage doubts about its value, representations of credit as being creditworthy could reinforce belief in it. Here, again, is the entrenched circularity that so often obtains in credit relations and that gave rise to the power of such "belief-producers" as political economists and economic journalists, in whose writings "credit" became synonymous with "confidence" and became more credible as a result. Thus, while J. R. McCulloch observed, in his oft-reprinted *Principles of Political Economy* (1825), that "credit is the term used to express the trust or confidence placed in one individual by another when he assigns him property . . . without stipulating for its immediate payment" (70), by the 1850s, influential journals like *The Economist* treated the terms interchangeably, asserting, for example, that "confidence or credit" was "essential to all future production" and that this was "advantageous . . . in the natural system of society" (8 November 1856).

Of course, "confidence" itself is not unequivocal. It is also fundamental to the swindle, as Merdle, the proprietor of the "wonderful Bank" (*LD,* II, ch.25) well knows. Just as he is about to extort Mr. Dorrit's fortune, Merdle observes: "'There must be the strictest integrity and uprightness in these transactions; there must be the purest faith between man and man; there must be unimpeached and unimpeachable confidence; or business could not be carried on'" (*LD,* II, ch.16). This is an utterance precisely—and no different, on the face of it, from the position taken by *The Economist*. But then, as both Merdle and *The Economist* pointed out, business had to go on, even if "there [was] nothing, and c[ould] be nothing, to rely on but . . . honesty" (*The Economist,* 25 October 1856), and the grounds for confidence—"nothing"?—were in essence quite thin.

This became apparent in 1857, when a growing international economic crisis exposed the "hollowness" of the credit system.[25] Generated by a significant number of British joint-stock banks, which "'never possessed adequate capital, but carried on extensive transactions by fictitious credit'" (Evans,

71),[26] the crisis escalated as the press reported "once and once again . . . the story of reckless mismanagement on the part of directors, and of the sacrifice of helpless depositors" (Evans, 36). With confidence being shaken by the very medium that had sustained it and the crisis threatening to bring the economy crashing down, Parliament passed emergency legislation authorizing the extension of the Bank's fiduciary issue by £2 million "'for the purpose of sustaining commercial credit in a period of extreme pressure'" (Evans, 67). The expedient had the desired effect and eventually restimulated the re-extension of credit and the renovation of the economy on the basis of paper inscribed with symbols and signs. That the credit system could—and did—regain and for the most part maintain the confidence on which the economy and society depended is a testament to the power of the (mere) sign to generate belief and create the very substance of the real.

## A CAPITAL NAME

Dickens knew the potentiality of the symbolic economy full well. Its uncertainties were among the liberating conditions that made it possible for him to write in a "language with the shackles removed," language that "becomes capable of constant, rapid, and virtually illimitless multiplications of its own effects and forms in new inventions and combinations and configurations."[27] This language is play—"'Capital fun!'" (*MC*, ch.27)—and it is speculative— "'A capital idea!'" (*MC*, ch.27). Circulating in the literary market and the money market, it is the self-generating, self-authenticating, self-sustaining, self-enhancing source of identity and value through which Dickens continually created and recreated himself and acquired what literally became a "capital name" (*LCD*, 8 May 1855).

To be sure, the making of Dickens was as much the result of his remarkable ardor for achievement and his extraordinary capacity for self-discipline as it was of his ability to recognize, create, and exploit "contingent opportunities."[28] The writer whose first novel instigated a "Bozmania" always required of himself that he "Work" and "Do."[29] This tension persisted throughout his career, but in the late 1840s, its features began to change. During this period when the economy was becoming more "literary," as it were—more dependent on the representation and the production of value through the exchange of written symbols and signs—Dickens himself became a literary capitalist in the full sense of the phrase, conducting his growing enterprises in a way that had close parallels with the "new art" (*The Economist*, 25 October 1856) of commerce, as the City itself did not fail to note.

Reviewing the first installment of *Dombey and Son* (1846–48), *The Economist* observed that although "genius and observation are all the store [Dickens] possesses"—he was judged to be "deficient" in "all [the] requisites" of erudition—"with the wand of an enchanter he may turn these gifts into gold" (*CH*, 214). Whatever the merits of this judgment of Dickens's capacities, the prediction was not far off the mark: sales throughout the serial run were consistently "brilliant" (*LCD*, 2 September 1847), and by June of 1848, *Dombey and Son* had brought Dickens the considerable sum of £9,165, which, for the first time in his career, was not tied to paying off debts.[30] Nor was *The Economist*'s view of the facility with which he could covert his "genius" to hard cash entirely mistaken. Although Dickens had planned *Dombey and Son* with an unprecedented degree of shrewdness—capitalizing on the sensation that had been created by the improvised death of Little Nell and by the carefully contrived death of little Paul—the "magic" of advertising and publicity also played a significant role.[31] Remarkable for its aggressiveness, the promotional campaign extended to the United States, where *Dombey and Son* far surpassed *The Old Curiosity Shop* in popularity and sales. Closer to home, the novel garnered widespread acclaim, summed up in the pronouncement that this was "the masterpiece of Charles Dickens" (*CH*, 299) and augmented by Forster, whose elaboration of the "power" the novel manifested, which "is even yet not fully developed in its higher and more ideal tendencies," could "raise the interest" (*CH*, 233, 232) for future novels as much as little Paul's death had for the next number of *Dombey*. Dickens was more than satisfied (for the time being). "The profits, brave indeed, . . . are more than the utmost I expected"; "Dombey has been the greatest success I have ever achieved" (*LCD*, 5 September 1847; 17 June 1848).

While one of the direct consequences of *Dombey and Son* was that Dickens began saving money for the first time, another was the increasingly indirect way in which he came to gain more of it. After 1848, he started buying Consols—a prudent investment, given that they were issued by the government and yielded only 3¼ percent interest.[32] Still, this was interest—it was money that accrued effortlessly (magically?) from past earnings—and this tendency to capitalize on his savings extended to the republication of his previous novels in a Cheap Edition, which was the first venture in which Dickens put the imaginary capital he had amassed to work. Set in motion in 1847, when the success of *Dombey and Son* was certain, the Cheap Edition brought in £800 in 1848 alone. After that, "Dickens's significant earnings for his writing [came] from the four reprint series, the 'Cheap,' 'Library,' 'People's,' and 'Charles Dickens' editions"—earnings that Dickens gained with hardly any new investment in work.[33]

## 9: Funny Money

Naturally, he did continue to "Work" and to "Do," starting in on *David Copperfield* (1849–50) soon after the conclusion of *Dombey*. The "favourite child" (1867 Preface) in which Dickens vested one of his favorite and most enduring views of himself, *David Copperfield* was, of course, a crucial item in his reputation, which, though peerless, was not untarnished. Indeed, the amount of money Dickens was making could reflect poorly not only on him but on other men of letters, who feared that his example could make literature "tempt[ing] to speculators" and reduce it to being no more than "a trade."[34] Thus, inasmuch as *David Copperfield* was Dickens's contribution to the contemporary debate surrounding the "honour and dignity" of "Literature,"[35] it was also a novel in which he was personally concerned with establishing that writing was a "worthy . . . avocation"[36] and, even more fundamentally, that it was, in fact, work. In this last particular, however, Dickens was singularly unsuccessful, as several critics have noted.[37] What I suggest here is that it was Dickens's very failure to represent work that, paradoxically, contributed to the credit and confidence he gained at the time.

■ ■ ■

Although David, like Dickens, straggles into literature more out of a need to make money than out of any particular sense of vocation, David's becoming "fortunate in worldly matters" (*DC,* ch.42) does call attention to a question that could be pressing for Dickens, as well as for a society suffused with the "magic" of credit: namely, how it is that money is made? Understandably, Dickens makes no recourse to genius, a quality that can be as readily deflated to imply no more than a knack as it can be inflated to suggest singular aptitude. Nor does he treat the notion of talent, which is inherently problematic by virtue of its association with money. Thus, in "review[ing] his life," David affirms, "I have never believed it possible that any natural or improved ability can claim immunity from the companionship of the steady, plain, hard-working qualities, and hope to gain its end" (*DC,* ch.42); and in "review[ing] his life" again in a speech twenty years later, Dickens would say, "My own invention or imagination, such as it is, I can most truthfully assure you, would never have served me as it has, but for the habit of commonplace, humble, patient, daily, toiling, drudging attention" (*Speeches,* 406).

Yet even as Dickens espoused the value of work, he could also speak with some embarrassment about "the labours (if I may call them so) that you hold in such generous esteem" (*Speeches,* 20). Echoed by Agnes when she says, "'The labour [of teaching] is so pleasant, that it is scarcely grateful in me to call it by that name'" (*DC,* ch.60), this view finds another expression in

David, for whom "writing, has its own charms" (*DC,* ch.62). David's references to the "wear and tear" (*DC,* ch.42) of his occupation notwithstanding, if writing, along with its correlative, teaching, is "labor" in *David Copperfield,* it is singularly unlaborious, and the manner of David's becoming "fortunate in worldly matters" is rather unlike anything that resembles "Work."

Whether writing is a form of "Do[ing]" is another question—or do fortunes accrue "as if by magic"? According to David and Dickens, the answer to the latter question is no: "Perseverance" is "the source of his success" (*DC,* ch.42). Writing is not just "Do[ing]"; it is "How to Do It." Nevertheless, this writing remains undone in *David Copperfield,* which begins with David's merely "record[ing]" the record of his birth and proceeds with few other references to the act of writing.[38] Apart from this contradiction, there is a further peculiarity in the affirmation that writing is an exemplary form of "Do[ing]" in that it takes the static form of the noun "perseverance." This nominal form, which contravenes the gist of what Dickens is affirming, also suggests something more: it gestures toward that condition of Victorian society in which character was coming to be divorced from action, and worth could accrue from the attributes of individuals rather than from direct investment in work.

While Dickens would come to regard this segregation as crippling and divisive, in *David Copperfield,* the priority given to character over action[39] contributed, paradoxically, to conferring on the novelist what Carlyle defined as "the first and chief characteristic of a Hero: he is heartily *in earnest.*"[40] A word that conveys the "importance of work to character"[41] (Welsh, 75), as well as integrity of character, "earnest" is what David proclaims himself to have been and to be: "There is no substitute for thorough-going, ardent, and sincere earnestness" (*DC,* ch.42). In view of the absence of "Work[ing] or "Do[ing]" by writing in the novel, the gospel that David so vehemently preaches—and that finds a peculiar echo in Dickens's later assertion "as earnest as I and David Copperfield" (*LCD,* 15 February 1855)—does, of course, ring rather hollow. However, far from discrediting David, or Dickens, the lack of earnestness in action can have quite the opposite effect. Indeed, it is the very erasure of the process of writing that contributes to the seeming presence of the writer and to his apparent "earnestness."

This erasure and its effects are determined by the way in which the first-person narrative not only solicits identification with David but also, in situating the reader to participate with David in the recollection of his life (which is also a recreation of it), suppresses the act of creating a representation (in the very act of that creation). Thereby overcoming the degrees of mediation between reader and protagonist, the form of the novel further creates an effect of immediacy and intimacy with David that extended to Dickens. "It is

## 9: Funny Money

the whole world rather than a bit of it which you see before you" (*CH*, 261), said one reviewer; "there is, moreover," wrote another, "an air of reality pervading the whole book" (*CH*, 246); "there is a candour and fair play in him" (*CH*, 270), observed a third, conflating novelist and protagonist entirely and attesting to both characters' "earnestness" ("as earnest as I and David Copperfield")—or to a thoroughly credible effect of "earnestness" created through fiction.

Little wonder, then, that this is the Charles Dickens who was the focus of the recent £10 note—the novelist whose "earnestness" seemed not just exemplary but unassailable (for the moment) and who was also credited at that time with "comprehending the national character" (*CH*, 244). In effect, what the Bank's representation of Dickens amounted to was a re-invention of his invention of his character and a re-accreditation of the terms in which it was accredited. But for all the degrees of mediation involved therein, the Bank also presented this image of Dickens as real.

For it was the "real" Dickens who backed the currency, officially speaking. Although no existing visual materials could simply be reproduced—to do so would facilitate counterfeiting—graphic elements that appear on the £10 note were modeled as closely as possible on items collected in the Dickens House Museum—on details of lampshades, pen nibs, and the like. The images that dominate the note reiterate this commitment to visual accuracy. Thus, while the cricket illustration is virtually R. W. Buss's own, only in reverse, the portrait is based not on a painting but on a more mimetic medium, a photograph from 1862. And, having moved this close to reality, we arrive, at the bottom of the portrait, to the real thing: Dickens's signature, which *is* one of Dickens's own. It is also the singular and necessary exception to the rule of close approximation that governs the note. For, had the bank produced an imitation—that is, a forgery—it would not only have committed the offense of uttering but also subverted its own project of issuing currency that will "'command . . . confidence'" by violating one of the primary foundations on which the creditworthiness of this note rests: the imprimatur of the "real" Dickens, the "authenticity" of the cultural icon who backs it and whose written character—in the multiple, converging senses of the word—confers symbolic value on the £10 note and contributes to sustaining confidence in the paper pound.

■ ■ ■

Dickens had a name for the logic that obtains on the banknote. He called it "the Forge-bellows of Puffery" (*LCD*, 15 July 1854), compressing in this figure the uncanny power of language to manufacture, as it were, out of nothing, the very reality it purports to represent. Unpacked further, this figure also suggests how writing confers credibility, how interest and further accreditation accrue from circulation, how trust becomes confidence, and how the outcome of all of this (mere) "Puffery" is the very substance of worth. That the workings of these "Forge-bellows" can be consonant with those of forgery is certainly critical, but at the same time not quite to the point at this particular juncture in Dickens's career, when his reputation was at an apex and his name could itself do the work of those bellows.

More pertinent is the increasing ambivalence with which Dickens's growing capacity to forge credit and confidence through fiction was coming to be regarded in some quarters. As one reviewer observed, "Dickens's very name gives a sanction to everything to which he lends it. He could *do* many things among his fellow creatures, for no other reason than that he wrote *Pickwick* and *Copperfield*" (*CH*, 294). While this critic points to the authority Dickens had acquired from his earlier works, the stress here is not on his achievements, but rather on what Dickens might "do" by virtue of the name that he had gained "for no other reason" than he had written popular novels; and although the commanding influence of the name "Charles Dickens" appears to be certain, the "doing" remains an open field.

What Dickens did was to launch *Household Words,* through which he became a veritable construction conglomerate in the belief-building industry and bolstered his bank account even more. Providing Dickens with a steady income for the first time in his career, the journal also established him as a literary capitalist as he became an employer of writers, whose labors, though remunerated, brought the proprietor the lion's share of the profits. Of course, Dickens himself did work: he wrote scores of articles, reviewed hundreds of manuscripts, and closely followed the business of the weekly. But as one of his regular contributors remarked, "'all good things in *Household Words* were credited to Dickens,'" and, for all his efforts, Dickens's credit exceeded the investment he put in.[42] Moreover, where the policy of anonymity was more like one of "'*mono*nymity'" (ibid.), not only did Dickens's name acquire greater influence through (mere) circulation, but also "Charles Dickens" could, in itself, perform "the Whole Duty of Man in a commercial country" (*LD,* ch.13), as the advertisers who came to flock to the enterprise well knew. But it was just as his name was becoming "as much a 'Household Word' in every sequestered hamlet lying between the most extreme points of our *home* islands, as it [was] in the metropolis" (*CH,* 382), and "Charles Dickens" was coming to be identified with anything the topically exhaustive journal covered, that one of the associations its proprietor promoted was that of his enterprise with the Bank of England and of its issue with his denomination.

One such account, "The Old Lady in Threadneedle Street," written with W. H. Wills, is typical of those articles in which Dickens set out to reveal the inner workings of a variety of enterprises and institutions of mid-Victorian Britain. At the same time, however, "The Old Lady" calls as much attention to the act of testifying to the reality behind the public field of perception to which the investigative reporter has gained privileged access as it does to the facts themselves. Thus, while Dickens notes that "no tyro need be told that ["flimsies"] are representatives of weightier value," he *does* go about informing John Bull that they really are backed by the "piles of gold bars" that the reporter has seen "set cross-wise" in the Bank's vaults "like sandwiches at supper." Moreover, although the familiar shape that money takes certainly does demystify the aura surrounding gold, as well as reinforcing the public's "habit of trusting" in paper money, the testimony itself appears to draw on another habit—John's "habit of trusting" the novels that he regularly consumed at home after supper and that typically presented themselves as being "substantially true" (*BH*, Preface). If the credit Dickens was enjoying at the time tends to weigh in his favor in his reassurances concerning the Bank, the scales tip even further in his direction as that venerable institution, rather than being the model for literature to copy, is instead notable for its resemblance to the model enterprise of Dickens.

The Bank, Wills goes on to explain in "The Old Lady," is "an extensive printer, engraver, bookbinder and publisher," involved in a "publishing business as extensive as it is profitable and peculiar"—but not that peculiar since it publishes "Numbers," "serials," and "popular prints," which are produced on "steam-printing machines" just like those "we use for this publication." That the processes of printing money and periodical literature are similar is perfectly plausible, but in the terms of this analogy, one of the "great distinction[s]" of the Bank turns out to be its likeness to *Household Words*. Deflating the Bank's mystique, much as those "sandwiches" domesticate gold, the comparison simultaneously inflates the interest of Dickens's publication, which not only "reviews" "the Great Woman's literature" but also, it turns out, issues the "flimsies" that are "sought" with an "eagerness" that "surpasses that displayed for the productions of the greatest geniuses who ever enlightened the world."

"Reviewing is, alas, too often mere surface work," Wills observes in "A Review of a Popular Publication, In the Searching Style," a self-consciously witty analysis of a banknote that examines its face and then "penetrate[s] below it," where "we shall ... set a bright example of profundity" by "speak[ing] of the paper." While paper itself was (and remains) crucial to the authenticity of banknotes, Wills gets to such technicalities only after the critical business of reading "the superficies" of the banknote has been done. For it is, of course, on the surface that the inscriptions that constitute the value of this "popular publication" appear. "Few can rise from a critical examination of the literary contents of this sheet without being forcibly struck by the power, combined with the exquisite fineness of the writing," Wills writes:

> It strikes conviction at once. It dispels all doubts, and relieves all objections. There is a pithy terseness in the sentences; a downright, direct, straight-forward, coming to the point, which would be wisely imitated in much of the contemporaneous literature that obtains currency (though not as much). Here we have no circumlocution, no discursive pedantry, no smell of the lamp; the figures, though wholly derived from the East (being Arabic numerals), are distinct and full of purpose; and if the writing abounds in flourishes, which it does, these are not rhetorical, but boldly graphic: struck with a nervous decision of style, which, instead of obscuring the text and meaning, convinces the reader that he who traced them when promising to pay the sum of five, ten, twenty, thirty, forty, fifty, one hundred, or a thousand pounds, means honestly and instantly to keep his word: that he *will* pay it to the bearer on demand, without one moment's hesitation.

In short (!), the banknote materializes the epistemological and ethical ideal of the word as a bond. But while this "Review" regards Bank of England notes as epitomizing a gold standard of representation that all "contemporaneous literature" should emulate, the superiority of this model is superseded by the superiority of the critic: they are "judged by the golden rule of our greatest bard"—Shakespeare, presumably, but it is equally possible that this bard is Dickens, who appears here not just as the arbiter of the value of this publication, but as the author of the note. For what the written characters described in the "Review" attest to is the character of Charles Dickens: standing out "boldly graphic," they bear the impress of Dickens's consciousness of the pictorial, physical quality of writing[43] and his distinctive mid-century style—the parataxis, the momentum, the driving, emphatic will of his writing. It is as though *his* substance were embodied in the signs themselves, in the way that a signature is shorthand for a person and acts "like a thumbprint guaranteeing the aura of the authentic."[44]

Whether Wills consciously imitated Dickens is not clear.[45] This uncertainty gives one pause and calls attention, again, to how readily authenticity can be struck up in the marketplace of representation. If the pirated "Inimitable" was well aware of this problem, the Bank of England became newly alert to it at mid-century, when it decided to produce notes on which the signature of the chief cashier was no longer handwritten and addressed the problem of the greater liability of "flimsies" to forgery by introducing an image of high artistic quality that would make counterfeiting less likely. In 1850, the Bank commissioned Daniel Maclise to design a vignette, and in 1855, the new notes featuring his Britannia went into circulation.

Although Dickens makes no mention of Maclise in this connection, the fact that Maclise had painted the *Nickleby* portrait (1839) is already suggestive: described as a "'looking-glass . . . facsimile'" by Thackeray, the image, reproduced and circulated for sale, had contributed earlier to the public transformation of the eponymous Boz into the "real" Charles Dickens.[46] Ten years later, Dickens was undoubtedly aware of his friend's role in the Bank's latest efforts to prevent forgery. They were traveling companions in June of 1850, and a number of articles concerned with the Bank appeared in *Household Words* in July and September of that year. Several of these detail the Bank's costly experiments in the "art-manufacture" of banknotes, pursued with a view toward baffling forgers; others retell notorious schemes in the "art of Bank note forgery"; all reflect the earlier preoccupation of "the only true Boz" with preventing piracy; and some repeatedly remind readers that the Bank's goal was to produce what the Bank itself called "inimitable notes."[47] The opportunity to point out that Dickens and the Bank shared a denomination, as it were, appears to have been too good for the self-styled "Inimitable" to pass up. Given the facts of "inimitability," this particular conceit appears to be written tongue-in-cheek. At the same time, though, not only does the conceit point to an interchangeability of Dickens and money; it also identifies Dickens with a standard of authenticity and suggests that the value of truth is conferred by Dickens himself—or by his own (mere) "capital name."

To observe that this actually became the case over a century later—that the representation of the Inimitable serves to ensure what the Bank continues to call the "inimitability"[48] of notes—is to point to a development that was, once again, fitting with regard to the position that Dickens was taking at the time: at a peak of confidence, he was exploiting, even flaunting, his ability—or talent or genius—to be a source and arbiter of value. Indeed, although Dickens's direct identification of himself with money may be surprising in view of his recent efforts in *David Copperfield* to affirm that he earnestly earned it, the difference between Dickens's representation of money in *Household Words* and his representation of his character in the novel is more a difference in degree than in kind. The novelist who was committed to reproducing "the exact truth" was always equally capable of giving an "air of reality that would oblige the reader to believe in his fictions" (*LCD*, 13 May 1857).

Believe for the most part we do. Dickens's capacity for closing the fault line between perdurable reality and abstract textuality is one of the most palpable effects of his will and his style. Dickens "imparts to a fictitious being an absolute and visible reality" (*CH,* 228), one reviewer had written in 1848. In 1850, Dickens had imparted his individuality not only to David Copperfield but also to paper money—to literary characters, both. And in both cases, it was Dickens's invention of himself, his writing, his "capital name" that served as the "solid ground" for these representations. What occurs in this kind of "realism" is not so much a representation of an existing reality as a substitution for and a displacement of it. Dickens's works—his words—come to stand in for the "real," much as the paper money that circulates takes the place of the gold that remains locked away in the Bank's vaults.

But while the Bank could point to the gold in those vaults, that dimension of reality is flattened out elsewhere in the realm of representation, where any authority can be contested. "It is useless to discuss whether the conduct and character of the girl seem natural or unnatural, probable or improbable, right or wrong," Dickens had written in exasperated reply to critics of *Oliver Twist;* "IT IS TRUE" (*OT,* Preface). Maybe yes; maybe no. But where "blustering assertion goes for proof, half the world over" (*LD,* ch.10), how could the truth—the *real* thing—be ascertained? Dickens's own capacity for "blustering assertion" may have been ample, his power to prove consequential, but where the authority to assert "the" truth is constituted by the inherently uncertain power of writing, any testimony concerning this truth is borne by the same media that can confer credit and destroy it. And for all of his power to wield the "Forge-bellows of Puffery," Dickens soon found the degree to which the "Engine of Puffery" (*LCD,* 30 May 1854) was beyond his control, as his reputation became caught up in a vicious cycle of hostile critical opinion,[49] one outcome of which was that he was charged with uttering—that is, with profiting from "Mr. Merdle's Complaint."

Dickens brought this charge on himself to some extent by calling attention to *Little Dorrit*'s unprecedented sales: "In the Preface to Bleak House, I remarked that I had never had so many readers. In the Preface to its next successor, Little Dorrit, I have still to repeat the same words." At least one reviewer took up the cue: "Apart from the question of taste . . . the very prominent announcement of a large sale of books looks a little like latent suspicion that it was not quite deserved. 'Oh, I am very well,' replied Mr. Merdle, after deliberating about it; 'I am as well as I usually am!' and the man went and cut his throat forthwith. This may serve to remind Mr. Dickens that uncalled-for asseverations of well-doing do not prove the heart to be quite at ease."[50] It was not at ease: the "'*Restlessness*'" that was "'always driving'" Dickens did not relent; nor did his "'low spirits'" lift (quoted in Forster, 3:184). Whether he was afflicted with "Mr. Merdle's Complaint" was another matter, however. Near the end of his life, Dickens said that he was.

In "A Fly-Leaf in a Life" (1869), in which Dickens recalled the crisis that beset him in the mid-1850s—his feeling "giddy, jarred, shaken, faint, uncertain of voice and sight and tread and touch, and dull of spirit"—he transcribed, word for word from *Little Dorrit,* the "Pressure" that was "so entirely satisfactory" an explanation for "Mr. Merdle's Complaint" and that "literally" explained Dickens's own frame of mind at the time: the "Pressure" "you brought yourself to by work! work! work!," by "devot[ing] yourself to the pursuit of wealth" and "overdoing it" (*UT,* 353-44). Noting "the remarkable coincidence between my case, in the general mind, and one Mr. Merdle's" (*UT,* 353), Dickens appears to have been remarking—through the peculiar phrase "the general mind"—on the accuracy of some critics' perception of a "coincidence" between himself and Merdle. "To be sure," Dickens added immediately, "Mr. Merdle was a swindler, forger, and thief, and my calling had been of a less harmful (and less remunerative nature); but," he continued, even more ambiguously, "it was all one for that" (*UT,* 353). "It": does this word refer to the "complaint" or to the "calling"—or to both, since they were in so many respects linked? Looking back at his career, continuing to practice his own highly equivocal forms of utterance, Dickens could see himself and the confidence artist becoming indistinguishable. This is where "you brought yourself to"; "There you were!" (*UT,* 354).

■ ■ ■

And here we are, faced with an ineluctably ambiguous character on the Dickens £10 note, which now looks even more like "an apt symbol for the way the features of the past may be hidden *and* distorted in the present."[51] In fact, some are not entirely hidden: Dickens's multifarious modes of utterance are represented by the titles of his novels, which appear in small, faint print on the front of the note, swirled behind the crucial text "I Promise to Pay," thereby recapitulating the way that his representations could, and did, stand in place of and produce the value of the real. To be sure, this banknote is no longer current. The peculiar moment of exchanging its particular representation of Dickens for any number of representations by Dickens (*David Copperfield? Little Dorrit?*) has passed and with it any vertiginous implications that may have arisen from such a moment of exchange. But then the moment of Dickens and the currency of Dickens have not passed, so it is fitting that a prototypically modern Dickens should utter the never-final word:

*Tatiana M. Holway*

I do not strain the truth. . . . a mere spoken word—a mere syllable thrown into the air—may go on reverberating through illimitable space for ever and ever. (*Speeches*, 399)

## NOTES

1. Derrick Byatt, 9, quoting the Governor of the Bank of England at the time. Byatt's *Promises to Pay* is an official publication of the bank.
2. Quoted in Philip Collins, *Dickens: The Critical Heritage*, 205. Subsequent references are made parenthetically in the text, cited as *CH*.
3. Roger Withington and B. R. James, *The New £10 Note*, 24, 21.
4. Byatt, *Promises to Pay*, 7.
5. T. J. Brown, Communications Officer for the Bank of England, letter of 19 May 1997.
6. *Nicholas Nickleby* Advertiser, no. 12, in *The Life and Adventures of Nicholas Nickleby*, ed. Michael Slater, facsimile edition.
7. See Gerard Curtis, "Dickens in the Visual Market"; Curtis mentions the Dickens £10 note in his conclusion.
8. Marc Shell, *Art and Money*, 84.
9. J. S. Mill, *Collected Works*, 4:79. Subsequent references are made parenthetically in the text.
10. Byatt, *Promises*, 132.
11. Shell, *Money, Language, and Thought*, 7.
12. Discussion of the incredulity with which paper money had earlier been regarded and the many reasons for the lack of confidence in commerce as well as currency is beyond the scope of this chapter. Likewise, the creation of confidence is a much more complex matter than can be treated here. For particulars regarding the development of mid-Victorian attitudes toward paper money, see Patrick Brantlinger, *Fictions of State*, chapter 3.
13. Simmel, *The Philosophy of Money*, 179.
14. Bagehot, *Collected Works*, 9:307. Subsequent references are made parenthetically in the text.
15. Factors contributing to the growth of the joint-stock banking system are usefully summarized by Mary Poovey in her Introduction to *The Financial System in Nineteenth-Century Britain*. For changes in laws concerning indebtedness, which were as crucial as those that encouraged joint-stock banking, see V. Markham Lester, *Victorian Insolvency*.
16. These included promissory notes, bills of exchange, accommodation bills, and others, which are explicated in detail in Mill, *Principles*, 3:527ff., as well as John Eatwell et al., eds., *The New Palgrave Dictionary of Economics*.
17. T. H. Williams, "Observations on Money," 66.
18. Shell, *Money*, 4.
19. J. R. McCulloch, *Principles of Political Economy*, 76.
20. Jean-Joseph Goux, *Coiners of Language*, 149.
21. Shell, *Money*, 7.
22. Quoted in George Robb, *White Collar Crime*, 62.

9: *Funny Money*

23. Thomas Carlyle, "The Hero as Man of Letters," 189.
24. Karl Marx, *Capital*, Vol. 1, 648.
25. D. Morier Evans, *History of the Commercial Crisis*, 1. Subsequent references are made parenthetically in the text.
26. Here and further down, Evans is quoting a Parliamentary Select Committee appointed to inquire into the causes of the crisis.
27. Steven Marcus, "Language into Structure," 24. I am indebted to Steven Marcus for his comments on an early version of this chapter, and for much else.
28. Robert L. Patten, *Charles Dickens and His Publishers*, 333.
29. There are fifteen such entries of "Work" and "Do" in Dickens's diary of September of 1839. The diary is reproduced in Volume 1 of the Pilgrim Edition of his letters (*LCD*).
30. Patten, *Charles Dickens*, 188.
31. David Musselwhite, "Dickens: The Commodification of the Novelist," 144.
32. Patten, *Charles Dickens*, 186.
33. Ibid., 198.
34. "The Condition of Authors in England, Germany, and France," 285–95.
35. See, for example, Poovey, "The Man-of-Letters Hero: *David Copperfield* and the Professional Writer" (in *Uneven Developments*), as well as Mark Cronin, "Henry Gowan, William Makepeace Thackeray, and 'The Dignity of Literature' Controversy."
36. K. J. Fielding, ed., *The Speeches of Charles Dickens*, 20; henceforth cited in the text as *Speeches*.
37. See, among others, Alexander Welsh, *The City of Dickens*, 78.
38. An apparent exception occurs in the famous passage in which David describes his struggles with stenography, but the exception is only apparent, since what we get here is, typically, product without process, "a procession of new horrors, called arbitrary characters" (ch.38).
39. Cf. Jonathan Arac's discussion of the development of character at "the expense of action" in "Hamlet, *Little Dorrit*, and the History of Character," 93.
40. Carlyle, *Hero as a Man of Letters*, 225.
41. Welsh, *City of Dickens*, 75.
42. John Hollingshead, quoted in Schlicke, *Oxford Reader's Companion*, 284.
43. For discussion of Dickens's acute awareness of the physical, graphic qualities of writing, see, for example, Marcus, "Language into Structure," 228–32.
44. Shell, *Art*, 86.
45. The "Review" is not in any collection of Dickens's writings from *Household Words*. Anne Lohrli attributes it to Wills in her index to the journal.
46. See Curtis, "Dickens in the Visual Market," 217ff.
47. W. H. Wills and George Dodd, "I Promise to Pay"; W. H. Wills, "Two Chapters on Banknote Forgeries: 1"; Charles Dickens and H. W. Wills, "Two Chapters on Bank-Note Forgeries: 2."
48. Byatt, *Promises*, 205.
49. See Collins's introductory essay to *Dickens: The Critical Heritage* for an account of this "onslaught" (13), which came from many different sources and had many diverse features, as well as George Ford, *Dickens and His Readers*, chapter 7.
50. Quoted in Ford, *Dickens and His Readers*, 87.
51. Jay Clayton, *Dickens in Cyberspace*, 160.

# 10

# Enumeration and Exhaustion

Taking Inventory in *The Old Curiosity Shop*

JAMES BUZARD

> He excels in inventories of poor furniture, and is learned in pawnbrokers' tickets.
> —WALTER BAGEHOT
>
> Mr. Shandy's clock was nothing to mine [i.e., Master Humphrey's Clock], wind, wind, wind, always winding I am; and day and night the alarum is ringing in my ears, warning me that it must not run down.
> —CHARLES DICKENS
>
> Of the making of many books there is no end.
> —ECCLESIASTES

Inventory: traceable to Late Latin *inventarium,* "a finding out," or "enumeration," from the Latin *invenire,* "to come upon, find, invent." The word preserves the archaic meaning of invention, whose modern sense of "devising, contriving, or making up" rests upon this buried, contrary idea of "coming upon or finding . . . of finding out; discovery (whether accidental, or the result of search and effort)" (*OED*).

■ ■ ■

*Item.*

Coming upon, or making up?
Charles Dickens's novel *The Old Curiosity Shop,* serialized between April 1840 and February 1841, begins with Master Humphrey's account of meet-

## 10: Enumeration and Exhaustion

ing by chance a lost little girl in the London street, of escorting her back to her grandfather's shop, of conversing with the grandfather and mingling with the dissolute Fred Trent and Dick Swiveller, the loyal Kit, the fiendish Quilp. Yet if we are to believe what he says upon concluding his narration, none of that ever happened. I refer here to Master Humphrey's notorious announcement (in the dialogue ensuing *The Old Curiosity Shop* in Dickens's periodical *Master Humphrey's Clock*) that his "share ... in the pages we have read" was not, after all, that of the chance discoverer of Nell and her old grandparent, that his initial appearance was "fictitious," and that he is in fact the "single gentleman" who entered the narrative in its thirty-fourth chapter, that old grandparent's long-expatriated younger brother who searches England—too late—in hopes of being reunited with his kin.[1]

It has been easy for critics and editors to discount this "confession" as an afterthought irreconcilable with the tale it follows up, but then a standard of narrative consistency would seem ludicrously misapplied to such a wayward and improvised text as *The Old Curiosity Shop*. And to engage in the thought-experiment of taking the confession seriously for even one minute is to realize that its being "true" would mean that the narrator of this work never saw Nell Trent alive—for the "single gentleman" arrives with his search party at Nell's final resting place (ch.72) two days after her death, to find her lying in state and his brother insensible to anything but Nell. Between his entrance into the story and this tardy arrival, he personally interacts with most of the other characters, but a living Nell has no place on any inventory of those he has dealt with. He made her up. And knowing her only as a corpse, he has retrospectively invented an illusion of a walking and talking and weeping and laughing Nell that seems permanently out of place in the world of the living. Inventing her, he has made a "oner," something wonderful and unique. Nell is a "wax-work child" (ch.31) of "classical" repose (ch.27), placed in the domain of mutability and history, "surrounded and beset by everything that was foreign to its nature" and endowed with a spiritual prestige befitting her incipient angel-hood, an allure by contrast with which all the contents of that historical domain fade into undifferentiated "heaps of fantastic things," all its actors into "a crowd of wild grotesque companions," all its events into so much "useless strife" (ch.17).[2] "It would be a curious speculation," Master Humphrey says to himself at the end of the opening chapter, "to imagine her in her future life, holding her solitary way among a crowd of wild grotesque companions; the only pure, fresh youthful object in the throng. It would be curious to find" (*OCS*, ch.1)—but he interrupts himself there. If Master Humphrey is the single gentleman, then the speculation is a sham: he already knows that Nell has no future life, no way to make. However many pages are

James Buzard

heaped up, however much narrative invention is expended to distract us from the fact, there is nothing to find: Dickens seems to have abidingly felt as much in the writing of this most curious of books, a tale that makes a mockery of the curiosity on which narrative feeds. Or rather, there is only one thing: but whether that one thing is the black hole of Nell's always inevitable absence or the surviving "single gentleman" who creates and destroys her—who else but Dickens, terribly alone at his desk?—neither of these "oners" can make up a narrative, or an inventory, all by itself.

■ ■ ■

*Item.*
  "The author's object in this work was to place before the reader a constant succession of characters and incidents; to paint them in as vivid colours as he could command; and to render them, at the same time, life-like and amusing." So wrote Dickens in the Preface to the 1837 volume edition of *Pickwick Papers,* a work of episodic serial fiction whose miraculous comic inventiveness may be described by the trope of the inventory—a list of separate items ("characters and incidents") placed one after another, preserved in their plurality. All the items on an inventory contribute to a total value, but, arrayed in succession, they are amenable to line-item evaluation, and the value of the whole is nothing more than the sum of their separate worths. "The publication of this book in monthly numbers," Dickens noted, "rendered it an object of paramount importance that, while the different incidents were linked together by a chain of interest strong enough to prevent their appearing unconnected . . . the general design should be so simple as to sustain no injury from this detached and desultory form of publication" (*PP,* Preface). A collection of installments essentially "complete in [themselves]" might strive for only the modest aim of a "tolerably harmonious whole" (*PP,* Preface); literary creativity simply meant, in this instance, the capacity for continual production of new material, the capacity to keep extending a list. "And if it be objected to the Pickwick Papers, that they are merely a series of adventures, in which the scenes are ever changing, and the characters come and go like the men and women we encounter in the real world," Dickens added, "they claim to be nothing else" (*PP,* Preface).
  Inventory proliferates: it implies a point of view alert to differences, interested and indeed invested in the difference it makes to move from one item to another and to tally each judiciously. If one pays close enough attention and is sufficiently discriminating, missing no chance to exploit a distinction and so add a new line, there is no intrinsic reason why an inventory, like a picaresque

191

## 10: Enumeration and Exhaustion

novel, cannot be prolonged almost indefinitely. This was a consideration that arose during the serial run of *Pickwick,* once the work's phenomenal success was assured—for, surely, there was no internal logic in the text, no constraining plot, requiring the rounding off and closure of its narrative at any particular point: why should it not be extended as long as the market would bear? ("Which nothing but death will terminate" are, in fact, the last words of *Pickwick Papers.*) Yet in an announcement accompanying the tenth installment (in December 1836), the author made clear "his intention to adhere to his original pledge of confining his work to twenty numbers," in spite of his having received, as he no doubt took pleasure in recounting, "every temptation to exceed the limits he first assigned to himself, that brilliant success, an enormous and increasing sale, the kindest notice, and the most extensive popularity, can hold out." (Dickens here indulges in a little inventory of "reasons for self-satisfaction.") Having to make this decision probably heightened Dickens's awareness that, short of death, and as long as the work enjoyed its success, nothing but his authorial fiat would put a stop to the story and bring its wayfaring characters to rest. His situation was like that of Mr. Codlin in *The Old Curiosity Shop,* the Punch-and-Judy patterer on whom alone rests "the responsibility of deciding on [the puppet show's] length and of protracting or expediting the time for the hero's final triumph over the enemy of mankind, according as he judged that the after-crop of halfpence would be plentiful or scant" (*OCS,* ch.17). In the event, a death did halt the forward progress of the Pickwick juggernaut for awhile—Dickens's sister-in-law Mary Hogarth's death, in the spring of 1837, which caused Dickens to miss his deadline for the only time in his career, and, of course, supplied the germ of Nell, the always-already-an-angel heroine of *The Old Curiosity Shop*—a lavishly idealizing piece of work that is also prone to Codlin-esque cynicism about its creator's inventive genius.

■ ■ ■

*Item.*
"He was for some days restrained by business from performing any particular pranks, as his time was pretty well occupied [in] taking . . . a minute inventory of all the goods in the place" (*OCS,* ch.11). This is the villain Quilp, newly in possession of Nell's grandfather's property and for once, it seems, doing something rational: for even he, with his demonic energies and that abiding "taste for [always] doing something fantastic and monkey-like" (*OCS,* ch.9), appears to defer, at least for a time, to another exigency, subordinating his usual malign acrobatics to the business of sorting and counting

and record keeping. Still at this point believing the old man he has ousted to be a miser with a cache of treasure hidden amongst the miscellaneous oddities of the shop, Quilp settles down to determine, item by item, exactly what it is he now owns. So what is there in the old curiosity shop—or in *The Old Curiosity Shop*?

Master Humphrey says—and remember, he may be making this up, since he may never have been there—that "there were suits of mail standing like ghosts in armour here and there, fantastic carvings brought from monkish cloisters, rusty weapons of various kinds, distorted figures in china and wood and iron and ivory: tapestry and strange furniture that might have been designed in dreams" (*OCS*, ch.1). But this is inefficient inventory, exhibiting only the most minimal discriminating energy: a halfhearted gesture at enumeration employing a few rough-and-ready distinctions to form fuzzy, unhelpful classes (such as "tapestry and strange furniture"). The point of view expressed here is one almost entirely lacking in the commitment, the curiosity, to delineate more and yet more items, to extend the catalogue and avoid lumping possibly distinguishable items together, so as to miss no opportunity of extracting value. As Henry James would say, we have been given "the circumstances of the interest," "but where is the interest itself?"[3] Indeed, one gets the feeling that even if Master Humphrey were to tell us in greater detail what the shop contained, the effect of his doing so would be comparable to the one that arises from John Bunyan's description, in *Pilgrim's Progress*, of the Vanity Fair of this fallen world, where (says Bunyan) "all such merchandise [is] sold, as houses, lands, trades, places, honours, preferments, titles, countries, kingdoms, lusts, pleasures, and delights of all sorts, as whores, bawds, wives, husbands, children, masters, servants, lives, blood, bodies, souls, silver, gold, pearls, precious stones, and what not."[4] To the Nell-fixated gaze—and how many of this novel's characters, as well as readers, have it?—spin the list out as one may, it all reduces in the end, and even before that, to a mass of "what not," or to what the single gentleman sums up as "the wreck of life," the assorted, heaped-together, unworthy-to-be-delineated contents of history's old curiosity shop (*OCS*, ch.71). Bunyan says that one might see in Vanity Fair "jugglings, cheats, games, plays, fools, apes, knaves, and rogues, and that of all sorts" (125): a pretty fair description, one might be disposed to think, of the narrative business, the narrative busy-ness, set serially before us between our first view of Nell, as she lies sleeping in the shop, and our last, as she lies dead upon her bier. The uncanny sameness-and-difference of these two well-known illustrations, the seemingly typological relationship in which the former appears inevitably to forecast the latter, threatens to reduce "reading" this novel to the act of flipping back and forth between the two framing, static images, and to evacuate all significance from the in-between.

In *The Old Curiosity Shop,* Dickens hurls against his own narrative-propagating powers, so gloriously deployed in *The Pickwick Papers,* the story-negating inertia of Nell. With our eyes fixed on her in her passage from one picture to another, we will be inclined to regard all the energetic comings and goings of The Old Curiosity Shop and, for that matter, of mortal existence as such, in the manner Master Humphrey attributes to a bedridden man listening to the foot traffic outside his window: as just so much maddeningly pointless "pacing to and fro," as an "incessant tread of feet," a "stream of life that will not stop [but] pour[s] [senselessly] on, on, on" (*OCS,* ch.1) in the delusion that there is anywhere to get to other than where we always knew we were always headed.

Tennyson, in the fifty-sixth poem of *In Memoriam,* fills out an inventory that is just as pointlessly, tragically prolonged as the narrative of *The Old Curiosity Shop* might seem to us, when he responds to the evidence of a suspectedly indifferent Nature by asking:

> And he, shall he,
> Man, Her [Nature's] last work, who seem'd so fair,
> Such splendid purpose in his eyes,
> Who roll'd the psalm to wintry skies,
> Who built him fanes of fruitless prayer,
> Who trusted God was love indeed
> And love Creation's final law—
> Tho' Nature, red in tooth and claw
> With ravine, shriek'd against his creed—
> Who loved, who suffer'd countless ills,
> Who battled for the True, the Just,
> Be blown about the desert dust,
> Or seal'd within the iron hills?[5]

As this single sentence grows and grows, the poet unwinds and unwinds the whole long scroll of human history, its prayers, loves, sufferings, battles, ideals, theories, purposes—what not—as if to defer his arrival at the terminus he has seen lying before him all along.

In *The Old Curiosity Shop,* if we are really to pay attention to what fills up the middle, to inventorize, delineating and involving ourselves in the affairs of Quilp and Dick Swiveller and the Punch performers and Mrs. Jarley's waxworks and the factory fire-watcher and the impoverished unemployed and the bereft old schoolmaster—and what not—we must distract ourselves from the static spectacle of Nell, must practice what James Kincaid calls "the massive . . . evasion" of the dying or already dead child: our challenge as readers of this unreadable novel, Kincaid says, is to "show Nell and her corpse that they can't claim all the attention."[6] Because to look at Nell is to miss everything else. Witness Nell's grandfather, a man blasted loose from all attachment to the world by the experience of living with an angel. By the end of the book, he has come to inhabit a condition in which "whatever power of thought or memory he retained, was all bound up in her," such that he can feel "no love or care for anything in life" (*OCS*, ch.72). His plight may remind us of the opening lines of Rilke's *Duino Elegies,* where the poet writes,

> Who, if I cried, would hear me among the angelic
> orders? And even if one of them suddenly
> pressed me against his heart, I should fade in
> the strength of his
> stronger existence. For Beauty's nothing
> but the beginning of a Terror we're still just
> able to bear,
> and why we adore it so is because it serenely
> disdains to destroy us. Each single angel is
> terrible.[7]

Nell's is the image, as her grandfather puts it, that "sanctifies the game" (*OCS*, ch.31), but to look upon that image is to forget the point of playing. By the end, this curiosity shop keeper has been rendered "quite incapable of interest or curiosity" (*OCS*, ch.71).

■ ■ ■

*Item.*

"Inventory," Roland Barthes once wrote, "is never a neutral idea; to catalogue is not merely to ascertain, . . . but also to appropriate."[8] Quilp's attention to the business of reckoning the value of his new property restrains him from fully indulging in his usual menacing monkey business. To be sure, even while conducting his inventory Quilp manages to make a thorough nuisance of himself to both Nell (whose bed he commandeers with salacious glee) and his own lawyer, Mr. Brass (whom he compels to smoke as incessantly as himself). But whereas most of the time he functions in this novel as a superlatively busy and finally self-defeating devil incarnate who merely moonlights as a businessman, here the calculative protocols of the latter assume temporary priority, making this maliciously mobile enemy of peace and rest accept temporary confinement in the shop, for as long as the process of counting and assessing lasts. And confinement is something "foreign to [his] nature." Like the book in which he appears, and like all the other houses and buildings in that book, and indeed like Quilp's small body itself, the shop and its rooms and furniture seem scarcely able to hold his errant energy. When he goes to sleep in the very coziest of the book's enclosures, Nell's little bed, Quilp "hang[s] so far out of [it] that he almost seem[s] to be standing on his head" (*OCS*, ch.12).

A parodic reflection of Quilp's inventory taking can be found a few chapters earlier, when a character who is destined to counterbalance Quilp in the novel—Dick Swiveller—takes "a greasy memorandum-book from his pocket and [makes] an entry therein" (*OCS*, ch.8). Having just consumed another delivered dinner and incurred another debt he cannot defray, Dick explains, "I enter in this little book the names of the streets I can't go down while the shops are open. This dinner to-day closes Long Acre. I bought a pair of boots in Great Queen Street last week, and made that no thoroughfare too. There's only one avenue to the Strand left open now, and I shall have to stop up that to-night with a pair of gloves. The roads are closing so fast in every direction, that in about a month's time, unless my aunt sends me a remittance, I shall have to go three or four miles out of town to get over the way" (*OCS*, ch.8). Where Quilp finds it necessary to take stock of what he owns, his comic counterpart defers to calculative rationality so far as to keep careful track of what, and where, he owes. In both cases, on the credit side of the ledger and on the debit, concession to the necessity of accounting requires that a character defined by his capacity for movement—the restless troublemaker and the constantly "swiveling" evader of debt—accept or acknowledge a measure of limitation, checking or at least redirecting his steps.

Like other villains in early Dickens, Quilp achieves his primary effect through his apparently incessant and unpredictable motion: not only does his body jerk and caper its way through every scene, as if unable to control the force it harbors; more than this, whenever Quilp is compelled to remain indoors, he tends to smoke so volcanically as to suggest he is liable to erupt. He also exhibits the alarming tendency (visible as well in the behavior of Oliver Twist's Monks and Fagin) suddenly to materialize from out of nowhere. When Kit is arrested on the trumped-up charge of stealing from the lawyer Brass, the innocent dupe looks out the window of the carriage bearing him away and sees "all at once, as though it had been conjured up by magic, ... the face of Quilp" (*OCS*, ch.60). Here again—and strikingly captured in the accompanying illustration—the baleful power in Quilp shows itself straining against enclosure: "It was from the open window of a tavern that [Quilp] looked out," we read; "and the dwarf had so spread himself over it, with his elbows on the window-sill and his head resting on both his hands, that what between this attitude and his being swoln with suppressed laughter, he looked puffed and bloated into twice his usual breadth" (*OCS*, ch.60). In another passage, Nell has a close call when Quilp turns up unexpectedly, seeming "to have risen out of the earth," in the town she has just arrived in with Mrs. Jarley's traveling waxworks show, and the fright makes her feel "as if she were hemmed in by a legion of Quilps, and the very air were filled with them" (*OCS*, ch.27). It appears as if the driving force in Quilp is something, to borrow language Dickens will later apply to the detective Bucket of *Bleak House,* that "time and space cannot bind" (*BH*, ch.53).

As for Dick Swiveller, he is reminiscent of figures like Jingle and Bob Sawyer in *Pickwick Papers,* men of boundless appetite and verbal self-invention who love the wide world for its ample provision of more and more places in which to contract new obligations and escape having to repay them. For such locomotive appetites, as for Tennyson's Ulysses in the dramatic monologue of that name, "all experience is an arch wherethro' / Gleams that untravell'd world, whose margin fades / For ever and forever as [they] move" (lines 19–21). From the mouths of such men comes an outflow of chatter proportionate to the amount of free food and drink that goes in. Other people exist, for such characters, for the almost exclusive purpose of affording them what Swiveller is looking for from Nell's grandfather when he first appears in the novel: "The watch-word to the old min," Dick says, "is—fork" (*OCS,* ch.3)—as in fork over, or provide the means of feeding me. Embodied in Swiveller is the comic potential so rapturously exploited in Dickens's inaugural novel, that of the man self-invented on the move, unfettered by relationships, by institutions, and most of all by the women who control them: the man who makes it up as he goes along, his creative powers seemingly equal to the variety of the world. When Jingle announces that his place of residence is "No Hall, Nowhere" (*PP*, ch.7), he defines himself and his ilk as the instruments of a boundless, unhouse-able desire, the radical extension of that cornerstone of English liberty, the principle of habeas corpus. As Sam Weller memorably puts it, "The have-his-carcase, next to the perpetual motion, is vun of the blessedest things as wos ever made" (*PP,* ch.40).

Yet in *The Old Curiosity Shop,* as Dick perceives, the roads are closing fast in every direction. By the middle of the novel he finds himself installed in a kind of curiosity shop, that lawyer's trap for ensnaring the innocent,

## 10: Enumeration and Exhaustion

the House of Brass. Here he takes up his station alongside other oddities such as (in a kind of inventory) "she-dragons in the business, conducting themselves like professional gentlemen [Sally Brass]; plain cooks of three feet high appearing mysteriously from under ground [the Marchioness]; strangers walking in and going to bed without leave or license in the middle of the day [the single gentleman]" (*OCS*, ch.34). No better able to bear confinement than Quilp is, Swiveller is liable to burst into "the performance of a maniac hornpipe" (*OCS*, ch.34) when left alone, and to play at attacking his jailer (Sally Brass) when her back is turned. For this comic law-unto-himself, being compelled to serve as clerk to a lawyer is tantamount to being what he imagines his destiny will make him next: "a convict . . . trotting about a dockyard with [his] number neatly embroidered on [his] uniform, and the order of the garter on [his] leg" (*OCS*, ch.34).

When these restless characters stay inside and pay attention to their lists, they acknowledge the power that places them on a list—the power that constructs and manages the dramatis personae. They defer, that is, to the narrator, who enumerates, apportions, and delimits the domains of his characters.

■ ■ ■

***Item.***

"Everything in our lives, whether of good or evil, affects us most by contrast" (*OCS*, ch.53). As Audrey Jaffe observes in her excellent study *Vanishing Points: Dickens, Narrative, and the Subject of Omniscience,* the Dickensian narrator possesses his authorizing mobility and freedom "in relation to and at the expense of" its characters, producing the effect of omniscience and omnipresence by opposition to characters who are, finally, made to remain in their places, however much they may long to roam free.[9] Narrative omniscience, Jaffe maintains, is not just a phenomenon of Dickens's fiction but perhaps *the* project of that fiction, and *The Old Curiosity Shop* in particular shows us that project in faltering and self-conscious operation, revealing "not the unproblematic achievement of distance and detachment, but rather a blurring of the boundaries that define and separate narrator and narration" (Jaffe, 49–50). As readers cannot help noticing, the Master Humphrey who participates in the narrative of the book's opening chapters removes himself from the story's action at the end of chapter three in what seems the most ham-fisted of manners, announcing his intention of "detach[ing] [him]self from its further course" (*OCS*, ch.3). Subsequently he will make full and ironically knowing use of the omniscient narrator's unique ability to leap from setting to setting and story line to story line, demonstrating and indeed flaunting the narrator's privilege in such passages as the following:

> As the course of this tale requires that we should become acquainted, somewhere hereabouts, with a few particulars connected with the domestic economy of Mr Sampson Brass, and as a more convenient place than the present is not likely to occur for that purpose, the historian takes the friendly reader by the hand, and springing with him into the air, and cleaving the same at a greater rate than ever Don Cleophas Leandro Perez Zambullo and his familiar travelled through that pleasant region in company [in Le Sage's play *The Devil on Two Sticks*], alights with him upon the pavement of Bevis Marks. (*OCS*, ch.33)

And yet, as we have seen, he will make a "return" to the domain of the story's participants that feels just as clumsy as his exit from it, as if he is unsatisfied with having to choose only one side of the opposition between teller and told. As Jaffe puts it, "the status of the narrator—whether he is 'in' or 'out'—is not fully settled by his departure" at the end of chapter three (Jaffe, 49). It cannot be settled, that is, whether the narrator should be listed on or omitted from an inventory of *The Old Curiosity Shop*, whether he intends to accept the self-erasure that is the price of omniscience or whether he considers that price too high.[10] Not content with being the peripatetic student of human affairs, he ambivalently occupies a position we might label *peripathetic,* at once free to move about the fictional landscape he surveys and affectively involved in it. He cannot just stay "out."

At the same time, the characters whose limitation and inventoriability define the narrator's mobility and invisibility by contrast can appear to chafe, as we have already begun to see, against the restriction they are obliged to accept under the terms of their fictional contract. When Quilp encounters and then taunts to fury a chained dog, the interaction travesties the Dickensian differential relationship of narrator and characters: from a position of "perfect safety," Quilp "triumph[s] over [the dog] in his inability to advance another inch" (*OCS*, ch.21). "The dog tore and strained at his chain with starting eyes and furious bark," we read, "but there the dwarf lay, snapping his fingers with gestures of defiance and contempt. When he had sufficiently recovered from his delight, he rose, and with his arms a-kimbo, achieved a kind of demon-dance round the kennel, just without the limits of the chain, driving the dog quite wild" (*OCS,* ch.21). In a later passage, we need hardly ask the true identity of the "figure-head of some old ship," "much too large for the apartment which it was . . . employed to decorate," which is propped in a corner of Quilp's room "like a goblin or hideous idol whom the dwarf worshipped" (*OCS*, ch.62). Quilp says it looks like Kit, but to say so is to screen himself from what stares him in the face: who else but his creator and confiner, the narrator, could provoke such a torrent of aggression as he rains down upon the colossal effigy? The churl "batter[s] the great image until the perspiration stream[s] down his face with the violence of the exercise"; he boasts of "screwing gimlets into him, and sticking forks in his eyes, and cutting [his] name on him," intending "to burn him at last" (*OCS*, ch.62).

A comparable effect arises from the fact that our attention is repeatedly directed, by both the text and its accompanying pictures, to the permeability of the spaces characters occupy. If we recall that illustration of Quilp emerging from the tavern window to crow at the captured Kit, we confront just one of this novel's images of a barely successful restraint or an endangered threshold, with the frame of an insufficiently large window coming to suggest the frame of the illustration itself and the frame of the book that contains it. If you see a window in this book, chances are that Quilp will be thrusting himself through it. Similarly, there appears to be no half-opened doorway in this novel without its eavesdropper or unexpected entrant. And doors that are closed are often being pounded upon, a situation that more than once stirs up a threshold anxiety about what might happen if they are suddenly opened.

For example, the morning after Nell and her grandfather abscond from the shop they have forfeited to Quilp, the antagonist and the lawyer Brass are awakened by "a knocking at the street-door, often repeated and gradually mounting up from a modest single rap into a perfect battery of knocks, fired in long discharges with a very short interval between" (*OCS*, ch.13). It is Dick Swiveller, laying siege to the shop—in answer to whom Quilp, "opening the door all at once, pounce[s] out upon the person on the other side" (*OCS*, ch.13), whom he mistakenly believes to be his wife, a sort of substitute Nell he delights in terrorizing. This sequence involves the replacement of Quilp's opposite and victim (Mrs. Quilp; Nell) by a figure who at this point in the narrative is his rival pursuer of Nell (for Swiveller is acting here on Fred Trent's plan that he woo Nell to get hold of the grandfather's supposed fortune). A line of demarcation between opposed characters' spaces is crossed with an explosive sense of release, and a distinction temporarily collapses, as two men with similar aims engage in the one activity this novel provides in plenty: pointless violence, "useless strife" (*OCS*, ch.13).

Later on, once Swiveller has become something of a victim himself, entrapped in the House of Brass, he hears "a loud double knock" at the street door that is "repeated with increased impatience" up to the point at which "the door [is] opened, and somebody with a very heavy tread [goes] up the stairs and into the room above" (*OCS*, ch.34). This is followed by a further "rapping of knuckles at the office door" (*OCS*, ch.34), which Dick, who ignored the first summons, is compelled to answer. In walks the small servant—her very existence a surprise—whom Dick will eventually rechristen the Marchioness (and later, Sophronia Sphynx), to announce the arrival of the "single gentleman" who has come to take the room for rent upstairs. A complex transaction is taking place here. Though he does not yet recognize the fact, just as he does not admit the knocker into the house, Dick is himself a "single gentleman" in search of a loved one; and insofar as we are willing to entertain the idea that the brusquely intrusive single gentleman is Master Humphrey, we might also observe that Dick Swiveller is the poet, the story-maker, the word-spinner, in this novel. Had he opened the street door, he would have looked into a mirror, he would have been a mirror to the single gentleman who looked at him, and the narrative would have foundered on the spectacle of a Dick(ens) "all alone," a "Swiveller solus" (*OCS*, ch.56). But the Marchioness mediates, helping to keep apart the teller and the told, to keep narrative going and to ensure a different, happier destiny for Dick Swiveller than the one that awaits his fellow bachelor.

Nor is this the last of the door-business. A few pages later, the new lodger's preternatural powers of sleeping have so disturbed the other inhabitants of the house that they gather outside his chamber determined to roust him out, even though they fear "it would be an extremely unpleasant circumstance if he was to bounce out suddenly" (*OCS*, ch.35). "Hallo there! Hallo, hallo!" shouts Mr. Brass,

> as a means of attracting the lodger's attention, and while Miss Brass plied the hand-bell, Mr Swiveller put his stool close against the wall by the side of the door, and mounting on the top and standing bolt upright, so that if the lodger did make a rush, he would most probably pass him in its onward fury, began a violent battery with the ruler upon the upper panels of the door.... [He] rained down such a shower of blows that the noise of the bell was drowned....
>
> Suddenly the door was unlocked on the inside and flung violently open. (*OCS*, ch.35)

One can imagine a passage like this in an acutely self-reflexive modern text such as Flann O'Brien's *At Swim-Two-Birds,* in which we would not be surprised to find a group of characters laboring to awaken their slumbering storyteller so that he might invent something for them severally to do, might divide and distribute and mobilize them by means of an efficacious fictional plot. Perhaps they just want him to tell them whether he intends to stay "in" or go "out."

But perhaps the uncanniest instance of this threshold anxiety in *The Old Curiosity Shop* occurs when Mrs. Jarley's carriage is put in motion at the end of chapter twenty-six. Nell is on board, the recipient of the waxwork proprietress's hospitality, and as the vehicle takes to the road we read that "away they went, with a great noise of flapping and creaking and straining, and the bright brass knocker, which nobody ever knocked at, knocking one perpetual double-knock of its own accord as they jolted heavily along" (*OCS*, ch.26). Ask not for whom the invisible knocker knocks. The north-by-northwest journey Nell is on makes a gloomy rejoinder to the sunny picaresque of *Pickwick,* in which the road and the book always promise something new, something more around the next bend. In *The Old Curiosity Shop,* as Hilary Schor has put it, "the central activity of any reader . . . is watching Little Nell walk herself to death."[11] Even when she gets to ride for a time, her foreordained fate is out there, importunately knocking.

The inventoriable world of Dickens's early fiction, like the whole universe as John Milton imagined it in his *Doctrine and Discipline of Divorce,* requires what Milton called the "divorcing command" of its creator if it is to rise, and remain, "out of Chaos": it requires the exertions of a power capable of drawing a line between and "separating . . . unmeet consorts" like Light and Dark, dry land and water, Nell and Quilp.[12] But in *The Old Curiosity Shop,* as Robert Frost put it, "something there is that doesn't love a wall."[13] And so we face a catalogue of items exhibiting what seems a compulsive failure to stay distinct from one another. There is Abel Garland—Abel without a Cain, a clone of his father, down to the clubfoot. There are the brother and sister Brass, of whom it is said that "so exact . . . was the likeness between them, that had it consorted with Miss Brass's maiden modesty and gentle womanhood to have assumed her brother's clothes in a frolic and sat down beside him, it would have been difficult for the oldest friend of the family to determine which was Sampson and which Sally" (*OCS*, ch.33). There are Mrs. Jarley's waxwork figures, so malleable to their mistress's hand that "Mr Grimaldi as clown" can be transformed into "Mr Lindley Murray as he appeared when engaged in the composition of his English Grammar," that "a murderess of great renown" can undergo wholesale moral revision and turn into "Mrs Hannah More," that "Mr Pitt in nightcap and bedgown, and without his boots" can represent "the poet Cowper with perfect exactness," and "Mary Queen of Scots in a dark wig, white shirt-collar, and male attire" can become "a complete image of Lord Byron" (*OCS*, ch.33). There is the "I and five hundred other men" of the desperate unemployed, the pitiful aggregate never permitted to diversify into individuals (*OCS*, ch.45). There are Nell, and Mrs. Quilp, and Miss Edwards, and her sister, and perhaps the Marchioness, all versions of each other. There are Quilp and Swiveller, two masks for "the uncontainable." There is Kit, who surrenders his separate consciousness entirely to his image of Nell, determining his conduct by the principle of "always try[ing] to please her," of "always be[ing]," as he puts it, "what I should like to seem to her if I was still her servant" (*OCS*, ch.69). There is Nell's grandfather, who convinces himself that his gambling addiction is a selfless service to Nell and who winds up so thoroughly lost to himself that, as we have seen, "whatever power of thought or memory he retained, was all bound up in her" (*OCS,* ch.72). There are Nell and Quilp—but then, as Steven Marcus noted, the one exists not just as the antithesis but as the other half of the other.[14] The exaggerated carnality that must shadow Nell's exaggerated purity, Quilp without Nell is a rebel without a cause. There is Nell's family tree, which generates generations without differences and which features "the same sweet girl through a long line of portraits—never growing old or changing—the Good Angel of the race" (*OCS,* ch.69). And then, of course, there are the bachelors.

■ ■ ■

***Item.***
   "When Death strikes down the innocent and young, for every fragile form from which he lets the panting spirit free, a hundred virtues rise, in shapes of mercy, charity, and love, to walk the world, and bless it. . . . In the Destroyer's steps there spring up bright creations that defy his power, and his dark path becomes a way of light to Heaven" (*OCS,* ch.72). The narrator of *The Old Curiosity Shop* here imagines a vibrant growth economy of goodness rooted in the fertile soil of buried Nell. Yet by the end of this novel, Dickens's own capacity for bringing hundreds of new shapes and bright creations into the world is straining to its utmost. In the last scene in which we see Nell alive, the old sexton tells her that the deep, dry well into which he compels her to gaze is "to be closed up, and built over" (*OCS,* ch.55). In a later work, such as *Bleak House,* what is meant to get constructed over the gaping hole left by a child's passing is a revitalized national culture determined to prevent the neglect that condemned the child to penury, ignorance, and disease. In dying, Jo the street-sweeper assumes a nation-energizing power comparable to that of the "Unknown Soldier": he becomes a site of commemoration and rededication for an entire people, belonging to all of them equally, since he is both theirs and none of theirs in particular. One can discern a

tentative gesture in this direction in *The Old Curiosity Shop,* in the nation-implying, center-to-periphery radius that Nell's itinerary draws from London to a Shropshire hamlet "within sight of the primeval heart of Britain, 'the blue Welch mountains far away.'"[15] *Bleak House* describes a similar circuit in reckoning the Chancery Court's baleful effect upon Mr. Gridley, "the man from Shropshire," and so suggesting that the evil it concerns itself with is fully national, infecting not just the metropolis but "every shire" (ch.1). But in the earlier novel, any progress we might want to make toward this expansive vision is checked by the vision of the little community, if we can call it that, constituted around Nell's grave. In seeming mockery of his celebrated fecundity and variety as a storyteller, Dickens turns and turns his crank and gives us a series of insufficiently distinguishable deformed or wounded aged bachelors: Master Humphrey, the single gentleman, the old schoolmaster, the "little old gentleman" called "the bachelor," the old sexton, another old man who talks with him, and while we are at it why not include Nell's grandfather (so long ago married it hardly counts), and the village clergyman (ditto), and Mr. Garland (surely a bachelor, even though married), and Quilp (who in the course of the story leaves his wife and declares himself a bachelor), and, of course, the other members of Master Humphrey's club, that "bizarre distortion of the Pickwickians."[16] Thinking about this self-negating inventory of spent men gathered around the figure of Nell can call to mind the obscure mechanical and fruitless ritual taking place in Marcel Duchamp's so-called Large Glass, that masterpiece of twentieth-century conceptual art whose full title, in English, is *The Bride Stripped Bare by her Bachelors, Even.*

■ ■ ■

*Bottom line.*

What saves us, and Kit, and Dick Swiveller—insofar as Dickens considers any of us worthy of salvation—is the little servant Dick names, the woman for whom he harrows the hell of Brass's kitchen-dungeon. Without her, his only possible future is that of the single gentleman, condemned to join the queue. As Dick learns through his near-fatal illness and recuperation under her care, he must have someone else to play off, and play with. Until he has the Marchioness, all he can do is give a self-pleasuring solo performance, like his performance of the tune "Away with Melancholy," which he plays—one blushes to recall—"very slowly on [a] flute in bed" for "half the night, or more" (*OCS*, ch.58). Whatever gratification he gets from this, his neighbors may prefer not to know about it. G. K. Chesterton called the union of Swiveller and Sophronia Sphynx "the one true romance in the whole of Dickens," and John Bowen has more recently contended that in this couple the cold "spiritual heaven" of Nell "is answered and outplayed" by the more mundane, material satisfactions, such as they are, "of having enough to eat and drink, and some fun."[17] Both of these critics take a more sanguine view of the matter than I am able to take. For me, the fascination of this breathtaking Dickensian antinovel, or anti-Dickensian Dickens novel, can be summed up by saying that the whole gaudy apparatus it parades before us can be, exactly, summed up—in a slogan. Innumerable writers undergo crises of creativity; Dickens turned his into a substantial work of fictional narrative that questions in the most radical and remorseless fashion the very principles he understood his art of fictional narrative to follow. It is a work that, by repeatedly threatening to negate that divorcing power with which Dickens's imagination multiplied characters and incidents, brought the novelist again and again to the brink of his terrible singleness. The slogan? I imagine Dickens muttering it to himself as he wound and wound and wound his Clock and churned out page after page: stop sniveling; keep swiveling.

## NOTES

1. The quotation is from the Appendix to the Penguin edition (page 680), which gives the material preceding and immediately following *The Old Curiosity Shop* in *Master Humphrey's Clock* (673–80).

2. The three quotations in this sentence (not otherwise referenced) can be found toward the end of chapter one in the Penguin edition. Penguin reproduces the original text of the first volume publication, in 1841, which differs from the serial publication in the addition of three penultimate paragraphs in chapter one.

3. James, "The New Novel," 319: "These are the circumstances of the interest—we see, we see; but where is the interest itself, where and what is its centre, and how are we to measure it in relation to *that*?" (emphasis added).

4. Bunyan, *Pilgrim's Progress*, 125. Subsequent references are made parenthetically in the text.

5. Tennyson, *In Memoriam*, poem #56, in Christopher Ricks, ed., *Tennyson: A Selected Edition*, 399.

6. Kincaid, *Annoying the Victorians*, 36, 37.

7. Rainer Maria Rilke, *Duino Elegies*, 21.

8. Barthes, "The Plates of the *Encyclopedia*," in Susan Sontag, ed., *A Barthes Reader*, 222.

9. Jaffe, *Vanishing Points*, 12. Subsequent references are made parenthetically in the text.

10. A similar dubiety arises over the man in the mackintosh in James Joyce's *Ulysses*,

*10: Enumeration and Exhaustion*

who winds up listed as Mr. Mackintosh in the newspaper report of Paddy Dignam's funeral.
11. Hilary M. Schor, *Dickens and the Daughter of the House*, 32.
12. John Milton, *The Doctrine and Discipline of Divorce*, 420.
13. Frost, "Mending Wall," in *The Poetry of Robert Frost*, 33.
14. Marcus, *Dickens*, 151.
15. Ibid., 141.
16. Ibid., 131.
17. Chesterton, *Chesterton on Dickens*, 56; Bowen, *Other Dickens*, 156.

# Part Three

CONTEXTUAL READING

# 11

# Paterfamilias

EILEEN GILLOOLY

Like most of us, Charles Dickens seems to have found the work of parenting incomparably more difficult to manage in practice than in theory. Arduous, expensive, and emotionally demanding, even at its most rewarding: the caring for children—with whom one is always ineluctably related, far after the formal phase of rearing is over—is a lifelong endeavor, heavy with expectations and claims both social and psychological, prodigiously funded by ambivalence. From the very beginning, Dickens was acutely attentive to parental failings, though almost exclusively from the perspective of the suffering child, whose sense of neglect—in the interpolated tales of the *Pickwick Papers* as well as in *Oliver Twist*—is rendered nightmarish by the recognition of his own powerlessness. As Steven Marcus noticed long ago, inadequate parents are routinely killed off or otherwise psychically diminished in the early novels, replaced by idealized substitutes whose primary function (I would add) is to sustain the child at the center not only of Dickens's story, but, indeed, of narrative theory itself—the child being the raison d'être of the family romance and Freudian psychology more broadly, as well as of the Bildungsroman.[1]

Yet occasionally, even in the midst of a novel sharply focused on the excruciating vulnerability of his child-hero, Dickens pauses to consider other affective aspects of the parent-child relationship. Situated like Oliver in forlorn circumstances, but lacking the saving intervention of a Mr. Brownlow, Little Nell is bewildered to find herself (as, indeed, did Dickens, at the age of twelve), not simply without adult protection or financial support, but occupying the position of parent vis-à-vis her own guardian:

> [T]he child again summoned the resolution which had until now sustained her, and, endeavouring to keep steadily in her view the one idea that . . . her grandfather's preservation must depend solely upon her firmness, unaided by one word of advice or any helping hand, urged him onward and looked back no more.
>
> While he, subdued and abashed, seemed to crouch before her, and to shrink and cower down as if in the presence of some superior creature, the child herself was sensible of a new feeling within her, which elevated her nature, and inspired her with an energy and confidence she had never known. There was no divided responsibility now; the whole burden of their two lives had fallen upon her. (OCS, ch.43)

This "new feeling within her, which elevated her nature, and inspired her with an energy and confidence she had never known"—which, like a religious conversion experience, temporarily overcomes conflicts of will and desire ("there was no divided responsibility now") and even a stable sense of separate existence ("the whole burden of their two lives had fallen upon her")—describes what Dickens's contemporaries would have termed "the feelings of a parent." If, on the one hand, Dickens never completely outgrew his own desire for such self-denying love—fostering a domestic emotional economy fueled by idealization and devaluation, in which affection and attention were largely invested in himself—on the other, he imaginatively understood that the urgency of one's own narcissistic needs might at least temporarily recede in a swell of parental feeling. Nor was this feeling exclusively accessible to biological parents or even adoptive ones. Indeed, children themselves, as Nell discovers, might occasionally experience the phenomenon.[2]

## THE RELUCTANT PARENT

That Dickens was beleaguered to an unusual degree by a vast number of dependent relations is hardly disputable. He supported either in whole or in part—until his death or theirs—not only all of his children, but also his parents and his siblings, and *their* spouses and offspring as well. And yet, at least part of his frustration with his sons in particular seems to have arisen less from their personal failures of temperament or ambition than from his own tendency (not uncommon among parents, certainly) to allow empathy for his children to collapse into overidentification at moments when sympathy would doubtless have been more productive.³ Although *sympathy* and *empathy* are notoriously approximate and mobile terms—often used interchangeably, to the utter befuddlement of local meaning—there exist at least some conceptual distinctions between them. Empathy is a ubiquitous emotional response—as common to the reader as to the parent—but sympathy in its most radical form, as symbiotic feeling, occurs rarely, even within parental experience. Empathy requires imagination: "I imagine myself in your position and I feel what I imagine you must feel." As Adam Smith puts it in *The Theory of Moral Sentiments,* we "place ourselves in [the] situation" of another, "enter[ing] as it were into his body" and thus coming "to *conceive* . . . what he feels" (emphasis added).⁴ Overidentification, too, requires imagination, but empathy is almost completely evacuated in the process: "I imagine myself in your position; but, actually, I am much less interested in what you feel than what *I* feel when I imagine myself in your position." Distinct, too, is projection, a psychic skill that is indispensable to the novelist but generally counterproductive in everyday life: "You feel this way because that is how *I* feel and because I say you do."⁵ If empathic identification is an imaginative, ethical act that arouses feeling—appropriately characterizing our response to others' narratives of suffering, for example—sympathetic identification is a condition of largely unwilled responsiveness, predicated upon the heightened state of emotional vulnerability and receptivity that obtains at moments in the closest of relationships: "I am feeling your feeling."

This is sympathy as Hume theorizes it—less a sentiment in itself than the faculty by which sentiments are communicated between individuals. The greater the resemblance between individuals, the greater their tendency to share the other's feelings; thus, as Darwin would come to argue in *The Descent of Man,* social sympathy (what we now usually term empathy) evolves from the primary, physiological sympathy that a parent feels for his child.⁶ However, as Hume noted, too much similarity—as in the case of family members—can also breed "uneasiness" and interfere with the desire to sympathize. This is so because "entering into or sharing the feelings of another" (sympathizing, as defined by the *OED:* 3b) is particularly threatening to the integrity of the self—to one's sense of an individuated ego—in circumstances where, as in the family, the boundaries separating and defining the self from others are already psychologically blurry.⁷

Endowed with an extraordinary capacity for sympathetic identification—unique, according to Forster ("no man had ever so surprising a faculty . . . of entering into mental phases and processes so absolutely")—Dickens apparently found it less menacing to "become himself what he was *representing*" (Forster, 2:116–17; emphasis added) than to enter into the feelings of his children, easier to sympathize, that is, with his imaginative offspring, created by projection, than with his biological issue: by his own admission, he was "chary of showing my affections, even to my children, except when they are very young" (*LCD*, 7:543). Producing children and novels in roughly equal numbers for the first fifteen years of his career, he fell into the habit of naming characters after his children, and his children after characters and other authors, creating a complex psychic landscape in which real-life and fictional offspring competed for affection and attention.[8] His children themselves noticed over time how unlike other fathers of their acquaintance he was—Thackeray, most notably—in his "reluctance to display his feelings" for them and in his "strange remoteness."[9]

If we fully credit the terrifying intensity of his emotional responsiveness—his fear "of feeling itself"—it is not surprising that Dickens should have sought relief in distance, in treating his children as though they were minor characters in his life narrative.[10] Rather than experiencing his children's joy and pain as his own—a state of sympathy appropriate, within limits, to the parental condition (think healthy symbiosis)—Dickens seems to have more frequently regarded his children with what he imagined *he* would have felt had he been in their shoes, indeed, often vividly recalling what he *had* felt at their age. So long as his sons were young, this inclination to overidentify with them appears not to have interfered greatly with their mutual affection, and the roles in which he cast them (their nicknames included "Flaster Floby," "Young Skull," "Ocean Spectre," and "The Jolly Postboy") enhanced his interest in them as well. His having virtually rechristened his youngest child "Plornish" ("Plorn" for short) in an affectionate nod to the memorable tenant of Bleeding Heart Yard attests to the power of this practice: by Dickens's own admission, Plorn remained his favorite son, despite the frustration he repeatedly occasioned as he grew older. Once his sons reached adolescence, however—evincing their mother's lethargy in the face of his own overpowering energy and will, failing to achieve scholastically, falling into debt, and otherwise disappointing his expectations and hopes for them—Dickens became increasingly disaffected: Oliver and Davy, he discovered, were considerably easier to idealize, identify with, and project upon.

Yet, even in the early years of his fatherhood, he seems to have found it more congenial to play the role of proud parent to his literary progeny than to his actual children. He announces Charley's birth in the following manner: "I was yesterday made—not a Member of the Garrick Club; but a father," and one week later he bids a friend to visit: "Come whenever you please.... [W]e are as quiet as if nothing had happened, and have been since the young gentleman's first appearance" (*LCD*, 1:221, 223). Just fourteen months later (and a miscarriage in the meantime), Mamie's arrival is first reported as simply "an instalment [sic] of posterity in the shape of a daughter" (*LCD,* 1:384). In contrast, Oliver Twist and Nicholas Nickleby—who also made their first appearances at this time—are repeatedly referred to by name and elicit relatively voluble pleasure and concern: "Have you seen Oliver Twist yet? I have taken a great fancy to him—I hope he deserves it" (*LCD,* 1:225); "I am sitting patiently at home waiting for Oliver Twist who has not arrived" (*LCD,* 1:387); "I would have joined you on the day you name, but I regret to say that if I were tempted to do so, Nicholas Nickleby and Oliver Twist would make a longer stay in London this month than is good for their health" (*LCD,* 1:398). Certainly, there is pleasure to be had and shared in this sort of rhetorical play. But there is little doubt, too, that consistently personifying figures of his imagination outside their fictional contexts—while underrepresenting his actual children—worked not only to displace onto his characters whatever real anxiety we might reasonably suppose he felt for his children, but also to displace the children themselves from the center of psychic awareness: whereas the unnamed "young gentleman," his first-born son, enters Dickens's life "as if nothing had happened," the pirating activities of the unnamed "literary gentleman" in *Nicholas Nickleby* deprive the true parent of what has "cost him many thoughtful days and sleepless nights" (*NN,* ch.48).

Oliver, indeed, was proving a grave worry during this period—Dickens being engaged at the time with his publisher, Richard Bentley, in a bitter legal battle over the custody of that child of his imagination. In this context, his "Familiar Epistle From a Parent to a Child Aged Two Years and Two Months"—which functioned as his editorial farewell upon resigning his editorship of *Bentley's Miscellany* in 1839—is strangely telling. After an opening, paragraph-length sentence in which the conceit of the editor-as-parent is vexatiously labored ("To recount with what trouble I have brought you up—with what an anxious eye I have regarded your progress,—how late and how often I have sat up at night working for you,—. . . to expatiate, in short, upon my own assiduity as a parent, is beside my present purpose, though I cannot but contemplate . . . your robust health, and unimpeded circulation [,] . . . without the liveliest satisfaction and delight"), Dickens rather astoundingly asserts that he will experience no sense of loss at "parting" from this "child" in whom he has invested so much "anxiety and tenderness," presumably because love, in this case at least, requires his narcissistic identification: "I resign . . . guardianship and protection" with "feelings of unmingled pleasure and satisfaction," for "you have always been literally 'Bentley's Miscellany,' and never mine."[11]

## PARENTS FROM HELL

Despite his reluctance to claim paternity—and even while he continued to dwell on his own feelings of having been parentally mistreated, especially during those few fateful months, at the age of twelve, when he was sent to work in Warren's Blacking factory—we find Dickens as early as *Nicholas Nickleby* beginning to think through in a sustained way what it might mean to be a good-enough parent.[12] Curiously, if not paradoxically, parents never cease to be children themselves, and the characteristically complex feelings generated by the parental condition often psychically resurrect vague, but nevertheless intensely felt, memories of one's own childhood—as they apparently did for Dickens (though, truth be told, his memories seem never to have been actually buried).[13] What might the "natural affections" of a biological parent *be* in a world where thousands of children were forced to fend for themselves in the streets of London and Manchester or were abandoned to the notorious Yorkshire schools?[14] What might constitute the social and ethical responsibilities of a parent—regardless of one's personal feelings for the embodied consequences (however unintended) of one's sexual behavior—especially for offspring whose mental and physical disabilities, whose "stunted growth, . . . hare-lip, . . . crooked foot, and every ugliness or distortion" tested even those parents most highly endowed with "natural affections" (*NN*, ch.8)? In *Nicholas Nickleby*, Dickens readily acknowledges—indeed, comically exploits—the gap between the sentimental ideology of parenting and the ambivalent feelings of parents, demonstrating not merely that "natural affections" are frequently weak or absent or counterfeit, but that even when strongly present they are no guarantee of parental success.

It perhaps goes without saying that all the "natural" or biological parents in the novel are underidealized by the narration: from the obsessively familial Kenwigses to the cold-blooded Ralph. And yet—though they fail in multiple ways and to varying degrees—all are spectacularly lacking in both sympathy and empathy. It is not just Wackford Squeers, that is, whose philosophy of parenting can be reduced to the following maxim: "'The only number in all arithmetic that I know of as a husband and a father is number one'" (ch.60). The Nicklebys, the Kenwigses, even the Crummleses treat their children as a capital investment—a present or future source of comfort, pride, and financial support—if not, as do the worst parents, as disposable property: "'I have come,'" Ralph informs Nicholas, "'to restore a parent his child,'" demanding that Nicholas relinquish possession of Smike to Snawley (ch.45). Ralph's is a rather curious locution, negatively calling to mind the more expected "I have come to restore a child to his parent"—which inflects the emotional bond as

Ralph's way of parsing the relation does not.

Ralph may be an early, unredeemed version of both Dombey and Scrooge, but the narrative suggests that even *his* villainy can be traced back to a lack of parental sympathy.[15] Speaking of Nicholas, Ralph soliloquizes (Edmund-like) in the voice of the misunderstood: "'When my brother was such as he . . . the first comparisons were drawn between us—always in my disfavour. *He* was open, liberal, gallant, gay; *I* a crafty hunks of cold and stagnant blood, with no passion but love of saving, and no spirit beyond a thirst for gain'" (ch.34). Yet this "love of saving," we are told, was inspired by his *mother's* "long accounts of their father's sufferings in his days of poverty, and of their deceased uncle's importance in his days of affluence": Ralph "deduced from the often repeated tale the two great morals that riches are the only true source of happiness and power, and that it is lawful and just to compass their acquisition by all means short of felony" (ch.1). Dickens thus not only acknowledges that Ralph's upbringing has had a heavy hand in deforming his character: he also sentimentally proposes that had Ralph "known his child to be alive, . . . he might have been otherwise" (ch.62)—redeemed by a second-chance opportunity to parent. And while such a reversal seems improbable even in this highly melodramatic novel, there is little doubt that Ralph's having "persecuted and hunted down his own child to death" (ch.60) can only pass for verisimilitude—however laxly conceived—by his having done so unwittingly. By insisting on this point, Dickens raises the question of limits: how bad must parenting be before it is legally understood to violate "natural" law—to be monstrous and inhuman? When will exiling one's son to a Yorkshire school or putting him to labor in a blacking factory to support his prodigal parents come to be judged socially intolerable, if not felonious, behavior?

Bad parenting takes less lethal shape elsewhere in this novel. Perhaps the worst charge that can be reasonably brought against the Kenwigses is that of overzealous identification. Indeed, their identification with their children is so extreme as to preclude their recognizing them—either psychologically or rhetorically—as differentiated beings. The little Kenwigses are most often represented either by synecdoche (eight "flaxen tails" requiring continual monitoring and tight control) or by metonymy (they collectively constitute Mr. and Mrs. Kenwigs's "tenderest point," being their point of pride): "Mrs. Kenwigs, rightly deeming that the honour of the family was involved in Miss Morleena's making the most splendid appearance . . . and testifying . . . to all fathers and mothers present that other people's children could learn to be genteel besides theirs, had fainted away twice under the magnitude of her preparations, but [was] upheld by a determination to sustain the family name or perish in the attempt" (ch.52). Although certainly an attentive and demonstrably affectionate mother, Mrs. Kenwigs nevertheless psychically represents her daughters not simply as an extension of herself—enlarging her territory for ego investment and increasing her family claim on Uncle Lillyvick's fortune—but sometimes as a physical appendage under fierce threat of amputation: "'I will consider my child! I will consider my child! my own child, that no uncles can deprive me of, my own hated, despised, deserted, cut-off little child'" (ch.52). As John Bowen has noted, there are both "murderous and affectionate impulses" afoot here.[16] Quite "overpowered by the feelings of a mother" upon witnessing "the blaze of their combined beauty," the sobbing Mrs. Kenwigs memorably declares them to be "'too beautiful to live, much too beautiful'"—to which "alarming" and Medea-like "presentiment" the "four little girls" respond by "burying their heads in their mother's lap simultaneously and scream[ing] until the eight flaxen tails vibrated," in Medusa-like fashion (ch.14).

However reprehensibly the Squeerses may treat other people's children, their response to their own offspring is strikingly—indeed, alarmingly—like the Kenwigses'. They double each other not only in the way that the Kenwigses' dinner party for Uncle Lillyvick "transforms the violence of the preceding Dotheboys chapter into 'slaps on the head' for the infant Kenwigses,"[17] but also in their shared inability to discriminate between a "fondling" and a "foundling"—between an object of affection and an object of abandonment—to imagine children, that is, as having subjectivity or even distinct sentience (ch.9; ch.36). In both cases, parental pleasure is thoroughly narcissistic:

> "Oh my eye, won't I give it to the boys!" exclaimed the interesting child, grasping at his father's cane. . . .
>
> It was a proud moment in Mr Squeers's life to witness that burst of enthusiasm in his young child's mind, and to see in it a foreshadowing of his future eminence. He pressed a penny into his hand, and gave vent to his feelings (as did his exemplary wife also), in a shout of approving laughter. The infantine appeal to their common sympathies at once restored cheerfulness to the conversation, and harmony to the company. (ch.9)

The Nicklebys, too—both living and dead, and for generations back—are found severely wanting as parents. However much Kate's tender recollection of her father's "broken heart" works to soften the destitution he has brought upon them (ch.43) or however much Nicholas's reclaiming the ancestral home helps to vindicate his father's memory, Nicholas Senior, as Helena Michie notes, "fail[s] to act as a father should" by providing adequately for his family.[18] His "horror of little babies, . . . because he couldn't very well afford any increase to his family" (ch.41) may be forgivable, but his financial fecklessness and his clinging to the role of victim cannot altogether be erased from the narrative or from filial consciousness—as Dickens (whose own parents were at the time—and not for the first time—running up debts against his name) was himself painfully aware.

Although Mrs. Nickleby is not without her virtues (she certainly cannot be accused of being a *withholding* mother, in any sense of that word), her completing inverting the parent-child paradigm by demanding almost infantile attention (we are told she dribbles her water [ch.35]) rather than protecting her children constitutes one of the most grievous parenting offenses in the book. Indeed, in order for us not to read her narcissism as villainy, we, like Nicholas, must come to see her as a child of limited understanding, who requires strong coaxing to be cooperative: "[A]lthough the good lady . . . was now addressed in most lucid terms both by Nicholas and his sister, she . . . could by no means be made to comprehend the necessity of . . . [their immediately leaving the lodgings Ralph had provided for them]. At last Nicholas, in a condition of absolute despair, ordered the coachman to drive away, and in the unexpected jerk of a sudden starting, Mrs Nickleby lost a shilling among the straw, which fortunately confined her attention to the coach until it was too late to remember anything else" (ch.33). Even before she colludes in pandering, however unwittingly, for Sir Mulberry Hawk ("'If I had not put them in the right track today,' thought Ralph [speaking of Verisopht and Hawk], 'this foolish woman would have done so'" [ch.27]), Mrs. Nickleby is implicated in another sort of child selling: like Mrs. Dickens, she seems never to have questioned the morality of sending her child out to "work" (cf. Miss La Creevy, who, though impoverished, is nonetheless self-supporting). That Mrs. Nickleby is a reliable, if sometimes tedious, source of humor does much to mitigate the emotional suffering her maternal failures cause: Nicholas, as well as the reader, is often caught smiling at his mother's vertiginous chatter. But he achieves this state of detached amusement only by playing, as it were, the adult in their relationship.

When a talent for parenting is missing, imagining oneself feeling the emotions of the neglected child can sometimes elicit a corresponding urge to mother. This is called empathic identification in one idiom and method acting in another. Mrs. Nickleby, however, always "considering herself foremost," querulously assumes the opposite: "'nobody knows what my feelings are—nobody can—it's quite impossible!'" (ch.61)—a sentiment exposed as hollow when echoed meaningfully some twenty pages later by a tender and tearful

Newman Noggs: "'you don't know what I feel today; you can't and never will!'" (ch.63). While Mrs. Nickleby's "natural affections" for her children are real enough, "after her own peculiar fashion" (ch.61), they are of a self-gratifying sort: "'it's a very delightful and consoling thing to have a grown-up son that one can put confidence in, . . .—indeed I don't know any use there would be in having sons at all, unless people could put confidence in them'" (ch.37).[19]

And, then, of course, there are the Crummleses. Although doubtless the most appealing biological parents of the lot, they are also the most ethically problematic from a readerly perspective. For despite the romantic attraction of their peripatetic domestic life and the forgiving humor that accompanies their every appearance ("'Look at her—mother of six children—three of 'em alive, and all upon the stage!'" [ch.25]), the Crummleses are guilty not simply of putting their children to labor, but of bona fide child abuse: distorting their only living daughter, Ninetta—by means of sleep deprivation and "an unlimited allowance of gin-and-water from infancy" (ch.23)—into the freakish Infant Phenomenon.

## ROLE REVERSALS

Although all of the biological parents in *Nicholas Nickleby* fail to varying degrees, other characters—all childless themselves: the spinster, the elderly bachelor twins, the alcoholic clerk, and perhaps even the loyal, sober one—by *affecting* the role of parent in effect affectively perform it. What seems to me most unusual is not that Nicholas and Kate so easily find any number of surrogates at the ready to undertake reparative parenting work as needed (however unusual that indeed may be), but rather that these child protagonists discover that in acting the loving parent toward others they come in the process to recuperate their own (perhaps always-already) lost sense of being deeply cared for, closely held, themselves.

Judith Kegan Gardiner suggestively remarks that "to mother maturely, a woman must develop an identity sufficiently flexible that she can merge empathically with her child and still retain an adult sense of herself as nurturing yet independent."[20] Such an identity may be gendered feminine, but, as Nicholas comes to learn, its performance is not restricted to biological mothers. The challenge is to maintain a sense of oneself as separated and individuated yet nevertheless deeply related, either by sympathizing (in the Humean sense of feeling the feelings of the other as one's own) or empathizing with one's child (imagining oneself to be in the child's position and to feel in that position what one supposes the child to feel). In either case, the result is that in the act of nurturing, one comes to feel nurtured oneself. As Dickens writes of Kate Nickleby, hers was "a young heart," one "stored with every pure and true affection that women cherish," though "almost a stranger to the endearments and devotion of its own sex, *save as it learnt them from itself*"—a heart "rendered by calamity and suffering keenly susceptible of the sympathy so long unknown and so long sought in vain" (ch.55; emphasis added). (Mrs. Nickleby herself admits, "'I have no sympathy,'" though, as usual, she has an entirely different signification in mind [ch.41].)

While Kate comes herself, by means of empathic identification, to experience the affectionate care she bestows upon her mother, Nicholas learns how to mother, and to feel mothered in return, by means of his radical, unwilled sympathy for Smike, whose anguish (in the following example) Nicholas proleptically feels: "the unhappy being had established a hold upon his sympathy and compassion, which *made his heart ache* at the prospect of the suffering he was destined to undergo" (ch.13; emphasis added). The maternal quality of that sympathy attracts Miss Snevellicci's notice: "'How kind it is of you . . . to sit waiting here for him night after night, night after night, no matter how tired you are; and taking so much pains with him, and doing it all with as much delight and readiness as if you were coining gold by it!'" (ch.30). Smike's "single-hearted" (ch.30) love for Nicholas—the first person he can remember to have ever shown him affectionate care—elicits maternal love in response. Nicholas teaches Smike, who has "not the intellect" of an adult (ch.30), how to speak his lines—how to form his first words, as it were (ch.25)—and nurses him with reciprocal single-heartedness through his fatal illness: "By night and day, at all times and seasons, always watchful, attentive, and solicitous, and never varying in the discharge of his self-imposed duty. . . . He never left him; to encourage and animate him, administer to his wants, support and cheer him to the utmost of his power, was now his constant and unceasing occupation" (ch.58).[21] If we thus understand Nicholas to be playing the part of mother to Smike (which elicits maternal feelings from Smike in response), then the bond pledged in the following exchange comes to look less homoerotic than preoedipal:[22]

> "You grow," said the lad, laying his hand timidly on that of Nicholas, "you grow thinner every day; your cheek is paler, and your eye more sunk. Indeed I cannot bear to see you so, and think how I am burdening you. I tried to go away today, but the thought of your kind face drew me back." . . . [H]is eyes filled with tears, and his voice was gone.
>
> "You are my only comfort and stay. I would not lose you now, for all

the world could give. The thought of you has upheld me through all I have endured. . . . Give me your hand. My heart is linked to yours." (ch.20)

## DICKENS IN 1851

The tableau of household harmony with which *Nicholas Nickleby* concludes belongs more appropriately to family romance than to realism or even melodrama: a charming rural property with two large residences and "a little cottage" for Newman Noggs, "whose chief pleasure and delight was in the children, with whom he was a child himself, and the master of the revels" (ch.65); a large and protean family, whose inhabitants move easily between country and city, and in so doing gather the Cheerybles and Linkinwaters into their communal life as well. Theirs is an extended and inclusive ménage, brimming with members of three generations—all of whom are accomplished caregivers. For in this domestic idyll, even the unnamed, uncounted "lovely children" produced by the marriages of Nicholas and Kate have affective labor to perform: speaking "low and softly of their poor dead cousin," they tend Smike's grave with "infant hands" (ch.65).

As early as 1838, then, Dickens—a new father of two small children, with another on the way—was already imagining alternative forms of domesticity. Indeed, his own household—always including, as it did, one of his wife's sisters—had from the beginning experimented with such alternatives.[23] But by 1851, the dissonance between his ideal of household harmony and the actual conditions prevailing at home was jarring. Even for Dickens, the months during which he ruminated upon, composed, and published *Bleak House* were remarkably hectic and emotionally taxing. His correspondence shows him struggling to move his substantial household from Devonshire Terrace to Tavistock House—the new London residence requiring such thorough renovation, in Dickens's estimation, that he was forced to extend the family's summer rental in Broadstairs, a seaside town in Kent, until late November 1851, while he himself shuttled back and forth so as to oversee the Tavistock alterations personally. Although annoyed to distraction by the usual delays, Dickens was pleased with the results: according to one of his biographers, "the house was exactly as he—and he only—had determined that it should be."[24] At the same time, Dickens was energetically "conducting" *Household Words*—an enterprise demanding that he perform a host of roles, including (though not limited to) acquisitions and copy editor, bookkeeper, writer, and publicist. He was also caught up in managing (and acting in) an amateur theatrical troupe engaged in staging a play, written by his friend Edward Bulwer Lytton, to benefit the Guild of Literature and Art, his most recent charity project. One of these performances, commanded by Queen Victoria and originally scheduled for the end of April 1851, was postponed for two weeks following the sudden death of Dickens's nine-month-old daughter, Dora, on 14 April—just nine days after he had buried his father.

Although Dickens had been joking tendentiously for years about his wife's fertility (what he unkindly called her habitual "anti-Malthusian state"), his irritation with the ever-increasing size both of their family and of Catherine herself—whose weight, clumsiness, lassitude, and "nervous illnesses" were becoming intolerable to him—was particularly in evidence in March 1852, when the first number of *Bleak House* appeared in print.[25] Three days after the birth of his tenth and last child, Edward Bulwer Lytton Dickens (aka Plorn), on 13 March, Dickens informed his friend the philanthropist Angela Burdett-Coutts: "I am happy to say that Mrs. Dickens and the seventh son—whom I cannot afford to receive with perfect cordiality, as on the whole I could have dispensed with him—are . . . in a most blooming state. I had been in an unsettled and anxious condition for a week or so, but may now shut myself up in Bleak House again" (*LCD*, 6:627). A few days later—in a letter to Mrs. Richard Watson, whose Rockingham Castle residence served as the model for Chesney Wold—he again lamented his advanced parental state. Referring to a recent encounter with an old friend, Dickens declares that (wondrously) "when he talked to me," "my uncountable children disappeared"—a feat of conjuration that evokes from Dickens at least as much gratitude as it does admiration (*LCD*, 6:630).[26]

These months also mark the beginning of what was to become a lifelong disappointment in his sons. Charley, his oldest child, at age fourteen was of special concern, being an indifferent student and in an "unsettled state" that suggested to Dickens that "retaining him" at school "might be a mere loss of time" (*LCD*, 6:792). He left Eton in 1852, first thinking he would like to be a soldier, later a businessman—a choice that he pursued until the bankruptcy of his firm in 1867. The second son and fourth child, Walter Landor Dickens, eleven years old in 1852, was already being trained (unsuccessfully) for a military career: "going to India bye and bye" (as Dickens rather tendentiously spelled it in a letter to Lydia Sigourney), where he died, in debt, at the age of 22.[27] And Frank, the next in line and in Dickens's estimation "the cleverest of all the children," who had recently begun to "stammer so horribly as to be an afflicted spirit," as well as Alfred Tennyson D'Orsay Dickens—although only nine and eight years old, respectively—were left behind to school in Boulogne at the end of the family vacation there in September 1853, when the last number of *Bleak House* was published.[28]

As the boys grew, Dickens found their daily presence harder to bear—an irritating reminder not only of their infuriating lack of will and energy, but also of his having failed dismally to teach them self-reliance, whatever their natural inclination.[29] In a letter to Wilkie Collins (1866), he laid claim to the unenviable achievement of "having brought up the largest family ever known with the smallest disposition to do anything for themselves" (*LCD*, 11:252). Constantly fretting over his own financial security, he found his sons' apparent insouciance about their academic success and later about their professional futures as bewildering as it was maddening. By 1867—eight years after the publication of *The Origin of Species*, when his oldest son was thirty; his youngest, fifteen—Dickens feared that the children had inherited from their mother a fatal weakness of character: "my boys," he wrote to his subeditor, W. H. Wills, have "the curse of limpness on them. You don't know what it is to look round the table and see reflected from every seat . . . some horribly well remembered expression of inadaptability to anything" (*LCD*, 11:377).

Frustration and regret now clung implacably to associations of home life. Not only did Devonshire Terrace (where the Dickens family had been living ever since *Nickleby*'s volume publication in 1839) seem in 1851 insufferably cramped, but so too did the very idea of the nuclear family—where parents and children were culturally imprisoned in their biologically determined relationships, where parents (who were no more than grown children themselves) were morally obligated to support and compassionate even the most exasperating of offspring.[30] The adolescent Charley—though "a clever, well-educated boy" of "fine feeling" (*LCD*, 6:832, 808)—was proving almost as difficult to impress upon, whip into shape, or empathize with as Richard Carstone.

> Charley and I had a great talk at Dover about his going into the Army, when I thought it right to set before him fairly and faithfully the objections to that career. . . . The result was, that he asked in a very manly way, for time to consider. So I appointed to go down to Eton on a certain day . . . and resume the subject. . . . [H]e came to the conclusion that he would rather be a merchant, and try to establish some good house of business, where he might find a path perhaps for his younger brothers, and stay at home, and make himself the head of that long, small procession. (*LCD*, 6:808)

We held many consultations about what Richard was to be . . . ; but it was a long time before we seemed to make any progress. Richard said he was ready for anything. . . . When Mr. Jarndyce asked him what he thought of the Army, Richard said he had thought of that too, and it wasn't a bad idea. When Mr. Jarndyce advised him to try and decide within himself, . . . Richard answered, Well, he really *had* tried very often, and he couldn't make out. (*BH,* ch.13)

Richard . . . with his quick abilities, his good spirits, his good temper, his gaiety and freshness, was always delightful. (*BH,* ch.17)

[But his] energy was of such an impatient and fitful kind. (*BH,* ch.17)

Shutting himself up in Bleak House provided Dickens not simply with a temporary escape from a household overrun by a slew of "uncountable children" and a wife distinguished for her "impracticable torpor" (*LCD,* 6:363), but with the psychic space to imagine home as something other than the site of incessant emotional and financial demands. In *Bleak House,* as in *Nicholas Nickleby,* home is "'the place where . . . those I love are gathered together'" (*NN,* ch.35). But the particulars of the ideal domicile had altered somewhat in the intervening years: fewer residents, for one thing. Recall the final pages of the novel: three adorable and ageless little ones; a young man beloved and respected for his tireless attention to the public good; and two lovely, sweet-tempered young women, devoted to the benevolent father figure who has made their life together possible—one of whom demonstrates an extraordinary talent for housekeeping.[31]

## MR. DICKENS BUILDS HIS DREAM HOUSE

In its first book edition, *Bleak House* announced itself thus: "dedicated, as a remembrance of our friendly union, to my companions in the Guild of Literature and Art." The Guild—the brainchild of Dickens and a few friends (Forster and Bulwer Lytton helped to write the prospectus)—was officially "a Branch Insurance and Provident Society, solely for the Professors of Literature and Art" (*LCD,* 6:852). Its mission was not only to provide life insurance ("at rates of premium"), annuities, and widows' pensions, but also, innovatively, to establish a writers' and artists' colony as well as a number of nonresidential fellowships. Moreover—so as to raise the necessary funds to build domestic "lodges" on the land donated by Bulwer Lytton for the purpose—the Guild proposed to offer a series of "Dramatic Representations," performed by some of its originating members, including Dickens, who was also designated the theatrical "Manager."

Despite the financial success of the "Dramatic Representations," the construction of this idyllic community—composed of "painters, sculptors, and writers, of either sex" (*LCD*, 6:852), living together in harmony and joint purpose—never came to pass. For though the residential project was meant to encourage the "independence" of struggling writers and artists by releasing them from "the necessity of stooping their ambition to occupations at variance with the higher aims of their career," the proviso that Members (who received free housing) were "elected for life" must have felt to some potential candidates constraining—less suggestive of a pastoral utopia than a model prison (*LCD*, 6:854). And this feeling was likely to have shaded into resentment under the oversight of the "Warden," who, though "elected from among the Members," was "to superintend all the internal discipline and arrangements; . . . to conciliate any differences that may arise," to command "the personal respect and attachment of those by whom his opinions should be regarded as an authority, and over whose comforts" he could "not fail to have a certain degree of influence."

If an artists' colony so conceived constituted one blueprint of ideal domesticity for Dickens, another model of more makeshift design could be found in the theatrical troupe formed to support it. For no matter how praiseworthy were the charitable goals of the Guild, the project also provided Dickens—an inveterate stager of home theatricals—with an excellent excuse to create, manage, perform in, and direct a company of amateur actors composed almost entirely of friends (including Forster, Mark Lemon, Douglas Jerrold, Augustus Egg, and Wilkie Collins) and, on some occasions, his daughters, Mamie and Katie, and their aunt Georgina. Brought into being and sustained by his vigor and determination, this temporary "family"—each member of which was individually chosen by Dickens—not only came together at his bidding, but (rather magically, really) said and did just as he told them to do. Compared to the occupants of Tavistock House—whom despite his strenuous efforts he managed, by his own estimation, with very limited success—his theatrical family was tractable, compliant, and properly appreciative: "[A]t dinner and supper I am never absent from my post at the head of the table," Dickens wrote to Gaskell, declining her invitation to dinner during the Manchester performances. "I can't imagine what the Company would think, if the Manager were away" (*LCD*, 6:583). In marked contrast to child management, with its myriad contingencies and uncontrollable variables, "stage management," Dickens once noted with relief, was remarkably "like writing a book in company."[32] Characters could be created merely by dint of desire, energy, and will—and exiled or killed off by such means as well. Playing favorites and pitting one character against another (effective, but highly controversial, strategies for maintaining parental control) were perfectly acceptable in managing stage action and narrative economies.[33]

Reminiscing with a fellow (female) trouper about a recent theatrical tour—traipsing, like Crummles's company, about the United Kingdom for a number of far-flung limited runs—Dickens grumbles: "I loathe domestic hearths. I yearn to be a Vagabond. . . . Why have I [so many] . . . children—not engaged at sixpence a night apiece, and dismissible for ever, if they tumble down, but taken on for an indefinite time at a vast expence . . . ? A real house like this is insupportable after that canvass [sic] farm wherein I was so happy.'"[34] Tavistock House was indeed barely supportable, in more ways than one, as Dickens well knew. But what about an *unreal* house like Bleak House? Might one construct an imaginative refuge for an idealized self and a few carefully selected, equally idealized relations? Might one be, as Esther Summerson calls herself, "the happiest of the happy" in that perfectly designed domestic retreat (ch.67)? And what might the ideal household look like? What if, shutting himself up in Bleak House, he were to rewrite his own domestic script with an altered cast of characters—to redistribute roles among a reduced number of players who would perform as directed, willingly taking on the personalities and responsibilities he assigned to them?[35]

First and foremost, make Catherine the Torpid disappear. Split up the normative maternal functions between two adoring daughterly types—though greatly enlarge the household capacity for sympathy generally and disburse it among other family members, bonded not by blood but by mutual care and "inextinguishable affection" (*BH*, ch.55). And, being already engaged in expansion, create in the final chapters, *two* Bleak Houses—in supplementary rather than antagonistic relation—so as to counteract the restlessness that confinement to any single dwelling (however comfortable and commodious) would inevitably cause. Include, however, for purposes of Manichean comparison, a nightmare vision of the "insupportable" "real house," with all those "uncountable children"—who could be neither idealized nor identified with—and who were scandalously neglected (along with the housekeeping) by their mother, to tumble up on their own.[36] Limit the overall number of young children to three (the size he had planned for his own family),[37] and make the oldest a boy (named after his father) and the younger ones, girls. Kill off the limp, exasperating adolescent son (who shows little "disposition to do anything" for himself), but redeem the loss by creating another adolescent character (this time female)—obedient, devoted, energetic, and competent—and give *her* the name of one's own exasperating eldest child (who also happens to be one's own namesake). For if the role of Esther is played by Dickens in drag, then Charley Neckett is Charley Dickens sufficiently feminized to be associatively included in this fantasy of the ideal household. Give one of the dutiful daughter figures a frisson of erotic attraction—but make sure it is only a frisson: she must remain foremost, as Dickens described Mary Hogarth, a "perfect creature," "the grace and life" of the home, and, like Georgina Hogarth, a consummate homemaker (*LCD*, 1:259, 263).

Lastly, split the narrative function into two, and take on both roles oneself. Also split the hero function into two, and inhabit both those parts as well: one a young, kind-hearted, self-sacrificing, professional man, dedicated to bettering the lives of the poor; the other a kind-hearted, self-sacrificing fatherly figure, dedicated to bettering the lives of his family. But keep the younger man's part small, and let him remain in the shadows for most of the narrative. Under no circumstances whatsoever allow him to displace the older in the affections of the heroine, but let the older man be sustained by the affectionate care of the idealized young women, even as his affection sustains them. And make him as close to Inimitable as possible: "the fondest father," the "best and dearest friend," "the object of our deepest love and veneration"; "a superior being," yet "easy" and "familiar" (*BH*, ch.67).

## POSTSCRIPT

Playfully re-imagining his own "insupportable" "real house" helped no doubt to ease the tensions, losses, and disappointments that pressed so forcefully upon Dickens during the writing of *Bleak House*. Perhaps it was his stupendous professional success at imagining such alternative realities—combined with his propensity for sympathizing and identifying with his own personified mental projections more easily than with family members—that encouraged him five years later to try to market another domestic fantasy as a work of nonfiction.[38] In his narrative of their marital separation in 1858, Dickens unsuccessfully cast Catherine in the role of "unnatural mother"—a Gorgon, whose own daughters "harden into stone figures . . . when they can be got to go near her" (*LCD*, 8:559). This was a role—and a performance—that utterly failed to persuade either the public or the other dramatis personae of its probability or verisimilitude. For although the children were helpless to resist their father's "indomitable will" or to marshal the forces of character and energy necessary to break out of *his* narrative of their lives and establish their own, they nevertheless played with growing reluctance the roles he imagined for them, seldom fulfilling his expectations for them, though often (like Catherine) perfectly enacting the failures he came in time grimly to anticipate.

## NOTES

1. See Steven Marcus, *Dickens from Pickwick to Dombey*, especially chapters 1 and 2.

2. Amy Dorrit, age eight, undergoes a similar awakening when she sees her father a widower: "From that time the protection that her wondering eyes had expressed towards him, became embodied in action, and the Child of the Marshalsea took upon herself a new relation towards the Father" (*LD*, 1, ch.7).

3. Fred Kaplan emphasizes Dickens's propensity to overidentify with his children: "Their pattern of vocational indecisiveness made him anxious . . . [as did] the thought that some of them had inherited both their mother's laziness and his own father's tendency toward chronic indebtedness. . . . He felt himself potentially the indefinite financial guarantor of a family of unpromising sons, whose insufficiencies rose up before him" (*Dickens*, 423).

4. Smith, *Theory of Moral Sentiments*, 9–10.

5. An American cartoon of 1867 detected Dickens projecting himself into the shoes, so to speak, of his characters. Showing Dickens in various guises (as Copperfield, Sam Weller, Pickwick, Little Nell, and Dombey), the cartoon carries the following caption: "The great novelist appears in various characters, all, however, showing the same prolific 'head'" (reprinted in Kaplan, *Dickens*, illustration #99).

6. Darwin, *Descent of Man*, 80–82.

7. See Hume, *Treatise on Human Nature*, 4–11. "Uneasiness" quotation is found on page 9.

8. While writing *Dombey and Son*, Dickens confessed that "the fading life of little Paul" seemed "'the only reality . . . and all the realities [but] shortlived shadows'" (Johnson, *Charles Dickens*, Revised and Abridged, 326; subsequent references are to this edition).

9. Peter Ackroyd, *Dickens*, 879. Such remoteness must have been accentuated for his children by his oft-reported technique of composing characters by acting them out before mirrors—which were strategically placed in Dickens's household. Ackroyd reports that most of Dickens's children noted at one time or another his fear "of feeling itself, . . . that curious reserve which he exhibited towards those closest to him" (828). See also Henry Dickens, *Memories of My Father*. On the closeness Kate Dickens felt for Thackeray, see Johnson, *Charles Dickens*, 505–6.

10. The more distant the relation, the less discomfort he apparently felt in acknowledging the intensity of his feeling. According to Forster, Dickens's "genius was his fellow-feeling with his race; his mere personality was never the bound or limit to his perceptions, however strongly sometimes it might colour them" (2:117). It was the opportunity to indulge without restraint his "peculiar personal relation with his audience" (almost a "tangible link") that made his readings and theatrical performances so necessary to him in later years (Ackroyd, *Dickens*, 905).

11: *Paterfamilias*

11. Dickens, "Familiar Epistle From a Parent to a Child," 552–54, passim.

12. As Marcus points out, "The prodigal parent and the influence of his improvidence on his children is one subject Dickens never abandons for long" (*Dickens from Pickwick to Dombey*, 122).

13. In the "Autobiographical Fragment," Dickens twice mentions his fatherhood in the context of his reliving childhood feelings of pain, shame, and betrayal generated by the memory of Warren's Blacking factory: "even now, famous and caressed and happy, I often forget in my dreams that I have a dear wife and children; even that I am a man; and wander desolately back to that time of my life"; "My old way home by the Borough made me cry, after my eldest child could speak" (Forster, 1:23, 33).

14. Nicholas makes an analogy between Bray's "monstrous" treatment of his daughter Madeline and Britain's shocking treatment of its fatherless poor: "Last night the sacrifice of a young, affectionate, and beautiful creature to such a wretch and in such a cause, had seemed a thing too monstrous to succeed. . . . But now, . . . he thought how regularly things went on . . .—how many those who lay in noisome pens, . . . generation upon generation, without a home to shelter them or the energies of one single man directed to their aid . . .—how ignorance was punished and never taught—. . . how much injustice, and misery, and wrong" (ch.53). Dickens also touches in this novel on a point that he was to press more urgently later in his career: that sympathy "expended on out-of-the-way objects" rather than on one's own personal offspring or the homeless children of Britain, who "are constantly within the sight and hearing of the most unobservant person alive," was "diseased" (ch.18).

15. It is probably worth remembering that Dickens not only shared with Ralph Nickleby a sense of grievance against his parents, but that he, too, found himself irritated by the appeals of his prodigal relations, even if he characteristically answered those appeals with considerably more generosity and dutiful good will.

16. Bowen, *Other Dickens*, 122.

17. Ibid., 121–22. Moreover, the interpolated tale of the "Five Sisters of York" (chapter six) reworks tragically the sentiment of the Kenswigs's girls being "too beautiful to live."

18. Michie, "The Avuncular and Beyond," 85.

19. Mrs. Nickleby is also guilty of projection: misreading Kate's agitation at seeing her mother at the theater in the company of Hawk as "symptoms" of "violent love" (ch.27), Mrs. Nickleby imagines what *she* would feel in her daughter's position and attributes that feeling to Kate: "she expressed her entire approval of the admirable choice she had made" in Sir Mulberry Hawk (ch.28). The ambiguous referent of the second "she" (she Kate or she Mrs. Nickleby?) grammatically assists the projection.

20. Gardiner, "On Female Identity and Writing by Women," *Critical Inquiry* 8 (1981): 356.

21. Johnson remarks that for all of Dickens's resentment against his father for having reversed their roles, what he remembered at the time of his father's death was a "tenderness that throughout many a night had nursed a sick child" (*Charles Dickens*, 376).

22. At the very least, "the reciprocity and chastity of Nicholas's love for Smike seems a good deal more interesting to Dickens than his perfunctory passion for Madeline Bray" (Bowen, *Other Dickens*, 124).

23. Although as Eileen Cleere has recently reminded us, the nuclear family in

nineteenth-century Britain—given the high mortality rate—might be more accurately described as the normative ideal rather than the majority experience. See *Avuncularism*.

24. Johnson, *Charles Dickens*, 389.

25. Quoted in Johnson, *Charles Dickens*, 362. At the time of Dora's death, Catherine was convalescing at the health spa of Great Malvern, where Dickens had placed her a month or so earlier, from a "nervous illness" resembling severe and prolonged postpartum depression. Her habitual "anti-Malthusian state" meant that such depression had become virtually chronic.

26. The letter is worth quoting from at greater length: "'The manner in which my uncountable children disappeared when he talked to me, and I stood again upon the enchanted Island of those brilliant old proposals of my own (accepted in the most fervent manner, and never coming to anything) which graced the thousands of years (as they seem to me now) when I was yet an infant in the eye of the law—is proof to me, in itself, of the goodness of such a character.'" I am grateful to Rosemarie Bodenheimer for bringing this letter to my attention.

The trope of innumerability also occurs several weeks earlier, before the last of his children had made his appearance: "I begin to count the children incorrectly, they are so many; and to find fresh ones coming down to dinner in a perfect procession, when I thought there were no more" (*LCD*, 6:591).

27. Dickens's letter to Sigourney (*LCD*, 6:400) lists all of the children and their ages, but, except for noting that Charley was "at school at Eton," comments only on Walter.

28. Quoted in Kaplan, *Dickens*, 288.

29. For a brief account of Dickens's child-rearing habits and his diminishing affection for the children as they aged, see Ackroyd, *Dickens* (877–80). Ackroyd claims that "self-reliance" was second only to "absolute neatness" as the virtue Dickens most wanted to teach his sons and the one they almost unanimously failed to learn (879).

30. As Fred Kaplan succinctly puts it, for Dickens, parental "concern" was "inseparable from exasperation" (*Dickens*, 427). In his last years, Dickens seems to have considered all of his children, with the exception of Henry, to be failures. Walter and Sydney had become dissipated, though the former, by dying from fever shortly after acquitting himself well during the Indian Mutiny, had done something to soften his father's judgment of him; Sydney, however, had finally been forbidden to return home. Frank, who proved "of little use" to Dickens in the offices of *All the Year Round*, was sent to join the Bengal Mounted Police (Johnson, *Charles Dickens*, 494). Plorn, who like his brother Alfred was at constant loose ends, was, like that brother, packed off to Australia.

31. Sylvère Monod and George Ford point out that "there are at least twenty-four different households pictured" in *Bleak House* ("Introduction," *Bleak House*, xi).

32. Quoted by Johnson, *Charles Dickens*, 811.

33. With both his children and his friends, Dickens tended first to idealize and then, when they failed to live up to his expectations, to allow disappointment to slide into devaluation. The example of Plorn illustrates this point. First cast as Benjamin, whom "'of all his children he loved . . . best . . . truly his Benjamin,'" Plorn later was considered to be just one more Prodigal Son (quoted by Kaplan, *Dickens*, 531).

34. *LCD*, 5:374. This letter to Mary Cowden Clarke is dated 22 July 1848, a week after touring the Amateur Company (a precursor to the Dramatic Representations of the Guild) to raise money for a Shakespeare museum curatorship.

*11: Paterfamilias*

35. Near the end of his life, Dickens confided to a friend that "one of my most cherished day-dreams" is to "hold supreme authority" over a company of actors: "the pieces acted should be dealt with according to my pleasure, and touched up here and there in obedience to my own judgement; the players as well as the plays being absolutely under my command" (quoted in Johnson, *Charles Dickens*, 577).

36. As others have noted, the portrayal of the Jellyby household was likely inspired by Dickens's visit to the home of Caroline Chisholm, founder of the Family Colonization Loan Society, whose "bad housekeeping and her children's dirty faces haunted him" (Kaplan, *Dickens*, 287).

But Dickens had firsthand experience of boys tumbling on the stairs. He writes to Wilkie Collins (17 July 1855): "Walter goes back to School on the first of August. Will you come . . . [the day before], for that is the day on which he leaves us and we begin (here's a Parent!) to be able to be comfortable. Why a boy of that age should seem to have on at all times, 150 pair of double soled boots, and to be always jumping a bottom stair with the whole 150, I don't know. But the woeful fact is within my daily experience" (*LCD*, 7:675–76).

37. In a letter to the actor William Macready, announcing the impending birth of his namesake, Kate Macready Dickens, Dickens writes: "I . . . must solicit you to become godfather to that last and final branch of a genteel small family of three which I am told may be looked for" in a few months time (*LCD*, 1:571).

38. As Johnson remarks, with Dickens's "desire to control the participants, to determine negotiations and even to manipulate the reactions of onlookers, he was, in a sense, attempting to write a book out of real people and real events" (*Charles Dickens*, 811–12).

# 12

# Reading with Buzfuz

Dickens, Sexuality, Interrogation

**JAMES ELI ADAMS**

Over the past two decades or so, the work of literary and cultural criticism has come to be widely described as a project of *interrogation*. This is a striking and outwardly perplexing development. Why should a discipline that so insistently professes resistance to authority and power find its idiom in the activity of police and prosecutors? One answer to this question would explore the recent provenance of the usage, which seems to derive mainly from France, particularly the example of Althusser. Another path, however, would take us to a more remote genealogy: within the Victorian novel. The novel has been an especially fruitful ground for interrogation, largely because Victorian fiction seems to generate the very archetype of human identity on which the procedure depends. In the wake of broadly Foucauldian readings, the Victorian novel has been associated with the effort to produce a fundamentally private subjectivity anchored in an integral, "deep" psyche, which is defined against the hostile glare of publicity, or the universalizing, abstracting dynamics of instrumental reason. Viewed thus, the novel always has much to hide. As it attempts to screen its characters from surveillance (so the official story runs), the novel inevitably reinscribes the power it ostensibly resists. The critic must then elicit from the fictional artifact its complicity in a web of oppressive forces. We read for the pleasure of scandalous exposure—a pleasure borne out in the titles of a number of important studies: "Caught in the Act," "Secret Subjects, Open Secrets," "Sex Scandal."

12: *Reading with Buzfuz*

Such critical engagements tend to reserve pride of place for interrogations of sexuality. The Victorian novel, it is presumed, produces erotic desire as the very archetype of privacy—a realm of "inwardness" that can only be intimated through a rhetoric of obliquity and circumspection, a strategy which in itself suggests the high stakes in being found out. This interrogation of the private self typically extends to the agency of the author, who is seen to be enmeshed in sexual discourses or desires that elude his or her awareness and control—a further mode of complicity in orders of power that await the triumphant exposure of the critic. Recently, however, this understanding of sexuality and subjectivity has been challenged on two very different fronts. Within queer theory, critics (most notably Eve Kosofsky Sedgwick) have objected that symptomatic or paranoid modes of exegesis have obstructed richer, suppler understandings of human identity and experience that might be derived from what Sedgwick calls "reparative reading."[1] Within study of the Victorian novel proper, critics, including Judith John and Elaine Hadley, have contested notions of the Victorian subject as a radically privatized self, by pointing to the countervailing power of theatricality, particularly melodrama, within Victorian culture.

These conflicts, I will argue, are in fact centrally and cannily rehearsed within the novels of Charles Dickens, who found an especially resonant forum for them in the Victorian courtroom. This is not as somber as it may sound, for the courtroom in Dickens is notoriously sparing in gravitas; indeed, for my purposes the most telling courtroom drama occurs in *The Pickwick Papers*, in the memorable trial of Bardell versus Pickwick. The famous performance of Serjeant Buzfuz, counsel for the plaintiff, may seem to subject our own strategies of interrogation—or something very much like them—to withering parody. Yet the misplaced ingenuity of Buzfuz's interpretation points us to a suggestive clash between two different models of sexuality, and of novelistic character, that will resonate throughout Dickens's career and in much of Victorian culture. Reading with Buzfuz helps us to see the point of familiar distinctions between early and late Dickens; at the same time, his performance suggests important continuities between those two bodies of work. The forms of suspicion anatomized in *David Copperfield*, for example, are far more somber and momentous than those of Buzfuz, but they share with the earlier work an understanding of sexuality as a markedly public transaction, a collective construction at odds with the conjuring of a "deep" private self. In this light, Buzfuz's example repays more serious reflection.

■ ■ ■

In his famous courtroom interrogation of two messages from Pickwick to the widow Bardell, Serjeant Buzfuz sets a daunting example for close readers everywhere. "These letters," he exhorts the jury, "bespeak the character of the man."

> They are not open, fervent, eloquent epistles, breathing nothing but the language of affectionate attachment. They are covert, sly, underhanded communications, but, fortunately, far more conclusive than if couched in the most glowing language and the most poetic imagery—letters that must be viewed with a cautious and suspicious eye—letters that were evidently intended at the time, by Pickwick, to mislead and delude any third parties into whose hands they might fall. Let me read the first:—"Garroway's, twelve o'clock. Dear Mrs B,—Chops and Tomata sauce. Yours, PICKWICK." Gentlemen, what does this mean? Chops and tomata sauce. Yours, Pickwick! Chops! Gracious heavens! And Tomata sauce! Gentlemen, is the happiness of a sensitive and confiding female to be trifled away, by such shallow artifices as these? (*PP*, ch.34)

This travesty bears on the way we read now, first of all, as it captures the risk that our own pursuit of deep meaning may end up sounding like that of Buzfuz. Never more so than now, perhaps, when so much exegesis, particularly that dealing with sexuality, similarly relies on the raised eyebrow, the insinuating quotation, the portentous repetition of some outwardly banal phrase. But the more pointed relevance, I think, is not that this could seem a comic travesty of our own procedures—or that the line between those procedures and travesty is sometimes difficult to draw. Instead, I want to stress the sheer canniness of Dickens's mockery, on a subject on which he is often thought to be profoundly evasive or unknowing, at best uncanny. For the comedy here allows Dickens to represent with hyperbolic insistence a concerted, deliberate construction of transgressive desire.

The comic travesty of a breach-of-promise suit may seem an unhelpfully oblique approach to sexuality. But for Dickens's contemporaries, the sexual dimension would have been underscored by an unmistakable allusion to recent news, a notorious trial on which Dickens had reported for the *Morning Chronicle* just weeks before. "The memorable trial of Bardell against Pickwick" recasts the action brought by the Hon. George Norton against Lord Melbourne, the Prime Minister of Great Britain, alleging "criminal conversation"—that is, adultery—with Norton's wife, the Hon. Caroline Norton. The social prominence of the parties naturally created quite a stir, but

## 12: Reading with Buzfuz

what caught the young Dickens's ear as a court reporter was the plaintiff's counsel's interpretation of what passed for evidence. Here, for example, is (in toto) one of the notes introduced at the trial: "I will call about half past 4. Yours, Melbourne." And here is the argument of Norton's attorney, Sir William Follett, as taken down by Dickens himself: "The style and form of these notes, Gentlemen, seems to impart much more than they contain. Cautiously, I admit, they are worded; there are no professions of love . . . but still they are not the letters of an ordinary acquaintance."[2] And the same line of interrogation was reported in a different paper, *The Morning Advertiser*:

> They state that Lord Melbourne would be there by such an hour, and nothing more; but there is something in the style of the notes that seems to me to lead to something like a suspicion of what was going on. The first note merely said, "I will call about half-past four. . . ." This letter has no beginning; it has no commencement. It does not commence as letters actually do which are written by gentlemen to ladies. The next letter was in these words: "How are you? I shall not be able to call today, but I probably shall tomorrow.—Yours" This is not the note of a mere acquaintance.[3]

And on it goes.

This lofty but willful insinuation clearly echoes in Buzfuz's virtuoso turn with "Chops and tomata sauce." And the echo brings home a larger design and historical resonance in what commentators tend to call vaguely Buzfuz's "absurd manipulation" of evidence.[4] Dickens's target is less aristocratic transgression than the legal system itself—or, more precisely, the modes of suspicion that the legal system engenders and enforces. Like the plaintiff's counsel in *Norton v. Melbourne*, Buzfuz transforms a seemingly mundane communication into a textual field of erotic insinuation. "Why is Mrs. Bardell so earnestly entreated not to agitate herself about a warming-pan, unless (as is no doubt the case) it is a mere cover for hidden fire—a mere substitute for some endearing word or promise, agreeably to a preconcerted system of correspondence, artfully contrived by Pickwick with a view to his contemplated desertion?" (*PP*, ch.34) For Dickens's earliest readers, the joke drew added point from awareness that Buzfuz corresponded to a world outside the novel, a world in which a very substantial and weighty judicial apparatus was dedicated to doing just that—to producing from textuality a trove of (among other things) carnal knowledge.

In treating writing as an encryption of desire, Buzfuz's mode of engagement has an enduring resonance in Victorian culture. Here is an excerpt from another cross-examination, this one drawn from a real courtroom some thirty-five years later, in which a prosecuting attorney produced a letter that begins, "My darling Ernie, I had another cry in the train after leaving you, then lay back and managed to get to sleep." The Queen's Counsel was deeply troubled: "Gentleman, what language is this! A man crying at parting for a few weeks from another man. 'I had a cry in the train!' What language is that? Is it the language of friendship, or is it the language of love? It seems to me very strange. . . . Gentlemen, you may put your own interpretation upon that, but it seems to me very strange and I do not understand it, I confess."[5]

This is an excerpt from the Crown's prosecution in 1870 of Boulton and Park, two young men arrested for dressing as women and subsequently tried for conspiracy to commit sodomy. William Cohen, who has incisively analyzed this prosecution in his book, *Sex Scandal: The Private Parts of Victorian Fiction,* notes that the defense counsel attempted to rebut such insinuation by insisting that it was merely fanciful projection—that the counsel's inability to distinguish between friendship and love was, in effect, merely Buzfuzian. But Buzfuz is never mentioned in Cohen's book. Indeed, I have never come across Buzfuz in accounts of Victorian sexuality. And this is perplexing: Buzfuz's address of what he imagines to be encrypted desire seems so importantly congruent with current literary analysis that we might expect work on Victorian sexuality to cite him at every turn. Could one find a more fundamental example of the interpretation of obliquity (or opacity) as an insinuation of transgressive desire?

We have overlooked the relevance of the episode because of its context. Until very recently, critics have understood sexuality almost entirely in terms of psychic depth; indeed, sexuality probably still remains, in the wake of Freud, our very paradigm of inwardness. *Pickwick Papers,* on the other hand, persistently refuses our yearning for the illusion of interiority, of "deep" and mysterious psychic regions. "It's like a dream . . . a hideous dream," Pickwick remarks at one point; "The idea of a man's walking about, all day, with a horse he can't get rid of!" (*PP,* ch.5). The deflationary gesture here is exemplary of most of the novel: we may yearn for insinuations of momentous self-recognition, or glimpses of frightening desire, but we get the sheer inanity of walking around all day with an unwanted horse.[6] Now, of course, the truly ambitious exegete might labor to elicit some deeper erotic fantasy in Pickwick's exclamation, but the result, I daresay, would merely reproduce the example of the master, Buzfuz.[7]

This is *not* to say, however, that *The Pickwick Papers* offers us a world without sexuality. On the contrary, the novel is absolutely saturated with it. Most obviously, Sam Weller and his father trade in an offhand, comic denaturing of aggression, which frequently takes the form of erotic violence: "I think he's the wictim o' connubiality, as Blue Beard's domestic chaplain said, with a tear of pity, ven he buried him" (*PP,* ch.20). More subtly, however, Pickwick himself comes to seem enveloped in sexual desire. Not that Pickwick ever *expresses* such desire; his innocence in this regard, as commentators often note, is a central feature of the idyllic quality of the novel. Less often noted, however, is that Pickwick's innocence is brought home through his seeming immunity to the sexual contagion that circulates throughout the novel. That circulation is evoked not only by Buzfuz but also by a host of colleagues—including the narrator—who join in an effort to discover erotic desire in even the most outwardly innocent of Pickwick's gestures. So, for example, during the famous Eatanswill election scenes, when Pickwick kisses his hand to Mrs. Pott, wife of the renowned editor of the Eatanswill Gazette, "this very innocent action," the narrator tells us, "was sufficient to awaken [the crowd's] facetiousness."

> "Oh you wicked old rascal," cried one voice, "looking arter the girls, are you?"
> "Oh you wenerable sinner," cried another.
> "Putting on his spectacles to look at a married 'ooman!" said a third.
> "I see him a winkin' at her, with his wicked old eye," shouted a fourth.
> "Look arter your wife, Pott," bellowed a fifth;—and then there was a roar of laughter.
> As these taunts were accompanied with invidious comparisons between Mr. Pickwick and an aged ram, and several witticisms of the like nature; and as they moreover tended to convey reflections upon the honour of an innocent lady, Mr. Pickwick's indignation was excessive. (*PP,* ch.13)

"Facetious" they may be, but the crowd's taunts clearly anticipate Buzfuz's more earnest interrogation. Not only Pickwick's letters but also his every gesture seem to become in their very lack of hidden depth a screen onto which observers are invited to project erotic fantasy. And this collective enterprise generates a current of insistently sexualized reference—such as the striking allusions to *Othello.* "Pickwick and an aged ram" recalls the opening scene, where Iago torments Brabantio, "an old black ram / Is tupping your white ewe" (lines 88–89), and this allusion is in turn taken up, I think, in the very surname of Pickwick's good friend, Tracy Tupman. (Later, in chapter seventeen, a minor character, recalling Othello's demand for "ocular proof," gains "ocular demonstration" of another character's wealth).

At moments, even the narrator reproduces the sexualizing dynamic of Buzfuz and the Eatanswill crowd, with yet more potent and subtly prurient gestures, reinforced as they are by the authority of his privileged vantage. So, for example, as Pickwick departs from Manor Farm at Dingley Dell, the narrator coyly remarks, "He kissed the young ladies—we were going to say, as if they were his own daughters, only as he might possibly have infused a little more warmth into the salutation, the comparison would not be quite appropriate" (*PP,* ch.11). The narrator thus amplifies even the faintest erotic vibrations that might animate the Pickwickian kiss, by associating it with the whisper of incest. All of this, of course, eludes Pickwick himself; it is the narrator, not Pickwick, who envisions the young ladies as his own daughters.

Pickwick thus not only "blunders into erotically pregnant situations," as one commentator puts it;[8] the other characters in the novel seem joined in an effort to envelop Pickwick in sexuality. Their chorus incarnates energies most arrestingly focused in the grotesque figure of the "Fat Boy," whose embodiment of seemingly unbounded appetite also points up the somatic investments in various scenes of romantic affection. After suddenly materializing in the midst of a romantic assignation in the arbor at Dingley Dell, where Mr Tupman is wooing Mrs Wardle with fervent extravagance, the Fat Boy subsequently recounts the scene to Mrs. Wardle's elderly mother, prefacing his narration with the remark, "I wants to make your flesh creep" (*PP,* ch.8). Which is, in another context, precisely what Buzfuz seeks to do. Buzfuz wishes to arouse his courtroom audience in a twofold sense, evoking their indignation by appealing to their appreciation of (as he imagines it) predatory desire.

This sustained current of sexual insinuation of course recalls the novels of Fielding and Smollett, from which *The Pickwick Papers* draws so much inspiration. Like those works, Dickens's novel is hardly lacking in sexuality. What is missing is psychology—the psychology, that is, associated with the forms of interiority that we are accustomed to in high Victorian realism. In *Pickwick Papers,* sexuality is a widely dispersed surface effect, or (more precisely) an affect cut adrift from structures of deep psychology. In the scenes I have noted, Pickwick's sexuality never seems to reside in Pickwick himself—indeed, it hardly seems to belong to him. Instead, it is a collective, public experience, a shared projection onto a character defined largely through resistance to the premises of Buzfuz's paranoid interpretation.[9] Put differently, Dickens shows us a world in which sexuality is emphatically constructed, but in which sexuality does not constitute a private self. As Buzfuz's interrogation seeks a hidden, "deep" Pickwick, it only underscores the absence of such a being. And yet Buzfuz thereby sheds unexpected light on the very different model of sexuality that becomes increasingly prominent in Dickens's later work.

In *The Pickwick Papers,* Buzfuz's interrogation is comically misplaced because it presumes a deep psychology at odds with the dominant mode of characterization in the novel—which is the dominant mode throughout early Dickens (the phase that is typically presumed to end with *Martin Chuzzlewit*). The lawyers presume a world of hidden and therefore sinister design that is alien to the novel, where desire is nearly always transparent, is indeed insistently performed, and is misread only by the utterly foolish or facetious. In this vein, Dickens throughout his early writings calls upon varieties of suspicion to organize fairly consistent and clear-cut moral oppositions. Within the fundamentally melodramatic framing of the major characters, suspicion is an index of villainy, a self-implicating projection of characters who harbor their own damning secrets. One need only think how often the word "deep" is invoked as invective (as in Arthur Gride's account of Ralph Nickleby) to see how profoundly (as Juliet John has pointed out) the early work resists a model of psychology associated with the alienated self of romanticism. The paranoid interpretive stance that pursues, and thereby reinforces, a solitary, withdrawn selfhood finds an acme of sorts in *The Old Curiosity Shop*, where Mr. Brass recalls the leading maxim of his father, "Foxey": "Always suspect everybody" (*OCS*, ch.66).

This comic tension offers a suggestive fulcrum for distinguishing early and late Dickens. Over the course of Dickens's career, the comedy in Foxey's imperative grows increasingly unstable, as Dickens's own writing more openly and pervasively trades in its own momentous secrets—and conjures up its own hermeneutics of suspicion. Buzfuz and his fellow representatives of the law, in and out of fiction, not only depend on but also help to generate a model of psychology increasingly prominent in Dickens's later fiction—and, more broadly, in Victorian realism. The misplaced ingenuity of Buzfuz, I am suggesting, throws into especially sharp relief a fictional technique in which the illusion of psychic depth depends on evoking an aura of mystery or reserve, which not only accommodates but often incites the discovery of transgressive desire. In *Pickwick* itself, the seductions of "mystery" are treated light-heartedly, as an appeal to traditionally feminine curiosity: "the temptation ... of hearing something at present embellished in mystery" is what calms the agitated residents of the seminary for young ladies in chapter sixteen. In *Barnaby Rudge,* curiosity grows more portentous but remains harnessed by moral and rhetorical authority. "To surround anything, however monstrous or ridiculous, with an air of mystery, is to invest it with a secret charm, and power of attraction which to the crowd is irresistible," the narrator remarks. "Curiosity is, and has been from the creation of the world, a master-passion" (*BR*, ch.37). In immediate context, the comment indicts the demagogue who would inflame "the unthinking portion of mankind," but it also points to the fascinations of the novelist. In Dickens's later novels, the two callings are less securely distinguished. In *A Tale of Two Cities,* for example, critics have noted an unsettling complicity of the novelist's interests with those of the revolutionary conspirators: both thrive on the fantasy that dangerous secrets lurk everywhere.[10] Within this pursuit of dangerous secrets, sexuality tends to become similarly associated with hidden, private recesses of a character's psyche.

As Buzfuz points us to this momentous shift, the familiar conjunction of fiction and the law—the novel and the police—is demonstrated with startling clarity in a novel that New Historicists rarely notice. We miss the import of Buzfuz's interrogation because we devalue "early" Dickens, reading these works as if they were failed efforts at the techniques that predominate from roughly *Dombey* onwards—as if, for example, the characters of Pickwick and Nicholas Nickleby represented a psychology of the same order as that of David Copperfield or Eugene Wrayburn in *Our Mutual Friend.* Nonetheless, crucial continuities exist between the two modes of characterization, which suggest that throughout Dickens's writing, sexuality remains a complexly public dynamic, its association with a private, "secret" self more qualified and self-conscious than received wisdom allows. This fact emerges when one sets the comic preoccupation with breach of promise in the early novels against the far more somber and consequential suspicion directed toward hints of adulterous or "fallen" sexuality in women. Buzfuz, it turns out, has a great deal to tell us about *David Copperfield.*

■ ■ ■

*David Copperfield* has become something of a *locus classicus* for the study of Dickens and sexuality, largely through the influence of D. A. Miller's scintillating reading in *The Novel and the Police.* I want to dwell on an important subplot of *David Copperfield* that Miller does not mention—that involving Annie Strong, the young wife of David's schoolmaster, Dr. Strong, to whom David, in concert with virtually every character acquainted with the couple, suspects Annie of being unfaithful. (As it turns out—I hope I am not giving too much away—she is innocent.) This subplot is emphatically a drama of knowledge, whose psychological involutions in many ways epitomize what critics find most compelling about later Dickens. The self-conception of the protagonist is obscurely related to his radical ambivalence toward the figure of a young woman who, as she stands on the verge of "fallenness," unwittingly expresses what David takes up as a kind of personal blazon, a mantra of self-recognition for his own errors in object choice: "my undisciplined heart." The forms of recognition brought about through this subplot evoke a sense of psychic depth that is alien to *Pickwick,* and the tonal register is dramatically different, as the suspicion brought to bear on Annie is far more momentous than that of Buzfuz's interrogation. For all of these differences, however, this subplot recasts Dickens's concerns in the account of *Bardell v. Pickwick.* The suspicion of "breach of promise" is importantly congruent with the suspicion of sexual transgression in Annie: she is suspected, as it were, of breach of promise after the fact. And this congruence in turn reveals Dickens's persistent concern with forms of interpretation that, in an effort to discover illicit sexuality, in fact construct it.

The two episodes differ most tellingly, for my purposes, in their differing understandings of the mechanisms of interpretation. The Annie Strong subplot in effect develops the preoccupation in Pickwick with "the force of circumstances." This is a phrase Pickwick utters soon after he is served with notice of the widow Bardell's lawsuit, an event that prompts Mr. Tupman to recall an incident in chapter twelve, when he and other friends had burst in on Pickwick with Mrs. Bardell "reclining in his arms." "Gracious powers," the innocent Pickwick responds, "what a dreadful instance of the force of circumstances!" (*PP,* ch.12). The comic possibilities of the scene echo, of course, throughout the domestic intrigues of the novel. Pickwick's remark, "We are all the victims of circumstances" (*PP,* ch.18), is truer than he realizes. As the novel repeatedly stages collisions between character and context, agency and circumstance, breach of promise comes as near as any structure can to organizing its notoriously diffuse action. The accusation of breach of promise underscores the often vexed relation between desire and obligation that organizes modern "respectable" domesticity.[11] It also links erotic yearning to an insistent preoccupation with social appearances—a preoccupation that may readily shade into the paranoid and even at lesser intensity obviously may compromise the autonomy of the actors thus preoccupied. At their most extreme, banal domestic anxieties can thus enforce rituals of suspicion, interrogations of fidelity, rivaling those that Buzfuz deploys in the courtroom.

This deference to "circumstances" may seem to endow them with an agency of their own. Not merely a misleading frame, circumstances seem to exert an active power over the human beings entrapped within them. "Is it not a wonderful circumstance," a bewildered Pickwick announces just before the lawsuit is served, "that we seem destined to enter no man's house without involving him in some degree of trouble?" (*PP,* ch.18)—the "trouble" that typically turns on sexual misunderstanding. Here, in effect, "circumstance" itself seems to be doing the work I have noted in the commentary of observers throughout the novel. "Circumstance" mimics the sexualizing dynamic in, for example, the reference to Pickwick kissing young women as if they were his daughters. Accordingly, when "the force of circumstances" seems to compromise a character's virtue, the idiom conjures up an agency at odds with the character's own. Circumstances themselves seem to be indicting Pickwick, quite apart from any legal assistance. We have, in essence, a comic version of a fantasy that powerfully unites legal argument and narrative, as Alexander Welsh has shown in *Strong Representations:* the fantasy that sufficient evidence speaks its own truth, that facts cannot lie.

In a sense, then, Pickwickian "circumstances" comically externalize a form of paranoia, and it is not hard to imagine someone doing a Foucauldian number on this structure analogous to the Freudian reading of Pickwick's dreams—with similarly disconcerting results. For in Pickwick the comic mode disarms the potentially dire consequences of misplaced suspicion. "Circumstances" shape judgment in a form that does not determine character but merely frames it—in the dual sense that it both isolates and distorts a character's actions. Put differently, comedy ultimately disables the consequentiality of "circumstances": the force of circumstances is the power of accident, that power which so often vexes, but ultimately redeems, heroes of the picaresque.

*David Copperfield,* however, brings a new weight and complexity to the force of circumstances in understanding human action and identity. Here Dickens is interested not only in the way in which that power may abridge autonomy and agency but also in the complicity of human beings in constructing and sustaining what in the early novels is a more impersonal dynamic.[12] Although the alleged transgressions of Pickwick and Annie are outwardly congruent, in *David Copperfield* the suspicion of sexuality is understood as an interpretive project requiring analysis in its own right—unlike Buzfuzian interrogation, whose weaknesses are presumed to be self-evident. The suspicion directed at Annie Strong therefore elicits scrutiny not only because it is more consequential than that of Buzfuz—particularly as it is focused on "fallen" womanhood rather than male transgression—but also because its complexity, as a mode of interpretation, makes it subject to momentous error, which is precisely what entraps Annie. As it entraps Annie, however, suspicion also underscores her affinities with Pickwick—and David's with Buzfuz. In this epistemological drama, the guilty party turns out to be not Annie but David, and the locus of desire turns out to be less any particular character than (once again) the interpretive project itself.

That the drama surrounding Annie is as much epistemological as sexual emerges from her first appearance in the novel, in chapter sixteen, "I am a New Boy in more Senses than One." In a chapter centrally concerned with forms of knowing, Dr. Strong, master of the school at which David is newly arrived, is a figure highly reminiscent of Pickwick. He is "the least suspicious of mankind," Mr. Wickfield remarks (*DC,* ch.16)—one of the many remarks that inevitably generate suspicion of Annie, who is so much younger than her husband that David presumes she is his daughter. Set against Strong's innocence, David's guilty knowledge is thrown into sharp relief. Acutely conscious of his lack of formal schooling, he nonetheless reflects that "in what I did know, I was much farther removed from my companions than in what I did not" (*DC,* ch.16). The other boys, David thinks, are so "innocent" that he shrinks from their discovering "how knowing I was"—knowing in "some of the meanest phases" of London life and London streets (ch.16). While David quails before his own knowledge, however, Uriah Heep, taken on as Mr. Wickfield's assistant, is busy gleaning and storing whatever compromising evidence falls his way, apparently as befits an aspiring attorney: when David first encounters him in this chapter, he is reading Tidd's Practice, "improving my legal knowledge." Yet for all his alliance with the legal powers of darkness, Heep is also—as many readers have observed—something of a double to David. David is riveted by "a sort of fascination" for Heep (ch.16), "attracted to him in very repulsion" (ch.25), and later, when Heep in chapter forty-two springs his trap to expose (as he imagines) Annie's waywardness, there is a virtual melding of the two characters: "I saw so plainly, in the stealthy exultation of his face, what I already so plainly knew; I mean that he had forced his confidence upon me." The exasperated David slaps Heep, who "caught the hand in his, and we stood in that connexion looking at each other. We stood so, a long time" (ch.42). When Heep then berates Copperfield for so losing his self-possession as to strike someone of Heep's lowly status, the turn of the knife is complete: "He knew me better than I knew myself."

There are, of course, many grounds of identification here, and one might interpret this strange exchange as a screen for all sorts of intimacy—including homoerotic desire. But one common ground is suspicion of both Annie and one another. David's own suspicions are projected onto Heep, as the unwitting observer tries to distance himself from the eagerly grasping spy, a character in whom both suspicion and sexuality can be disowned as perversion, the distinguishing attributes of (yet again) the predatory legal mind. Yet the effect of this structure is to join the two characters more closely than ever. Hence the striking fact that the sense of interiority generated in this episode characterizes the interpreters of sexuality rather than the character who ostensibly embodies transgressive sexuality. Initially, when Annie's red ribbon inexplicably disappears along with her cousin Jack Maldon, it seems an emblem of her guilt, and David senses in her face, "such a face as I never saw," a psychic complexity alien to the world of Pickwick: "It was beautiful in its form, it was so ashy pale, it was so fixed in its abstraction, it was so full of a wild, sleep-walking, dreamy horror of I don't know what" (*DC*, ch.16). Ultimately, however, Annie remains, like Pickwick, a screen for projection rather than a harbor of psychic depth. Moreover, the interiority that develops in this episode is not that of a radical privacy but instead is emphatically intersubjective. David discovers himself, and the desire that rules his project, by seeing himself in the eyes of Uriah Heep.

Far from enacting a disjunctive break with strategies in Dickens's early novels, then, the management of suspicion and innocence in *David Copperfield* in fact suggests the enduring relevance of Buzfuz. What in *The Pickwick Papers* is mocked as a delirious paranoia is reconstituted in the later fiction as a far more unsettling, because more pervasive, habit of social reading, which has the power to constitute the sexuality it purports to discover. The persistence of this structure, moreover, complicates the view that in *David Copperfield* (and "the Novel") "the self is most itself at the moment when its defining inwardness is most secret, most withheld from writing."[13] On the contrary, Annie's self is most itself when it is being acquitted in something akin to an informal tribunal, a tacit interrogation. And David's self is most itself as he is participating in that process. David's inchoate recognition of his own investments in the interrogation does develop an interiority not to be found in *The Pickwick Papers*. But as it also reveals a fundamental continuity with earlier, broadly melodramatic structures of recognition, the novel resists an association of identity with radically alienated interiority.

That continuity also confounds the premise in so much recent criticism that sexuality in the Victorian novel is a largely unwitting or uncanny production, an effect generated by novelists unable to grasp their own dynamics of representation. The axiom that Victorian novelists could never be masters in their own house of fiction is a difficult one to relinquish, not least because it sustains so many performances of our own critical mastery. In the wake of Freud, with sexuality as our archetype of knowledge, we pursue meaning as an inadvertent disclosure, an unwitting insinuation or an uncanny eruption of buried energies or systems of meaning that eluded the writer—and that only the daring and subtlety of the modern critic can elicit. To be sure, no fictional design is entirely transparent to its author. But the example of Buzfuz suggests that Dickens's engagement with sexuality, however circumspect or oblique, is a good deal more canny, more knowing, than we tend to allow. We might derive an importantly different history of both sexuality and the Victorian novel by attending to the reading of Buzfuz.

## NOTES

1. Eve Kosofsky Sedgwick, "Paranoid Reading and Reparative Reading," 5.
2. John Butt and Kathleen Tillotson, *Dickens at Work*, 71.
3. James Kinsley, Introduction, *Pickwick Papers*, lxiv.
4. Ibid.
5. William Cohen, *Sex Scandal*, 117.
6. The one exception, as many readers have noted, is the so-called interpolated tales, which open onto a world more akin to gothic, but for that reason have always seemed something of a discord in the novel.
7. Readings that seek the requisite depth for psychoanalytic interpretation of the characters typically appeal to forms of doubling, as in John Glavin's recent account of the novel (*After Dickens*, 88–89). Karen Chase offers the most supple alignment of the novel with psychoanalysis, conceding that psychoanalysis has encouraged a misplaced impulse "to look for depths even in the shallow," but arguing that in *Pickwick* the dispersal of "personality" among disparate fragmentary characters anticipates a Freudian questioning of "the sovereignty of the individual subject" (*Eros and Psyche*, 32).
8. Glavin, *After Dickens*, 89.
9. Judith John points up a similar effect in the work of melodrama, in which "emotions do not 'belong' to the individual experiencing them but to common experience" (*Dickens's Villains*, 30). In *The Pickwick Papers*, however, the projective, communal grounding of sexuality is all the more apparent in Pickwick's ultimate resistance to it.
10. See Catherine Gallagher, "The Duplicity of Doubling in *A Tale of Two Cities*."
11. The burdens of obligation are illuminated in Randall Craig's account of the legal grounds of Mrs. Bardell's lawsuit—an action, Craig argues in *Promising Language*, that under contemporary legal constructions (Buzfuz's special pleading aside) would have been highly plausible.
12. My emphasis here complements Amanda Anderson's incisive reading of this episode in *Tainted Souls and Painted Faces*, in which she sees the "fallen" woman as a figure of "attenuated autonomy"; to be fallen is to be fated, to have lost one's powers of self-determination. David's powerfully vicarious response to Annie not only reflects as Mary Poovey comments, that "woman is the site at which sexuality becomes visible" (*Uneven Developments*, 97) but also worries over the extent and durability of human freedom. As she doubles the anxiety that besets David in worries over the exposure of his contamination in the blacking warehouse, Annie also figures "the threat that coercive narrative forms are perceived to pose to the recovery and representation of the self" (94–95). In this sense, the narrative of "falling" is one version of "the force of circumstances" as I have described them. My main interest, however, lies in Dickens's meditation on how this suspicion generates its own forms of subjectivity, in both the observers and their object.
13. Miller, *The Novel and the Police*, 200.

# 13

# *Little Dorrit*'s Theater of Rage

DEIRDRE DAVID

> "*Little Dorrit* is a more seditious book than *Das Kapital.*"
> —GEORGE BERNARD SHAW (1862)

## ANGRY "ATTITUDES"

Almost at the close of *Little Dorrit,* Amy Dorrit, Flora Finching, and that extraordinary bundle of rage, Mr. F's Aunt, repair to a pie-shop where Flora orders "three kidney ones." In her genuinely good-hearted way, Flora confides to Amy that she harbors no more nonsensical feelings about Arthur and that she wishes them to be happy: "The withered chaplet my dear . . . is then perished the column is crumbled and the pyramid is standing upside down. . . . I must now retire into privacy and look upon the ashes of departed joys" (*LD,* 2, ch.34). Mr. F's Aunt takes a less happy view of the impending marriage and, having eaten her pie with great solemnity, declares to Flora: "Bring him forward, and I'll chuck him out o'winder!" This is not a new demand on her part since she has, almost from the moment she meets Arthur Clennam, demanded that she be allowed to hurl him to the street; as justification for him to be brought "for'ard," she proclaims, "I hate a fool!" (*LD,* 1, ch.13). Always staring, she refuses to acknowledge any individual, and every man retires "cowed and baffled" after attempting to engage her in rational conversation, which is understandable since there can be no response to such opaque announcements that when she lived at Henley, "Barnes's gander was stole by tinkers." Already half-broken by the emasculating rule of his mother, Arthur is absolutely terrified when in her presence.

At the pie-shop, Mr. F's Aunt stages a remarkable scene of unappeasable female rage. When Arthur fails to be produced so that he can be pitched through the plate-glass window, she folds her arms, sits down in a corner, and refuses to budge until such time as "the chucking portion of his destiny" can be accomplished. She remains in place throughout the afternoon, during which time Flora fortifies herself with a tumbler brought from a neighboring hotel in order to fight off embarrassing rumors of an old lady's having sold herself to the pie-shop "to be made up" and now refusing to complete the bargain. Allowing for the fact that Mr. F's Aunt is a superbly comic figure (and, of course, a minor character), the enraged image of this furious old lady, her bonnet "cocked up behind in a terrific manner" and her "stony reticule" as rigid "as if it had been petrified by the Gorgon's head" (*LD*, 2, ch.34), suggests the powerful feeling of injury and injustice that seems to infect the social order in *Little Dorrit*.

In particular, *Little Dorrit* seethes with the resentment of angry women, and what interests me in this chapter is the creation of a theater of rage by three characters who share the fury and animosity for the male sex that is exhibited by Mr. F's Aunt: Tattycoram, Miss Wade, and Mrs. Clennam. They construct vivacious performances of the role of enraged and vengeful woman, and in scripting their shared desire to destabilize oppressive ideologies of social class, complacent domesticity, and lax male sexual morality, they reject rules of behavior for dependent servants, orphaned governesses, and betrayed middle-class wives and mothers. In their rebellion, they may be said to attempt a rewriting of the social roles to which they are relegated, and in staging their theater of rage, they cast their shadows upon what Dickens terms, in *Little Dorrit,* "the great social Exhibition" (*LD*, 1, ch.13). As we know, throughout this novel, characters move into and out of literal and metaphorical shadows, and, at the end, Arthur Clennam and Amy Dorrit walk out of the church after their marriage into "the autumn morning sun's bright rays" (*LD*, 2, ch.34).[1] The darkness of Mrs. Clennam's adamantine and punitive refusal to disclose the secret of Arthur's parentage; William Dorrit's miserable exploitation of his daughter; Merdle's dubious financial operations; and the malevolent manipulations of that "smooth polished scoundrel," Rigaud: all fade in the somber union of Arthur and Amy as they go down into "the roaring streets, inseparable and blessed" (*LD*, 2, ch.34). What fades, too, in the autumnal brightness of the Clennam/Dorrit marriage is the destructive passion of *Little Dorrit*'s angry women.

That Dickens chooses to represent the anger of these women in a theatrical mode is not surprising given the pervasive incorporation of such tropes into his fiction, the staging of highly theatricalized public readings of his novels, and the abundance of his writings about and for the theater. In a speech delivered at the thirteenth anniversary dinner of the Royal General Theatrical Fund, held at the Freemasons Tavern on 29 March 1858 (ten months after the first edition of *Little Dorrit* appeared on 30 May 1857), Dickens proposed an after-dinner toast to Thackeray in which he declared, "Every writer of fiction, although he may not adopt the dramatic form, writes in effect for the stage."[2] In his own fiction, Dickens often mounts lengthy, elaborate monologues that dramatize extreme passions (think, say, of Edith Granger's speech to her mother in *Dombey and Son* about having been "hawked and vended" on the marriage market[3]), and he often embellishes his staging with the arrangement of characters in positions that recall an important motif of early-nineteenth-century theater: the adoption of various physical "attitudes."

In *Little Dorrit,* Dickens's deployment of this theatrical trope has a significant dual effect. First, and most obviously, it places the reader in the position of spectator, with the result that we become, in a sense, members of the audience for whom the performance is intended. When Tattycoram rants against the condescending benevolence of the Meagles family, we are imaginatively grouped with them as witnesses of her rage; similarly, when Mrs. Clennam stages her Calvinist drama of self-denial (the meager supper of rusks and port, the virtual entombment in her black bolsters), we stand with Affery in a dark corner, half appalled and half terrified by what we witness. And, it may be said, we press our noses against the pie-shop window to witness the spectacle of Mr. F's Aunt: furious, recalcitrant, waiting for Arthur to be brought "for'ard." Second, Dickens's theatrical presentation of his characters as a means to intensify their passion has significant political consequences: paradoxically, he tempers the fury that fuels the performance. By virtue of the ephemeral and transitory nature of all performance, a threat to the social order embodied in female fury is fragmented, scattered to the shadowy corners of the novel from whence it came: Dickens employs theatrical effects to express extreme emotion *and* to neutralize its potential to disrupt the order of "the great social Exhibition." If, as Michael Slater argues, in the decade 1847 to 1857 Dickens was "preoccupied with women as the insulted and injured of mid-Victorian England" (243–44), then by the end of that decade, he seems, at least temporarily, to dispatch their insult and injury to the wings.[4] When the curtain falls at the end of *Little Dorrit,* the female theater of rage has played itself out, the actors' vengeful desire to punish the oppressive structures that have stoked their fury having been exhausted by its presentation.

Although fundamental Romantic concepts of dramatic character were not altered by the innovations in mid-nineteenth-century theater enabled by technical advances and demanded by changing audiences, the stylized "attitudes," which involved the assumption of exaggerated positions and the extended articulation of speech, had lost favor by the time Dickens began composing *Little Dorrit* in 1855.[5] Theatrical performances that followed a specific taxonomy of elaborate poses had given way to a more spontaneous and psychologized mode favored by such actors as Dickens's good friend, William Macready. The earlier fashion for actors to hold a physical position indicating intense emotion—supplication, astonishment, anger, disgust, grief, and so on—was derived from classical modes of rhetorical gesture, and the "attitudes" served a very real practical purpose: only those in the pit and in the boxes closest to the stage could expect to hear and see the nuances of speech and facial expression perfected by such famous actors as John Philip Kemble and Sarah Siddons, who were renowned for the broad physicality of their acting, for being skilled practitioners of the art of the "attitudes."

Sometimes, early-nineteenth-century actors also relied upon what was ridiculed as the "teapot school," a label derived from the fashion for actors to place one hand on the hip, the other extended and moving in curved lines, with a gradual descent to the side.[6] But whether favoring fancy, unnatural movements or remaining frozen in place and articulating the text to the point of distortion, actors needed to hold the audience in theaters that were fully lit by gas chandeliers, where people in the pit munched on meat pies and swigged ale, and where those in the upper galleries often roared and shrieked and indulged in debaucheries "so openly," according to a shocked Walter Scott, "that it would degrade a bagnio."[7] Dickens's fictional arrangement of his angry women in riveting positions serves much the same purpose for his readers as did the exaggerated "attitudes" assumed by early-nineteenth-century actors for the theater audience: both the novel and the drama aim to hold reader and spectator in a state of enthralled attention, eager either to buy the next number or to remain rooted to the spot in the pit or in the galleries.

## VICTORIA'S FEMALE SUBJECTS

At the time Dickens was writing his novel of literal, psychological, and social incarceration, contemporary public discussion of women's rights was critiquing, in a more formal but no less impassioned way, the patriarchal order that infuriates a number of women in *Little Dorrit*. Dickens planned the novel in the first five months of 1855 and began to write in May of that year; the first number appeared in December 1855, and the last, the nineteenth, appeared in June 1857.[8] It was in 1855 that Caroline Norton composed her pamphlet, "Letter to the Queen on Lord Chancellor Cranworth's Marriage and Divorce Bill," in which she declared that she wished to point out to the queen "the grotesque anomaly which ordains that married women shall be 'non-existent' in a country governed by a female sovereign."[9] Victoria's female subjects cannot make a will, cannot legally claim their own earnings, cannot leave their married homes or divorce their husbands—but can be divorced if found guilty of infidelity—cannot prosecute for libel, and cannot sign a lease. Seething with indignation and grounded in an observation of the ironic disjunction between a female sovereign and oppressed female subjects, Norton's pamphlet was a crucial text in the 1850s development of a politicized feminist movement that gathered strength throughout the rest of the century and that led, in the next, to significant advances in the cause of women's rights.

In her argument about the serious absence of gender equality in relation to the nineteenth-century claim that economic individuals were equivalent in the marketplace, Mary Poovey notes that feminists such as Caroline Norton and Barbara Bodichon challenged the naturalization of female virtue and by association, one might add, the saccharine domesticity that saturates the Meagles family in *Little Dorrit*: "This challenge was articulated in the 1850s in a self-consciously politicized feminist movement, which was itself a response to the increasing numbers of women entering the workforce. . . . Even though the 1857 Married Women's Property Bill did not become law, the controversy it aroused interjected the issues of women's rights, property, and work into parliamentary discussion, quarterly review articles, and popular novels as well."[10] Nowhere in *Little Dorrit* do we find explicit reference to women's rights: no one demands more and better opportunities for women to enter the workforce; no one inveighs against hobbling codes that prohibit women from owning property, divorcing their husbands, and so on; no one refers to a country-wide campaign taking place in 1855 to gather proof of hardship under the law and to collect signatures on a petition to Parliament requesting reform. Such reference would be severely anachronistic given the setting of the novel in the mid-1820s, the same period in which Dickens's father was imprisoned for debt.[11] Yet it is a woman's fierce feeling of injustice and betrayal that drives the plot of *Little Dorrit*: the violent shame of Arthur Clennam's parentage endured by Mrs. Clennam and her vengeful secretion of a codicil that would have sprung the Dorrit family from the Marshalsea are the forces that, in essence, propel the action. By the same token, it is the recovery and return of this codicil to its rightful place by a tamed and repentant Tattycoram that enables a restoration of familial and social order.

## 13: Little Dorrit's Theater of Rage

In a note to the first sentence of the most recent Penguin edition of the novel ("Thirty years ago, Marseilles lay burning in the sun, one day"), Helen Small observes that as is so often the case in his fiction, "Dickens's concerns in *Little Dorrit* included those of the time in which he was writing: financial fraud, bureaucratic inefficiency, 'the Sunday question,' the new Poor Law and others."[12] I would include in "others" an ambiguous concern with the position of women registered in the presentation and consequences of their anger, and in this way *Little Dorrit* may be said to participate in the heated public discussion of women's rights taking place during the months of the novel's composition. In that participation, the novel seems to offer an implicit warning about the class and sexual resentment felt by Tattycoram, Miss Wade, and Mrs. Clennam, since each of these women, in her own destructive way, disrupts the domestic harmony of the Victorian family. Tattycoram, the girl taken by the Meagles family from the Thomas Coram Foundling Hospital in Bloomsbury to become a maid to Pet, burns with resentment against the bourgeois benevolence practiced by Mr. Meagles; her desire is to be recognized as an autonomous individual rather than to be treated as a dependent functionary, a lesser version of Pet's dead twin, Minnie Meagles. Miss Wade nurses a deep-seated grudge against the class system that has relegated her to the position of governess, and she aids and abets the roguish Rigaud in defiance and blackmail of the middle class; the grudge is compounded by the experience of a tumultuous love affair with Henry Gowan, and Wade seeks revenge upon patronizing families such as the Meagles, and, in particular, punishment for Pet, who marries Gowan. Mrs. Clennam exhibits none of the forgiveness and stoical forbearance that the Victorian wife might be expected to display in the face of marital infidelity, or in the face of an arranged and loveless marriage; she chooses instead to imbue her husband's illegitimate son with the "wholesome repression, punishment, and fear" that were the "themes" of her own childhood (*LD,* 2, ch.30).

In enacting their scenes of dramatized female rage, these three women embody a symptom of what Caroline Norton (in her "Letter to the Queen") sees as a society infected from within: "Madam," she concludes, "in families, as in nations, Rebellion is a disease that springs from the *malaria* of bad government" (151). If Dickens does not aim explicitly to present women's anger and rebellion against patriarchal rule as a sign of Caroline Norton's "bad government," it is clear that the angry women in *Little Dorrit* are deeply dissatisfied with the workings of Victorian society: their anger is a sign of something wrong, somewhere. We are prompted to consider the cause of their fury and to wonder about its justification.[13] Their injuries are open wounds, their passions transparent, and in this sense they are unlike such opaque characters as the financial conjurer Mr. Merdle or the deceptively benign landlord Mr. Casby—"a mere Inn signpost without any Inn" (*LD*, 1, ch.13).

Caroline Norton's image of a diseased government is, of course, the primary theme and the controlling metaphor of *Bleak House*, yet in many ways the world of *Little Dorrit* is equally infected. With less of the fierce indignation with which he invests scenes of metropolitan misery in *Bleak House*, Dickens, in a more somber, even resigned, mode that seems to match the emotional temperature of Arthur Clennam, discloses in *Little Dorrit* many symptoms of diseased government. Instead of a corrupt legal system, we find the addled bureaucracy of the Circumlocution Office; in place of the cholera-infested Tom-All-Alone's, we find "fifty thousand lairs . . . where people lived so unwholesomely, that fair water put into their crowded rooms on Saturday night, would be corrupt on Sunday morning" (*LD*, 1, ch.3); and just as we recoil from the grease-smeared cave of Krook's rag-and-bottle shop, so we shrink from the "turbid tide" of the Thames as it wards off "the free air and the free country swept by winds and wings of birds" (*LD*, 2, ch.10). Where Esther Summerson discovers her mother lying dead in a burial ground "hemmed in by filthy houses, with a few dull lights in their windows, and on whose walls a thick humidity broke out like a disease" (*BH,* ch.59), Amy Dorrit endures her so-called party—a night spent locked out of the Marshalsea, huddled with Maggy in a doorway, where they are surrounded by the "shame, desertion, wretchedness, and exposure, of the great capital: the cold, the slow hours, and the swift clouds, of the dismal night" (*LD*, 1, ch.14). As is so often the case in Dickens's fiction, the remedy for all this political corruption, urban pollution, and sheer misery is to be found in the private, domestic sphere: Arthur and Amy go down into the roaring secular world to do the best they can to live "a modest life of usefulness and happiness" (*LD*, 2, ch.34) and the festering anger of resentful women is imaginatively drowned out in the roar of the teeming city. Tattycoram returns chastened to the Meagles family; Miss Wade fades away into some kind of French obscurity; and Mrs. Clennam is felled by a stroke, a suitable punishment for her stony cruelty. And Mr. F's Aunt is eventually removed from the pie-shop by its owner, wedged into a carriage by Flora, and taken home, rigid as ever, to the Gray's Inn Road.

In terms of the threat to a social order controlled, in essence, by men, it is significant that the audience for the theater of rage mounted by angry women in *Little Dorrit* is more often male than female. Mr. Meagles watches helplessly as Tattycoram tears her hair and stamps her feet; Arthur Clennam gloomily witnesses his mother's melodramatic ritual of eating her rusks and reading her Bible, and he becomes the passive reader of Miss Wade's

"History of a Self-Tormentor," a text designed specifically for his eyes only; and the demonic fury of Mr. F's Aunt freezes Arthur in the position of virtually paralyzed audience for her wildly uninhibited spite. It seems as if certain male characters in *Little Dorrit* are either implicitly punished for a more general social inattention to women's needs and rights (even if they possess no direct responsibility) or function as the vehicles of warning to Dickens's readers about the consequences to the social order if those rights and needs are ignored. Either way, women's anger with male governance is admitted into the novel and then dispatched through repentance, exile, and death.

## THE MALE AUDIENCE

*Little Dorrit* is not the first of Dickens's novels in which male spectators witness the drama of female rage. Rosa Dartle in *David Copperfield,* for instance, nurses a grudge as fierce as that of Miss Wade. Bearing upon her lip a sign of Steerforth's own childhood fury, she assumes upon his death an "attitude" of desperate grief as she stands before David and Steerforth's mother. Smiting herself theatrically upon her breast and lip (where the ugly mark remains of a hammer thrown by Steerforth), she cries, "Look at me! Moan, and groan, and look at me! Look here! [at her scarred lip] at your dead child's handiwork!" A captive audience for Rosa's rewriting of the role of docile, dependent companion, David watches fearfully as she stamps her feet and releases years of suppressed resentment against both mother and son for the mother's condescension and the son's treatment of her as "a mere disfigured piece of furniture . . . having no eyes, no ears, no feelings, no remembrances" (*DC,* ch.56). Fated to be Rosa's principal audience, when he goes in search of Emily in the shady dockside streets of East London, guided by Martha Endell, he witnesses another sensational scene of female rage that could have been lifted from any contemporary melodrama featuring a "fallen woman." Remaining hidden behind a door from Rosa, yet able to hear every word and to see almost all the action, he watches as Emily crouches quivering on the floor and Rosa stands over her, laughing contemptuously, gesturing theatrically, and drawing away her skirt from the "contamination" of Emily's fallen touch. Stretching out her hands in a pose of jealous fury and seeming to address her unseen audience, David (although she is at this moment unaware of him), she points to Emily as a "piece of pollution, picked up from the waterside, to be made much of for an hour, and then tossed back to her original place!" (*DC,* ch.50). As David recounts the scene, Rosa strikes Emily with a face of "such malignity, so darkened and disfigured by passion, that

I had almost thrown myself between them." But he does not. His passivity suggests that Dickens means to station him to the very last moment as a male spectator of Rosa's melodrama, even allowing for the fact that David wishes Peggoty to be Emily's rescuer and not himself.

Critics have long noted that in *Great Expectations,* almost all of Pip's life, from the marshes and the forge to London and a gentlemanly pursuit of leisure, is characterized by passivity. His emotional fear and uncertainty are compounded by his unsought-for position as spectator for women's fury, a training in subjugation that begins, of course, in early childhood at the rough hands of Mrs. Joe Gargery. Always on a "rampage," "tickler" in hand and bottle of castor oil at the ready, Mrs. Joe bullies Pip and Joe: they are her cowed audience as they huddle by the fire (with Orlick dropping in occasionally) for her theater of rage at having to take care of Pip and having to manage a husband whose passivity, goodness, and patience drive her to distraction. A frightened boy who brings Magwitch "vittles," Pip quickly becomes the toy of Miss Havisham, then a bewildered young man mysteriously elevated to the life of gentleman, and, finally, a plaything for Estella.

On his first visit to Satis House, Pip witnesses a more stylized and sumptuous performance than that enacted by his sister. Led by Estella as if by an usher in a darkened theater into a room lit dramatically by wax candles, he finds Miss Havisham posed in an "attitude" that signals resigned dejection: she sits with her head resting on the hand of an arm that is draped across her dressing table. Dressed all in grubby white, wearing white satin shoes, and adorned with a few dried bridal flowers, she garbs herself in a theatrical costume that displays her rejection at the altar, and she surrounds herself with the props of her jilting: trunks half-packed with her trousseau, a watch stopped at twenty to nine, handkerchief and white kid gloves, and a prayerbook. The consummate manager of her long-ago rejection, Miss Havisham maliciously stages scenes in which Pip must play the role she herself plays to perfection: casting him as victim, she uses Estella as her human prop to play an allotted part in the cruel theater of his humiliation.

Tellingly, Joe Gargery refuses to assume any part in Miss Havisham's revenge tragedy, and he rejects the role of humble beneficiary of her charity when she pays Pip for his painful attendance at Satis House: ignoring the script, he wants none of her manipulative posturing and persists in speaking only to Pip. Pip, though, remains a willing, if increasingly disillusioned, audience to the very end, her confessor as she asks for forgiveness and her savior (at least for a little while) as he sees her transformed into tinder by her moth-eaten wedding dress: she runs at him, "shrieking, with a whirl of fire blazing all around her and soaring at least as many feet above her head as she was high" (*GE,* ch.49).

In *Our Mutual Friend,* Dickens raises the theatrical curtain on the last and most comical of his enraged women characters, Mrs. Reginald Wilfer. Driven to almost demented self-stagings of class resentment by the "sprat-like" appearance of her husband, she is a woman of gloomy majesty who presents to the world an "attitude" of perpetual injury and disappointment. As armor against misfortune, she dons a carefully planned costume of gloves within doors and a handkerchief on her head; she speaks in tones of severe monotony and favors biting sarcasm (the Boffins are "much too kind and too good for *us*"). Skilled at putting on a show for her despised Holloway neighbors, she calls loudly for the "male domestic of Mrs. Boffin" when Bella leaves the humble Wilfer home to return to the home of the "Golden Dustman": she delivers her to the footman "like a female Lieutenant of the Tower relinquishing a state prisoner. The effect of this ceremonial was for some quarter of an hour afterwards perfectly paralysing on the neighbours, and was much enhanced by the worthy lady airing herself for that term in a kind of splendidly serene trance on the top steps" (*OMF,* 2, ch.8).

Her animated performance of the role of Holloway housewife is magnificent. She declares the Boffin mansion to be "the halls of slavery," and she addresses a polished rebuke to Bella's sister Lavinia (who has announced that such references are nonsensical) that projects her words into the Wilfer parlor as if she were declaiming from the stage at Covent Garden: "I say, presumptuous child, if you had come from the neighbourhood of Portland Place, bending under the yoke of patronage, and attended by its domestic in glittering garb to visit me, do you think my deep-seated feelings could have been expressed in looks?" (*OMF,* 3, ch.16). Her adoption of idiosyncratic roles expressing class envy and female disgust with pretty much all the men in the novel runs the gamut from appearing "like a frozen article on sale in a Russian market" (*OMF,* 3, ch.16), through going to bed in the manner of Lady Macbeth, to conducting herself when she visits the Boffin mansion at the end of the novel with the bearing of a Savage Chief. When she takes her leave at last, she departs magisterially in the self-assigned role of neglected mother-in-law, her audience a bewildered Mr. Boffin, an amused John Harmon, and the henpecked cherub Reginald Wilfer.

## TORMENTED "ATTITUDES"

In her contribution to a discussion among her fellow-travelers about being quarantined in Marseilles, Miss Wade declares that if she had "been shut up in any place to pine and suffer," she would "always hate that place and wish to burn it down, or raze it to the ground" (*LD*, 1, ch.2). Immediately afterwards, she walks to her room and spots Tattycoram, an enraged incarnation, at this moment, of her own contemptuous anger: Tattycoram's face is flushed and hot, and she sobs and rages, plucks at her lips unsparingly, and pinches her neck so that it comes out in great scarlet blots—all as self-punishment for her cry that the Meagles family are "Selfish brutes... Beasts! Devils! Wretches!" (*LD*, 1, ch.2). Presciently, she cries out to Miss Wade, "You seem to come like my own anger, my own malice, my own—whatever it is" (*LD*, 1, ch.3). In this scene, and throughout the novel, the older woman figures as the enraged shadow of the younger: both are driven by a powerful and self-destructive sense of injustice.

Mr. Meagles's remedy for Tattycoram's rages is to instruct her to count to five and twenty, a disciplinary tactic that several critics suggest Dickens appropriated from the system of a "Mark Table" at Urania Cottage, the "Home for Homeless Women" in Shepherds Bush (principally for seduced and abandoned girls and prostitutes), which he managed for its founder, Angela Burdett-Coutts.[14] Counting to five and twenty, however, eventually fails with Tattycoram, as Arthur Clennam discovers one day after coming home to find Pa Meagles lamenting her loss: "Wouldn't count to five-and-twenty sir; couldn't be got to do it; stopped at eight and took herself off" (*LD*, 1, ch.27). Burning with hatred of Pet as the one always to be "cherished and loved," Tattycoram takes herself off to Miss Wade, and when Clennam and Meagles arrive in search of her, Dickens stages a theatrical scene in which Clennam plays a supporting role in the Meagles family drama and in which Miss Wade gets all the good lines. She thunders forth to her cowed apprentice in female rage: "You can be, again, a foil to his pretty daughter, a slave to her pleasant wilfulness, and a toy in the house showing the goodness of the family.... You can again be shown to this gentleman's daughter, Harriet, and kept before her, as a living reminder of her own superiority and her gracious condescension" (*LD*, 1, ch.27). Pa Meagles's parting lines also ring with a melodramatic warning for Tattycoram: Miss Wade's influence over her is grounded in a passion and a temper fiercer and more violent than hers. "What can you two be together? What can come of it?" he asks (*LD*, 1, ch.27)—questions for which the reader already has one ready answer: together, the two women will not enjoy the cozy heterosexual domesticity of Twickenham.

At the close of this scene, Miss Wade puts her arm around Tattycoram "as if she took possession of her for evermore" (*LD*, 1, ch.27). Whether they enjoy a lesbian relationship has been the subject of much critical speculation, from assertions that Miss Wade's "History of a Self-Tormentor" should be read metaphorically as a wish to create social havoc, not as a confessional narrative of lesbian desire,[15] to assertions that even if Miss Wade is a lesbian, to read her purely in terms of sexual identity is to ignore the fact that she embodies a much larger threat of "political rebellion."[16] It seems to me that Miss Wade may, all at once, be read as a lesbian, a metaphor, and a political insurgent: her aim to seduce Tattycoram away from the normative bourgeois domesticity of the Meagles family signals an overdetermined passion to disrupt the Victorian social order, whose stability rested, at core, upon the family. An outsider by virtue of being an orphan, an unhappy governess, and an unmarried woman severely disappointed in her relationships with men, for whom she seems to have nothing but contempt: she is bent on destroying the forces that have placed her in these miserable positions. Seducing unhappy young women is a powerful weapon in her arsenal.

Frozen in the theatrical "attitude" of rage, Miss Wade is described by Pancks as a woman "who writhes under her life. A woman more angry, passionate, reckless, and revengeful never lived" (*LD*, 2, ch.9). Her face is the dramatic register of her feelings, as we see when she sits apart from her fellow-travelers in Marseilles, her indifference to them signaled in her "proud eyes, the lifted nostril ... the handsome, yet compressed and even cruel mouth" (*LD*, 1, ch.1). Late in the novel, when Clennam confronts her in Calais, her rage rivets his attention, keeps him rooted to the spot, and emphasizes his passivity: "It flashed out of her dark eyes as they regarded him, quivered in her nostrils, and fired the very breath she exhaled; but her face was otherwise composed into a disdainful serenity, and her attitude was as calmly and haughtily graceful as if she had been in a mood of complete indifference" (*LD*, 2, ch.20). Dickens means "attitude" here, of course, not in the sense of assuming a theatricalized position, yet Miss Wade's immobility, her inclination to assume inflexible poses of indifference, suggest her psychological hypersensitivity to how she appears to others. That hypersensitivity feeds her resentment, and this is disclosed to Clennam, the male audience for her "History." Thoroughly stylized in her movements and gestures, and in textual presentation of herself, she writes "The History of a Self-Tormentor" as a textual performance fashioned for a male audience: she gives Clennam this text—her autobiographical fragment—with the words that she has written it explicitly for *his* perusal, and no one else's. On the packet back to England, he reads her extraordinary "History."

At an early age, she declares she began to "see" how she was patronized by others; made wild with jealousy by "an unworthy girl," she obtains revenge by reducing her to hysterical tears and then holding her in her arms until morning, "loving her as much as ever, and often feeling as if, rather than suffer so, I could hold her in my arms and plunge to the bottom of a river—where I would hold her, after we were both dead" (*LD*, 2, ch.21). When Miss Wade becomes a governess, she admits she is treated decently by the family, something she meets with studied rejection; in another family, she attracts the attention of a nephew and persists in repulsing him, which rather peculiarly leads to their engagement. Henry Gowan's arrival at the house encourages her paranoid self-consciousness, and she departs in a display of prideful injury in which she believes herself degraded by the affectionate concern of the woman who employs her. In Tattycoram, she writes, she found a girl much like herself, feeling much of the resentment she has felt against "swollen patronage and selfishness, calling themselves kindness, protection, benevolence, and other fine names" (*LD*, 2, ch.21). Consistent with her self-absorption, she is drawn to Tattycoram because she sees within her no one but herself: both are illegitimate orphans; both lack privilege; and both possess volatile temperaments. As several critics have noted, their shared spite and jealousy serve to highlight the lives of other women in the novel, most particularly Pet Meagles and Amy Dorrit: Pet enjoys the material comfort and parental indulgence they lack, and Amy displays an angelic acceptance of deprivation that is foreign to their natures.[17]

While the flaming anger of Tattycoram and Miss Wade stems primarily from class envy and patriarchal condescension, the anger nursed by Arthur's mother from before his birth derives more from resentment of patriarchal despotism and sexual betrayal. Married off by her father to the orphan nephew of old Gilbert Clennam and discovering that her husband within a year of their marriage has "held a guilty creature" in her place, she takes it upon herself to "lay the hand of punishment upon that creature of perdition" (*LD*, 2, ch.30). Her indignant announcement that Arthur's mother "fell hiding her face at her feet" reveals her adoption of an "attitude" of self-righteous injury reminiscent of Rosa Dartle's position as Emily cowers in fear beneath her wrathful accuser. Mrs. Clennam also forms a pair with Mr. F's Aunt, who, as we know, bears herself with an "extreme severity and grim taciturnity" that anticipates the stern majesty of Mrs. Wilfer; the physical rigidity of Mr. F's Aunt serves as a comic parody of the paralyzed body of Mrs. Clennam (just as she refuses to budge from the pie-shop, so Mrs. Clennam becomes a "statue" in her final paralysis); and, lastly, the vituperative shouts of Mr. F's Aunt form a demonic, crazed, and jumbled analogue to Mrs. Clennam's recitation of biblical creed.[18]

At the beginning of *Little Dorrit,* Arthur has returned to Europe after some twenty years in China working in the family business, and in a revealing response to Mrs. Meagles's question as to what he plans to do next, he says, "I have no will.... Trained by main force; broken, not bent; heavily ironed with an object on which I was never consulted and which was never mine; ... what is to be expected of *me* in middle life? Will, purpose, hope? All those lights were extinguished before I could sound the words" (*LD*, 1, ch.2). His mother's rage and perverse pleasure in becoming the instrument of punishment for Arthur's true parents ensure that as a young child he is terrified by warnings of perdition, that as a boy at school he is marched to chapel three times a day on Sundays, and that as a young man he is sentenced to listen to his mother's reading from the Bible, "sternly, fiercely, wrathfully."

As Miss Havisham arranges the soured bridal theater of her jilting—replete with costumes, props, and appropriate lighting—so Mrs. Clennam constructs her tragedy of martyrdom in the face of sexual betrayal. Going out perhaps once a year, she is confined to a wheelchair with a paralysis never fully explained by the novel. She inhabits a "dim bedchamber, the floor of which has so sunk and settled, that the fireplace was in a dell" (*LD*, 1, ch.3), as if the house itself is giving way, one imagines, under the weight of its family secrets (as indeed it does). Where Miss Havisham dresses herself in grimy white as mourning for the husband who never appeared, Mrs. Clennam dresses in dusty widow's black for the husband who betrayed her; where Miss Havisham sits moodily by her dressing table, Mrs. Clennam sits on a black bier-like sofa "propped up behind with one great angular black bolster, like the block at a state execution in the good old times." Neither woman will forgive, and both are driven by self-consuming vengeance to present their tableaux of female martyrdom to their male audiences, surrogates for those who have abandoned them: Pip and Arthur. Mrs. Clennam's props consist of several devotional texts, her handkerchief, a pair of steel spectacles, and an old-fashioned gold watch in a heavy double case. As terrified by his mother as he is by the implacable hostility of Mr. F's Aunt, Arthur retreats to a dark and damp room in the house, curious only about why his mother would have Little Dorrit sewing in the corner and feeling the "shadow of a supposed act of injustice, which had hung over him since his father's death" (*LD*, 1, ch.27).

In a chapter aptly entitled "Closing In," Mrs. Clennam stages the last act in her family melodrama. The stage is taken first by Rigaud, complete with "evil leer," who is arranged by Dickens in the fashion of a theatrical villain, as if he were directing amateur theatricals at Gad's Hill: "Leaning over the sofa ... his right hand sometimes arranging his hair, sometimes smoothing his moustache, sometimes striking his nose, always threatening her with whatever it did; coarse, insolent, rapacious, cruel, and powerful; he pursued his narrative at his ease" (*LD,* 2, ch.30). For the benefit of Affery and Jeremiah Flintwinch, he maliciously relates the dreadful history of the Clennam marriage and Arthur's birth and childhood, whereupon Mrs. Clennam, desperate to be the narrator of her own tragedy, cries out, "I will tell it myself!," which she proceeds to do in bone-chilling detail. In a gesture symbolic of the release of years of suppressed anger that has "preyed upon itself evenly and slowly" (*LD,* 1, ch.15), the fingers that have long remained virtually immobile suddenly become looser; she vigorously hits the table with a clenched hand and raises her whole arm in the air in the classical "attitude" of defiance.

The confession to her audience that she has withheld a codicil to old Gilbert Clennam's will that would have benefited Arthur's true mother is followed by an extraordinary scene in which Mrs. Clennam makes her gaunt way west through the London streets to the Marshalsea—unearthly pale, "a spectral woman." Bent on reclaiming the codicil and letters from Amy Dorrit, to whom they have been sent by the crafty Rigaud, she stages a dramatic confrontation in which the vengeful mother who is not a mother begs the woman who loves her adopted son to keep secret the narrative of anger and revenge until she is dead. In turn, Amy, positioned in the softened light of the window, begs Mrs. Clennam, relegated to a dark corner of the room, to put aside a punitive Old Testament god of retribution and to be guided by a New Testament god who heals, raises from the dead, and sheds tears of compassion for man's infirmities.

As they go through the streets together, back to the rotting house, the light of the summer evening falls upon the clear steeples of the City churches, and Dickens paints a backdrop saturated with Christian imagery devoted to the pure goodness of Amy Dorrit, who possesses not a theatrical bone in her little body: "great shoots of light" stream "among the early stars, like signs of the blessed later covenant of peace and hope that changed the crown of thorns into a glory" (*LD,* 2, ch.31). Amy transforms the thorns of Mrs. Clennam's bitterness and rage into the glory of remorse and compassion for the man who is, and is not, her son. They arrive at the house just in time to see it heave, surge outward, open asunder, collapse, and fall to the ground—a spectacular moment worthy of any of the elaborate pantomimes offered in the mid-nineteenth-century theater that featured such things as "The Battle of Waterloo" complete with cavalry advances, bugle calls, and cannon fire. With the collapse of the house, its owner falls to the ground—never to move again and to die three years later as she has lived, "a statue."

Mrs. Clennam, then, is punished by a fatal paralysis for her construction of a revenge tragedy, just as Tattycoram is punished for her lack of gratitude by enduring the obsessive jealousy of Miss Wade; and Miss Wade is punished, one may assume, by living out her life in French exile, gnawed from within by her unappeasable rage at having been wounded by all and sundry. *Little Dorrit* admits their resentment of oppressive ideologies of class and gender and occasionally allows the reader to understand the origin of that resentment, even to sympathize with it. As we have seen, much of this understanding and sympathy, and the eventual erasure of women's anger from the novel, gains imaginative force from Dickens's deployment of theatrical tropes, particularly the "attitudes." Male characters are very often the principal audience for female performance, and they also become agents for the social change that, in the imaginative economy of *Little Dorrit,* will dispense with women's grievances.

## WOMAN'S DUTY

While Arthur Clennam lies ill in the Marshalsea, Mr. Meagles in his characteristically good-natured way travels to Calais in search of Miss Wade. He is eager to clear up the mystery surrounding Arthur's childhood and to retrieve the box of papers deposited, he discovers correctly, by Rigaud with Miss Wade for secrecy and safekeeping. She claims to know nothing of such things, and Pa Meagles returns to England disappointed, only to be astonished when Tattycoram bursts in carrying the iron box. Overhearing the conversation between Miss Wade and her old protector, she takes the box and travels back to England (hidden in a cloak) on the same boat as Mr. Meagles, and now she falls on her knees and begs to be re-admitted to the family, vowing to count not just to five and twenty but to five and twenty hundred and twenty thousand, if she must.

In a quasi-sermon that offers a familiar Victorian remedy to neutralize the destructive rage wreaked upon so many characters in *Little Dorrit,* Mr. Meagles asks Tattycoram to look at Amy Dorrit gliding out of the Marshalsea, a "little, quiet, fragile figure." Think, he admonishes her, that if Amy had constantly thought of herself, she would have led an "irritable and probably useless existence"; rather, she chose a life of "active resignation, goodness, and noble service" founded in a dedication to duty (*LD,* 2, ch.33). The familiar imperative directed at Victorian women to be good, to be dutiful, and to resign themselves to whatever the social order might assign them is rejected by Tattycoram, Miss Wade, and Mrs. Clennam—and, as we have seen, is also rejected by a notable number of Dickens's other discontented women characters. As antidote to the anger of women that, at the historical moment he was composing *Little Dorrit,* was finding expression in the public sphere in the form of pamphlets, demonstrations, and petitions, Dickens characteristically offers the benevolent interventions of a jolly patriarch, Pa Meagles, and the devotion to duty of a saintly young woman, the resigned Amy Dorrit. His tepid dispatch of the female fury that has given life to so much of *Little Dorrit* suggests a faint-hearted retreat from a postulation of a politically more feasible (if fictional) remedy for the social malaise that is the origin of women's anger. As for Amy Dorrit: even as she witnesses her father at his most abject and degraded, after he has pitifully suggested she accept John Chivery as her husband to ensure his own continued comfort in the Marshalsea, she has "no doubts," asks herself no questions, feels no anger. For a woman to doubt and to ask questions is often to discover legitimate causes for resentment, both within *Little Dorrit* and in the Victorian public debate about women's rights. In Dickens's imaginative resolution of social discontent, even if the power of women's rage might direct the plot and force men to become passive, often frightened spectators, that power is eventually vanquished by a delicate woman who harbors no resentment against a father who casts his selfish shadow over her young life.

## NOTES

1. In "Guilt, Authority, and the Shadows of *Little Dorrit*," Elaine Showalter explores in detail the imagery of light and darkness. She also points to the remarkable amount of doubling and pairing in the novel, which, she claims, suggests that "characters have their shadows—doubles who enact their repressed roles and desires" (21). As instances of the doubling and pairing, Showalter notes the Meagles twins, the Flintwinch brothers, and Casby and Pancks, adding that the pervasive presence of doubling in *Little Dorrit* reveals "the underside of Victorian authority, the shadows behind the sunny promise of bourgeois self-help, parliamentary democracy, and private charity" (21).

2. Quoted by Renata Kobetts Miller, "Imagined Audiences," (208). Miller notes that Dickens, along with other Victorian novelists, incorporates theatrical motifs into his work as a means of conceiving "of the place of the novel in relation to audiences, to other genres, and to Victorian culture" (208). Deborah Vlock in *Dickens, Novel Reading, and the Victorian Popular Theatre* argues that Dickens "regularly borrowed characters, dramatic idioms, even stories from the melodrama" (3), doing so, she claims, with "an evident confidence" in the familiarity of theatrical tropes to his readers—tropes such as stylized patterns of physical gesture and staged physical enactment of character (9). In a paper delivered at the Third Annual Conference of the North American Victorian Studies Association, David Kurnick explored what he describes as "a gradual 'novelization' of the theater," a "disciplining of theatrical culture" that reflects "the new prominence of the private, domestically oriented, psychologically absorbed form of the realist novel." See "Empty Houses: Thackeray's Theater of Interiority" (258). In *Little Dorrit,* Dickens

*13: Little Dorrit's Theater of Rage*

may be said, I think, to theatricalize the novel, in a reverse process to that described by Kurnick.

3. Assuming a theatrical "attitude" of bitter anger, Edith delivers her impassioned speech with "burning brow" and "flashing eyes" and with a "terrible tremble" creeping over her "whole frame" (*DS*, ch.27).

4. Slater, *Dickens and Women*, 243–44.

5. See Joseph Donohue, *Dramatic Character in the English Romantic Age*, 5.

6. Alan S. Downer discusses the "teapot" style in his essay, "Players and Painted Stage: Nineteenth-Century Acting," 528–29.

7. Quoted in H. Barton Baker, *The London Stage*, 1:162.

8. The first number was a great success. Dickens wrote to John Forster, "*Little Dorrit* has beaten even *Bleak House* out of the field. It is a tremendous start, and I am overjoyed at it" (Forster, 2:182).

9. Norton, "Letter to the Queen," 144. Subsequent references are made parenthetically in the text.

10. Poovey, *Making a Social Body*, 173. See Lee Holcombe, "Victorian Wives and Property," for a comprehensive discussion of the work of these women and others in agitating for the legal reform of women's rights.

11. Deborah Vlock finds it remarkable that *Little Dorrit* is a novel that "seems to concern itself with almost every contemporary social issue except the problem of redundant women. . . . [N]owhere, despite the fact that the single woman problem was bandied about while this novel was in progress, does Dickens explicitly engage with the debate over redundancy" (*Dickens, Novel Reading*, 180).

12. Helen Small, note 1, *Little Dorrit* (Penguin, 2003), 923.

13. Lionel Trilling argues, "No reader of *Little Dorrit* can possibly conclude that the rage of envy which Tattycoram feels is not justified in some degree, or that Miss Wade is wholly wrong in pointing out to her the insupportable ambiguity of her position as the daughter-servant of Mr. and Mrs. Meagles and the sister-servant of Pet Meagles. Nor is it possible to read Miss Wade's account of her life, 'The History of a Self-Tormentor,' without an understanding that amounts to sympathy." Trilling points to the fact that both Tattycoram and Miss Wade are orphans and that they are illegitimate. He believes that their bitterness "is seen to be the perversion of the desire for love" ("*Little Dorrit*," 287–88).

14. Dickens is thought to have modeled the character of Tattycoram upon a young woman named Rhena Dollard who was living at Urania Cottage when he began writing *Little Dorrit*. For Dickens's description of the young women taken in at Urania Cottage, see his 1853 *Household Words* article, "Home for Homeless Women," reprinted in Slater, ed., *Dickens' Journalism: "Gone Astray*," 127–41. See also Jenny Hartley, "Undertexts and Intertexts."

15. Anna Wilson, "On History, Case History, and Deviance: Miss Wade's Symptoms and Their Interpretation," 196–97. Wilson argues that the paradoxical narrative position of Miss Wade's narrative (both at the heart of the novel and also excisable) parallels her position in social history.

16. Janet Retseck, "Sexing Miss Wade," 217. That this character threatens the social order is undeniable; I would extend this point, however, to argue that the specific nature of what Retseck terms "political rebellion" is clearly resistance to normative heterosexual

domesticity. Inevitably, Miss Wade must be read as a lesbian.

17. Barbara Black argues that the defeat of Dickens's violent women allows "the triumph of the good Dickensian heroines" ("A Sisterhood of Rage and Beauty: Dickens's Rosa Dartle, Miss Wade, and Madame Defarge," 103).

18. Elaine Showalter believes that this character is the darkest of all in *Little Dorrit*—stony, omnipotent, her power is "quite simply emasculating" (34). For Lionel Trilling, Mr. F's Aunt is "one of Dickens' most astonishing ideas, the embodiment of senile rage and spite, flinging to the world the crusts of her buttered toast" ("*Little Dorrit*," 290–91).

# 14

# The Making of Dickens Criticism

DEBORAH EPSTEIN NORD

When Lionel Trilling was an undergraduate at Columbia in the early 1920s, he and his classmates were astonished to hear their eccentric professor John Erskine declare "with a smile of saying something daring and inacceptable" that plot and melodrama were "good things for a novel to have and that *Bleak House* was a very good novel indeed." "I took this," Trilling recalls in the 1952 essay "The Dickens of Our Day," "to be at best a lively paradox of Erskine's, intended to shock his young listeners, at worst an aberration of his critical intellect."[1] For the young Trilling, raised to regard Dickens as what he calls a "familial figure," something homey and ultimately banal, one of those "great authors" who, as George Orwell put it, was "ladled down" the throats of young children, this Victorian author of sentimental, undisciplined fictions could not possibly have real merit in the eyes of an "intelligent and advanced" person.[2] To be "advanced" in the 1920s was to be dismissive of Dickens. Not so by the 1950s, when Trilling wrote not only the "Dickens of Our Day" but also, a year later, his influential Introduction to *Little Dorrit*. What had happened in the interim and, beyond that, in the 1960s, when a prodigious amount of critical writing on Dickens by scholars and literary intellectuals appeared?[3] What were the critical, historical, and intellectual forces that transformed Dickens the novelist from what Edmund Wilson referred to as an article of faith for the English middle class—"a favorite fish, a familiar joke, a favorite dish, a beloved Christmas ritual"—into a brilliant and prescient literary figure, so secure in his place in the pantheon of writers that Trilling felt he could safely say in 1952 that Dickens and Austen were "the two greatest novelists of England"?[4]

I will answer these questions by looking, first of all, at the terms in which some of the most interesting naysayers in the critical canon evoked and depreciated Dickens's fiction. These important detractors—George Henry Lewes, Virginia Woolf, Henry James, the F. R. Leavis of *The Great Tradition*—reveal a particular strain of disparagement that not only serves as an explanation for their ambivalence but also hints at a source for rehabilitation by later critics. Their emphasis on the childishness of Dickens's appeal, in particular, explains both their revulsion against his talent and the rediscovery of his work by subsequent generations. I turn next to an examination of the seminal critical contributions of those who re-imagined Dickens through the filter of a mid-twentieth-century sensibility, an American sensibility, it is fair to say, one that understood itself in opposition to an English mindset that, with certain important exceptions, was too close to Dickens to see him afresh.[5] It can be said, in not-so-flippant shorthand, that it was Marx and Freud (as seen from Cape Cod or Morningside Heights) who were responsible for the new Dickens criticism just before and during the mid-century, but that would make for a very short essay indeed and would neglect the historical and cultural specificity of the moment, the interesting continuities between detractors and celebrants, and the particular psychological investment of readers and critics in the Dickens they either dismissed or revered.

## INFANTILE DICKENS

In an article in the *Fortnightly Review* published only two years after Dickens's death, George Henry Lewes sounded some of the keynotes of Dickens criticism that would reverberate for decades to come. Ostensibly defending Dickens against the common objections of critics more shortsighted than himself, Lewes offered up a novelist who, though incapable of conjuring anything "ideal" or "heroic," had within his grasp "all the resources of the bourgeois epic."[6] He could touch the "domestic affections," but his work was absent any real thought or ideas: "He never was and never would have been a student," Lewes remarks, as if considering Dickens for admission to university rather than assessing his fiction (151). Dickens the nonintellectual emerges here: a sentimental writer, not cerebral or educated, with no interest in philosophy, science, or what Lewes calls "the higher literature," but with an instinctive sense of middle-class domestic drama—in other words, the "familial figure" of Trilling's youth.

As if trying to establish Dickens as the antithesis of his companion, George Eliot, Lewes reserved his sternest criticism for Dickens's lack of realism, particularly in relation to the rendering of character. Failing to have any real understanding of human psychology—the "complexity of the organism," as Lewes puts it, in a scientific key—Dickens created characters with verbal and physical tics, as if behavior and speech "in nature" could ever be precisely repeatable (149). Only as the result of "hallucination" could Dickens have believed such compulsive repetition to be "real." That Lewes should have thought Dickens did believe in the absolute "reality" of his characters is perhaps attributable to the way the novelist tended to talk about them in his prefaces and elsewhere. That Lewes homed in on hallucination as part of Dickens's creative process, however, is more interesting, and it is, as we shall see, in tune with later characterizations of the effect and quality, rather than the mode of production, of Dickens's fiction. Finally, Lewes concedes that, though we do not seek "thought, delicate psychological observation, [or] grace of style" in Dickens's novels, "we enjoy them like children at a play, laughing and crying at the images which pass before us" (154). When we read him, we become children.

In a theme related to Lewes's charge of an absence of ideas, late-nineteenth- and early-twentieth-century critiques of Dickens's fiction harp on the novelist's lack of seriousness and his insufficient maturity. Virginia Woolf complains that Dickens's otherwise capacious sympathies fail in two instances: when a character is well off, or is upper class, or has been to university and when he has to treat "mature emotions" and submerged feelings that require the writer's penetration.[7] Henry James's well-known review of *Our Mutual Friend,* written in 1865 when he was only twenty-two, labels Dickens memorably as "the greatest of superficial novelists." He has "added nothing to our understanding of human character," James declared with youthful certainty, nor is "[any]thing of a philosopher."[8]

In 1930 Aldous Huxley reproduced this portrait of Dickens as a stunted man—a creator of "infantile" male characters such as Mr. Pickwick and a writer prone to losing any spark of intelligence when in the throes of emotion.[9] Even George Santayana, who defended Dickens eloquently against the common indictment of exaggeration, took a cue from Lewes in admitting that Dickens had no interest in "ideas on any subject" and was, in this regard, "like a sensitive child."[10] By the time the curious reader of Dickens criticism gets to F. R. Leavis's explanation for omitting Dickens from the "great tradition" of English novelists, the Cambridge don's rhetoric takes on the ring of caricature. Dickens may have influenced Conrad, who, along with Eliot and James, marked one of the three pinnacles of the great tradition, but what was "profoundly serious" in Conrad had been mere melodrama in Dickens. Indeed, in relation to Conrad, the Victorian was "at the other end of the scale from sophistication." The "*adult* mind," Leavis goes on, does not usually find in Dickens "a challenge to an unusual and sustained *seriousness*," though children might profit from hearing the works read aloud.[11] Except for *Hard Times,* which as we know Leavis singled out as worthy of a chapter in *The Great Tradition,* the novels lacked coherence and discipline: they were overdone, repetitive, and out of control.

The rhetorical pattern that begins to emerge here—language that evokes the novelist's childishness, his inappropriateness for the adult reader, the infantile quality of his characters, and his instinctive or automatic talents—gives us a clue to the detractors' own psychic need to distance themselves from, indeed repress, the love of Dickens's work. Sometimes casually and sometimes more passionately, these critics confess to the importance of Dickens to their child selves. His association with childhood *tout court* is also, then, a deep association with their own childhoods, and it emerges as an obstacle to adult appreciation. The hard work of achieving intellectual, aesthetic, and critical maturity, especially for those embarked on the voyage of modernism, necessitates the sloughing off of infantile joys and tastes.

At the beginning of Virginia Woolf's essay on *David Copperfield,* the novel most closely associated with childhood experiences of Dickens, she declares that no one living in 1925 could actually recall reading the novel for the first time. Expanding on this point in a letter to *The Nation* that Leonard Woolf later appended to the essay, she explains that she did not mean to suggest that *Copperfield* made a negligible impression on its readers but rather that "parents will read it aloud to their children before they can quite *distinguish fact from fiction,* and [so] they will never in later life be able to recall the first time they read it" (69; emphasis added). It is one of those books, she concludes, that belong to "the memories and myths of life, and not to its aesthetic experiences" (65). Like many others born in the second half of the nineteenth century and even later, Woolf's first experience of Dickens was an aural one, with the reader-aloud most likely a parent. The process of absorbing Dickensian prose was part of the child's relationship to her mother or father, an aspect of the infantile state, and so automatic that the reality of the experience itself—its status as fact or fiction—is questionable. For Woolf, this experience is allied with the passive modes of memory, listening, and reception and not with the active, adult mode of aesthetic appreciation.

Woolf does credit Dickens with visual power: he had a genius for seeing (to the extent that he possessed "subtlety and complexity," it came through the eye) and for lodging his own creations in the visual memories of his readers—or listeners. His people, she writes, are "branded upon our eyeballs" (68). For Henry James, writing not as the young reviewer and fledgling novelist but as a memoirist in his seventies, the impress of Dickens's characters on his mind's eye was also overpowering. Repeatedly in *A Small Boy and Others,* James evokes people from his childhood as Dickensian types, as figures drawn by Phiz or Cruikshank. His childhood dentist was "empurpled" like Phiz's Joey Bagstock, his cousin Henry "another Mr. Dick."[12] And he was haunted by the "vividly terrible images" that Cruikshank had drawn for *Oliver Twist* (120). These allusions to the indelible nature of Dickensian types and to their status as points of reference for later experience illustrate James's visceral connection to his Victorian predecessor. James speaks of the "force of the Dickens imprint . . . in the soft clay of our generation," of Dickens's "la[ying] his hand on us" and "enter[ing] so early into the blood and bone of our intelligence" (117).

The lasting mark of the novelist's influence is physical, felt on the body, absorbed in the bloodstream, tied to the eye and the ear: it is not, once again, self-conscious or intellectualized, accessible to rational analysis or introspection. Like Woolf, James can trace his bond to Dickens to hearing *David Copperfield* read aloud as a child, except that, in James's case, the memory of first hearing is altogether specific. His cousin from Albany had come to visit the family in lower Manhattan and, after seeing the boy Henry sent to bed, proceeded to read the first installment of the novel to his aunt, Henry's mother. Like the proverbial child on the stairs looking down between railings at an adult gathering, James did not go to sleep but eavesdropped, in this instance hiding under a table and behind a cloth. But, in a scene that would not have been out of place in *David Copperfield* itself, his boyish identification with David and his resultant grief betray him. "I listened long and drank deep while the wondrous picture grew," James recalls, "but the tense cord at last snapped under the strain of the Murdstones and I broke into the sobs of sympathy that disclosed my subterfuge" (118–19). The phenomenon of first hearing or reading *Copperfield*—and sometimes *Oliver Twist*—is repeated time and again by critics, memoirists, and other novelists, but James's version has an especial force and poignancy.[13] The depth of feeling, the overpowering physical sensation of sadness, and the betrayal by his own body in an ostensibly privileged state of seeing but not being seen underscore the indelible and even primitive nature of the Dickens imprint.

This imprint, freighted with emotion and memory, became for many an embarrassing rather than a desirable feature of development, an obstacle to mature aesthetic appreciation. It served as a reminder of the child within, the remnant of immaturity that needed to be overcome, left behind, denied altogether. The most overt articulation of this is to be found in a footnote to the 1962 edition of Leavis's *The Great Tradition,* in which Leavis interrupts the flow of his dismissal of Dickens as "a great entertainer" best suited to reading aloud, in Santayana's words, "of a winter's evening." The astonishing content of the note, composed fourteen years after *The Great Tradition* first appeared, is as follows: "Rather, childhood memory and the potent family-reading experience must be invoked to excuse what is absurd in this paragraph. Others will testify to the power of the 'interference.' I now think that, if any one writer can be said to have created the modern novel, it is Dickens."[14] With the sweep of a pen and the insertion of a note Leavis takes it all back. This would be breathtaking enough, but he does so on the grounds that the psychic residue of early familial experience had previously clouded his critical judgment. The rhetoric of "seriousness" and the "adult mind," so prevalent in Leavis's original discussion, masks or compensates for a potent emotional connection to Dickens—a connection forged in childhood and consequently discarded as puerile.

## AMERICAN DICKENS

In his discussion of *The Pickwick Papers* in *Dickens from Pickwick to Dombey* (1965), Steven Marcus asserts that this first novel of Dickens presents a challenge to "current preconceptions about the conditions and possibilities of greatness in literature."[15] How can the modern critic, so geared to discussions of symbolic and thematic complexity, acknowledge the greatness of *Pickwick,* a work that has been "enjoyed and loved" by so many people of varying ages, classes, and national cultures? "The very words 'enjoy and love,'" Marcus writes, "whose use we cannot avoid in describing what has always been so much a part of the essential response to *Pickwick Papers,* evoke something of the uneasiness and equivocation which this book regularly elicits from the modern critic" (*Dickens,* 14). "Uneasiness and equivocation": these words capture well certain aspects of the critical responses of Lewes, Woolf, James, and Leavis, whose accusations of childishness obscure their embarrassment at the pleasure they associate with Dickens. The American critics Edmund Wilson, Lionel Trilling, and Steven Marcus, beginning in the late 1930s and extending through the '50s and '60s, recast the essential experience of reading Dickens by acknowledging its fundamental link with the child and childishness and, partly through Freud, by explicating

Dickens's preoccupation with the persistence of childhood within adulthood. In other words, the embarrassing flaws discerned in Dickens's work by late-nineteenth- and early-twentieth-century critics became the basis for a wholesale reevaluation.

Why do I identify this critical renewal as an American phenomenon? Philip Collins, author of *Dickens and Crime* (1962) and *Dickens and Education* (1963), was surely right in naming three critics—two British and only one American—as the initiators of the "modern re-assessment of Dickens": Edmund Wilson, George Orwell, and Humphry House, who wrote about Dickens independently of one another around 1940.[16] Orwell's essay, perhaps the least influential of all of these in its lasting effect on academic criticism, cast Dickens as a revolutionary writer, not in *"the accepted sense,"* but in the sense that Blake was revolutionary—the purveyor of a "merely moral criticism of society."[17] Orwell, filtering Dickens through the political mesh of his own moment, sees him as the quintessential nineteenth-century liberal—"a free intelligence"—yet also (contra Edmund Wilson, as we shall see) warns against overstating Dickens's sympathy for the criminal outcasts of society.[18] Perhaps the most trenchant and valuable observations in Orwell's essay concern nuances of class. He is able to place Dickens's characters socially with great precision and to identify the novelist's own class feelings, whether directly or indirectly expressed, in a way that, for the most part, American readers could not do so masterfully.

Humphry House's *The Dickens World* (1941), a slim but powerful treatment of Dickens's oeuvre as a whole in relation to the "social and economic environment" that produced each of the novels, made its mark as a key text for Victorian studies generally. House's historical approach and interest in political reform marked a profound sea change in Dickens criticism on his side of the Atlantic: from a focus on the narrowly biographical (who was the real-life model for which character?) and topographical (where did such-and-such an event in the novels occur?), House shifted the reader's attention to broader social issues of Dickens's day and to the complex temporal relationship between the novels and specific historical moments.[19] While House opened up an interdisciplinary method that combined literary analysis with historical scholarship, he also advanced a view of Dickens as the creator of a fictional world that was to influence some of his most purely textual critics (most notably J. Hillis Miller, who titles his 1958 monograph *Charles Dickens: The World of His Novels* in homage to House). House wanted to enable his readers to "trace the process of *imaginative transformation* from the supposed original to the fiction" and noted strands of evolution across the novels (a bad smell is a bad smell in *Pickwick,* but a social problem in *Our Mutual Friend*).[20]

As innovative and important as Orwell and especially House might have been, however, their relationship to the American strain of Dickens criticism I focus on here must be seen as contemporaneous and even, in the end, complementary but essentially separate and intellectually divergent. The psychological, indeed psychoanalytic, impulse of this American Dickens distinguished it from counterparts across the Atlantic and often prompted British critics to respond with overt hostility. Even after rethinking his position on Dickens in *Dickens, the Novelist,* Leavis makes clear that he has little use for what he calls "the trend of American criticism of Dickens, from Edmund Wilson onwards, [which is] in general wrong-headed, ill-informed ..., and essentially ignorant and misleading."[21] It is the psychological emphasis of American criticism that Leavis most dislikes, both the interest in Dickens's own life and the tendency to locate the source of his art in "childhood impressions."[22] Although Leavis means to include others in his screed, his initial target is Wilson, who cast his "Two Scrooges" essay as an American vision. The English, Wilson implies, had lost the ability to separate Dickens from what Steven Marcus called "Early English *Kitsch*" and had produced only one "admirable" pre-1900 critic of Dickens, George Gissing.[23]

It was precisely in the context of an American intellectual climate receptive to psychoanalytic ideas that Dickens was remade as a critical subject in the middle decades of the twentieth century. The influx into the United States, beginning in the 1930s, of European intellectuals and psychoanalysts, mainly Jews in flight from Nazism, made America the richest environment for such ideas in the English-speaking world.[24] American intellectuals and writers in certain northeast circles, especially the group associated with the *Partisan Review,* imbibed the influence of European Freudians and took psychoanalytic scholarship and research in their own directions.[25]

Trilling offers an additional clue about the reasons for a connection between American literary critics' approach to Dickens and Freudian paradigms. In "The Dickens of Our Day" (1952), when he recalls the stigma Dickens carried as "so familial a figure," he goes so far as to identify the novelist's works as "a sort of surrogate for the family hearth itself." No wonder, Trilling continues, that these works should be thought of "rather vindictively" by "young men [who] detached themselves from their homes" (43). Of course, each generation detaches itself from the generation of its parents and re-creates itself in some fashion, but for the children of immigrants and for mid-twentieth-century intellectuals bent on defying the professional expectations of their fathers, oedipal struggles were often especially vexed and the Freudian schema of father-son conflict compelling.[26] Looking again at Dickens as a surrogate for the family, Trilling sees that Dickens's own most powerful representations of the hearth are bitter rather than anodyne, modern and caustic in their tenor and not sentimental or kitschy. Wilson, Trilling, and Marcus were in a position both to understand the rejection of Dickens by early-twentieth-century critics and novelists as part of an oedipal rebellion and to see in Dickens himself—and in his novels—the working out of oedipal, as well other psychic, dramas.

What, then, of Marx? Or, put another way, what was the role of a particular social and historical vision in the making of Dickens criticism in the middle decades of the twentieth century? However powerful was the influence of Freud and a general intellectual culture steeped in psychoanalytic thought on Wilson, Trilling, and Marcus, the psychological dimension of their criticism is only half the story. The accusations of childishness, primitive emotion, irrationality, and exaggeration that were leveled at Dickens by his late-nineteenth- and early-twentieth-century detractors were addressed not only by a complex understanding of the human psyche, but also from the perspective of a historical moment fraught with tragedy and yet tinged with political idealism.

The promise of social renewal through Marxian revolution—or even through a reformed Western capitalism in the manner of the New Deal—stimulated a literary critical sensibility that emphasized social criticism and social transformation. In the 1930s Edmund Wilson turned his attention as a writer first to the effects of the Great Depression on political and social life in the United States and then to the drama of the Russian Revolution.[27] He was finishing *To the Finland Station* (1940) as he undertook the essay on Dickens, as well as another called "Marxism and Literature."[28] His Dickens turns out to be "of all the great Victorian writers ... probably the most antagonistic to the Victorian age itself," a man identified with social rebellion, who set his energies against almost all social institutions, and the creator of a "new literary *genre* ... the novel of the social group."[29] Wilson credits Dickens with a perception of exploitation and hypocrisy congruent with that of Karl Marx, offering Mr. Spenlow, Mr. Casby, and Fascination Fledgeby as illustrations of the capitalist principle that the exploiter always distances himself from those he exploits and delegates the "face-to-face encounters to someone else who is paid to take the odium" ("Two Scrooges," 35). Marx theorized that this "falsifying of human relations" was inherent in a particular economic organization of society, and Dickens illustrated this insight in his parasitical and self-righteous "squeezers" and those underlings who do their bidding.

Lionel Trilling's essay "The Dickens of Our Day" was published in the early years of the 1950s, in the aftermath of World War II, and, despite its title, pays little attention to the moment of its writing. The reader is, therefore, particularly struck by one paragraph tucked into the middle of the piece that touches, briefly but poignantly, on events of the recent past and ideologies still then present. He is commenting on how contemporary literature casts a particular light on Dickens's fiction, rendering it more profound and more accurate than had heretofore been understood. But contemporary literary texts do not do this alone:

> In that last difficult matter of accuracy, events have played their part in setting the question in Dickens's favor. We who have seen Hitler, Goering, and Goebbels put on the stage of history, and Pecksniffery institutionalized in the Kremlin, are in no position to suppose that Dickens ever exaggerated in the least the extravagance of madness, absurdity, and malevolence in the world—or, conversely, when we consider the resistance to these qualities, the amount of goodness. "When people say Dickens exaggerates, it seems to me that they can have no eyes and ears. They probably have only *notions* of what things and people are"—thus, in justified irritation, Santayana: and who now, with the smallest experience of life, would fail to agree with him? ("Dickens of Our Day," 44)[30]

Fascism and totalitarianism, and the desperate struggles against them (I think Trilling uses the word "resistance" with its full topical force), offer evidence to the postwar world that demonic and angelic extremes of human behavior do exist and that the unimaginable is possible. Just as Kafka's nightmare vision of modern bureaucracy lent credence to the Circumlocution Office, so too did the experience of the Second World War convince Trilling's generation that the grotesqueries of the Dickensian universe were believable, and not the products of a childish, hyperbolic imagination. In a time of gross irrationality and irrationality masquerading as rationality, what had seemed exaggeration in Dickens now seemed familiar.

## WILSON'S DIVIDED MAN

The new Dickens critics tended to differ about whether modern fiction had obscured or illuminated the Victorian novelist's greatness as an artist. Steven Marcus pointed out in *Dickens from Pickwick to Dombey* that Dostoevsky admired and learned much from Dickens, but that the Russian's own work had made it impossible for us to do likewise, principally because Dostoevsky convinced us that "the powers of truth" appear always in concert with "the powers of suffering, negation and outrage" (13–14). Whereas Lionel Trilling believed that contemporary literature had the effect of "bringing to light, of developing as on a photographic film, our sense of [Dickens's] importance and profundity," Edmund Wilson argued in "The Two Scrooges" (39) that readers of Kafka, Mann, and Joyce seldom recognized in Dickens the same force of symbolic writing they found in the modernists.[31] But Wilson's own reading of Dickens clearly comes not only from Freudian interest in unconscious authorial conflict but also from his reading of *Crime and Punishment, Dr. Jekyll and Mr. Hyde,* and *The Picture of Dorian Gray.*[32] For Wilson, Dickens was above all a divided and self-alienated man, and his emphasis in "The Two Scrooges" is—as the title suggests—on the dualism of Dickens's nature and impulses. The novelist's works reveal him to be both social rebel and criminal, virtuous and perverse, seeker of justice and murderer, victim and perpetrator. Wilson regards the last part of Dickens's career as a turn toward the psychological and toward an increasing identification with the criminal—Bradley Headstone and finally John Jasper being the exemplary cases in point. Jasper leads Wilson directly to Dorian Gray and Dr. Jekyll, but these latter two also reveal retrospectively the split and tormented nature of Jasper and other Dickensian protagonists.

Though Wilson's interest ultimately centers on Dickens's novels—his symbolism, and especially his mode of characterization—he begins, as is already clear, in biography and the author's own psychology. Less overtly concerned with the oedipal struggle than subsequent critics, Wilson instead underscored the importance of trauma—the "wound" that would account for Dickens's greatness as an artist and make him both pariah and being of prodigious creativity. Like Philoctetes, after whose story Wilson named the *The Wound and the Bow,* the collection in which the Dickens essay would eventually appear, the novelist sublimated into artistic invention an injury he suffered in early life. Murderous rage, repression, hallucinatory imagination, resourcefulness, and neurotic single-mindedness all played roles in the career of the Dickens conjured by Wilson. He plotted a coherent narrative for Dickens's life—"the life of the artist as a story with a single burden," as David Bromwich puts it—and identified a series of defining episodes or crises by which we continue to map Dickens's life.[33]

Each episode marked an instance either of formative trauma or of its neurotic seepage into adult life. In the former category, John Dickens's imprisonment for debt and Charles's employment in Warren's Blacking factory loom largest, and, in the latter, the public readings Dickens performed at the end of his life have the most dramatic, the direst, consequences. Extending the pattern of monomania he displayed in his novels (Wilson offers Mr. Dick's obsession with King Charles's head as an example), Dickens read the scene of Nancy's murder by Bill Sykes compulsively, over and over, until the recitals took on the quality of "an obsessive hallucination" ("Two Scrooges," 85). Wilson proposes to give us nothing less than a reading of Dickens's death. Giving in finally to the feeling that he was "a creature irretrievably tainted" and to the overwhelming guilt associated with his past, the novelist turned on himself. Just as Bradley Headstone bloodied his own knuckles and John Jasper destroyed himself, Dickens "put . . . his own nerves to the torture by enacting the murder of Nancy [and] invoking his own death" ("Two Scrooges," 91). Wilson argues that Dickens's identification with the social rebel—that is, the iconoclast who harnesses his rage in the service of social change—had dropped away by the end of his life and his fixation on the criminal had taken the upper hand. His unfinished final novel shares more with the focused, psychologically freighted stories of murder and underworld vice of Stevenson and Wilde, Wilson suggests, than with Dickens's own magisterial, wide-ranging narratives of society.

In Wilson's hands Dickens's life becomes a drama of psychic torment and ultimate self-immolation. But seeing him as a man, Wilson argued, served to strip away the misleading late- and post-Victorian mythology that had stuck, to "exorcise the spell which has bewitched him into a stuffy piece of furniture" ("Two Scrooges," 17). And by aligning his work with *fin-de-siècle* narratives in this way, Wilson made Dickens into a modern man and a modern writer. One of the notable aspects of Wilson's method is his focus on many of the elements that interested detractors like George Henry Lewes, especially those plot and character elements that appeared irrational and aesthetically primitive. The "hallucinatory" evocation of character, which Lewes levels as a serious criticism, becomes in Wilson's hands a productive habit of fixation. Only through hallucination and ignorance of human psychology, Lewes observes, could Dickens possibly believe in the credibility of figures like Quilp or Mr. Dick or the reality of compulsively repeated gestures and phrases. Whereas Lewes associates this "hallucinatory" writing with a kind of anti-intellectualism, even ignorance, Wilson reinterprets its meaning in relation both to the complex psychological dynamic of self-division and to what he calls "imprisoning states of mind" ("Two Scrooges," 54). Aiming for a wholly different level and mode of realism, Dickens creates characters locked in neurosis, an instance of "remarkable pre-Freudian insight," that derives from the novelist's own struggles. The psycho-biographical approach allows Wilson to return to the excesses and apparent childishness of Dickens's art and claim them for modernity.

## TRILLING: THE PRISON TAINT

Thirteen years after the initial publication of "The Two Scrooges," Lionel Trilling wrote an introduction to *Little Dorrit* that revived serious interest in the one novel of Dickens's late period that, since the writer's death, had been consistently undervalued and underread. Of the three great novels of this phase of Dickens's career, *Bleak House* had emerged as the most celebrated, and *Our Mutual Friend* had recently been rediscovered.[34] By some lights the greatest of all the novels, *Little Dorrit* had fallen into near obscurity, perhaps because of the bleakness of its vision. Trilling recasts the novel by looking at the nature of the symbol at its center. The prison-house, with its important biographical resonances and powerful historical reality, becomes, in Trilling's analysis, a symbolic rendering of the human psyche and, beyond that, of "the ineluctable condition of human life in society" ("Little Dorrit," 282).

Trilling gets to this wholly integrated understanding of the novel, in which all of its aspects are seen from a single point of vision, through Freud or, rather, through a drawing Freud used as a frontispiece for the original version of the *Introductory Lectures on Psychoanalysis*.[35] The drawing, by the Austrian painter Moritz von Schwind (1804–71), shows a man reclining on bales of straw, probably asleep, in a medieval dungeon or prison cell.[36] In a ray of light that extends from the man's head to the small window at the top of the cell, the artist represents the prisoner's dream of escape: a gnome, standing on the shoulders of three others, saws at the bars of the window, while a long-haired maiden (not mentioned, by the way, in Trilling's description of the image, though wholly consistent with his sense of its meaning) floats toward the little men while pouring some refreshment from a pitcher into a goblet. Here, says Trilling, is a perfect illustration of Freud's idea of wish fulfillment: that the "impulses of the will" expressed in dream or fantasy cannot be realized in actuality ("Little Dorrit," 282). But why, Trilling asks, does Freud choose incarceration as the way to represent wish fulfillment? Why, we might add, does he introduce his entire volume on psychoanalysis with this image?

The answer is partly historical and involves the power and ubiquity in nineteenth-century culture of the prison as an emblem of human experience. Trilling wants us to consider this, of course, in relation to *Little Dorrit* as a way of confirming the wide significance of the symbol Dickens chose for his novel. But he also wants to suggest that Dickens anticipated Freud in the way he conceptualized the mind and its self-defeating, self-imprisoning mechanisms. In *Little Dorrit,* and especially in the story of the Clennam family, we have the working out of "the essential theory of the neurosis" ("Little Dorrit," 283). Arthur Clennam believes that his mother's paralysis is an imprisonment that she unconsciously inflicts on herself out of guilt for what he thinks she has done to the Dorrit family—that is, caused them to be shut up in the Marshalsea. Arthur himself feels tainted by this particular guilt, as well as by a general, pervasive sense of culpability that has multiple causes, and later, when he is imprisoned for debt in the Marshalsea following the fall of Merdle, he feels that such punishment is his due. For Freud and for Dickens, Trilling tells us in words reminiscent of Edmund Wilson's theory of the novelist's multiple selves, the mind "is at once the criminal, the victim, the police, the judge, and the executioner" ("Little Dorrit," 284).

This proto-Freudian way of understanding the human condition is to be found in all aspects of *Little Dorrit*: from the self-tormenting Miss Wade, locked in rage, to the self-deluding Mr. Dorrit, fixated on deference, to the subtly smug Mr. Meagles, unaware of the condescension he directs at both Tattycoram and Daniel Doyce, and to the array of neglectful or punishing parents, both figurative and real, who appear in the novel. Trilling's Freud is the tragic Freud, the thinker who perceives one's inability to escape self-defeat, who understands the inevitability of human failure and yet perceives as well the human impulse toward affirmation.[37] The sad, modest ending of the novel—absent both Dickensian jocularity and attempted transcendence—seems to reflect such a muted vision of the human condition. Arthur Clennam is a man suffering from a crisis of the will, a kind of modern angst born of guilt and "sickness unto death" ("Little Dorrit," 291). His helpmate Amy Dorrit, whose small size, modesty, and self-effacing stance reflect the subdued vision of redemption in the novel, also takes on a symbolic role in Trilling's view. If the prison represents the constraining will of society and the self-imprisoning human psyche, Amy represents resistance to these forces of oppression or, as Trilling puts it, "the negation of the social will" ("Little Dorrit," 293). Her resistance is at once modest and overwhelming, making her for Trilling a religious figure or spiritual symbol. He invests Dickens's Christian vision with new meaning by linking it, perhaps improbably, to a Freudian understanding of human neurosis. The unrealistic, exaggerating Dickens and the saccharine, kitschy Dickens are revised, the former through emphasis on symbolism and psychology and the latter by celebrating forbearance and love as heroic means of opposing tyrannies of both self and society.

## MARCUS: OEDIPAL STORIES

Like Edmund Wilson and Humphry House before him, Steven Marcus approached Dickens's works as a coherent whole with a number of identifiable themes, impulses, and obsessions running throughout. J. Hillis Miller, whose critical study *Charles Dickens: The World of His Novels* preceded Marcus's *Dickens from Pickwick to Dombey* by seven years, also claimed as his subject the novelist's entire oeuvre. His purpose, Miller declared, was to assess "the specific quality of Dickens's imagination in the totality of his work, to identify what persists throughout all the swarming multiplicity of his novels as a view of the world which is unique and the same, and to trace the development of his vision of things from one novel to another throughout the chronological span of his career."[38] Much the same could be said of Marcus's aims, but, unlike any of his predecessors, he took the early novels as his focus, making the argument that the consistency detected by critics mainly in the later novels might be better understood by examining the novelist's development from the start of his career. Marcus wished to argue that here, too, was a kind of unity, a set of interests and methods launched as early as *Pickwick* and predictive of what was to come in the second half of Dickens's oeuvre. In identifying the overwhelming psychic and literary impulses of the first half, he married the perspectives of Wilson and Trilling. Taking the biographical narrative of unresolved childhood trauma from the former and the dominant image of the prison-house from the latter, Marcus deepened the psychoanalytic investigation of Dickens's work and placed the triangle of father, son, and prison at the center of his analysis. Indeed, if Marcus shares with Hillis Miller the impulse to read the novels as a totality, he differs most dramatically from Miller in his use of a Freudian and biographically oriented approach.[39] In *Dickens from Pickwick to Dombey*, Marcus reads early Dickens as it had never before been read, as an oedipal story that had not yet emerged as full-blown crisis (as it would later, in the novelist's middle age) and as a rendering of neglect and deprivation still subject to mastery and transcendence.

Beginning at the beginning, then, Marcus gives us a *Pickwick Papers* with emphasis on paternity and imprisonment—or, rather, self-imprisonment—all in a "Pickwickian" key. Dickens here imagines a world in which the ordeals of his early life could be represented as benign and transitory. Mr. Pickwick lands in Fleet Prison for the gentlest of crimes: breach of promise, proved in court via the prose of dinner instructions left for his landlady, the aggrieved party. But the misery he sees around him once in the Fleet compels him to take to something like solitary confinement for three months (the length of time, Marcus reminds us in a footnote, on page 47, that John Dickens spent in the Marshalsea as a debtor). This self-incarceration, bound up with the shame and guilt induced in Dickens by his father's imprisonment and his own employment in the blacking factory, marks the end of *Pickwick Papers* though not of its irrepressible buoyancy. The novel descends into the despair of the Fleet but reemerges, the wickedness of the world registered briefly, but finally held at bay. It is as if Dickens finds the introduction of this autobiographical detail irresistible, partly because it burdens him and partly because it poses no threat, so sure is he of his ability to manage and contain its menace.

So it is with the story of paternal negligence, at the center of which is Sam Weller. Marcus points out the bravado with which Dickens first introduces Sam: he is polishing boots (with Warren's blacking?) at the White Hart Inn. Not satisfied with this allusion to his time of child labor or with having made Sam's character a "boots," Dickens mentions his erstwhile employer by name. Sam's work, he adds, "would have struck envy to the soul of the amiable Mr. Warren" (Marcus, *Dickens*, 31; *PP,* ch.10). The joke—for it is clearly that—is only for himself, a wink for his own benefit at the distance he has come despite the humiliation of having been forced to do work demeaning for a boy of his class. Neither Sam's labor—an echo of Dickens's own—nor his neglect at the hands of his feckless father, Tony, disturbs him. "Vagrant parenthood," as Marcus puts it, is here regarded with humor and equanimity. And beyond this, Sam is given two fathers, Tony and his namesake, Samuel Pickwick, to compensate for the failures of either one. "Standing between [them]," Marcus writes, "Sam receives the several kinds of affection a parent can give, without having to endure any of the pains. . . . Sam's relation to his two fathers repairs the deficiencies of which Dickens would later accuse his own father so bitterly" (35).

The motifs of imprisonment, oedipal strife, and paternal doubling reappear as crucial elements in Marcus's interpretations of the novels leading up to *Dombey.* In *Oliver Twist* the eponymous hero suffers abandonment and multiple captivities, reflections of that "ineradicable feeling of humiliation, of having been violated, degraded and declassed" that Dickens endured as a child (*Dickens,* 82). Less obvious, perhaps, is the case of *Nicholas Nickleby,* with its two abandoned sons, Nicholas and Smike, and their two fathers, Nicholas's beneficent one and Smike's hideously cruel one, Ralph, who, as Nicholas's uncle, also serves as his father-surrogate. The novelist mitigates the flaws of John Dickens through Nicholas's long-dead and therefore safely idealized father, repeating the exculpatory gesture he had made in the cases of Tony Weller and Samuel Pickwick and reserving all opprobrium for Ralph Nickleby. Marcus brilliantly traces the version of the oedipal story implicit in Smike and Ralph's relationship, in which all of the vengeful feelings kept out of the other father-son relations in the early novels is lethally concentrated. The son's wrath is unleashed on the father in a death and a place that the son had always desperately feared. In a cell where Smike had cowered as a child, Ralph hangs himself—going self-incarceration one better—and thus fulfills his discarded son's worst imaginings and wishes.

Although the essay "Who Is Fagin?" appears in *Dickens from Pickwick to Dombey* as an appendix, it is in some respects the final working through of the book's engagement with the Dickensian oedipal story and so is an integral part of Marcus's approach to the early works. The essay is, however, both more directly biographical and more deeply psychoanalytic than the rest of the book and takes as its point of departure the episode of Dickens's employment wrapping and pasting labels onto bottles of shoe-black at Warren's factory. His workmate and instructor in preparing the bottles was a boy named Bob Fagin, after whom Dickens named the London fence in *Oliver Twist*. As Marcus tells us, describing a number of instances in which Bob went out of his way to help the boy Dickens, "Bob Fagin's protectiveness is transformed [in the novel] into Fagin's treacherous maternal care" (*Dickens*, 367). In the autobiographical fragment that Dickens wrote in the 1840s and showed only to his friend and biographer, John Forster, the novelist recalls one instance during this period that Marcus regards as crucial for an understanding of *Oliver Twist*. John Dickens had been released from debtor's prison while his son continued to work at Warren's and one day entered the factory to see Charles and Bob Fagin seated at the window tying up pots of blacking with great expertise. The boys were visible not only to the elder Dickens but also to passersby who sometimes congregated to see the dexterity and speed of the young workers. Thus exposed and on display as a working boy, Dickens wondered how his father "could bear it" (*Dickens*, 369). Marcus observes that Dickens wrote about this scene with intense feeling of a mixed kind: pride and pleasure in his skill and the appreciation of the crowd at the window together with "anxiety and humiliation" at being seen by his father. So much in excess of the circumstances of the occasion is Dickens's response, Marcus concludes, that the memory must be a "screen" for something else, some memory deeper, buried, and more powerful in its effect.

He then moves to the novel itself, singling out two anomalous scenes that seem in some sense inexplicable and extraneous, unnecessary to the flow of plot, but that carry intense emotional weight. Both involve sleep, or rather a state somewhere between sleep and waking, and the condition of seeing and being seen. The first takes place early in the novel in Fagin's den, when Oliver is on the point of waking and sees Fagin looking at a small box of trinkets—loot from his band of small thieves. When Fagin realizes the boy has seen him, he grabs a bread knife threateningly and questions him about what he has observed. In the second scene, which takes place much later in the novel, Oliver is in a state of half-sleep in the country home of the Maylies, his benefactors. Overcome by a peculiar sensation, he thinks he sees the face of Fagin and of a second man—his half-brother, Monks—peering at him through the window. As in the first instance, Oliver is frightened and unable to understand what has occurred. Marcus continues, building his explanation of the screen memory:

> These scenes have in common several elements: a boy in a state of sleep or half-sleep in which conscious and unconscious impressions, fantasies and realities, dreams and recollections, tend to be fused and confused; supervening on this an intense experience of watching and being watched, which gives way to emotions of threat and terror. . . . I think that we are witness here to the decomposed elements of what Freud called the primal scene, to either a memory or fantasy of it: the child asleep, or just waking, or feigning sleep while observing sexual intercourse between his parents, and, frightened by what he sees or imagines, is either noticed by the parents or has a fantasy of what would occur if he were noticed. (*Dickens*, 373)

The crisis of watching and being watched at Warren's Blacking masks the earlier memory of the primal scene, a phenomenon delineated by Freud and closely tied to oedipal feelings of jealousy, fear, and aggression.[40]

To bolster his interpretation, Marcus offers other notable moments in *Oliver Twist* that involve disturbing and disembodied images of sight, watching, and being watched: Bill Sikes's flight through London, pursued by "'widely staring eyes, so lustreless and glassy,'" and the haunting of Fagin by peering human faces during his trial (*Dickens*, 375–76). Oliver's watchers and pursuers (and, we might add, potential castrators) are now the pursued. But the analysis is not done. Marcus ends by winding his way back to one of the most important episodes in the Dickensian biographical canon as outlined by Edmund Wilson: Dickens's compulsive and possibly self-destructive reading of the murder of Nancy at the end of his life. The importance of *Oliver Twist* to Dickens's psyche and the irresistible but dangerous emotions embodied in Sikes's murderous rage and Nancy's suffering are tied to the experiences of childhood humiliation and transgression that Marcus traces to the Warren's episodes and, beyond them, to a deeper memory of inchoate crisis. The overwhelming and ultimately self-punishing aggression that Wilson detects in the public readings is given a more specific interpretation by Marcus, at the center of which is Dickens's relation to his father. Contemplating various strata of memory and their literary re-imaginings, Marcus sees Dickens's profound resentment of, and yet identification with, John Dickens. The villains of *Oli-

*ver Twist*—Fagin and Bill Sykes—are deeply feared and then perceived, albeit briefly, as victims. And their victimhood is evoked through the phenomenon of being spied at, hunted down, and captured through the faculty of vision: the same phenomenon Dickens himself experienced and emphasized in his recorded memories of Warren's Blacking.

A final note on Marcus's unveiling of the oedipal story at the heart of Dickens's oeuvre and its relation to his method in "Who Is Fagin?": in a 1985 essay he wrote for a volume called *Introspection in Biography,* Marcus explores his own "biographical inclination" through a backwards and forwards process of memory.[41] Peeling back layers of recollection from his early academic career, student days, and childhood, he finds his way to the earliest (detectable) reason for his attraction to Dickens as a subject: a memory of reading, at age six, a chapter about *Oliver Twist* from a volume of abbreviated Dickens stories given to him by his mother, who had also taught him to read at a very young age. A particular Cruikshank drawing insinuated its way into the consciousness of Steven Marcus at age six: the illustration of Fagin and Monks staring at Oliver through a window that figures so importantly in "Who Is Fagin?" He recollects not only the drawing but Oliver's reaction upon waking up, in a "terrible scene of castration threats and fears" ("Biographical," 298). Despite, or perhaps because of, the powerful emotions associated with this episode, the actual memory of it "went underground" and did not reemerge until he finished writing his dissertation some decades later. "There is, I believe," Marcus writes, "a symmetry between the castration anxiety that I experienced in reading the story as a child and the assertion at a later date of potency and creativeness in writing a book [his first] about the figure that had been at the literary locus of that memorable experience" ("Biographical," 299).

We know from Marcus's brief intellectual autobiography that this "assertion ... of potency and creativeness" marked the overcoming of paternal disapproval. His father had wanted him to become a doctor, and he "went against [his] father's wishes" in pursuing literary studies. "That was the great early crisis in my life," Marcus observes, "because I lost my father's support and had to go ahead on my own" ("Biographical," 302). A second instance of discouragement, this time from the potential paternal figure, F. R. Leavis, presented another serious challenge to his aspirations. A student at Cambridge, Marcus approached Leavis about his intention of writing a book-length study of Dickens, and Leavis, still believing in the literary value only of *Hard Times,* "dismissed me." But this challenge, presumably like the first fatherly disavowal, also spurred him on ("'Well, I'm going to show you,'" Marcus recalls himself thinking at the time ["Biographical," 300]). Bolstered, we can imagine, by the memory of a maternal gift, Marcus was able to go on to prove himself as a critic and as a professionally successful man. He did so, as well, with the psychological and intellectual help of his "teacher and . . . surrogate father," Lionel Trilling, who "never wavered in his conviction that I had made the right choice, that I was on the right track" ("Biographical," 300). A second good father was Sigmund Freud, whose own revelatory and audacious work "gave [Marcus] the inner permission" to follow his inclination to pursue unconventional subjects and bold interpretations. From out of this oedipal drama and negotiation of multiple fathers—and one mother—Marcus became a critic able to write the following about Dickens, his first great subject: "That he remained until his death engrossed in his most primitive and vital conflicts may also add to our understanding of his extraordinary development as a novelist: to remain in touch with vital conflicts is to remain in touch with vital feelings, with one's roots in life" ("Biographical," 378).

## THE PSYCHE AND THE WORLD

It remains to be observed that the kind of criticism that Wilson, Trilling, and Marcus wrote in the middle decades of the last century insisted on the absolute interpenetration of the psychological and the social in Dickens's novels. In discussing their contributions, I have artificially separated the realm of the human psyche from the sphere of social, economic, and political life and emphasized the former. But these critics perceived that Dickens transformed personal experience into an understanding of the fundamental irrationality of both individual human behavior and social organization and that the two realms were fused in Dickens's narratives, imagery, and characters. Each critic sees the trajectory of the relationship between self and society a bit differently. Edmund Wilson argues that Dickens's private wound had become a "protest against the age" and that, ultimately, toward the end of his career, this had "turned into a protest against self" ("Two Scrooges," 44). He sees Dickens's rage against the indifference of powerful men and institutions rerouted toward self-punishment in his final, unfinished novel and in his public readings as well.

Trilling proposes a more dialectical relationship between historical reality, symbolism, and social criticism. Before the Victorian prison can become a psychic and social symbol, it is a lived reality, just as the dust mounds in *Our Mutual Friend* are also, in the first instance, a "social fact" ("Dickens of Our Day," 48). In the essay on *Little Dorrit,* Trilling initially identifies the prison as "the practical instrument for the negation of man's will which the will of society has contrived," but he expands its meaning to "the ineluctable condition of life in society" (282). Finally, via Freud, Trilling declares that for Dickens the mind is a prison, though not so simply. Dickens sees that the mind, "*having received the social impress, . . . becomes in turn the matrix of society*" ("Little Dorrit," 284; emphasis added). In this formulation, the mind and society are almost indistinguishable in their fundamental structures. The mind absorbs the patterns of social organization and then becomes readable as the template of society. For Marcus, the great project of Dickens's oeuvre was finding a way to connect his "personal experience and the experience of the age." In the end, the novelist could not imagine his own history in terms separable from "his imagination of society" (*Dickens*, 43–44).

The observation, apparently small but profound in its implications, that Dickens conflated the psychological and the social in his works helps to answer the indictments of Dickens's early critics. George Henry Lewes and others could not grasp that Dickens's "ideas," of which they found his novels to be void, presented themselves in just this form and that such ideas as the correspondence between mind and social structures presented themselves through symbol, image, and idiosyncrasies of character. The hypocrite Uriah Heep's unctuousness and bodily distortions themselves contain an idea, even a hypothesis: that the elaborate show of self-effacement masks class resentment and corrosive hostility. This is an idea about both psychic and social life, as are the nuggets of psychological and social observation embodied in the compulsive hand-washing of Jaggers in *Great Expectations* or the rapacious haircutting of Good Mrs. Brown in *Dombey and Son*.

In part because they had imbibed such exaggerated or hallucinatory truths in a visceral and automatic way in childhood, these examples and hundreds of others like them failed to penetrate the understanding of Dickens's early critics. Their disavowal of childhood and its attendant irrationality, both in themselves and in Dickens, hampered their ability to translate what they had absorbed as children into an adult critical sensibility. In an irony that would have no doubt pleased Dickens, the very persistence and indelibility of childhood that so embarrassed his detractors came in time to inspire the critical brilliance of his mid-twentieth-century admirers.

## NOTES

1. Trilling, "The Dickens of Our Day," 41. Subsequent references are made parenthetically in the text.
2. Orwell, "Charles Dickens," 90. Orwell added that, at the time, this force-feeding

causes "rebellion and vomiting" but may have different effects in later life.

3. In a 1962 symposium on Dickens, J. Hillis Miller cited Richard Altick and William Matthews's *Guide to Doctoral Dissertations in Victorian Literature, 1886–1958* to illustrate increased serious interest in the writer since 1950. Whereas fifty dissertations on Dickens had appeared before 1950, thirty-two had been produced in the eight years between 1950 and 1958. See *Dickens Criticism: Past, Present, and Future: A Symposium,* 25.

4. Wilson, "Dickens: The Two Scrooges," 11; and Trilling, "The Dickens of Our Day," 41. An invaluable source for the history of critical and popular responses to Dickens is George H. Ford, *Dickens and His Readers,* especially chapter 9, "The Common Reader," and chapter 12, "The Uncommon Reader." Ford's important work, first published in 1955, was part of the mid-century movement to recover Dickens's place in literary history. His efforts were more historically oriented than the work of Wilson, Trilling, or Marcus.

5. George Orwell's essay "Charles Dickens" (1939) and Humphry House's *The Dickens World* (1941) represent the two most significant exceptions to this view of the crucial importance of what I am calling "American Dickens." I discuss both briefly later in the chapter.

6. Lewes, "Dickens in Relation to Criticism," 147. Subsequent references are made parenthetically in the text. Orwell seemed to concur with this view when he wrote that in Dickens there is "no poetic feeling . . . , and no genuine tragedy, and even sexual love is almost outside his scope" ("Charles Dickens," 98).

7. Woolf, "David Copperfield," 66. Subsequent references are made parenthetically in the text.

8. James, "The Limitation of Dickens," 52–53.

9. Huxley, "The Vulgarity of Little Nell," 153–54.

10. Santayana, "Dickens," 137.

11. Leavis, *The Great Tradition,* 18–19; emphasis added.

12. James, *A Small Boy,* 64–65, 145. Subsequent references are made parenthetically in the text.

13. Orwell wrote of first reading *David Copperfield* when he was nine: "The mental atmosphere of the opening chapters was so immediately intelligible to me that I vaguely imagined they had been written *by a child* ("Charles Dickens," 60).

14. Leavis, *The Great Tradition,* 19.

15. Marcus, *Dickens from Pickwick to Dombey,* 20. Subsequent references are made parenthetically in the text.

16. Collins, *Dickens and Crime,* 16.

17. Orwell, "Charles Dickens," 64.

18. Philip Collins's own interest in the complexities of Dickens's positions on crime and punishment led him to feel more indebted to Orwell than to Wilson, though his most important influence was Humphry House. See *Dickens and Crime,* vii, 16.

19. House submits, for example, that the "mood" of *Great Expectations* does not belong to the "imaginary date of its plot"—the 1820s and '30s—but rather to the moment in which it was written—the early 1860s: "for the unquestioned assumptions that Pip can be transformed by money and the minor graces it can buy . . . were only possible in a country secure in its internal economy, with expanding markets abroad." See

House, *Dickens World*, 159.

20. House, *Dickens World*, 11, 135 (emphasis added).
21. F. R. and Q. D. Leavis, *Dickens*, ix.
22. Ibid., xv.
23. Marcus, "Dickens after One Hundred Years," 1; and Wilson, "Two Scrooges," 12. It is also interesting to note that Philip Collins, while mindful of and interested in Wilson's "Two Scrooges" throughout *Dickens and Crime*, refers with skepticism to "Wilson . . . and his American inheritors," who find an increasingly dark tone in the novels and see this as "betokening a more severe—and thus, by implication, a more comprehensive and just—judgment on contemporary society" (16). Collins departs from this "American" view in his analysis of Dickens's increasingly punitive attitude toward crime and criminals. Wilson's understanding of the trajectory of Dickens's career in relation to criminality could not be more different.
24. Gay, "Freud's America," in *America and the Germans*, 304–5. Gay refers to the 1950s as "the golden decade of psychoanalysis in the United States" (305).
25. For the *Partisan Review*, see Harvey Teres, *Renewing the Left*.
26. For Edmund Wilson on his profession and his parents, see Kazin, "The Great Anachronism: A View from the Sixties," 20; and for Lionel Trilling's immigrant parents, see Diana Trilling, *The Beginning of the Journey*, chapter 2. For Steven Marcus and his father, see 282–83 of this chapter.
27. Muchnic, "Edmund Wilson's Russian Involvement," 93–94.
28. Wilson, *The Thirties*, ed. Leon Edel, 714–16. Wilson had also been thinking about Dickens and Dostoevsky together (652).
29. Wilson, "Two Scrooges," 32–33, 37. Subsequent references are made parenthetically in the text. Wilson's essay was first delivered as a lecture to students at the University of Chicago in 1939. It was published in *The Wound and the Bow* in 1941.
30. Orwell ends his essay on Dickens by referring to the "smelly little orthodoxies which are now contending for our souls." Their proponents, he contends, would hate what Dickens was, a "liberal, a free intelligence" (104).
31. Trilling, "The Dickens of Our Day."
32. As J. Hillis Miller observed in a symposium in 1962, there was something to be gained by "a new generation that is brought up on Kafka coming to read Dickens": they could show us "things that were really there, but were invisible to earlier readers and critics" (*Dickens Criticism*, 36). Six years later, in *Dickens and Crime*, Philip Collins alluded to Miller's point of view and defended his own historicist approach by quoting George Ford's response to Miller on the occasion of the 1962 symposium. Would it not be "equally profitable," Ford asked, to compare Dickens to his own contemporaries, Carlyle, Thackeray, Browning, and even G. W. M. Reynolds (Collins, vii)?
33. Bromwich, "Wilson's Modernism," 200. Significant biographies of Dickens that appeared in the middle of the twentieth century were also, of course, part of the making of modern Dickens criticism. T. A. Jackson's *Charles Dickens, The Progress of a Radical* (1938) took a Marxist perspective, and Jack Lindsay's *Charles Dickens: A Biographical and Critical Study* (1950) a Freudian one. Edgar Johnson's authoritative two-volume *Charles Dickens: His Tragedy and Triumph* (1952) made use of the Nonesuch Press publication of Dickens's letters in 1938, an edition that was superseded by the twelve volumes of letters produced by Oxford University Press, starting in 1965 and edited by

Madeline House and Graham Storey (*LCD*).

34. Trilling, "Little Dorrit," 279. Subsequent references are made parenthetically in the text.

35. Sigmund Freud, *Vorlesungen zur einführung in die Psychoanalyse*.

36. Von Schwind, born in Vienna but active as an artist mainly in Munich, drew his subjects from fairy tales, folklore, and songs and was known primarily as an illustrator and muralist.

37. See two of Trilling's essays for his understanding of Freud's tragic vision: "Freud and Literature," 32–54; and "Freud: Within and Beyond Culture," 89–118.

38. Miller, *Charles Dickens*, viii.

39. Like Marcus, Miller claims Trilling as an intellectual precursor. Trilling's introduction to *Little Dorrit*, Miller writes, is "really one of the best examples of a kind of study closer to my own approach: the discussion of Dickens's novels as autonomous works of art" (viii). He carves out a critical space, however, that rejects the importance of the author's historical epoch or psychology as the dominant shaping forces of his fiction. On the contrary, he characterizes the conditions of a writer's life as "merely the *obstacles* or materials which he transforms and *vanquishes* by turning them into novels" (ix; emphasis added). Marcus, whose awareness of Miller's work is evident in a number of footnotes, gestures to the difference between their critical assumptions by indirectly attributing to Miller the belief that the novel—any novel—is "a self-enclosed and fully coherent system of discourse making statements about itself" (214). Marcus does not accept this idea of total self-referentiality except in a case like *Finnegans Wake*.

40. Hillis Miller's discussion of these scenes in *Oliver Twist* illustrates nicely both the similarities and the differences between his critical method and that of Marcus. Miller is interested in the phenomenon of "affective memory," which links one textual episode to another: "Here a peculiar psychological state caused by something directly present brings about the total recovery of a certain epoch of the past not as a faint memory but as an intimately lived experience" (*Charles Dickens*, 75). Though these words are consistent in important ways with Marcus's reading, Miller is not at all interested in the echoes of Dickens's own past in these episodes.

41. Marcus, "Biographical," 297–307. Subsequent references are made parenthetically in the text.

# Bibliography

Ackroyd, Peter. *Dickens*. New York: HarperCollins, 1992.
Anderson, Amanda. *Tainted Souls and Painted Faces: The Rhetoric of Fallenness in Victorian Culture*. Ithaca and London: Cornell University Press, 1993.
Anderson, Amanda and Joseph Valente, eds. *Disciplinarity at the Fin de Siècle*. Princeton: Princeton University Press, 2002.
Andrews, Malcolm. *Dickens and the Grown-up Child*. Iowa City: University of Iowa Press, 1994.
Anger, Suzy. "Introduction: Knowing the Victorians." In *Knowing the Past: Victorian Literature and Culture*, ed. Suzy Anger. Ithaca: Cornell University Press, 2001. 1–22.
———, ed. *Knowing the Past: Victorian Literature and Culture*. Ithaca: Cornell University Press, 2001.
———. *Victorian Interpretation*. Ithaca: Cornell University Press, 2005.
Arac, Jonathan. *Commissioned Spirits: The Shaping of Social Motion in Dickens, Carlyle, Melville, and Hawthorne*. New Brunswick: Rutgers University Press, 1979.
———. "Hamlet, Little Dorrit, and the History of Character." In *Critical Conditions: Regarding the Historical Moment*, ed. Michael Hays. Minneapolis: University of Minnesota Press, 1992.
Arnold, Matthew. *Culture and Anarchy and Other Writings*, ed. Stefan Collini. Cambridge: Cambridge University Press, 1993.
Bagehot, Walter. *The Collected Works of Walter Bagehot*, ed. Norman St. John-Stevas. 13 vols. Aylesbury, Bucks: Hazell Watson and Viney, Ltd., 1965–78.
Baier, Annette. "Hume, the Woman's Moral Theorist?" In *Moral Prejudices: Essays on Ethics*, ed. Annette Baier. Cambridge: Harvard University Press, 1994. 51–75.
Baker, H. Barton. *The London Stage: Its History and Traditions from 1576 to 1888*. 2 vols. London: W. H. Allen & Co., 1889.
Barthes, Roland. "The Plates of the *Encyclopedia*." In *A Barthes Reader*, ed. Susan Sontag. New York: Hill & Wang, 1982. 218–35.

"*The Battle of Life* and 'Mrs. Perkins's Ball.'" *Tait's Edinburgh Literary Magazine* 14 (January 1847): 55–60.
Baumgarten, Murray. "Writing and *David Copperfield*." *Dickens Studies Annual* 14 (1985): 39–59.
Benjamin, Walter. *Illuminations*. London: Fontana, 1973.
Bennington, Geoffrey and Jacques Derrida. *Jacques Derrida*. Chicago: University of Chicago Press, 1993.
Bentham, Jeremy. *The Principles of Morals and Legislation*. New York: Hafner Press, 1948.
———. *Utilitarianism*, ed. Oskar Piest. Indianapolis: Bobbs-Merrill, 1957.
———. *The Works of Jeremy Bentham*, ed. John Bowring. 11 vols. Edinburgh: W. Tait, 1838–43.
Black, Barbara. "A Sisterhood of Rage and Beauty: Dickens's Rosa Dartle, Miss Wade, and Madame Defarge." *Dickens Studies Annual* 26 (1998): 91–106.
Blake, Kathleen. "*Bleak House*, Political Economy, Victorian Studies." *Victorian Literature and Culture* (1997): 1–21.
Bodenheimer, Rosemarie. *The Politics of Story in Victorian Social Fiction*. Ithaca: Cornell University Press, 1988.
Born, Daniel. *The Birth of Liberal Guilt in the English Novel*. Chapel Hill: University of North Carolina Press, 1995.
Bourdieu, Pierre. *Distinction: A Social Critique of the Judgment of Taste*, trans. Richard Nice. Cambridge: Harvard University Press, 1984.
Bourne Taylor, Jenny and Sally Shuttleworth, eds. *Embodied Selves: An Anthology of Psychological Texts 1830–1890*. Oxford: Clarendon, 1998.
Bowen, John. *Other Dickens: Pickwick to Chuzzlewit*. Oxford: Oxford University Press, 2000.
Brantlinger, Patrick. "Did Dickens Have a Philosophy of History? The Case of *Barnaby Rudge*." *Dickens Studies Annual: Essays on Victorian Fiction* 30 (2001): 59–74.
———. *Fictions of State: Culture and Credit in Britain, 1694–1994*. Ithaca: Cornell University Press, 1996.
———. *The Spirit of Reform: British Literature and Politics, 1832–1867*. Cambridge: Harvard University Press, 1977.
Briggs, Asa. *Victorian Things*. Bury St. Edmunds: Folio Society, 1996.
Bromwich, David. "Wilson's Modernism." *Salmagundi* 113 (Winter 1997): 195–203.
Bunyan, John. *The Pilgrim's Progress*. 1678. Harmondsworth: Penguin, 1980.
Burgis, Nina. "Introduction." In *David Copperfield*. Oxford: Clarendon, 1981. xv–xxi.
Butt, John and Kathleen Tillotson. *Dickens at Work*. London: Methuen, 1957.
Butterworth, R. D. "Dickens the Journalist: The Preston Strike and 'On Strike.'" *The Dickensian* 89, no. 2 (Summer 1993): 129–38.
———. "Dickens the Novelist: The Preston Strike and *Hard Times*." *The Dickensian* 88, no. 2 (Summer 1992): 91–102.
Butwin, Joseph. "*Hard Times*: The News and the Novel." *Nineteenth-Century Fiction* 32, no. 2 (September 1977): 166–87.
Byatt, Derrick. *Promises to Pay: The First Three Hundred Years of Bank of England Notes*. London: Spink, 1994.
Campbell, Matthew, Jacqueline M. Labbé and Sally Shuttleworth, eds. *Memory and

*Memorials 1789–1914: Literary and Cultural Perspectives.* London: Routledge, 2000.

Carlyle, Jane Welsh. *The Collected Letters of Thomas and Jane Welsh Carlyle,* ed. Clyde de L. Ryals and Kenneth J. Fielding. Vol. 17. Durham: Duke University Press, 1990.

Carlyle, Thomas. "The Hero as a Man of Letters." 1841. *On Heroes, Hero-Worship, and the Heroic in History.* New York: Chelsea House, 1983.

———. *Sartor Resartus,* ed. C. F. Harrold. New York: The Odyssey Press, 1937.

Chase, Karen. *Eros and Psyche: The Representation of Character in Charlotte Brontë, Charles Dickens, and George Eliot.* New York: Methuen, 1984.

Chesterton, G. K. *Charles Dickens: A Critical Study.* New York: Dodd, Mead, 1913.

———. *Chesterton on Dickens.* London: Everyman, 1992.

Chow, Rey. "Fateful Attachments: On Collecting, Fidelity, and Lao She." *Critical Inquiry* 28:1 (Autumn 2001): 286–304.

"Christmas is Banned: It Offends Muslims." *The Daily Express,* 3 November 2005: 1.

Clark, T. J. *The Painting of Modern Life: Paris in the Art of Manet and His Followers.* New York: Knopf, 1985.

Clayton, Jay. *Dickens in Cyberspace: The Afterlife of the Nineteenth Century in Postmodern Culture.* New York: Oxford University Press, 2003.

Cleere, Eileen. *Avuncularism: Capitalism, Patriarchy, and Nineteenth-Century English Culture.* Stanford: Stanford University Press, 2004.

Cohen, William. *Sex Scandal: The Private Parts of Victorian Fiction.* Durham and London: Duke University Press, 1996.

Cohn, Dorrit. *The Distinction of Fiction.* Baltimore: Johns Hopkins University Press, 1999.

Collins, Philip, ed. *Charles Dickens: The Critical Heritage.* London: Routledge and Kegan Paul, 1971.

———. *Dickens and Crime.* Bloomington: Indiana University Press, 1968.

———. "Morality and Moral Issues." *Oxford Reader's Companion to Dickens,* ed. Paul Schlicke. New York and Oxford: Oxford University Press, 1999.

*Commons Preservation Society: Report of Proceedings, 1870–1876.* London: P. Grant, 1876.

"The Condition of Authors in England, Germany, and France." *Fraser's Magazine* (March 1847): 285–95.

Connelly, Mark. *Christmas: A Social History.* London: I. B. Tauris, 1999.

Connor, Steven, ed. *Charles Dickens.* London: Longman, 1996.

Craig, Randall. *Promising Language: Betrothal in Victorian Law and Fiction.* Albany: State University of New York Press, 2000.

Crary, Jonathan. "Spectacle, Attention, Counter-Memory." *October* (Autumn 1989): 96–107.

Crompton, Louis. *Byron and Greek Love.* Berkeley: University of California Press, 1985.

Cronin, Mark. "Henry Gowan, William Makepeace Thackeray, and 'The Dignity of Literature' Controversy." *Dickens Quarterly* 16, no. 2 (June 1999): 104–15.

Culler, A. Dwight. *The Imperial Intellect.* New Haven: Yale University Press, 1955.

Curtis, Gerard. "Dickens in the Visual Market." In *Literature in the Marketplace: Nineteenth-Century British Publishing and Reading Practices,* ed. John O. Jordan and

Robert Patten. London: Cambridge University Press, 1995.
*Daily Express*, Op/Ed, 3 November 2005: 12.
Daleski, H. M. "Imagining Revolution: The Eye of History and of Fiction." *Journal of Narrative Technique* 18, no. 1 (Winter 1988): 61–72.
Dallas, Eneas Sweetland. "The Hidden Soul." Excerpt from *The Gay Science* (1866). Rpt. in *Embodied Selves*, ed. Jenny Bourne Taylor and Sally Shuttleworth. Oxford: Clarendon, 1998. 149.
Dames, Nicholas. *Amnesiac Selves: Nostalgia, Forgetting and British Fiction 1810–1870*. New York: Oxford University Press, 2001.
Damrosch, Leopold. Jr. *God's Plot and Man's Stories: Studies in the Fictional Imagination from Milton to Fielding*. Chicago: University of Chicago Press, 1985.
Danto, Arthur. *Narration and Knowledge*. New York: Columbia University Press, 1985.
Darwall, Stephen. "Empathy, Sympathy, Care." *Philosophical Studies* 89 (1998): 261–83.
Darwin, Charles. *The Descent of Man, and Selection in Relation to Sex*. 1871. Princeton: Princeton University Press, 1981.
Debord, Guy. *Society of the Spectacle*. 1967. Trans. Donald Nicholson-Smith. New York: Zone Books, 2004.
de Grazia, Margreta, Maureen Quilligan, and Peter Stallybrass, eds. *Subject and Object in Renaissance Culture*. Cambridge: Cambridge University Press, 1996.
Delany, Paul. "Who Paid for Modernism?" In *The New Economic Criticism: Studies at the Intersection of Literature and Economics,* ed. Martha Woodmansee and Mark Osteen. London: Routledge, 1999. 335–51.
Dellamora, Richard. *Masculine Desire*. Chapel Hill: University of North Carolina Press, 1990.
de Mann, Paul. "The Rhetoric of Temporality." In *Blindness and Insight: Essays in the Rhetoric of Contemporary Criticism*. London: Methuen, 1983. 187–228.
Derrida, Jacques. *The Post Card from Socrates to Freud and Beyond*, trans. Alan Bass. Chicago: University of Chicago Press, 1987.
———. *Specters of Marx: The State of the Debt, the Work of Mourning and the New International,* trans. Peggy Kamuf. London: Routledge, 1994.
———. *The Truth in Painting,* trans. Geoffrey Bennington and Ian Mcleod. Chicago: University of Chicago Press, 1987.
Diamond, Cora. *The Realistic Spirit: Wittgenstein, Philosophy and the Mind*. Cambridge: MIT Press, 1991.
Dickens, Charles. "Christmas among the London Poor and Sick." *Household Words* (21 December 1850).
———. "Familiar Epistle From a Parent to a Child." In *Dickens' Journalism: Sketches by Boz and Other Early Papers, 1833–39,* ed. Michael Slater. London: Phoenix, 1994. 552–54.
———. "On Strike." *Household Words* (11 February 1854). Rpt. in *Hard Times,* 2nd ed., ed. George Ford and Sylvère Monod. New York: Norton, 1990. 285–97.
Dickens, Charles and Mark Lemon. "A Paper-Mill." *Household Words* (31 August 1850).
Dickens, Charles and W. H. Wills. "The Heart of Mid-London." *Household Words* (4 May 1850).

———. "The Old Lady in Threadneedle Street." *Household Words* (6 July 1850).

———. "Two Chapters on Bank-Note Forgeries: Chapter II." *Household Words* (21 September 1850).

Dickens Fellowship. *Dickens Criticism: Past, Present, and Future Directions*. A Symposium with George H. Ford, Edgar Johnson, J. Hillis Miller, Sylvère Monod, Noel Peyrouton. Cambridge, MA: Charles Dickens Reference Center, 1962.

Dickens, Henry. *Memories of My Father*. 1928. Rpt. in *Charles Dickens: Family History*, ed. Norman Page. London: Routledge/Thoemmes Press, 1999.

Dodd, George and W. H. Wills. "I Promise to Pay." *Household Words* (27 December 1856).

Donohue, Joseph W. *Dramatic Character in the English Romantic Age*. Princeton: Princeton University Press, 1970.

Downer, Alan S. "Players and Painted Stage: Nineteenth-Century Acting." *PMLA* 61:2 (June 1946): 522–76.

Eagleton, Terry. *The English Novel: An Introduction*. Oxford: Blackwell Publishing, 2005.

Easson, Angus. "A Novel Scarcely Historical? Time and History in Dickens's *Little Dorrit*." In *History and the Novel: Essays and Studies 1991 for the English Association*, ed. Angus Easson. Cambridge: D. S. Brewer, 1991. 27–40.

Eatwell, John, Murray Milgate, and Peter Newman, eds. *The New Palgrave Dictionary of Economics*. 4 vols. London: Macmillan, 1987.

Elmes, James. *Metropolitan Improvements; or London in the Nineteenth Century*. London: Jones & Co., 1828.

Engels, Friedrich. *The Condition of the Working Class in England in 1844*. 1892. Moscow: Progress Publishers, 1973.

Evans, D. Morier. *The History of the Commercial Crisis, 1857–58, and the Stock Exchange Panic of 1859*. London: Groombridge and Sons, 1859.

Everett, Charles. *The Education of Jeremy Bentham*. New York: Columbia University Press, 1931.

Felski, Rita. "Nothing to Declare: Identity, Shame, and the Lower Middle Class." *PMLA* 115:1 (January 2000): 33–45.

Ferguson, Frances. "Canons, Poetics, and Social Value: Jeremy Bentham and How to Do Things with People." *MLN* 110 (1995): 1148–64.

Fielding, K. J., ed. *The Speeches of Charles Dickens*. Atlantic Heights, NJ: Humanities Press International, 1988.

Fiering, Norman S. "Irresistible Compassion: An Aspect of Eighteenth Century Sympathy and Humanitarianism." *Journal of the History of Ideas* 37 (1976): 195–218.

Filonowicz, Joseph Duke. "Ethical Sentimentalism Revisited." *History of Philosophy Quarterly* 6:2 (1989): 189–206.

*First and Second Reports from the Select Committee on Open Spaces (Metropolis)*, June 1865, Parliamentary Papers, 1865.

Fleishman, Avrom. *The English Historical Novel: Walter Scott to Virginia Woolf*. Baltimore: Johns Hopkins University Press, 1971.

Ford, George H. *Dickens and His Readers: Aspects of Novel-Criticism since 1836*. New York: Norton, 1965.

Ford, George H. and Lauriat Lane, Jr. *The Dickens Critics*. Ithaca: Cornell University Press, 1961.

Ford, George and Sylvère Monod. "Introduction." In *Bleak House*, ed. George Ford and Sylvère Monod. New York: Norton, 1977. ix–xx.

Foucault, Michel. *The Archaeology of Knowledge*. New York: Pantheon, 1982.

———. *Discipline and Punish*, trans. Alan Sheridan. New York: Vintage Books, 1979.

———. *The History of Sexuality: Volume 1: An Introduction*. 1976. Trans. Robert Hurley. New York: Random House, 1980.

Freedgood, Elaine. *The Ideas in Things: Fugitive Meaning in the Victorian Novel*. Chicago: University of Chicago Press, 2006.

Freud, Sigmund. *Beyond the Pleasure Principle*. In *The Pelican Freud Library Volume 11: On Metapsychology; The Theory of Psychoanalysis*, ed. Angela Richards. Harmondsworth: Penguin, 1984. 269–338.

———. *The Standard Edition of The Complete Psychological Works of Sigmund Freud*. 24 vols. Trans. James Strachey. London: Hogarth Press, 1953–74.

———. "The Uncanny." 1919. In *The Pelican Freud Library Volume 14: Art and Literature*, ed. Albert Dickson. Harmondsworth: Penguin, 1985. 336–76.

———. *Vorlesungen zur einführung in die Psychoanalyse*. Leipzig & Vienna: Hugo Heller, 1918.

Frost, Robert. "Mending Wall." In *The Poetry of Robert Frost*. New York: Holt, Rinehart & Winston, 1974. 33–34.

Gager, Valerie. *Shakespeare and Dickens: The Dynamics of Influence*. Cambridge: Cambridge University Press, 1996.

Gallagher, Catherine. "The Duplicity of Doubling in *A Tale of Two Cities*." *Dickens Studies Annual* 12 (1983): 125–45.

———. "The Novel and Other Discourses of Suspended Disbelief." In *Practicing the New Historicism*, ed. Catherine Gallagher and Stephen Greenblatt. Chicago: University of Chicago Press, 2000. 163–210.

Gardiner, Judith Kegan. "On Female Identity and Writing by Women." *Critical Inquiry* 8 (1981): 347–61.

Gay, Peter. "Freud's America." In *America and the Germans*, ed. Frank Trommler and Joseph McVeigh. Philadelphia: University of Pennsylvania Press, 1985. 303–14.

Giddens, Anthony. *The Consequences of Modernity*. Stanford: Stanford University Press, 1990.

Girard, Rene. "Triangular Desire." In *The Girard Reader*, ed. James G. Williams. New York: Crossroad, 1996. 33–44.

Glavin, John. *After Dickens: Reading, Adaptation and Performance*. Cambridge: Cambridge University Press, 1999.

Golby, J. M. and A. W. Purdue. *The Making of the Modern Christmas*. London: Batsford Ltd., 1986.

Goldberg, Michael. *Carlyle and Dickens*. Athens: University of Georgia Press, 1972.

———. "From Bentham to Carlyle: Dickens' Political Development." *Journal of the History of Ideas* 33 (1972): 61–76.

Goux, Jean-Joseph. *The Coiners of Language*, trans. Jennifer Curtiss Gage. Norman: University of Oklahoma Press, 1994.

Grossman, Jonathan. "Representing Pickwick: The Novel and the Law Courts." *Nineteenth-Century Literature* 52 (1997): 171–97.

Hadley, Elaine. *Melodramatic Tactics*. Stanford: Stanford University Press, 1995.

*Hansard's Parliamentary Debates.*
Harrison, Ross. *Bentham, The Arguments of the Philosophers.* London: Routledge & Kegan Paul, 1983.
Hartley, Jenny. "Undertexts and Intertexts: The Women of Urania Cottage, Secrets and *Little Dorrit. Critical Survey* 17:2 (2005): 63–80.
Herschel, John. *Preliminary Discourse on the Study of Natural Philosophy.* 1830. Chicago: University of Chicago Press, 1987.
Hoffmann, E. T. A. "The Sandman." In *The Golden Pot and Other Stories,* ed. Ritchie Robertson. Oxford: World's Classics, 1992. 85–118.
Holcombe, Lee. "Victorian Wives and Property: Reform of the Married Women's Property Law, 1857–1882." In *A Widening Sphere: Changing Roles of Victorian Women,* ed. Martha Vicinus. Bloomington: Indiana University Press, 1980. 3–28.
Hollingshead, John. *Ragged London in 1861.* New York: Garland, 1975.
House, Humphry. *The Dickens World.* London: Oxford University Press, 1942.
"How Mr. Chokepear Keeps a Merry Christmas." *Punch, or the London Charivari* 1 (25 December 1841): 277.
Hume, David. *An Enquiry Concerning the Principles of Morals,* ed. J. B. Schneewind. Indianapolis: Hackett, 1983.
———. *Moral and Political Philosophy,* ed. Henry D. Aiken. New York: Hafner Press, 1948.
———. *A Treatise of Human Nature,* ed. David Fate Norton and Mary J. Norton. Oxford: Oxford University Press, 2000.
Hutcheson, Francis. "Reflections on the Common Systems of Morality." In *On Human Nature,* ed. Thomas Mautner. Cambridge: Cambridge University Press, 1993.
Huxley, Aldous. "The Vulgarity of Little Nell." In *The Dickens Critics,* ed. George H. Ford and Lauriat Lane, Jr. Ithaca: Cornell University Press, 1961. 153–56.
Jackson, T. A. *Charles Dickens: The Progress of a Radical.* New York: International Publishers, 1938.
Jacobson, Wendy S. *Dickens and the Children of Empire.* Basingstoke: Palgrave, 2000.
Jaffe, Audrey. "Spectacular Sympathy: Visuality and Ideology in Dickens's *A Christmas Carol.*" In *Victorian Literature and the Victorian Visual Imagination,* ed. Carol T. Christ and John O. Jordan. Cambridge: Cambridge University Press, 1995. 327–44.
———. *Vanishing Points: Dickens, Narrative, and the Subject of Omniscience.* Berkeley and Los Angeles: University of California Press, 1991.
James, Henry. "The Limitation of Dickens." In *The Dickens Critics,* ed. George H. Ford and Lauriat Lane, Jr. Ithaca: Cornell University Press, 1961. 48–53.
———. "The New Novel." In *Henry James: Selected Literary Criticism,* ed. Morris Shapira. Cambridge: Cambridge University Press, 1981. 311–42.
———. *A Small Boy and Others.* New York: Scribner's, 1913.
Jameson, Fredric. *The Political Unconscious: Narrative as a Socially Symbolic Act.* Ithaca: Cornell University Press, 1981.
Jann, Rosemary. "Fact, Fiction, and Interpretation in *A Child's History of England.*" *Dickens Quarterly* 4, no. 4 (December 1987): 199–205.
John, Juliet. *Dickens's Villains: Melodrama, Character, Popular Culture.* Oxford: Oxford University Press, 2001.

Johnson, Edgar. *Charles Dickens: His Tragedy and Triumph*. Revised and Abridged. New York: Viking Penguin, 1977.
———. *Charles Dickens: His Tragedy and Triumph*. 2 vols. New York: Simon & Schuster, 1952.
Jones, Ernest. *Sigmund Freud: Life and Work*. 3rd ed. London: Hogarth, 1978.
Jordan, John O., ed. *The Cambridge Companion to Charles Dickens*. Cambridge: Cambridge University Press, 2001.
Kaminsky, Alice R., ed. *Literary Criticism of George Henry Lewes*. Lincoln: University of Nebraska Press, 1964.
Kaplan, Fred. *Dickens: A Biography*. New York: Morrow, 1988.
———. *Dickens and Mesmerism: The Hidden Springs of Fiction*. Princeton: Princeton University Press, 1975.
———. *Sacred Tears*. Princeton: Princeton University Press, 1987.
Kazin, Alfred. "The Great Anachronism: A View from the Sixties." In *Edmund Wilson: The Man and His Work*, ed. John Wain. New York: New York University Press, 1978. 11–27.
Kincaid, James. *Annoying the Victorians*. New York: Routledge, 1995.
Kinsley, James. "Introduction." In *The Pickwick Papers,* ed. James Kinsley. Oxford: Clarendon Press, 1986. xv–xc.
Knight, Charles. *London*. Vol. 3. London: Charles Knight & Co., 1842.
Kristeva, Julia. *Strangers to Ourselves*. New York: Columbia University Press, 1991.
Kucich, John. *Excess and Restraint in the Novels of Charles Dickens*. Athens: University of Georgia Press, 1981.
Kumar, Krishnan. *The Making of an English National Identity*. Cambridge: Cambridge University Press, 2003.
Kuper, Adam. "The English Christmas and the Family." In *Unwrapping Christmas*, ed. Daniel Miller. Oxford: Clarendon, 1993. 157–75.
Kurnick, David. "Empty Houses: Thackeray's Theater of Interiority." *Victorian Studies* 48:2 (2006): 257–67.
*Lancet,* 11 March 1865.
Lane, Margaret, ed. *Christmas Stories. The Oxford Illustrated Dickens*. 1956. Oxford: Oxford University Press, 1987.
Langton, Robert. *The Childhood and Youth of Charles Dickens*. London: Hutchinson, 1912.
Larson, Janet. "Identity's Fictions: Naming and Renaming in *Hard Times*." *Dickens Studies Newsletter* 10 (1979): 14–19.
Leavis, F. R. *The Great Tradition*. New York: New York University Press, 1960.
——— and Q. D. Leavis. *Dickens the Novelist*. London: Chatto & Windus, 1970.
Lefebvre, Henri. *Critique of Everyday Life: Foundations for a Sociology of the Everyday*. Vol. II. Trans. John Moore. London: Verso, 2002.
Lefevre, G. Shaw. *English and Irish Land Questions*. London: Cassell, Petter, Galpin & Co., 1881.
———. "Our Common Land." *Our Common Land and Other Short Essays*. London: Macmillan and Co., 1877.
Lenard, Mary. "'Mr. Popular Sentiment': Dickens and the Gender Politics of Sentimentalism and Social Reform Literature." *Dickens Studies Annual* 27 (1998): 45–68.

Lester, V. Markham. *Victorian Insolvency: Bankruptcy, Imprisonment for Debt, and Company Winding-Up in Nineteenth-Century England.* Oxford: Clarendon Press, 1995.

Levinas, Emmanuel. *Entre-nous: On Thinking of the Other*, trans. Michael B. Smith and Barbara Harshav. New York: Columbia University Press, 1998.

———. *Totality and Infinity*, trans. Alphonso Lingis. Pittsburgh: Duquesne University Press, 1969.

Lewes, George Henry. "Dickens in Relation to Criticism." *The Fortnightly Review* XI (1872): 141–54.

Lindsay, Jack. *Charles Dickens: A Biographical and Critical Study.* London: Dakers, 1950.

Lodge, David. "How Successful is *Hard Times?*" 1981. *Hard Times,* 2nd ed., ed. George Ford and Sylvère Monod. New York: Norton, 1990. 381–89.

Lohrli, Anne. *Household Words: A Weekly Journal, 1850–59, Conducted by Charles Dickens. Index.* Toronto: University of Toronto Press, 1973.

"London in 1851." *Fraser's Magazine for Town and Country* 43:254 (February 1851).

Lucas, John. "Past and Present: *Bleak House* and *A Child's History of England.*" In *Dickens Refigured: Bodies, Desires, and Other Histories,* ed. John Schad. Manchester: Manchester University Press 1996. 136–56.

Luckhurst, Roger. *The Invention of Telepathy 1870–1901.* Oxford: Oxford University Press, 2000.

Lyell, Charles. *Principles of Geology.* Vol. 1. 1830. Ed. Martin J. S. Rudwick. Chicago: University of Chicago Press, 1990.

MacIntyre, Alasdair. *After Virtue.* Notre Dame: University of Notre Dame Press, 1981.

Mack, Mary. *Jeremy Bentham: An Odyssey of Ideas.* New York: Columbia University Press, 1963.

MacKenzie, A. D. *The Bank of England Note: A History of Its Printing.* Cambridge: Cambridge University Press, 1953.

Marcus, Sharon. *Between Women: Friendship, Desire and Marriage in Victorian England.* Princeton: Princeton University Press, 2007.

Marcus, Steven. "A Biographical Inclination." In *Introspection in Biography,* ed. Samuel H. Baron and Carl Pletsch. Hillsdale, NJ: Analytic Press, 1985. 297–307.

———. "Dickens after One Hundred Years." *New York Times Book Review* (7 June 1970): 1, 46–51.

———. *Dickens from Pickwick to Dombey.* New York: W. W. Norton, 1965.

———. *Engels, Manchester, and the Working Class.* 1974. New York: W. W. Norton, 1985.

———. "Homelessness and Dickens." *Social Research* 58 (1991): 93–107.

———. "Language into Structure: *Pickwick Papers.*" In *Representations: Essays on Literature and Society.* New York: Columbia University Press (Morningside Edition), 1990. 214–46.

———. *Representations: Essays on Literature and Society.* 1975. New York: Columbia University Press (Morningside Edition), 1990.

Martineau, Harriet. "How to Get Paper." *Household Words* 10, no. 11 (28 October 1854).

Marx, Karl. *Capital.* Vol. 1. *A Critical Analysis of Capitalist Production.* Vol. 3. *The*

*Process of Capitalist Production as a Whole*, ed. Friedrich Engels. Moscow: Progress Publishers, 1966.
Marx, Karl and Friedrich Engels. *The Communist Manifesto*. Harmondsworth: Penguin, 1967.
Mauss, Marcel. *The Gift: Forms and Functions of Exchange in Archaic Societies*, trans Ian Cunnison. London: Routledge and Kegan Paul, 1966.
Mayhew, Henry. *London Labour and the London Poor*. Vol. 2. London: Griffin, Bohn, and Company, Stationers' Hall Court, 1861.
McClure, Joyce. "Seeing through the Fog: Love and Injustice in *Bleak House*." *Journal of Religious Ethics* 31 (2004): 23–44.
McCulloch, J. R. *The Principles of Political Economy, with Some Inquiries Respecting Their Application*. 5th ed. Edinburgh: Adam and Charles Black, 1864.
McGinn, Colin. *Ethics, Evil, and Fiction*. Oxford: Clarendon, 1997.
McKeon, Michael. *Theory of the Novel: A Historical Approach*. Baltimore: Johns Hopkins University Press, 2000.
"Metropolitan Sewage Committee Proceedings." *Parliamentary Papers*. 1846.
Michie, Helena. "The Avuncular and Beyond: Family Melodrama in *Nicholas Nickleby*." In *Dickens Refigured: Bodies, Desires, and Other Histories*, ed. John Schad. Manchester: Manchester University Press 1996. 80–97.
Mill, John Stuart. "Bentham." In *The Collected Works of John Stuart Mill*. Vol. 10. Ed. J. M. Robson. Toronto: University of Toronto Press, 1963–. 90–100.
———. *The Collected Works of John Stuart Mill*. 21 vols. Ed. J. M. Robson. Toronto: University of Toronto Press, 1963–.
———. *Utilitarianism*, ed. Oskar Piest. Indianapolis: Bobbs-Merrill, 1957.
Miller, Andrew H. *Novels behind Glass: Commodity Culture and Victorian Narrative*. Cambridge: Cambridge University Press, 1995.
Miller, D. A. *The Novel and the Police*. Berkeley and Los Angeles: University of California Press, 1988.
Miller, Hugh. *Foot-Prints of the Creator, or, The Asterolepis of Stromness*. Boston: Gould and Lincoln, 1851.
Miller, J. Hillis. *Charles Dickens: The World of His Novels*. Cambridge: Harvard University Press, 1959.
———. "The Genres of *A Christmas Carol*." *The Dickensian* 89, no. 3 (Winter 1993): 193–206.
———. "Interpretation in Dickens' *Bleak House*." 1971. In *Victorian Subjects*. Durham: Duke University Press, 1991. 179–99.
Miller, Karl. *Doubles: Studies in Literary History*. Oxford: Oxford University Press, 1985.
Miller, Renata Kobetts. "Imagined Audiences: The Novelists and the Stage." In *A Companion to the Victorian Novel*, ed. Patrick Brantlinger and William B. Thesing. Oxford: Blackwell, 2002. 207–24.
Miller, William. "Dickens Reads at the British Museum." *The Dickensian* 43, no. 2 (Summer 1947): 83–84.
Milton, John. *The Works of John Milton*. Vol. III, Part II: *The Doctrine and Discipline of Divorce*. New York: Columbia University Press, 1931.
Mink, Louis O. "Narrative Form as a Cognitive Instrument." In *The Writing of His-

*tory: Literary Form and Historical Understanding*, ed. Robert H. Canary and Henry Kozicki. Madison: University of Wisconsin Press, 1978. 129–49.

Moretti, Franco. *The Way of the World: The Bildungsroman in European Culture*. London: Verso, 1987.

Muchnic, Helen. "Edmund Wilson's Russian Involvement." In *Edmund Wilson: The Man and His Work*, ed. John Wain. New York: New York University Press, 1978. 86–108.

Musselwhite, David. "Dickens: The Commodification of the Novelist." *In Partings Welded Together: Politics and Desire in the Nineteenth-Century English Novel*. New York: Methuen, 1987. 143–225.

Newey, Vincent. *The Scriptures of Charles Dickens: Novels of Ideology, Novels of the Self*. Aldershot: Ashgate, 2004.

Newman, John Henry. *Apologia Pro Vita Sua*, ed. David J. De Laura. New York: W. W. Norton, 1968.

Newsom, Robert. *Charles Dickens Revisited*. Twayne's English Authors Series. New York: Twayne, 2000.

———. "Fictions of Childhood." *The Cambridge Companion to Charles Dickens*, ed. John O. Jordan. 92–105.

———. "*Villette* and *Bleak House*: Authorizing Women." *Nineteenth-Century Literature* 46 (1991): 54–81.

Norton, Caroline. "A Letter to the Queen on Lord Chancellor Cranworth's Marriage and Divorce Bill." In *Victorian Prose*, ed. Rosemary J. Mundhenk and LuAnn McCracken Fletcher. New York: Columbia University Press, 1999. 143–55.

Nunokawa, Jeff. *The Afterlife of Property: Domestic Security and the Victorian Novel*. Princeton: Princeton University Press, 1994.

Nussbaum, Martha. *Love's Knowledge: Essays on Philosophy and Literature*. New York: Oxford University Press, 1990.

*Official Catalogue of the Great Exhibition of the Works of Industry of All Nations, 1851*. Corrected Edition. London: Spicer Bros., 1851.

Orwell, George, "Charles Dickens." In *A Collection of Essays by George Orwell*. New York: Harbrace, 1953.

———. *Keep the Aspidistra Flying*. New York: Harcourt, Brace, 1956.

Patten, Robert L. *Charles Dickens and His Publishers*. Oxford: Clarendon Press, 1978.

Pimlott, J. A. R. *The Englishman's Christmas: A Social History*. London: Harvester Press, 1978.

Pippin, Robert. *Henry James and Modern Moral Life*. Cambridge: Cambridge University Press, 2000.

Poovey, Mary, ed. *The Financial System in Nineteenth-Century Britain*. New York: Oxford University Press, 2003.

———. *Making a Social Body: British Cultural Formation, 1830–1864*. Chicago: University of Chicago Press, 1995.

———. "The Structure of Anxiety in Political Economy and *Hard Times*." In *Knowing the Past: Victorian Literature and Culture*, ed. Suzy Anger. Ithaca: Cornell University Press. 151–71.

———. *Uneven Developments: The Ideological Work of Gender in Mid-Victorian England*. Chicago: University of Chicago Press, 1988.

*Punch, or the London Charivari.* Vol. 1 (25 December 1841).
Qualls, Barry. *The Secular Pilgrims of Victorian Fiction.* Cambridge: Cambridge University Press, 1982.
Retseck, Janet. "Sexing Miss Wade." *Dickens Quarterly* XV:4 (December 1998): 217–25.
Richards, Thomas. *Commodity Culture in Victorian England: Advertising and Spectacle, 1851–1914.* Stanford: Stanford University Press, 1990.
Ridley, James. *The Tales of the Genii, translated from the Persian by Sir Charles Morell.* London: C. and J. Rivington, 1824.
Rilke, Rainer Maria. *Duino Elegies,* trans. J. B. Leishman and Stephen Spender. New York: Norton, 1963.
Robb, George. *White-Collar Crime in Modern England: Financial Fraud and Business Morality, 1845–1929.* Cambridge: Cambridge University Press, 1992.
Royle, Nicholas. *Uncanny.* New York: Manchester University Press, 2002.
Ruskin, John. "A Note on *Hard Times.*" 1860. *Hard Times,* ed. George Ford and Sylvère Monod. New York: Norton, 1990. 332.
Ryan, Alan. "Introduction." In *Utilitarianism and Other Essays, John Stuart Mill and Jeremy Bentham,* ed. Alan Ryan. Harmondsworth: Penguin Books, 1987. 7–63.
Rylance, Rick. *Victorian Psychology and British Culture, 1850–1880.* Oxford: Oxford University Press, 2000.
Sadrin, Anny, ed. *Dickens, Europe and the New Worlds.* Basingstoke: Macmillan, 1999.
Santayana, George. "Dickens." *The Dickens Critics,* ed. George H. Ford and Lauriat Lane, Jr. Ithaca: Cornell University Press, 1961. 135–50.
Schad, John, ed. *Dickens Refigured: Bodies, Desires and Other Histories.* Manchester: Manchester University Press, 1996.
Schaffer, Talia. "Craft, Authorial Anxiety, and the 'Cranford Papers.'" *Victorian Periodicals Review* 38, no. 2 (Summer 2005): 221–39.
Scheler, Max. *The Nature of Sympathy*, trans. Peter Heath. London: Routledge & Kegan Paul, 1954.
Schlicke, Paul, ed. *The Oxford Reader's Companion to Dickens.* Oxford: Oxford University Press, 1999.
Schneewind, J. B. *The Invention of Autonomy.* Cambridge: Cambridge University Press, 1998.
———. *Sidgwick's Ethics and Victorian Moral Philosophy.* Oxford: Clarendon Press, 1977.
Schor, Hilary. *Dickens and the Daughter of the House.* Cambridge: Cambridge University Press, 1999.
———. "Novels of the 1850s: *Hard Times,* Little Dorrit, and *A Tale of Two Cities.*" In *The Cambridge Companion to Charles Dickens,* ed. John O. Jordan. Cambridge: Cambridge University Press, 2001. 64–77.
Schramm, Jan-Melissa. *Testimony and Advocacy in Victorian Law, Literature, and Theology.* Cambridge: Cambridge University Press, 2000.
Sedgwick, Eve Kosofsky. "Paranoid Reading and Reparative Reading." In *Novel Gazing: Queer Readings in Fiction,* ed. Eve Kosofsky Sedgwick. Durham and London: Duke University Press, 1997. 1–37.
Semple, Janet. *Bentham's Prison.* Oxford: Oxford University Press, 1993.

Shaftesbury, Anthony Ashley Cooper, Third Earl of. *Characteristics of Men, Manners, Opinions, Times*, ed. Lawrence E. Klein. Cambridge: Cambridge University Press, 1999.
Shattock, Joanne, ed. *Cambridge Bibliography of English Literature Volume 4: 1800–1900*. Cambridge: Cambridge University Press, 1999.
Shaw, George Bernard. "Preface." 1862. In *Great Expectations*. New York: Modern Library, 2001.
———. *Collected Works*. 30 vols. New York: W. H. Wise and Company, 1930–32.
Shell, Marc. *Art and Money*. Chicago: University of Chicago Press, 1995.
———. *Money, Language, and Thought: Literary and Philosophical Economies from the Medieval to the Modern Era*. Berkeley: University of California Press, 1982.
Shklar, Judith. "The Liberalism of Fear." In *Liberalism and the Moral Life*, ed. Nancy L. Rosenblum. Cambridge: Harvard University Press, 1989. 21–38.
Showalter, Elaine. "Guilt, Authority, and the Shadows of *Little Dorrit*." *Nineteenth-Century Fiction* 34 (June 1979): 20–40.
Shuttleworth, Sally. "'The malady of thought': Embodied Memory in Victorian Psychology and the Novel." In *Memory and Memorials 1789–1914: Literary and Cultural Perspectives*, ed. Matthew Campbell et al. London: Routledge, 2000. 46–59.
Simmel, George. *The Philosophy of Money*. New York: Routledge, 1990.
Slater, Michael, ed. *A Christmas Carol and Other Writings*. Harmondsworth: Penguin, 2003.
———, ed. *Dickens' Journalism: The Amusements of the People and Other Papers: Reports, Essays and Reviews, 1834–1851*. Columbus: The Ohio State University Press, 1996.
———, ed. *Dickens' Journalism: "Gone Astray" and Other Papers from Household Words, 1851–1859*. Columbus: The Ohio State University Press, 1999.
———, ed. *Dickens' Journalism: Sketches by Boz and Other Early Papers, 1833–39*. London: Phoenix, 1994.
———. *Dickens and Women*. London: Dent, 1983.
———. "Introduction." In *The Haunted Man*, in *The Christmas Stories: Volume 2*, ed. Michael Slater. Harmondsworth: Penguin, 1971.
———, ed. *The Life and Adventures of Nicholas Nickleby*. Facsimile ed. 2 vols. Philadelphia: University of Pennsylvania Press, 1982.
Small, Helen, ed. *Little Dorrit*. Harmondsworth: Penguin, 2003.
Smith, Adam. *The Theory of Moral Sentiments*, ed. D. D. Raphael and A. L. Macfie. Indianapolis: Liberty Press, 1982.
Solomon, Robert C. "In Defense of Sentimentality." *Philosophy and Literature* 14 (1990): 304–23.
Spector, Stephen J. "Monsters of Metonymy: *Hard Times* and Knowing the Working Class." 1984. In *Modern Critical Views: Charles Dickens*, ed. Harold Bloom. New York: Chelsea House, 1987. 229–44.
Stone, Harry. *Dickens and the Invisible World: Fairy-tales, Fantasy, and Novel-Making*. London: Macmillan, 1980.
Stonehouse, J. H., ed. *Reprints of the Catalogues of the Library of Charles Dickens and W. M. Thackeray etc*. London: Piccadilly Fountain Press, 1935; facsimile reprint, Japan, 2003.

Taine, Hippolyte A. *History of English Literature.* Vol. 4. New York: Frederick Ungar Publishing Co., 1965.
Taylor, Charles. "Modes of Secularism." In *Secularism and Its Critics,* ed. Rajeev Ghargava. Delhi: Oxford University Press, 1998. 31–53.
Tennyson, Alfred Lord. *In Memoriam* and "Ulysses." In *Tennyson: A Selected Edition,* ed. Christopher Ricks. Berkeley and Los Angeles: University of California Press, 1989. 138–45, 321–484.
Teres, Harvey. *Renewing the Left: Politics, Imagination, and the New York Intellectuals.* New York and Oxford: Oxford University Press, 1996.
Thackeray, William Makepeace. "A Box of Novels." *Fraser's Magazine* 29 (February 1844): 153–69.
———. *Pendennis.* 2 Vols. London: Everyman's Library, 1959.
Trilling, Diana. *The Beginning of the Journey.* New York: Harcourt Brace, 1993.
Trilling, Lionel. "The Dickens of Our Day." In *A Gathering of Fugitives.* Boston: Beacon Press, 1956. 41–48.
———. "Freud and Literature." In *The Liberal Imagination.* Garden City: Anchor, 1953. 32–54.
———. "Freud: Within and Beyond Culture." In *Beyond Culture.* New York: Viking, 1968. 89–118.
———. "Little Dorrit." *The Dickens Critics,* ed. George H. Ford and Lauriat Lane, Jr. Ithaca: Cornell University Press, 1961. 279–93.
Van Ghent, Dorothy. *The English Novel: Form and Function.* 1953. New York: Harper & Row, 1961.
Vlock, Deborah. *Dickens, Novel Reading, and the Victorian Popular Theatre.* Cambridge: Cambridge University Press, 1998.
Walder, Dennis. *Dickens and Religion.* London: HarperCollins, 1981.
Watts-Dunton, Theodore. "Dickens and 'Father Christmas': A Yuletide Appeal for the Babes of Famine Street." *The Nineteenth Century* 62 (1907): 1014–29.
Weber, Max. *The Protestant Ethic and the Spirit of Capitalism.* 1930. Los Angeles: Roxbury Publishing Company, 1998.
Welsh, Alexander. *The City of Dickens.* Cambridge: Harvard University Press, 1986.
———. *Dickens Redressed: The Art of* Bleak House *and* Hard Times. New Haven: Yale University Press, 2000.
———. *Strong Representations: Narrative and Circumstantial Evidence in England.* Baltimore: Johns Hopkins University Press, 1999
Whewell, William. *Astronomy and General Physics Considered with Reference to Natural Theology.* 1833. London: H. G. Bohn, 1852.
White, Hayden. "The Historical Text as Literary Artifact." In *The Writing of History: Literary Form and Historical Understanding,* ed. Robert H. Canary and Henry Kozicki. Madison: University of Wisconsin Press, 1978. 41–62.
———. "The Value of Narrativity in the Representation of Reality." *Critical Inquiry* 7, no.1 (Autumn 1980): 5–27.
Wilde, Alan. "Mr F's Aunt and the Analogical Structure of *Little Dorrit.*" *Nineteenth-Century Fiction* 19 (June 1964): 33–44.
Williams, Raymond. *Marxism and Literature.* Oxford: Oxford University Press, 1977.
Williams, T. H. "Observations on Money, Credit, and Panics." *Transactions of the Man-*

*chester Statistical Society, 1857–58.* Manchester: J. Roberts, 1858.

Wills, W. H. "Review of a Popular Publication, In the Searching Style." *Household Words* (27 July 1850).

———. "Two Chapters on Bank-Note Forgeries: Chapter I." *Household Words* (7 September 1851).

Wilson, Anna. "On History, Case History, and Deviance: Miss Wade's Symptoms and Their Interpretation." *Dickens Studies Annual* 26 (1998): 187–201.

Wilson, Edmund. "Dickens: The Two Scrooges." In *Eight Essays*. Garden City: Doubleday, 1954. 11–91.

———. *The Thirties*, ed. Leon Edel. New York: Farrar, Strauss, and Giroux, 1980.

Withington, Roger and B. R. James. *The New £10 Note and Charles Dickens*. Essex: Debden Security Printing, n.d.

Woolf, Virginia. "*David Copperfield*." In *The Moment*. London: Hogarth Press, 1981. 65–69.

———. "Modern Fiction." In *The Common Reader*. Harcourt, Brace and Company, 1953. 150–58.

# Notes on Contributors

JAMES ELI ADAMS teaches in the Department of English at Cornell University, where he is Director of Graduate Studies. He is the author of *Dandies and Desert Saints: Styles of Victorian Masculinity* (1995), the coeditor, with Andrew Miller, of *Sexualities in Victorian Britain* (1996), and the editor-in-chief of the four-volume *The Encyclopedia of the Victorian Age* (2004). He is completing *A History of Victorian Literature*.

JOHN BOWEN is Professor of Nineteenth-Century Literature at the University of York. He is the author of *Other Dickens: Pickwick to Chuzzlewit* (2000) and has coedited, with Robert L. Patten, *Palgrave Advances in Charles Dickens Studies* (2006). He is a Fellow of the English Association and currently serves as President of the Dickens Society.

JAMES BUZARD is Professor and Head of the Literature Faculty at MIT. He has written two books, *Disorienting Fiction: The Autoethnographic Work of Nineteenth-Century British Novels* (2005) and *The Beaten Track: European Tourism, Literature, and the Ways to "Culture," 1800–1918* (1993), as well as numerous essays on nineteenth- and twentieth-century British literature and culture, the history of travel, and cultural theory. He is coeditor of a special *Victorian Studies* issue on "Victorian Ethnographies" and of *Victorian Prism: Refractions of the Crystal Palace* (2007). He is currently working on a second volume of the *Disorienting Fiction* study, covering United Kingdom fiction from George Eliot to Joyce.

KAREN CHASE is a professor in the department of English at the University of Virginia. She is author of *Eros and Psyche: Representations of Personality in Charlotte Brontë, Charles Dickens and George Eliot* (1984), *Middlemarch* (Cambridge Landmarks in World Literature Series, 1991), coauthor (with Michael Levenson) of *The Spectacle of Intimacy* (2000), and editor of *Middlemarch in the Twenty-First Century* (2005). She is currently completing a book, *Aging with Care: The Victorian Life Reviewed*.

Notes on Contributors

JOSEPH W. CHILDERS is Professor of English at the University of California, Riverside. He has published widely on Victorian literature and culture. Most recently he has edited *Victorian Prism: Refractions of the Crystal Palace* with James Buzard and Eileen Gillooly (2007) and *Sublime Economy: Intersections of Aesthetics and Economics* with Jack Amariglio and Stephen Cullenberg (Routledge, forthcoming).

DEIRDRE DAVID, Professor Emerita of English at Temple University, is the author, most recently, of *Fanny Kemble: A Performed Life* (2007). Her other publications include *Fictions of Resolution in Three Victorian Novels* (1981), *Intellectual Women and Victorian Patriarchy: Harriet Martineau, Elizabeth Barrett Browning, and George Eliot* (1987), and *Rule Britannia: Women, Empire, and Victorian Writing* (1995). She has also edited *The Cambridge Companion to the Victorian Novel* (2000) and is beginning work on her second biography, a study of the twentieth-century British novelist Olivia Manning.

ELAINE FREEDGOOD, Professor of English at New York University, is the author of *Victorian Writing about Risk: Imagining a Safe England in a Dangerous World* (2000) and *The Ideas in Things: Fugitive Meaning in the Victorian Novel* (2006), and the editor of *Factory Production in Nineteenth-Century Britain* (2002). Her new project concerns how things lived in the nineteenth century.

EILEEN GILLOOLY is Associate Director of the Heyman Center for the Humanities and the Society of Fellows and a member of the Department of English and of the Institute for Research on Women and Gender at Columbia University. Her publications include *Smile of Discontent: Humor, Gender, and Nineteenth-Century British Fiction* (1999), which was awarded the Perkins Prize by the International Society for the Study of Narrative, and *Victorian Prism: Refractions of the Crystal Palace* (2007), which she coedited with James Buzard and Joseph Childers. Current project include writing a book about parental feeling in nineteenth-century middle-class Britain and revising the Norton Critical Edition of *David Copperfield*.

TATIANA M. HOLWAY is a writer, editor, and independent scholar. She is currently working on a book about the *Victoria regia* water lily in nineteenth-century Britain, forthcoming from Oxford University Press.

MICHAEL LEVENSON is the author of *A Genealogy of Modernism: A Study of English Literary Doctrine, 1908–1922* (1984), *Modernism and The Fate of Individuality: Character and Form in the Modern English Novel* (1991), *Modernism* (Yale University Press, forthcoming), and, with Karen Chase, *The Spectacle of Intimacy: A Public Life for the Victorian Family* (2000). He is also the editor of the *Cambridge Companion to Modernism* (1999) and numerous essays on Victorian and Modernist subjects. Michael Levenson is William B. Christian Professor of English at the University of Virginia.

GEORGE LEVINE is Professor Emeritus at Rutgers University and Distinguished Scholar in Residence, New York University. His most recent books are *Darwin Loves You:*

*Natural Selection and the Re-enchantment of the World* (2006) and *How to Read the Victorian Novel* (2007). His *Realism, Ethics, and Secularism: Essays in Victorian Studies and Literature* will be published by Cambridge University Press in 2008.

RICHARD H. MOYE is Professor of English and Chair of the Department of English and Philosophy at Lyndon State College, a small college in northeastern Vermont. Although a specialist in nineteenth-century British literature and culture, he has taught a wide range of courses, from Mythology and the Bible as Literature to seminars on Dickens, Austen, Joyce, and Dante. His essays include "In the Beginning: Myth and History in Genesis and Exodus," "Thucydides' 'Great War': The Fiction in Scientific History," and "Silent Victory: Narrative, Appropriation, and Autonomy in *La Princesse de Clèves.*"

ROBERT NEWSOM is Professor Emeritus of English at the University of California, Irvine. He holds degrees from Columbia University (where Steven Marcus taught him freshman composition, and just about everything else about literature and society, and eventually supervised his dissertation) and Cambridge University. He is the author of *Dickens on the Romantic Side of Familiar Things* (1977), *A Likely Story: Probability and Play in Fiction* (1988), and *Charles Dickens Revisited* (2000), in addition to essays and reviews.

DEBORAH EPSTEIN NORD is a member of the English Department at Princeton University, where she also teaches in the Program in the Study of Women and Gender. She is the author of *The Apprenticeship of Beatrice Webb* (1985), *Walking the Victorian Streets: Women, Representation, and the City* (1995), and *Gypsies and the British Imagination, 1807–1930* (2006), and the editor of John Ruskin's *Sesame and Lilies* (2002).

NANCY YOUSEF is Associate Professor of English at Baruch College and the Graduate Center of the City University of New York. She is the author of *Isolated Cases: The Anxieties of Autonomy in Enlightenment Philosophy and Romantic Literature* (2004) and is currently at work on a book-length study of intimacy in literature, philosophy, and psychoanalysis.

# Index

*All the Year Round*, 20
Althusser, Louis, 98, 166, 231
Anderson, Amanda, 3
Anger, Suzy, 96
Anglicanism, 40–43
Anne, Queen, 145
Arac, Jonathan, ix
Arnold, Matthew, 40, 50, 104
Arnold, Thomas, 40
Austen, Jane, 22, 265
Austin, Henry (CD's brother-in-law), 85

Bagehot, Walter, 103, 159, 161, 172–74
Balfour, William, 14
Bank Charter Act (1844), 171
Bank of England, 169–72, 174, 176, 180, 182–85
banking, 169–87
bankruptcy, 28, 221
Barthes, Roland, 195
Benjamin, Walter, 86
Bennett, Arnold, 158, 163
Bentham, Jeremy, 38–40, 47, 54, 118, 122
Bentley, Richard, 213
*Bentley's Miscellany*, 213
Blake, William, 270

Bodichon, Barbara, 249
Born, Daniel, 123
Bourdieu, Pierre, 159
Bowen, John, 204
Brantlinger, Patrick, 98
Bromwich, David, 274
Brontë, Charlotte, 13, 36, 154; *Jane Eyre*, 22; *Villette*, 22, 52n14
Brontë, Emily, 36; *Wuthering Heights*, 16
Browne, Hablot Knight (Phiz), 268
Bulwer-Lytton, Edward, 223
Bunyan, John, 193
Burdett Coutts, Angela, Baroness, 49–50, 221, 255
Buss, R. W., 180
Butler, Joseph, Bishop, 19, 55
Butwin, Joseph, 101

Calvinism, 15, 18, 23, 25, 43, 247
Capra, Frank, 125
Carey, Peter, 13
Carlyle, Jane Welsh, 127
Carlyle, Thomas: attacks on utilitarianism, 39–40; and Christmas, 127–28; definition of "uttering," 174; history, 98; on the "earnestness" of heroes, 179; secularism, 14; view on society, 65, 100

## Index

Chadwick, Edwin, 39, 148
Chesterton, G. K., 114–15, 123, 204
Cholera Epidemic, 85, 135, 138, 148–49
Chow, Rey, 153
Christmas: in Dickens, 37, 88; and Englishness, 5, 113–29, 264; presents, 84; secularization of, 45–46
Clifford, W. K., 14, 16
Cohen, William, 235
Cohn, Dorrit, 95–96
Collins, Philip, 9, 44, 270
Collins, Wilkie, 222, 224
commodity criticism, 159–67
*Communist Manifesto*, 76
Connor, Steven, 2
Conrad, Joseph, 267
Cooper, Anthony Ashley. *See* Shaftesbury, Anthony, Earl of
Corelli, Maria, 13
Cowper, William, 202
Craik, Dinah Mulock, 13, 16
credit (financial), 1, 6, 171–76, 178
Crowe, Catherine, 85
Cruikshank, George, 137, 268, 282
Crystal Palace. *See* Great Exhibition of 1851

*Daily News*, 85
Dallas, Eneas Sweetland (E.S.), 90n17
Damrosch, Leopold, 17
Darwin, Charles, 14, 18, 211; *Descent of Man*, 211; *Origin of Species*, 18, 20, 222
Debord, Guy, 152, 154
Delany, Paul, 158
Diamond, Cora, 54, 71
Dickens, Alfred D'Orsay Tennyson (son), 221
Dickens, Catherine (wife), 221, 223, 225–26, 229n25
Dickens, Charles: banknote representing, 169–71, 180, 184, 186; charity and, 53, 60, 64–71, 86, 115; Christian moral framework, 16–17, 25–27, 277; critical reception, 239, 264–84; and the environment, 6, 139–41; history in his works, 96–100, 101, 283–84; influences, 35, 54, 73n19; journalism, 85, 94, 101, 108n5; and London, 131–32, 138, 141–44; and memory, 76–88, 132, 267, 269, 280–83; moral intuition, belief in, 47–49; moral views, 3–5, 107, 238; Protestant ethic, 31; reception of Christmas books, 115–17; religious beliefs, 37–38, 42–47, 51n9, 51n13; as religious novelist, 23–26; and secularism, 13, 16; sexuality and, 8, 231–37, 239–43, 281; and sympathy, 54–55, 63, 71; "thingfullness" of his novels, 153, 160
Works:
  *Barnaby Rudge*, 96, 98–99, 238
  *Battle of Life*, 116
  *Bleak House*: charity, 53; Christian morality in, 43, 46; city and country in, 138, 143; critical reception, 9, 264, 276; Dickens's defense of realism in, 16; and Dickens's family, 7, 220–27; compared to Engels, 102; happy ending in, 29; nature and art in, 136–37; and *Old Curiosity Shop*, 197, 203–4; paper and rags in, 144, 147, 149; and societal disease, 250–51; sympathy, 55, 60–71; systems of interpretation, 100
  *Christmas Carol*, 5, 77, 84, 86, 114–29
  *David Copperfield*: and charges of sentimentalism, 4; and Dickens's religious beliefs, 44; female rage in, 251–52; and *Haunted Man*, 5, 76–78, 85; and money, 169–70, 184–85; sanction given Dickens by, 181; sexuality in, 232, 239, 241–43; and the value of work, 178–79; Woolf on, 267–68
  *Dombey and Son*: history and the past in, 98–99; as later Dickens, 239; profitable for Dickens, 177–78; and psychological

criticism, 284; railways, 6, 134–36; theatrical moments in, 247
*Great Expectations,* 27, 86, 143, 253, 282
*Hard Times:* and commodities, 165; critical reception, 39–40, 267; fact and fiction in, 101–8; history and the past in, 96; as a moral fable, 5, 94
*Haunted Man,* 5, 75–88, 114, 116
*Little Dorrit:* Christian morality in, 4, 13; city and country in, 141–42; critical reception, 9, 264, 276–77, 283–84; criticism of Victorian financial institutions, 170, 175; fact and fiction in, 102; female rage in, 8, 245–52, 255–61; history and the past in, 96–98; nature cult in, 137; sales of, 185; tension between religion and secularism, 16, 23–31, 121
*Martin Chuzzlewit,* 174, 176
*Mystery of Edwin Drood,* 274–75
*Nicholas Nickleby:* anti-Catholicism in, 43; and concerns with authenticity, 170–71; internality in, 238, 239; parent-child relationship in, 7, 213, 214–20, 223
*Old Curiosity Shop:* and commodities, 164; domestic morality, 49; non-narrative style of, 7, 189–205; religious hypocrisy in, 43; sales in America, 177; suspicion in, 238
*Oliver Twist:* authorial naïveté in, 29; city and country in, 131, 136; critical reception, 268, 279–83; and Dickens's belief in innate moral intuitions, 48; parent-child relationship in, 209–10, 213; and realism, 185; tension between religion and secularism, 16; villains as predecessors of Quilp, 196
*Our Mutual Friend:* critical reception, 9, 266, 270, 276, 283; compared to Engels, 102; and the environment, 6, 143; ethical imperative in, 4, 36–37; female rage in, 253–54; internality in, 239; paper and rags in, 144–46, 149–50; as rare example of admirable clergy, 43; and the separation of spheres, 26–27; tension between religion and secularism, 16
*Pickwick Papers:* characters models for Dick Swiveler, 197; Christmas in, 45, 116; city and country in, 136; critical reception, 269, 270, 278–80; as early Dickens, 169; and the environment, 131; inventories in, 7, 191–92, 194; parent-child relationship in, 209; sanction given Dickens by, 181; satire of Evangelical Dissenters, 43; sexuality and, 8, 232–43; tension between religion and secularism, 16, 45
*Sketches by Boz,* 4, 6, 35, 132–34, 138–39
*Tale of Two Cities,* 43, 46, 96, 98–100, 239
*Uncommercial Traveller,* 42, 186
Dickens, Charles Cuillford Boz, Jr. (son), 221–22
Dickens, Dora Annie (daughter), 221, 229n25
Dickens, Edward Bulwer Lytton (Plorn) (son), 43, 49, 212, 221, 229n30, 229n33
Dickens, Elizabeth Barrow (mother), 78, 282
Dickens, Fanny (later Burnett) (sister), 75, 89n2
Dickens, Francis Jeffrey (Frank) (son), 221, 229n30
Dickens, Henry Fielding (son), 229n30
Dickens, John (father), 37, 77, 78, 228n21, 249, 274, 278–81

Dickens, Kate Mcready (daughter), 224, 227n9
Dickens, Mary (Mamie) (daughter), 213, 224
Dickens, Walter Savage Landor (son), 221
Dostoevsky, Fyodor, 1, 90n19, 273
Duchamp, Marcel, 204

Eagleton, Terry, 94
Easson, Angus, 96
Egg, Augustus, 224
Eliot, George: as critic, 94; critical agreement on, 93; *Daniel Deronda*, 30, 93; *Middlemarch*, 15, 22; realism, 36, 266; representation of clergy, 20; *Romola*, 93; and secularism, 14–16, 22
Elmes, James, 133
Engels, Friedrich, 76, 102–3
environmentalism, 6, 131–50
Erskine, John, 264
ethics: in *Bleak House*, 62–63, 67–71; and Christmas, 125–26; in *David Copperfield*, 77–78; in *Hard Times*, 107–8; in *Haunted Man*, 85–86; and history, 100; intuitionism and moral sense, 38, 41, 47–49, 55, 62; in *Little Dorrit*, 31; and narrative, 3, 4, 8; in *Nicholas Nickleby*, 218; and secularism, 14; sentimentalism, 40, 53–55, 72n7; Hume's theories, 57–60, 63–64; Smith's theories, 73n10, 77, 211; and sympathy, 35–50, 77–78, 211; utilitarianism, 37, 40–42, 47, 54–55, 103, 121; Victorian, 35–50

Fagin, Bob, 280
Felski, Rita, 162, 164
Fielding, Henry, 17, 21, 237
Follett, William, 234
Forster, John: anecdote about Dickens's father, 280; Dickens's capacity for sympathy, 211; Dickens's religion, 42–44; *Dombey and Son*, 177; Guild of Literature and Art, 223, 224; *Haunted Man*, 77

Foucault, Michel, 3, 9, 40, 231, 241
*Fraser's*, 128, 137, 140
Freud, Sigmund: admiration for Dickens, 91n20; Dickens's similarity to, 80–82; Freudian readings of Dickens, 8, 77, 241, 265, 271–72, 274, 283–84; parent-child relationships, 209, 270; primal scenes, 281; repetition, 87; sexuality and meaning, 235, 243; unconscious, 15; wish-fulfillment, Trilling's use, 276–78. *See also* psychoanalysis, and Dickens criticism
Frost, Robert, 202

Gallagher, Catherine, 161
Galsworthy, John, 158, 163
Gardiner, Judith Kegan, 218
Gaskell, Elizabeth, 224
George IV, King (previously Prince Regent), 133
gift-giving, 78–79, 84–86, 91n27
Girard, René, 82
Gissing, George, 94, 271
Golby, J. M., 116
Gooch, Daniel, 104
Great Depression, 272
Great Exhibition of 1851, 152, 154–56, 166
guilt, 122–26, 130n17, 275, 277–78

Hadley, Elaine, 232
Hazlitt, William, 35
Herschel, John, 18
history, and narrative, 94–101, 198–99, 256–57
Hobbes, Thomas, 55
Hoffmann, E. T. A., 81
Hogarth, Georgina (CD's sister-in-law), 224, 226
Hogarth, Mary (CD's sister-in-law), 192, 226
Hollingshead, John, 149
Hood, Thomas, 126
*Household Words*: Bank of England articles, 184; Christmas stories, 117, 127; Dickens taking credit for, 181; publication of *Hard Times*,

93, 96, 101; representation of city and country, 138, 146; review of Darwin, 20
Hume, David, 55–60, 63–65, 211, 218
Hunt, Leigh, 35
Hutcheson, Francis, 55
Hutton, James, 33n6
Huxley, Aldous, 266
Huxley, T. H., 14

Inclosure Acts, 140
intuitionism. *See* ethics
Islam, 50, 113
*It's a Wonderful Life*, 125

Jaffe, Audrey, 198–99
James, Henry, 8, 193, 265–67, 268
James, William, 16
Jameson, Fredric, 98, 166
Jerrold, Douglas, 224
Jews, 37, 41, 128, 271
John, Judith, 232
John, Juliet, 238
Jordan, John O., x, 1
Joseph, Gerhard, ix
Joyce, James, 158, 274

Kafka, Franz, 273, 274
Kant, Immanuel, 54, 73n21
Kemble, John Philip, 248
Kincaid, James R., 195
Kingsley, Charles, 40
Knight, Charles, 148
Kristeva, Julia, 78

Lamb, Charles, 35
Lamb, William. *See* Melbourne, Lord
Leavis, F. R., 8, 93–94, 265–67, 269, 271, 282
Lefebvre, Henri, 154
Lefevre, George Shaw, 140–41
Lemon, Mark, 90n14, 146, 224
Le Sage, Alain-René, 199
Lewes, George Henry, 8, 160–61, 265–66, 269, 275, 284
liberalism, 3–4, 50, 114–15, 122–23, 270
Luddism, 136

Lyell, Charles, 17–18

Macaulay, Thomas B., 98
Maclise, Daniel, 184
Mallock, W. H., 14
Malthus, Thomas, 118, 121, 221
Marcus, Sharon, 168n34
Marcus, Steven: on *Bleak House*, 62; and Dickens criticism, 9, 269, 270–73; Dickens's representation of reality, 101–2; Freudian readings of Dickens, 277–84; on *Old Curiosity Shop*, 203; past and memory in Dickens, 98–99; as teacher, ix
Martineau, Harriet, 145
Marx, Karl: and commodity fetishism, 153; ghosts in, 76; and history, 98; influence on Dickens criticism, 265, 272; and modernity, 155; Van Ghent's quasi-Marxist critique of Dickens, 162–63
Marxism: criticism of Victorian culture, 157, 159, 160; and literary criticism, 3, 8, 166, 272
Mauss, Marcel, 84. *See also* gift-giving
Mayhew, Henry, 147–48
McCulloch, J. R., 175
McKeon, Michael, 21
Melbourne, Lord, 233–34
Michie, Helena, 216
Mill, James, 29
Mill, John Stuart, 14, 39, 40, 47, 50, 96, 122, 171, 174; belief in progress, 50; and Bentham, 39, 122; on political economy, 171, 174; secularism of, 14; utilitarianism, 39, 40, 47; on Victorians as historical beings, 96
Miller, Andrew H., 155
Miller, D. A., 239
Miller, Hugh, 19–20, 33n12
Miller, J. Hillis, 9, 100, 270, 278, 286n32, 287n40
Milton, John, 202
Mink, Louis O., 95
moral philosophy. *See* ethics
moral sense. *See* ethics
Moretti, Franco, 22, 24
*Morning Chronicle*, 233

313

*Index*

Mumford, Lewis, 101

narratology, 95–96
Nash, John, 133, 135
natural theology, 18–19, 40. *See also* Paley, William
Nazism, 270, 271, 273
New Poor Law (1834), 39, 125
Newman, John Henry, Cardinal, 13, 40–42
Norton, Caroline, 250–52
Norton, George, 233–34
Nunokawa, Jeff, 153, 165

Oliphant, Margaret, 13
Orwell, George, 94, 162–63, 264, 270–71
Oxford Movement, 40. *See also* Newman, John Henry, Cardinal

Paley, William, 41, 47
paper, 6–7, 145–50; currency, 169–72, 176, 180, 182, 185
Pascal, Blaise, 16
Pater, Walter, 36
Phiz. *See* Browne, Hablot Knight (Phiz)
*Pilgrim's Progress. See* Bunyan, John
Pimlott, J. A. R., 123
Plato, 40
Poor Laws. *See* New Poor Law (1834)
Poovey, Mary, 26, 29, 100–101, 249
Protestant ethic, 15, 21–23, 27, 31, 170. *See also* ethics
psychoanalysis, and Dickens criticism, 3, 8, 271–72, 276, 277–83
Purdue, A. W., 116
Puritanism, 15, 17, 32–33n5, 43

Qualls, Barry, ix, 15

railway travel, 6, 99, 134–36, 139, 144
realism: comic realism, 26; commodities in, 165–66, 170; and the Great Exhibition, 154; and happy endings, 31; opposed to Dickens's didacticism, 36; psychology, 237–38, 275; and social context, 29; as substitute for real world, 185; as superior to allegory, 77
Reform Bill (1832), 39
Reynolds, Mary, 80
Ricardo, David, 39
Richards, Thomas, 154, 155
Richardson, Samuel, 17, 21; *Pamela*, 21, 26
Rilke, Rainer Maria, 195
Romanticism (English), 15, 77, 94, 137, 238, 248
Ruskin, John, 40, 93–94, 159

Sadlier, John, 174
Sadrin, Anny, 2
Santayana, George, 266, 269, 273
Schad, John, 2
Schaffer, Talia, 158
Scheler, Max, 56, 63. *See also* sympathy
Schneewind, J. B., 51n10
Schor, Hilary M., 202
Scott, Walter, 22, 23, 29, 97, 24
secularism: and Christmas, 45; in Dickens, 1, 4; and ethical thought, 47–48; in *Little Dorrit*, 23–25, 28, 31; as modern moral imperative, 32n1; and the novel, 13, 20, 22; Victorian, 14–17
Sedgwick, Eve Kosofsky, 232
sentimentalism. *See* ethics
Shaftesbury, Anthony, Earl of, 55–57, 68
Shakespeare, William, 1, 88, 183
Shaw, George Bernard, 114, 245
Shklar, Judith, 122–23
Siddons, Sarah, 248
Sigourney, Lydia, 221
Simmel, George, 155, 171
Slater, Michael, 247
Small, Helen, 250
Smith, Adam, 56, 73n10, 77, 211
Smollett, Tobias, 237
Spencer, Herbert, 14
Stanfield, Clarkson, 87–88
Stephen, Leslie, 14
Stevenson, Robert Louis, 275
sympathy: in *Bleak House*, 64–71 (*see also* ethics); in *Christmas Carol*, 123–24; in *Christmas Carol*,

214–15; Dickens's with his own creations, 226; eighteenth-century theories, 54–60; in *Haunted Man*, 77; as innate moral faculty, 47–48; and novelistic representation, 20, 38; opposed to empathy, 218–19

Taine, Hippolyte A., 159, 161
Taylor, Charles, 32n1
Tennyson, Alfred: *In Memoriam*, 194; "Ulysses," 197
Thackeray, William Makepeace: attentiveness to financial detail, 36; on Carlyle, 128; as father, 212; on Maclise's portrait of Dickens, 184; and novelistic conventions, 15; and secularism, 13, 22; *Vanity Fair*, 25, 29; on the weak hero, 23
Thucydides, 95
Trilling, Lionel: and Dickens criticism, 9, 264–66; on Dickens's "childishness," 8, 269; Freudian readings of Dickens, 271–72, 276–77; influence on Steven Marcus, 278, 283; on *Little Dorrit*, 276–77; Marxist readings of Dickens, 272–73
Tyndall, John, 14

Unitarianism, 37, 41, 42, 44
United States of America: Dickens's critical reception in, 269–73; Dickens's sales in, 177; display at Great Exhibition, 156; paper technology, 146; religious right in, 114

utilitarianism. *See* ethics

Valente, Joseph, 3
Van Ghent, Dorothy, 160–64
Victoria, Queen, 221, 249

Warren's Blacking factory, 37, 76, 78, 214, 280–82
Watt, Ian, 21
Watts-Dunton, Theodore, 115
Weber, Max, 19, 21–22, 27, 155
Wells, Herbert George (H. G.), 158, 163
Welsh, Alexander, 241
Whewell, William, 18–19
White, Hayden, 95
Wilde, Oscar, 36, 275
Williams, Raymond, 94, 115, 117
Wills, W. H., 138, 182–83, 222
Wilson, Edmund: and Dickens criticism, 9, 264, 283; on Dickens's "childishness," 8, 269; influence on Marcus, 278; psychological readings of Dickens, 271–72, 273–75, 281; similarity to Trilling, 277
Wilson, Thomas Maryon, 140
Woolf, Leonard, 267
Woolf, Virginia: as critic of Dickens, 8, 265; as critic of Victorian materialism, 158–59, 163; on Dickens's childishness, 267–68, 269; on the failure of Dickens's sympathies, 266

Zangwill, Israel, 128

www.ingramcontent.com/pod-product-compliance
Lightning Source LLC
Chambersburg PA
CBHW021135230426
43667CB00005B/131